Groups in contact

DATE DUE

Groups in Contact

The Psychology of Desegregation

Groups in Contact

The Psychology of Desegregation

EDITED BY

Norman Miller

Department of Psychology
University of Southern California
Los Angeles, California

Marilynn B. Brewer

Institute for Social Sciences Research
University of California, Los Angeles
Los Angeles, California

1984

ACADEMIC PRESS, INC.
(Harcourt Brace Jovanovich, Publishers)
Orlando   San Diego   San Francisco   New York   London
Toronto   Montreal   Sydney   Tokyo   São Paulo

ACADEMIC PRESS, INC.
Orlando, Florida 32887

United Kingdom Edition published by
ACADEMIC PRESS, INC. (LONDON) LTD.
24/28 Oval Road, London NW1 7DX

Library of Congress Cataloging in Publication Data

Main entry under title:

Groups in contact.

    Bibliograhy: p.
    Includes index.
    1. Segregation--Psychological aspects--Addresses,
essays, lectures. 2. Ethnic relations--Psychological
aspects--Addresses, essays, lectures. 3. Segregation
in education--Addresses, essays, lectures. 4. Culture--
Psychological aspects--Addresses, essays, lectures.
5. Prejudice--Addresses, essays, lectures. I. Miller,
Norman, Date   . II. Brewer, Marilynn B.,
HM291.G685   1984   305.8   83-9185
ISBN 0-12-497780-4 (alk. paper)

To the memory of Henri Tajfel (1919–1982)

Contents

4. Interethnic Relations and Education: An Israeli Perspective
Joseph Schwarzwald and Yehuda Amir

5. The Desegregated School: Problems in Status Power and Interethnic Climate
Elizabeth G. Cohen

6. Desegregation of Suburban Neighborhoods
David L. Hamilton, Sandra Carpenter, and George D. Bishop

7. The Trajectory of Local Desegregation Controversies and Whites' Opposition to Busing
David O. Sears and Harris M. Allen, Jr.

Part II. Improving Outcomes of Desegregation in Specific Settings

8. Cooperative Interaction in Multiethnic Contexts
Stuart W. Cook

9. Goal Interdependence and Interpersonal Attraction in Heterogeneous Classrooms: A Metanalysis
David W. Johnson, Roger T. Johnson, and Geoffrey Maruyama

10. Intergroup Acceptance in Classroom and Playground Settings
Marian Rogers, Karen Hennigan, Craig Bowman, and Norman Miller

11. The Role of Ignorance in Intergroup Relations
Walter G. Stephan and Cookie White Stephan

12. Training for Desegregation in the Military
Dan Landis, Richard O. Hope, and Harry R. Day

Part III. Conclusion

13. Beyond the Contact Hypothesis: Theoretical Perspectives on Desegregation
Marilynn B. Brewer and Norman Miller

Contributors

Numbers in parentheses indicate the pages on which the authors' contributions begin.

Harris M. Allen Jr. (124), The Rand Corporation, Santa Monica, California 90406

Yehuda Amir (53), Department of Psychology, Bar-Ilan University, Ramat-Gan 52100, Israel

J. W. Berry (11), Department of Psychology, Queen's University, Kingston, Ontario, Canada K7L 3N6

George D. Bishop (97), Division of Behavioral and Cultural Sciences, University of Texas at San Antonio, San Antonio, Texas 78285

Craig Bowman (214), Department of Psychology, University of Southern California, Los Angeles, California 90089–1111

Marilynn B. Brewer (1, 281), Institute for Social Science Research, University of California, Los Angeles, California 90024

Sandra Carpenter[1] (97), Department of Psychology, University of California, Santa Barbara, California 93106

Elizabeth G. Cohen (77), School of Education, Stanford University, Stanford, California 94305

Stuart W. Cook (156), Department of Psychology and Institute of Behavioral Science, University of Colorado, Boulder, Colorado 80309

Harry R. Day (258), Development Associates, Inc., Indianapolis, Indiana 46204

David L. Hamilton (97), Department of Psychology, University of California, Santa Barbara, California 93106

Karen Hennigan[2] (124), Department of Psychology, University of Southern California, Los Angeles, California 90089–1111

Richard O. Hope (258), Department of Psychology, Indiana University–Purdue University at Indianapolis, Indianapolis, Indiana 46205

David W. Johnson (187), College of Education, Department of Educational Psychology, University of Minnesota, Minneapolis, Minnesota 55455

Roger T. Johnson[3] (187), College of Education, University of Minnesota, Minneapolis, Minnesota 55455

Dan Landis (258), Office of the Dean, College of Liberal Arts, University of Mississippi, University, Mississippi 38677

Geoffrey Maruyama (187), Department of Educational Psychology, University of Minnesota, Minneapolis, Minnesota 55455

Norman Miller (1, 214, 281), Department of Psychology, University of Southern California, Los Angeles, California 90089–1061

Marian Rogers[4] (214), Department of Psychology, University of Southern California, Los Angeles, California 90089–1111

Peter Schönbach (29), Ruhr-Universität Bochum, Psychologisches Institut, 4630 Bochum 1, West Germany

Joseph Schwarzwald (53), Department of Psychology, Bar-Ilan University, Ramat-Gan 52100, Israel

David O. Sears (124), Department of Psychology, University of California, Los Angeles, California 90024

Cookie White Stephan (229), Department of Sociology and Anthropology, New Mexico State University, Las Cruces, New Mexico 88003

Walter G. Stephan (229), Department of Psychology, New Mexico State University, Las Cruces, New Mexico 88003

Ulrich Wagner (29), Ruhr-Universität, Bochum, Psychologisches Institut, 4630 Bochum 1, West Germany

[1]Present address: Department of Psychology, Ohio State University, Columbus, Ohio 43210.

[2]Present address: Health Behavior Research Institute, School of Pharmacy, University of Southern California, Los Angeles, California, 90033.

[3]Present address: Department of Curriculum and Instruction, Science Education, University of Minnesota, Minneapolis, Minnesota, 55455.

[4]Present address: American Telephone and Telegraph Information Systems, Lyncroft, New Jersey, 07748.

Foreword

The Society for the Psychological Study of Social Issues (SPSSI) has as one of its major goals the encouragement of research on important social concerns of the times. One of the ways in which this goal has been implemented is through its publication program. Thus SPSSI has a tradition of sponsorship of social science volumes that are topical and sound. This volume is an outstanding contribution to this program.

A predominant theory in social psychological studies of prejudice and desegregation has been the *contact hypothesis*, which states, in its simplest form, that attitudes toward a disliked social group will become more positive with increased interpersonal interaction. This hypothesis has been modified over the years as data have accumulated. This volume uses this elaborated theory as a point of departure and provides new data obtained in a variety of social contexts. The various chapters provide a picture of the desegregation process as a complex interplay between the cognitive processes within the individual and the structural features of the social environment. What emerges, in the final chapter, is an expanded theory of contact based on social categorization and social comparison processes. *Groups in Contact: The Psychology of Desegregation* is an important contribution to the study of intergroup conflict and prejudice and has considerable significance for the development of scientifically based intervention strategies. SPSSI is proud to be its sponsor.

Lois Wladis Hoffman
SPSSI President

Preface

Although this book is written primarily from the perspective of social psychology, it is intended for students of intergroup relations in all disciplines. The general starting point for each of the contributions in the volume is the *contact hypothesis*—the idea that prejudice and hostility between members of segregated groups can be reduced by promoting the frequency and intensity of intergroup contact. Each chapter then analyzes a specific contact situation, with particular emphasis on the perspective of individuals in that setting and the contact situation's impact on individual perceptions and interpersonal behavior. The chapters in the first part of the volume deal with issues of intergroup contact in a wide range of cultures and settings, each focusing on a particular social or political factor that influences receptivity to intergroup interaction and affects its outcomes. The chapters in the second part review the effects of specific interventions that have been introduced into desegregation settings with the intent of improving intergroup acceptance in those settings. The final chapter provides a systematic integration of the preceding chapters within a common theoretical framework. Although the volume as a whole takes a very broad view of intergroup contact and related research, the conclusions drawn in the various chapters should be readily applicable to specific situations involving the formation and implementation of desegregation policies. Thus the book is written with policymakers, as well as social science researchers, in mind.

It is particularly appropriate that this volume is sponsored by the Society for the Psychological Study of Social Issues (SPSSI), because its very existence is in many ways a product of SPSSI programs and activities. Several of the contributors have been recipients of SPSSI grants-in-aid (GIA), a program to provide seed money for socially relevant research efforts. The research reported herein by the Stephans (Chapter 11), Hamilton *et al.* (Chapter 6), and Rogers *et al.* (Chapter 10) resulted from GIA-supported projects. In addition, the chapter by Johnson *et al.* (Chapter 9) is part of a larger metanalysis project that received SPSSI's Gordon Allport Intergroup Relations Prize in 1982.

Apart from its role in supporting much of the research represented here, SPSSI also provided the forum for collaboration that resulted in the present volume. A SPSSI-sponsored symposium at the 1982 convention of the American Psychological Association created an opportunity for many of the contributors to get together and plan the content and organization of the book. The initial idea for the project grew out of discussions between the coeditors that took place when we were both serving on the SPSSI Council. Those early discussions revealed a number of common orientations toward the study of intergroup relations that have been incorporated in the themes in this volume. Some of those common perspectives derived from our respective experience with large-scale research on intergroup contact in naturalistic settings, experience that ranged from the study of the process and outcome of school desegregation in Riverside, California, on the one side, to the study of interethnic relations in East Africa on the other. The challenges and frustrations of working with large, field-based data sets led both of us to an appreciation of the need for analysis of intergroup behavior at the level of microprocesses as a route toward better understanding of group relations at the societal level. The diversity of intergroup settings with which we had been concerned also led us to a mutual appreciation of the need to step back from the immediate political contexts in which studies of intergroup relations are often embedded, in favor of a cross-cultural, transhistorical approach. This perspective also accounts for our shared conviction that common explanatory mechanisms can be applied to diverse contact situations. These assumptions are reflected in the range of social contexts and theoretical orientations represented in the contributions selected for inclusion in this volume, and in the content of the integrative chapter that concludes the volume.

Because this volume was truly a collective effort, a number of acknowledgments are in order. We are especially grateful to the contributors, whose cooperation in meeting deadlines and responding to editorial feedback was remarkable—a model of cross-cultural collaboration. Much appreciation is also due to those at SPSSI who helped put the project together, particularly to Jeff Rubin, cochair of SPSSI's publication committee, who coordinated the effort, and to the members of our editorial advisory committee—Harry Triandis, Janet Schofield, and James Jones—who read and reviewed early drafts of all the chapters and helped shape the final product. We also appreciate the input and direction of the editors at Academic Press, whose enthusiasm for the project helped get it off the ground and whose continuing efforts helped bring it to fruition.

Apart from those directly involved in the development of this volume, we are also deeply grateful to those whose influence and inspiration gave it form and substance: to Donald T. Campbell, our common mentor, whose intellectual influence pervades all of our work; to Henri Tajfel, to whom this volume is dedicated and whose contributions to the study and understanding of intergroup relations are reflected throughout the volume; and to our daughters, Carrie and Christine, who remind us why it is all worthwhile.

Groups in Contact
The Psychology of Desegregation

1

The Social Psychology of Desegregation: An Introduction

Norman Miller
and
Marilynn B. Brewer

Introduction

Research on the process and effects of desegregation lends itself to two very different views of the nature of the social science enterprise. The distinction between the two different approaches has been characterized as the difference between a "laws-and-instances ideal of explanation" and a "cases-and-interpretation one" (Geertz, 1980, p. 165). The former sees the goal of social research as the generation of generalized principles, abstracted from the context in which the phenomena of interest are embedded. The latter regards the goal of research as the understanding and interpretation of events in context, with an emphasis on what is distinctive rather than what is general (cf. Adams, Smelser, & Treiman, 1982).

Racial desegregation in the United States, particularly in school settings, has been subject to extensive analysis that takes into account the historical, political, and social circumstances in which it is embedded (e.g., Hawley, 1981; Orfield, 1978; Rist & Anson, 1977; Stephan & Feagin, 1980). The purpose of the present volume differs from most of these previous efforts. Though we do not believe that any social phenomenon such as desegregation can be fully understood outside its historical and social context, we do see some advantage in "stepping back" from particular instances and immediate political issues to assess the similarities and regularities that appear across events that may occur

1

in different times and places but that nevertheless share important commonalities. Certainly *desegregation*—defined as extended contact between previously isolated social groups that is brought on either by acute or gradual processes of change—cannot be regarded as limited to a single historical period or setting. We assume that many basic factors that determine the success or failure of such intergroup contact experiences are essentially the same across times and places, provided that the processes involved are conceptualized at an appropriate level of abstraction. The purpose of such abstraction is to contribute to the development of a social science theory of intergroup behavior and attitudes, which can in turn inform public policy in relevant instances.

The starting point for much of the research and theory represented in this volume is the so-called contact hypothesis. Basically, the hypothesis posits that one's behavior and attitudes toward members of a disliked social category will become more positive after direct interpersonal interaction with them. Numerous studies of intergroup contact in diverse settings such as the Merchant Marines (e.g., Brophy, 1946), the military (e.g., Mannheimer & Williams, 1949), housing projects (e.g., Wilner, Walkley, & Cook, 1952), and recreational sites (Williams, 1944), provided an empirical basis for this expectation. Although contact per se was sometimes thought to produce these positive effects, as research accumulated qualifications to the hypothesis seemed to be needed. Early work suggested that the nature of the contact was more relevant than its frequency or amount. Eventually, a number of specific stipulations became incorporated as part of the contact hypothesis. These are listed below:[1]

1. Contact must occur in circumstances that define the status of the participants from the two social groups as equal.
2. The attributes of the disliked group members with whom the contact occurs must disconfirm the prevailing stereotyped beliefs about them.
3. The contact situation must encourage, or perhaps require, a mutually interdependent relationship, that is, cooperation in the achievement of a joint goal.
4. The contact situation must have high acquaintance potential; that is, it must promote association of a sort that reveals enough detail about the member of the disliked group to encourage seeing him or her as an individual rather than as a person with stereotyped group characteristics.
5. The social norms of the contact situation must favor group equality and egalitarian intergroup association.

Although credit for the hypothesis is most frequently accorded to Gordon Allport as a consequence of his presentation of it in his eloquent, rich, and

---

[1]This summary of the contact hypothesis and its historical development has been adapted from Cook (1978). We appreciate his graciousness in making this material available to us.

influential book, *The Nature of Prejudice* (1954), earlier statements by Goodwin Watson (1947) and Robin Williams (1947) include these same qualifications in their integrations of research on intergroup relations. Undoubtedly, the relevant theoretical ingredients were in the air at the time. Brophy (1945) emphasized common goals as the explanation of his findings. Others noted the importance of equal status (Allport & Kramer, 1946; MacKenzie, 1948; Rosenblith, 1949). Newcomb (1947) cited personal communication and, earlier, Harlan (1942) stressed intimacy as important features of contact. Newcomb also suggested that social support from members of one's own group was important, thereby invoking the notion of normative support. Studies in residential settings strongly implicated cooperative interaction as critical (Deutsch and Collins, 1951; Wilner *et al.*, 1952). Thus any attempt to precisely fix credit for the elaborated hypothesis is probably inappropriate.

The contact hypothesis occupied an important role in the Social Science Statement that was appended to the plaintiffs' briefs in the Brown case, in which the Supreme Court declared that segregated schools were unconstitutional. Although it seems clear that the court responded as it did primarily because it viewed segregated schooling as an important contributor to the stigmatization of blacks, the Social Science Statement focused on three specific harms that it produced—impaired self concepts among minority children, poor academic motivation and learning among minority children, and intergroup hostility and prejudice. Further, it went on to argue that desegregated schooling would reduce prejudice if the process of desegregation (1) was swift and pervasive, (2) was consistently and firmly enforced, (3) provided equal status within the desegregated setting, and (4) minimized conflict between the groups.

Thus, the benefits anticipated in the Social Science Statement were clearly circumscribed by the specification of context conditions that were assumed to be necessary for positive intergroup contact. The difficulty in implementing them, or assessing their presence, however, was undoubtedly underestimated (Hennigan, Flay & Cook, 1980). Consequently, implementation of desegregation policies went forward with little or no attention to these moderating conditions. Perhaps as a result, findings from early research on cross-racial acceptance and social accommodation in desegregated classrooms were mixed at best. Much of this research was largely atheoretical. As data accumulated, however, and inconsistencies in findings emerged, the sheer number of relevant situational and dispositional factors to be taken into account mounted. So too did the need for theoretical clarification.

Among several qualifications listed above, for instance, equal-status contact has most frequently been stressed as critical. Although Allport emphasized the less restrictive stipulation that status need only be equal within the contact setting, Williams (1947) stressed the importance of equality of status across situations. In the school setting, this distinction became a particularly important point of controversy (e.g., see Cohen, 1980; Miller, 1980; and Pettigrew, Smith, Useem, & Norman, 1973). Would equal treatment of black and white children by teachers and administrators fulfill the necessary boundary requirements, or would average racial–ethnic differences in academic performance and social-class standing preclude salutory effects, despite fairness and equal treatment on the part of teachers and administrators? On the basis of careful analysis of studies purported to assess the importance of equal-status contact, Riorden (1978) concludes that it is indeed more difficult to implement equal-status contact than is implied by the social science statement, and that in many instances in which improvement in intergroup acceptance occurs, factors other than equal status explain the results.

In sum, the need for a theoretical framework to guide the conduct and interpretation of research has become obvious. The present volume focuses on such theory-guided research efforts and on attempts to reinterpret past research results in the light of current theoretical perspectives.

This volume is also focused on the social psychology of intergroup contact, that is, the intrapersonal and interpersonal processes involved in such contact as opposed to the institutional changes associated with desegregation. More specifically, we are interested in the consequences of desegregation for social acceptance at the interpersonal level, and in the conditions that promote positive intergroup interactions among individuals.

Overview of the Volume

The six contributions in Part I of this volume define issues for research on desegregation by identifying contextual features that are common to intergroup contact situations in a variety of settings. Collectively these chapters remind one that the process of desegregation rarely takes place in a political vacuum but that preexisting factors, such as status differentials between groups, ethnocentric values, educational practices, and prevailing government policies, almost always set the stage on which contact takes place. Each of the chapters in this section examines one or more of these contextual features and how they interact with contact itself to determine the outcomes of desegregation in naturalistic settings.

The lead chapter, by John Berry, provides a conceptual framework for succeeding chapters by identifying alternative ideological models for desegregation. In defining these alternatives, Berry makes two important distinctions that are implicit throughout this volume. One is the distinction between *desegregation* and *integration,* the former referring to the mere presence of extended contact between subgroups within a society and the latter to a particular outcome of such contact in terms of intergroup attitudes and relations. The second is the distinction between *integration* and *assimilation* as two different desegregation outcomes: integration preserves group distinctiveness whereas assimilation seeks to reduce intergroup differentiation through merging into a common culture. Focusing on the history of intergroup relations in Canada, Berry highlights the role of explicit government policies in determining which model of desegregation is pursued; at a different level of analysis, he also explores the correspondence between alternative models of intergroup relations and individual differences in cognitive complexity.

The relationship between individual cognitive capacities and intergroup attitudes is explored further in the chapter by Wagner and Schönbach. Within the framework of the West German educational system, the authors attempt to identify the cognitive and motivational factors that mediate the established correlation between educational status and attitudes toward outgroups. Their results suggest that some aspects of general intelligence and cognitive complexity predict prejudice against foreign workers in Germany both within and between educational tracks, and that this relationship holds regardless of amount of contact with the target outgroups. These findings raise the intriguing question of whether educational practices can alter the cognitive structures and processes that appear to underlie intergroup acceptance.

The role of educational institutions in intergroup relations is also the focus of the next two chapters in this section. Schwartzwald and Amir trace the history of official school desegregation policies in Israel and assess the effects of variation in implementation of those policies in different school systems. Their analyses suggest that the effectiveness of desegregation in promoting intergroup acceptance depends heavily on whether structural features of the educational environment tend to enhance or undermine preexisting status differentials between ethnic groups. The critical role of status differences is also examined in the chapter by Elizabeth Cohen within the framework of sociological "expectation states" theory. Basic to this theory is the prediction that status and power differences between groups on any one dimension are inappropriately generalized to new dimensions or settings. Based on evidence for such carry-over effects in school settings, Cohen predicts that intergroup contact, even under cooperative conditions, will tend to reinforce prior differences in status unless explicit efforts are made to reverse such differences in the contact situation.

The remaining two chapters in Part I deal with the course of desegregation itself and the conditions under which it is (or is not) achieved. The chapter by Hamilton, Carpenter, and Bishop reviews evidence on patterns of racial desegregation of residential neighborhoods in the United States as a context for presenting the results of a follow-up study of the effects of initial desegregation of neighborhoods in one suburban community. The apparently slow and irregular course of neighborhood integration in the absence of political intervention sets the stage for government policies designed to promote intergroup contact in institutional settings. Sears and Harris argue that the controversy surrounding the implementation of busing as a method of achieving school desegregation reflects a deep-seated ambivalence toward interracial contact derived from long-standing racist attitudes and beliefs in our society. To the extent that residual racism is manifested in organized resistance to busing and related policies, the gap between desegregation and integration is likely to remain unbridged.

The issues raised in Part I of this volume are grounded in research that is largely descriptive and correlational, undertaken in field settings with little or no intervention in ongoing processes. Analyses of natural variations in the course of desegregation, however, suggest types of intervention programs that might alter the nature of intergroup behavior and attitudes in such settings. The chapters in Part II of this volume report on research efforts that assess the effectiveness of such interventions in the contact situation. The first three chapters deal with interventions designed to alter the social structure within which intergroup interaction takes place, particularly by introducing cooperative interdependence among members of different groups. Stuart Cook summarizes the results of a program of research intended to test the expanded contact hypothesis in a variety of interracial settings. By introducing a task structure designed to maximize cooperative, equal-status cross-racial interactions, Cook assesses the effectiveness of such enriched contact experiences in improving interpersonal relations and reducing racial prejudice among initially highly prejudiced participants. A more general review of efforts to improve intergroup relations in desegregated schools through cooperative learning techniques is provided in the chapter by Johnson, Johnson, and Maruyama. Using metanalysis techniques, they summarize results of classroom experiments comparing specific cooperative interventions to interventions that involve competitive, individualistic, or mixed task structures, assessing and comparing effects on interpersonal acceptance in classes that are either racially heterogeneous or include the presence of handicapped children.

Although the studies summarized by Cook and by Johnson *et al.* uniformly support the effectiveness of cooperative task structure in improving intergroup acceptance *within* the contact situation, a question that remains unanswered is the generalizability of those effects to behaviors and attitudes toward outgroup members *outside* that controlled setting. Effects of cooperative learning structures, for instance, may be limited to intergroup behavior within the specific teacher-controlled classroom but not carry over beyond it. Such concerns form the basis for interventions that extend into alternative settings and behavioral contexts. The chapter by Rogers, Hennigan, Bowman, and Miller compares the patterns of intergroup behavior observed in playground versus classroom settings and reviews the results of research efforts to introduce cooperative game structures into playground activities. In addition, it presents new data that provide some understanding of mediating factors, such as group salience and perceived similarity, that determine the extent of cross-ethnic social acceptance in a given setting and its generalizability to new settings.

While interventions based on cooperative interaction focus on the *inter*personal aspects of the contact situation, the remaining two chapters in this section of the volume deal with *intra*personal factors that mediate intergroup acceptance. Specifically, both consider the role of knowledge about and familiarity with the outgroup as a primary determinant of positive intergroup relations. Stephan and Stephan provide a theoretical analysis of how knowledge of group differences may promote cross-ethnic acceptance in desegregated schools and suggest specific interventions that may enhance such effects. The chapter by Landis, Hope, and Day reviews the kinds of programs that have been introduced in military settings to increase intergroup understanding and reduce conflict in desegregated units. Although good experimental tests of the effectiveness of knowledge-based interventions in improving intergroup relations are still lacking, the successful use of specific techniques, such as the Cultural Assimilator, in cross-cultural settings encourages their development in other contact situations.

Collectively, the chapters in this volume provide a picture of the desegregation process as a complex interplay between cognitive processes within individuals and structural features of the social environment. The final chapter attempts to provide a single theoretical framework that encompasses these interactive effects and integrates the findings and conclusions of the preceding chapters. Taking the contact hypothesis as a point of departure, this chapter proposes an expanded theory of contact based on social categorization and social comparison processes. It concludes with an outline for a program of experimental research to clarify the processes underlying the effectiveness of cooperative interaction in promoting intergroup acceptance and the conditions under which this can be achieved. The ultimate goal of such a research program will be to contribute to the design of effective intervention strategies that are theory-based and grounded in empirical research.

References

Adams, R. M. Smelser, N. J., & Treiman, D. J. (Eds.) *Behavioral and social science research: A national resource. Part I.* Washington, D.C.: National Academy Press, 1982.

Allport, G. W. *The nature of prejudice.* Cambridge, MA: Addison–Wesley, 1954.

Allport, G. W., & Kramer, B. Some roots of prejudice. *Journal of Psychology,* 1946, *22,* 9–39.

Brophy, I. N. The luxury of anti-Negro prejudice. *Public Opinion Quarterly,* 1946, *9,* 456–466.

Cohen, E. G. Design and redesign of the desegregated school: Problems of status, power, and conflict. In W. Stephan & J. Feagin (Eds.), *School desegregation: Past, present, and future* (pp. 251–280). New York: Plenum, 1980.

Cook, S. W. Interpersonal and attitudinal outcomes in cooperating interracial groups. *Journal of Research and Development in Education,* 1978, *12,* 97–113.

Deutsch, M., and Collins, M. E. *Interracial housing: A psychological evaluation of a social experiment.* Minneapolis: University of Minnesota Press, 1951.

Geertz, C. Blurred genres—the refiguration of social thought. *American Scholar,* 1980, *49,* 165–179.

Harlan, H. H. Some factors affecting attitudes toward Jews. *American Sociological Review,* 1942, *7,* 816–827.

Hawley, W. D. (Ed.), *Effective school desegregation: Equity, quality, and feasibility.* Beverly Hills, CA: Sage, 1981.

Hennigan, K., Flay, B., and Cook, T. Give me the facts: Some suggestions for using social science knowledge in national policy making. In R. Kidd and M. Saks (Eds.), *Advances in applied social psychology.* Hillsdale, NJ: Erlbaum, 1980.

MacKenzie, B. K. The importance of contact in determining attitudes towards Negroes. *Journal of Abnormal and Social Psychology,* 1948, *43,* 417–441.

Mannheimer, D., and Williams, R. M. A note on Negro troops in combat. In S. Stouffer, E. Suchman, L. DeVinney, S. Star, and R. Williams (Eds.), *The American soldier.* Vol. 1. Princeton, NJ: Princeton University Press, 1949.

Miller, N. Making school desegregation work. In W. Stephan and J. Feagin (Eds.), *School desegregation: Past, present, and future* (pp. 309–348). New York: Plenum, 1980.

Newcomb, T. M. Autistic hostility and social reality. *Human Relations,* 1947, *1,* 69–86.

Orfield, G. *Must we bus? Segregated schools and national policy.* Washington, D.C.: Brookings Institution, 1978.

Pettigrew, T. F., Smith, N., Useem, E. L., and Norman, C. Busing: A review of the evidence. *Public Interest,* 1973, *30,* 88–118.

Riordin, C. Equal-status interracial contact: A review and revision of the concept. *International Journal of Intercultural Relations,* 1978, *2,* 161–185.

Rist, R. C., and Anson, R. J. (Eds.), *Education, social science, and the judicial process.* New York: Teachers College Press, 1977.

Rosenblith, J. F. A replication of "Some roots of prejudice." *Journal of Abnormal and Social Psychology,* 1949, *44,* 470–489.

Stephan, W. G., and Feagin, J. R. (Eds.), *School desegregation: Past, present, and future.* New York: Plenum, 1980.

Watson, G. *Action for unity.* New York: Harper, 1947.

Williams, D. H. *The effects of an interracial project upon the attitudes of Negro and white girls within the YMCA.* Unpublished M.A. thesis, Columbia University, 1944.

Williams, R. M., Jr. *The reduction of intergroup tensions.* New York: Social Science Research Council, 1947.

Wilner, D. M., Walkley, R. P., and Cook, S. W. *Human relations in interracial housing.* Minneapolis: University of Minnesota Press, 1955.

Part I

Issues in Desegregation Research

2

Cultural Relations In Plural Societies: Alternatives to Segregation and Their Sociopsychological Implications*

J. W. Berry

The concept of *desegregation* implies movement away from a particular condition, but it does not, in itself, indicate the direction or goals of this movement. This chapter conceptualizes some alternatives to segregation and considers their social and psychological implications.

A Model of Cultural Relations in Plural Societies

A model of group and individual relations in culturally plural societies has been developed over the past decade (Berry, 1974, 1980; Sommerlad & Berry, 1970). It is based upon the observation that in plural societies, individuals and groups must confront two important issues. One pertains to the maintenance and development of one's ethnic distinctiveness in society, deciding whether one's own cultural identity and customs are of value and to be retained. The other issue involves the desirability of ethnic contact, deciding whether positive relations with the larger society are of value and to be sought. These are essentially questions of values, including attitudes, even ideologies, and may be responded to on a continuous scale, from positive to negative. For conceptual

*I acknowledge various sources of financial assistance, including the Social Science and Humanities Research Council of Canada and the Multiculturalism Directorate, Government of Canada.

purposes, however, they can be treated as dichotomous ("yes" and "no") decisions, thus generating a fourfold model (see Table 2.1) that serves as the basis for our discussion in this chapter. Each cell in this fourfold classification is considered to be an option available to individuals and to groups in plural societies; these are *assimilation, integration, segregation–separation,* and *deculturation*. They define, in effect, four varieties of cultural relations and acculturation (Berry, 1980) and incorporate two basic dimensions of group relations: social differentiation (Tajfel, 1978) and contact (Amir, 1969, 1976). This model, although based upon responses to concrete issues, may best be viewed as an ideal because these four prototypes are not likely to be found in pure form in any cultural intergroup situation.

When the first question is answered "no," and the second is answered "yes," the assimilation option is defined, namely, relinquishing one's cultural identity and moving into the larger society. This can take place by way of absorption of a nondominant group into an established mainstream, or it can be by way of the merging of many groups to form a new society, as in the "melting pot" concept. In a detailed analysis of this form of acculturation, Gordon (1964) distinguishes a number of subvarieties or processes; most important among these are *cultural or behavioral assimilation,* in which collective and individual behaviors become more similar, and *structural assimilation,* in which the nondominant groups participate in the social and economic systems of the larger society.

The integration[1] option implies the maintenance of the cultural integrity of the group, as well as the movement by the group to become an integral part of a larger societal framework. Therefore, in the case of integration, the option taken is to retain cultural identity and move to join the dominant society. In this case there is a large number of distinguishable ethnic groups, all cooperating

TABLE 2.1

A Model of Possible Forms of Cultural Relations in Plural Societies

Question 2: "Are positive relations with the larger society of value, and to be sought?"	*Question 1:* "Are cultural identity and customs of value, and to be retained?"	
	Yes	No
Yes	Integration	Assimilation
No	Segregation–separation	Deculturation

[1]It should be clear from this definition that the term *integration* is being used in a specific way that derives from its etymology, rather than in the more usual and general way as a synonym for desegregation.

within a larger social system, described as the "mosaic" (Porter, 1965). Such an arrangement may occur where there is some degree of structural assimilation but little cultural and behavioral assimilation, to use Gordon's terms.

When there are no positive relations with the larger society, accompanied by a maintenance of ethnic identity and traditions, another option is defined. Depending upon which group, the dominant or nondominant, controls the situation, this option may take the form either of segregation or of separation. When the pattern is imposed by the dominant group, classic segregation to keep people in "their place" appears. On the other hand, the maintenance of a traditional way of life outside full participation in the larger society may derive from a group's desire to lead an independent existence, as in the case of separatist movements. In our terms, segregation and separation differ only with respect to which group or groups have the power to determine the outcome.

Finally, there is an option that is difficult to define precisely, possibly because it is accompanied by a good deal of collective and individual confusion and anxiety. It is characterized by striking out against the larger society and by feelings of alienation, loss of identity, and what has been termed *acculturative stress* (Berry & Annis, 1974). This option is *deculturation,* in which groups lose cultural and psychological contact with their traditional culture or the larger society. When imposed by the larger society, it is tantamount to ethnocide. When stabilized in a nondominant group, it constitutes the classical situation or marginality (Stonequist, 1935).

A number of points should be made with respect to the model in Table 2.1 First, these options pertain to both individuals and groups in plural societies. One individual may follow a course toward assimilation, whereas another may not; and one ethnic group through its formal organizations may opt for separation, whereas another may seek integration. It should be obvious, however, that choices among the options are not entirely independent. At the group level, if all of one's group pursues assimilation, one is left without a membership group, rendering the other options meaningless; and if group assimilation is widespread, the culturally plural character of the society is eliminated, again voiding the other options.

Second, the various options may be pursued by politically dominant or nondominant groups. For example, if assimilation is sought by a particular ethnic group, it is an example of the melting pot, whereas if it is enforced as national policy, we may characterize it as a "pressure cooker." Similarly, as we have noted, separation occurs when a group wishes to set up shop on its own, whereas the classic forms of segregation exist when such apartness is forced on it by the dominant groups.

Third, there can be flux and inconsistency with respect to which options are pursued within a society. Flux occurs over time as an individual or a group experiments with differing options; for example, French-Canadians, long in fear of assimilation, are currently exploring the relative merits of the integration versus separation options. Inconsistency occurs when, at a single point in time, for example, an individual may accept linguistic and economic assimilation but wish to avoid it in all other areas of daily life.

Despite these qualifications, the model proves to be conceptually and empirically useful as a framework for research on intergroup relations (Berry, 1976; Berry, Kalin, & Taylor, 1977; Berry, Wintrob, Sindell, & Mawhinney, 1982). Its presentation in this chapter provides a theoretical setting for the discussion of these and other studies in the following sections.

The Societal Context of Cultural Relations

The course or option that a particular individual or group takes may be influenced by a number of factors. One is the nature of current ideology and policy in the larger society. Obviously in a society with a strong assimilationist or mainstream ideology, groups will have difficulty in integrating or separating.

Another factor is the degree of voluntariness of a group's presence in the plural society; clearly a voluntary immigrant is more likely to seek relations with the larger society than those (like Native peoples) who have been imposed upon. This distinction is represented in Table 2.2, in which four types of groups are defined according to their freedom of contact and physical movement. This fourfold classification also represents an ideal typology, and some individuals may not fit neatly into a single category.

The purpose here is to suggest that the options chosen are likely to vary with the type of group under consideration. Free or voluntary contact, indicated by the desire to migrate or have positive relations with the larger society, suggests that immigrants and ethnic groups may be more likely to assimilate or integrate than refugees or Native peoples. Sedentary groups have greater possibility than mobile groups for establishing protective institutions and barriers that enhance the likelihood of maintaining distinct identity, language, and culture, and thus, of pursuing the integration or rejection options. To my knowl-

TABLE 2.2

A Model of Types of Groups in Plural Societies

Freedom of contact	Mobility	
	Mobile	Sedentary
Voluntary	Immigrants	Ethnic groups
Forced	Refugees	Native peoples

edge, no empirical studies have been carried out systematically that indicate which options are more likely to be followed by which type of group. The purpose of this analysis is merely to suggest that, with all four types present in most Western plural societies, one might reasonably expect to find different courses taken by different groups in various societies. Similarly, one can reasonably expect individual differences within groups; these can and have been assessed and are discussed in the next section of this chapter.

Returning to the question of ideology posed at the beginning of this section, the central issue is that of tolerance for diversity. Some societies are characterized by assimilationist expectations and policies that tend to reduce extant cultural diversity ("*e pluribus unum*"); in others the position is taken that diversity is valuable, a resource rather than a problem, and to be tolerated and even encouraged ("let a thousand flowers blossom"). The extent to which a society pursues one or the other of these extremes defines its degree of multiculturalism (Berry, 1979). This concept is not identical to that of cultural pluralism because even in plural societies, attitudes and policies may vary from efforts toward homogenization to those that support heterogeneity. In our view, for a society to be multicultural requires the presence of both pluralism and a positive multicultural ideology (Berry *et al.,* 1977) in public attitudes and policy.

Clearly the degree of tolerance for cultural diversity that is present in a society is a major factor in the options that are taken by cultural groups. In societies that attempt to reduce diversity, the options of assimilation or deculturation are more likely to be manifest, whereas in those more tolerant of diversity, integration or separation are more likely. However if intergroup attitudes are hostile in the larger society, segregation and deculturation are more likely than assimilation and integration.

Studies of Cultural Contact in Canada

This section does not attempt to review all the psychological literature on cultural contact in Canada; rather, some recent studies are used to illustrate some general trends.[2]

Population and Policy

The background to research on cultural contact in Canada is the diverse character of its population and the presence of an official policy of *multicul-*

[2]A recent bibliography (Désrochers & Clément, 1979) is a good general guide to much of the available information, and the texts edited by Gardner and Kalin (1981) and Samuda, Berry and Laferrière (1983) are useful compendia of current knowledge in the area.

turalism that is designed to maintain and develop this ethnic diversity. The Canadian population at the present time contains no single ethnic group that holds a numerical majority: the largest group is of French ancestry (28%), followed by English (26%), then Scottish (11%), Irish (10%), German (6%), Italian (4%), and Ukrainian (3%); and depending on how they are classified, Native (Amerindian and Inuit) peoples make up around 5%; others comprise the remaining 7%. Following the usage of Porter (1965), there are two charter groups, the French and the Angloceltic, who at the time of confederation together comprised 93% of the population. (Note that the Angloceltic group is a statistical amalgam of English, Scottish, Welsh and Irish, a practice not particularly favored by the Celtic groups themselves). The other ethnics (i.e., non-charter groups) have increased over the past century from around 7 to nearly 30% of the population.

The policy of multiculturalism was proposed in 1971 by the Federal Government, and now 5 of the 10 Canadian provinces have similar policy statements. Its historical roots lie in the recognition of the value of diversity as early as the 1956 UNESCO Havana Conference on "The Cultural Integration of Immigrants" (Borrie, 1959) in which the official Canadian paper argued that assimilation is impracticable as a general policy. In 1969 a Royal Commission on Bilingualism and Biculturalism produced a volume concerned with "the contribution made by the other ethnic groups to the cultural enrichment of Canada, and the measures that should be taken to safeguard that contribution" (Government of Canada, 1969 p. 4). Pointing out that Canada is a country of heavy immigration, the report further argues that the integration of the various elements: "does not imply the loss of an individual's identity and original characteristics or of his original language and culture. Man is a thinking and sensitive being; severing him from his roots could destroy an aspect of his personality and deprive society of some of the values he can bring to it" (1969, p. 5). Thus, a proposition of the Royal Commission is that immigration creates the possibility of cultural diversity; without it, ethnic groups would not have developed in Canada. A second proposition is that the maintenance of diversity is psychologically necessary for the well-being of the individual, and a third is that such diversity could be a valuable resource for the society as a whole.

From this position, a set of 16 recommendations was made to the federal government that led to the multiculturalism policy. Termed a "policy of multiculturalism within a bilingual framework" (Prime Minister's statement, 1971), it sought to encourage the retention of characteristic cultural features by those groups that desired to do so and the sharing of these cultural features with other members of the larger Canadian society. Based upon the assumption that if individuals are to be open in their ethnic attitudes and have respect for other groups, they must have confidence in their own cultural foundations, the policy is also designed to "help break down discriminatory attitudes and cultural jealousies" (1971, p. 2). In essence it asserts that in Canada, "although there are two official languages, there is no official culture, nor does any ethnic group take precedence over any other" (1971, p. 1). Further, other cultural communities are seen as "essential elements in Canada and deserve government assistance in order to contribute to regional and national life in ways that derive from their heritages, yet are distinctively Canadian" (1971, p. 3).

Thus, the policy makes explicit two points of view that have psychological importance. One is that an individual will be better off for having a culturally based social network. A sense of self-confidence and security, rooted in cultural attachment, are valuable characteristics for a population to have. The other, termed the *multiculturalism assumption* (Berry et al., 1977), is that by feeling culturally secure, an individual will be more able to accept the ethnicity of others by holding positive ethnic attitudes and will be more tolerant of diversity generally, accepting a multicultural ideology.

Multicultural Ideology

As part of the federal government's policy-related research, a national survey (Berry et al., 1977) addressed three aspects of this policy in its questioning: knowledge of the policy, perception of the policy, and an assessment of a person's multicultural ideology.

The survey question dealing with knowledge of the policy revealed that about 80% did not know of it, and almost three-quarters of those respondents had not even heard of it. Thus, an explicit knowledge of multicultural policy was relatively rare in 1974.

Perceptions of how Canadian policy deals with cultural diversity, however, were relatively accurate. Three statements were read out and respondents were asked to indicate which of the three alternatives represented the orientation of the Canadian government toward newcomers. Only 13% chose the alternative representing the assimilation option (see Table 2.1) in which people are encouraged to give up their life style and take on the customs of their new country. The balance chose either of two forms of the integration options: 60% of the respondents chose the permissive variety (in which people are allowed to maintain differences) and 26% chose the supportive variety (in which people are actually encouraged to do so). Thus, there is a fairly clear perception that uniculturalism is not being fostered by Canadian government policy; rather some degree of tolerance for diversity is perceived as a national goal.

In order to assess multicultural ideology, a new scale had to be developed. Items were created to reflect the Integration option (see Table 2.1); also included were items based upon the Assimilation and Separation options, representing opposing ideologies. Items in the multicultural ideology scale include statements such as: "Canada would be a better place if members of ethnic groups would keep their own way of life alive," and "If members of ethnic groups want to keep their own culture, they should keep it to themselves and not bother other people in this country." The first is positive whereas the second is negative with respect to multiculturalism. Total multicultural ideology scores were derived by averaging responses on a 7-point scale to the nine items (reversing negative items). The mean score for the total sample on this scale was 4.51, which indicates moderate acceptance of multicultural ideology, if one assumes that 4.00 represents the neutral point of the scale.

It is of interest to note that those respondents who perceived the official Canadian policy to be one of assimilation were less supportive of a multicultural ideology and of various programs designed to implement the policy than were those who perceived that integration was the official policy. Similarly, those who claimed a knowledge of the policy perceived it more accurately and were more favorable toward multicultural ideology and programs.

Ethnocentrism and Prejudice

Ethnocentrism is generally defined as the tendency to evaluate one's own ethnic group more positively than other groups. Evidence from studies of ethnic attitudes in Canada indicates that this pattern of attitudes is widely present (Berry & Kalin, 1979), and from this, we might conclude that ethnocentrism is a necessary, and perhaps an unwanted, element in a multicultural society. If we remember that the Canadian multiculturalism policy set out to encourage positive own group evaluation, we may wonder whether the policy might have opposite effects to those intended, that is, that it may encourage an ethnocentric pattern of attitudes rather than mutual tolerance. However, the policy also asserts that only when a person has confidence in his own cultural foundations can he also have respect for other groups. In this section we examine the relative merits of these two apparently opposing points of view and the empirical evidence relating to them.

Ethnocentrism is often thought of as a central element in ethnic prejudice; but the latter is more general and includes a wide variety of other attitudes and traits. In the national survey (Berry et al., 1977), many of these other aspects, such as Authoritarianism and attitudes toward immigration, were measured in addition to Ethnocentrism itself, Multicultural Ideology, and attitudes toward specific ethnic groups. All of these responses were subjected to a factor analysis from which two significant factors emerged. One includes all of the attitudinal measures that are of a broad and general nature, including Ethnocentrism and Authoritarianism, as well as all of the Immigration and Multicultural scales. In addition, attitudes toward "Immigrants in General" loaded on this general factor as well. We may label this factor as one of general tolerance (as opposed to prejudice): Multicultural Ideology anchors the positive pole (loading $+ .78$) whereas Ethnocentrism defines the negative end (loading $- .59$). A second factor loads the more specific attitudes towards particular ethnic groups and proved to be independent of this general tolerance–prejudice factor.

What can we say about the nature of prejudice in Canada on the basis of this analysis? First, the very existence of the first factor suggests that generalized attitudes cluster together in a way that indicates the presence of prejudice as an element in intergroup relations. Second, the presence of the Multicultural and Immigration scales on this first factor (rather than a factor orthogonal to Ethnocentrism and Authoritarianism) suggests that the dimension is appropriate to, and perhaps specific to, the assessment of prejudice in multicultural societies.

As we indicated in the preceding section, the Multicultural Ideology scale generally receives ratings in the positive range. This is also the case with respect to Ethnocentrism; with a mean of 3.53 for the total sample, ethnocentric statements are rejected on the average. However, the Authoritarianism scale mean is 4.86, indicating that Canadians tend toward acceptance of the sentiments expressed in this scale. Nevertheless, the general picture is one of moderate tolerance in the Canadian sample as a whole. But when examined by ethnicity of the respondent, a clear and consistent picture emerges: Angloceltic and other ethnic respondents are more tolerant across the board than are French-Canadian respondents.

This brings us back to the question posed earlier: Is such an inverse relationship between ingroup and outgroup attitudes inevitable and is such a relatively high level of prejudice always to be found in multicultural societies? The general answer, apparently, is no; but it does tend to be the case for French-Canadian respondents. This finding suggests two additional questions: Is such an ethnocentric pattern related to a lack of confidence or security in linguistic, cultural, or economic matters and can policies such as that of Official Languages and Multiculturalism change the pattern by increasing confidence?

The answer to the first question is that general intolerance is indeed related to feelings of cultural and economic insecurity (Berry et al., 1977, Chapter 7). French-Canadians do appear to feel less secure than Angloceltic Canadians, but more telling, these measures of cultural and economic security are significantly correlated with all general attitude scales. That is, at both the individual and group level, scores on the security measures allow us to predict and perhaps understand general tolerance levels.

An answer to the second question is not possible at the present time. The promise of the Canadian linguistic and cultural policies is to increase self- and ethnic-group feelings of confidence; but it is another matter to engineer a corresponding increase in tolerance. If increased levels of ingroup confidence lead to self-glorification, then the ethnocentric pattern may hold and lead to decreased tolerance. However, if it leads to a self-acceptance, a pride without glorification, then the multiculturalism assumption may be borne out.

Ethnic Contact

Are the various psychological orientations we have been discussing related to contact among ethnic groups in Canada? We may answer this by looking at three kinds of evidence: relationships between generalized contact outside one's own area and general prejudice; relationships between rated familiarity and evaluation of groups; and relationships between the ethnic composition of one's neighborhood and attitudes toward specific ethnic groups.

First, with regard to generalized contact and its relation to general prejudice, our analyses indicate that the more geographic movement (i.e., generalized exposure to diverse environments) individuals have experienced, the more generally tolerant they are (Kalin & Berry, 1980). This conclusion rests upon a supplementary analysis of the Berry et al., (1977) survey data, using some mobility variables derived from questions regarding experiences of visiting or living in other regions of Canada or abroad. Considering the total sample (n = 1277 respondents), who had been born in Canada, both Ethnocentrism and Authoritarianism were negatively correlated with the geographic mobility variable ($-.23$ and $-.16$) whereas Immigration Attitudes and Multicultural Ideology were positively correlated ($+.23$ and $+.20$) with Mobility; the Tolerance factor score (made up of all variables that loaded on the general attitudinal factor) was also correlated significantly and positively with Mobility ($+.25$).

Given that income as a status indicator is also related to Mobility and to Tolerance, partial correlations were also computed; the relationship between Mobility and Tolerance remained firm ($+.21$), holding income constant. A similar pattern of results were obtained for all three ethnic subsamples; it was generally strongest for French-Canadian respondents and least strong but still significant for most variables, among other ethnic Canadians.

The interpretation of this overall relationship between one's experience of mobility and generalized tolerance is not entirely clear. One possibility is that prior tolerance motivates one to seek new experiences. Another is that both variables are related to some third characteristic; however, partialling out the most obvious of these, status, left the relationship intact. A third possibility is that tolerance actually comes about as a result of mobility. Just as specific contact with an ethnic group can lead to greater acceptance of that group, so general contact with ethnic diversity, whether at home or abroad, may lead to general tolerance for diversity.

A second approach to the contact question may be made by examining the correlation between familiarity and attitudes toward specific ethnic groups. In our studies of intergroup evaluation in Canada (Berry & Kalin, 1979), correlations between scores in an evaluation matrix and those in a familiarity matrix were over $+.9$. In the general sample, correlations between evaluation of and rated familiarity with each ethnic group were all positive and significant, ranging from $+.55$ for ratings of French-Canadians to $+.26$ for Chinese-Canadians. Thus, at this global level, we find evidence that ethnic groups who are said to be more familiar by the respondent are also evaluated more positively.

These results could, in part, arise from common method variance because assessments of both favorability and familiarity were derived from scores obtained on a similar 7-point scale. What is needed is some more objective measure of contact than that of rated familiarity; the analysis by Kalin and Berry, (1982) attempts to provide such an objective measure.

The Canadian census has, for years, included a question on ancestral country of origin, which is used by officials to estimate the ethnic composition of the population. These ethnic proportions are available for small census units, similar to an urban neighborhood or a rural township. The Berry et al. (1977) survey also obtained this ethnicity information from each respondent, as well as attitudes toward particular ethnic groups. It thus becomes possible to examine the social ecology of ethnic attitudes by determining the proportion of a particular ethnic group in a respondent's immediate vicinity (as the objective measure we are seeking) and then to relate this to both the ratings of familiarity (the subjective measure used up until now) and to the evaluations made of each group.

Considering the relationship between actual ethnic proportion and familiarity ratings by respondents who are not members of the subject group, there is a strong and consistent pattern that for even small increases in ethnic proportion, there is a corresponding increase in rated familiarity. This is true for all seven groups included in this analysis and applies even to groups that are not racially or linguistically distinctive (i.e., differing from the respondent only in ethnicity). Ethnicity is clearly signaled to others in Canadian neighborhoods, and the relationship is one that does not depend on visible or audible difference. Indeed, there appears to be operating a "law of ethnic perception" that closely approximates classical psychophysical functions in the judgement of physical stimuli. This finding partially substantiates our earlier use of the subjective familiarity ratings as a probable index of actual familiarity.

The crux of the analysis, however, is the relationship between neighborhood ethnic composition and ethnic-group evaluation. Here the relationships are all significant, positive and linear, with one exception—that for Canadian-Indians. The greater the proportion of an ethnic group (from 0% to over 20%), the more positively is that group evaluated by individuals who are not members of the group. Moreover, the relationship is group specific (e.g., more Ukrainians in the area is associated with more liking for Ukrainians) and not general (e.g., more Germans in the area does not predict liking Ukrainians better).

How to interpret this relationship is not clear from correlational data alone. One possibility is that there is in- or out-migration from a neighborhood because of its ethnic character. However, there is no evidence that in-migration occurs for this reason (e.g., a Chinese-Canadian settling in an Italian neighborhood because he likes them), and our own evidence suggests that out-migration does not occur for ethnic reasons: if it did, then one might have found signs of lower evaluation as proportions increased, but this did not appear. The other obvious interpretation once again, is, that ethnic contact leads to positive ethnic-group evaluation. Because a neighborhood is generally cohesive with respect to status, there is present status equality, one of the major conditions for contact to work, according to Amir's (1969, 1976) analysis of contact effects. Moreover, having discounted internal migration as a major factor, the situation of involuntary contact or invasion may not be present to turn contact into conflict.

On the basis of these three analyses (geographic mobility, familiarity-evaluation ratings, and social ecology), we are of the opinion that contact with ethnic groups within a multicultural society such as Canada is likely to be generally associated with positive ethnic attitudes and general ethnic tolerance. This appears to be true for relationships between the two charter groups, French and Angloceltic; (Clément, Gardner, & Smythe, 1977), and among these groups and the other ethnic groups included in our study. The one partial exception to this generalization is the social ecology of ethnic attitudes toward Canadian-Indians. Here we come closest to the presence of institutionalized segregation and racism in Canada, and this result appears to parallel that found for similar situations elsewhere (Perry, Clifton, & Hyrniuk, 1982).

Attitudes toward Native peoples in general, and as a function of contact, need to be much more fully researched before the reasons underlying this important exception can be identified. The other side of the coin, the study of Native contact with and attitudes toward the larger society, is the focus of some recent work, and we turn to this in the following section.

Native Contact

A review of the relations between Native peoples and the larger society (Berry 1981) shows that a general process of cultural contact and change has been taking place among the Native peoples in northern Canada for centuries. Recently, though, an event of great speed and magnitude has occurred in northern Quebec: the unheralded announcement, and almost immediate construction of, a massive hydroelectric project on the hunting and trapping territory of the Cree people of the region.

The proposal of the hydroelectric project stimulated a collective reaction that included political organization and court proceedings to halt the intrusion. Following the granting of an injunction against its construction, which was later lifted, a negotiated settlement was achieved that provided for a Cree regional government, a school board, health and social services board, and a set of economic measures (e.g., land claims settlement, guaranteed income from trapping, and royalties on resources). Within a period of 5 years, the political and institutional structure of Cree society was radically transformed in a way that transferred institutional control to the Cree people themselves.

At the individual level, many persons became involved in these new structures. It is at this individual level that our interests lie in the present discussion. More specifically, an attempt was made to assess a number of experiences and attitudes of individuals in three Cree communities at two different times, just before construction began and about 9 years later. In all, 230 persons were studied at Time I and 199 were studied at Time II, 102 of whom were longitudinal. All were over the age of 16, and there were approximately equal numbers of males and females.

The variables that are relevant to our discussion fall into five classes: *contact* variables (schooling, wage employment, ownership of Eurocanadian goods, language use, literacy in French or English, and mass media exposure); *attitudes toward cultural relations* (assimilation, integration, separation, and scales that assess preferences for types of relations in Table 2.1); *attitudes toward cultural change* (continuity, synthesis, change, and scales that assess modernity preferences); *stress* variables (psychosomatic stress and feelings of marginality); and *cognitive* variables (Kohs Blocks, Ravens Matrices, and Cree Picture Vocabulary Test). Details of these variables and the rationale for them can be found in Berry *et al.* (1982).

The questions of interest here concern the relationships, after the major changes took place in the Cree area, between individual experience of contact and the various attitudes and characteristics of the Cree people. The clearest way to express these relationships is by way of factor analysis of the various measures included in the study; this is presented in Table 2.3.

A clear Factor I appears that contains all of the contact variables except wage employment (which loads only .28, marginally below the .3 cutoff). In addition, Factor I loads age and attitudes toward assimilation and separation. A clear Factor III also appears that loads attitudes toward continuity with traditional Cree ways and change toward Eurocanadian life; a parallel but weaker loading appears for assimilation and rejection.

These two factors suggest a number of important features about the Cree contact situation. First, virtually all measures of contact cluster together, and these are inversely related to age. Younger people have been experiencing a dose of contact that is relatively pervasive. Schooling seems to be by far the most important element in the contact package, followed closely by language use

TABLE 2.3

Factor Analysis of Acculturation and
Psychological Variables (Loading above .30)

| Variable | Factor | | |
	I	II	III
Age	−.78	—	—
Schooling	.91	—	—
Wage Employment	(.28)	.30	—
Ownership	.39	—	—
Language	.76	—	—
Literacy	.51	—	—
Mass media	.38	—	—
Assimilation	.47	—	(−.28)
Integration	—	.38	—
Separation	−.59	—	(.25)
Continuity	—	—	.82
Synthesis	—	.45	—
Change	—	—	−.73
Stress	—	−.56	—
Marginality	—	−.54	—
Kohs	—	.34	—
Ravens	—	.39	—
Vocabulary	—	.38	—

(Cree vs. English or French), whereas ownership of Eurocanadian goods, media use, and wage employment (all economic indicators) are less important.

Second, the two opposite cultural relations attitudes (assimilation and separation) appear on Factor I; assimilation loads positively, whereas separation loads negatively. Thus, we may say that the younger, those with most contact, tend to favor assimilation; whereas the older, those with least contact, tend to favor separation.

Interestingly, the modernity scales, dealing with attitudes toward cultural continuity and change, do not load on this first factor; rather they appear by themselves in a separate Factor III, although the two cultural relations attitudes do appear on this factor with a weak loading. Even more interesting, however, is the fact that the middle way, the relational attitude of integration and the modernity attitude of synthesis, do not appear on Factors I and III with these other attitudes, but both load on a separate one Factor II.

Turning to this Factor II, we find a varied set of psychological indicators, along with one contact variable (wage employment). Although at first glance, they seem too disparate to interpret, such a pattern was expected on the basis of earlier research (Berry, 1976; Berry & Annis, 1974). Specifically, the two acculturative stress variables (psychosomatic stress and feeling of marginality) were previously shown to be clustered together; they are now shown to be negatively related to a sense of cognitive control over the cultural contact situation, and positively related to integration and synthesis. Put in another way, those individuals who prefer the middle way (high on integration and synthesis attitudes) tend to be those who are less stressed by the contact and the change and have the cognitive and employment resources to cope with it.

Interestingly, it is the integration option that is preferred over assimilation or rejection among the Cree; this is also generally true among other Native groups who are in contact with Eurocanadian society (Berry, 1976). In contrast, synthesis is not the preferred orientation among the Cree: change is preferred over synthesis, with continuity being least preferred. The conceptual and empirical independence of these two sets of attitudes, cultural relations and change attitudes, are thus not only evident from the factor analysis (Table 2.3) but also in this differential preference pattern. It is apparent that high contact has led to an assimilationist orientation (Factor I) but that positive attitudes toward cultural and technical change are now in keeping with the maintenance of one's identity and values, combined with positive group relations (Factor II). Within a multicultural society this makes sense; the loss of Cree identity and values should not be the price paid for access to the economic and technical benefits available from the larger society.

In contrast, one might have expected a different pattern of results in an unicultural society: preference for assimilation and change might have been evident, and these may have been associated positively with all contact variables and cognitive resources and negatively with stress. In a sense, the Cree have taken the optimal path through the realities with which they are confronted: integration in the face of contact with a multicultural society and a combination of synthesis and change in the face of massive economic and technical intrusions into their area.

On the basis of this study of cultural contact in the Cree area, it is apparent that as a people, and as individuals, the Cree have not been wiped out, as so many initially feared. In the face of massive intrusion (forced contact) that is more at the economic, technical and political level than at the personal level, the Cree have managed to avoid the two extreme reactions of rejection or assimilation. From an initial position of partial segregation, they have taken the integration route, which is consistent both with current policy and associated with the avoidance of stress and marginality.

Indeed, in the circumstances, it is difficult to see how, in sociopsychological terms, they could be better situated than they are now. With a Cree regional government that has control over their own education, health and social services, and economic development, with current funds and future royalties to help them pursue their goals, and with positive attitudes both toward Cree identity and relationships with the larger society, the only difficulty appears to be the reciprocal attitude, that of the larger society toward Native peoples in general. Clearly this is a problem of major national importance. If we wish to pursue multiculturalism as a national policy, we have to somehow keep the current Native preference for integration from turning to one of separation; however, if negative attitudes toward Native peoples continue in the larger society, they are likely to be reciprocated by Native peoples, and in turn lead to a preference for separation. This example illustrates the difficult balance that integration requires between assimilation and rejection, but it shows that the contact of cultures is manageable, if not easy, in a society guided by a multicultural ideology.

Acknowledgments

This chapter contains ideas and data generated over a period of time in collaboration with a number of students and colleagues. Among these are: Elizabeth Sommerlad, with whom a first version of the cultural relations model was developed; Rudy Kalin and Don Taylor, with whom the multicultural attitudes study was conducted; and Ron Wintrob, Peter Sindell, Tom Mawhinney, and Bob Annis, with whom the Cree acculturation studies were done.

References

Amir, Y. Contact hypothesis in ethnic relations. *Psychological Bulletin*, 1969, *71*, 319–341.

Amir, Y. The role of intergroup contact in change of prejudice and ethnic relations. In P. Katz (Ed.), *Towards the elimination of racism*. New York: Pergamon, 1976.

Berry, J. W. Psychological aspects of cultural pluralism: unity and identity reconsidered. *Topics in culture learning*, 1974, *2*, 17–22.

Berry, J. W. *Human ecology and cognitive style: Comparative studies of cultural and psychological adaptation*. New York: Sage–Halsted, 1976.

Berry, J. W. Research in multicultural societies: Implications of cross-cultural methods. *Journal of Cross-Cultural Psychology*, 1979, *10*, 415–434.

Berry, J. W. Acculturation as varieties of adaptation. In A. Padilla (Ed.), *Acculturation: Theory, models and some new findings*. Washington, D.C.: AAAS, 1980.

Berry, J. W. Native peoples and the larger society. In R. C. Gardner and R. Kalin (Eds.), *A Canadian social psychology of ethnic relations*. Toronto: Methuen, 1981.

Berry, J. W. & Annis, R. C. Acculturative stress: the role of ecology, culture and differentiation. *Journal of Cross-Cultural Psychology*, 1974, *5*, 382–406.

Berry, J. W. & Kalin, R. Reciprocity of inter-ethnic attitudes in a multicultural society. *International Journal of Intercultural Relations*, 1979, *3*, 99–112.

Berry, J. W., Kalin, R. & Taylor, D. M. *Multiculturalism and ethnic attitudes in Canada*. Ottawa: Ministry of Supply and Services, 1977.

Berry, J. W., Wintrob, R., Sindell, P. & Mawhinney, T. Psychological adaptation to culture change among the James Bay Cree. *Le Naturaliste Canadien*, 1982, *109*, 965–975.

Borrie, W. D. (Ed.) *The cultural integration of immigrants*. Paris: UNESCO, 1959.

Désrochers, A. & Clément, R. *The social psychology of inter-ethnic contact and cross-cultural communication: An annotated bibliography.* Quebec: Centre International de Recherche sur le Bilinguisme, 1979.

Gardner, R. C. & Kalin, R. (Eds.) *A Canadian social psychology of ethnic relations.* Toronto: Methuen, 1981.

Gordon, M. *Assimilation in American life.* New York: Oxford University Press, 1964.

Government of Canada. *The cultural contributions of the other ethnic groups: Report of the Royal Commission on Bilingualism and Biculturalism, Book IV.* Ottawa: Queen's Printer, 1969.

Kalin, R. & Berry, J. W. Geographic mobility and ethnic tolerance. *Journal of Social Psychology,* 1980, *112,* 129–134.

Kalin, R. & Berry, J. W. Social ecology of ethnic attitudes. *Canadian Journal of Behavioural Science,* 1982, *14,* 97–109.

Porter, J. *The vertical mosaic.* Toronto: University of Toronto Press, 1965.

Perry, R. P., Clifton, R. A. & Hryniuk, S. M. *Multiculturalism in Winnipeg schools: A preliminary analysis of selected student, teacher and school characteristics.* Paper presented at Canadian Psychological Association, Montreal, June 1982.

Prime Minister's Statement, House of Commons, October, 1971.

Samuda, R., Berry, J. W., & Laferrière, M. (Eds.). *Multiculturalism in Canada: Social and educational perspectives.* Toronto: Allyn and Bacon, 1983.

Sommerlad, E. & Berry, J. W. The role of ethnic identification in distinguishing between attitudes towards assimilation and integration of a minority racial group. *Human Relations,* 1970, *23,* 23–29.

Stonequist, E. V. The problem of the marginal man. *American Journal of Sociology,* 1935, *41,* 1–12.

Tajfel, H. (Ed.). *Differentiation between social groups: Studies in the social psychology of intergroup relations.* London: Academic Press, 1978.

3

Links between Educational Status and Prejudice: Ethnic Attitudes in West Germany

Ulrich Wagner
and
Peter Schönbach

Overview

Interventions for the reduction of prejudice presuppose a theoretical analysis of prejudiced attitudes and their determinants. Our aim here is to present some theoretical perspectives based on two studies of prejudice among German schoolchildren toward foreigners in the Federal Republic of Germany. We are particularly interested in finding explanations for the frequently noticed negative correlation between the educational status of respondents and their degree of prejudice against outgroups. Our studies were guided by the hypothesis that this relationship can be explained in part by differences in cognitive abilities and/or habits between students in different educational tracks. In addition, we investigated whether the relationship is mediated by differences between the groups of students in self-esteem, as suggested by Tajfel's (1978) social identity theory.

Before we summarize our two studies[1] we should provide some background information on the situation of workers from abroad in the Federal Republic of Germany and on the origins of our approach. Subsequent to the presentation of our main hypotheses and some relevant data, we discuss the alternative hypothesis that persons from the higher and the lower educational strata might

---

[1]A detailed presentation of study I is available in Schönbach, & Gollwitzer, Stiepel, Wagner (1981). Study II is presented in detail in Wagner (1983).

have different contact experiences with foreigners that in turn foster different potentials of prejudice toward this outgroup.

Background

In the 1950s and 1960s the rapidly expanding West German economy needed more labor than was available at home. The gap was filled at increasing rates with workers from abroad. Recruitment treaties were negotiated with Italy (1955), Spain and Greece (1960), Turkey (1961), Morocco (1963), and several other countries, Yugoslavia (1968) being the last one. The number of foreigners in the Federal Republic of Germany rose to 4.7 million in 1982, representing about 7.6% of the West German population.

The recruitment treaties assumed that a rotation process would occur, that is, that most workers from abroad would stay and work in West Germany for only a few years and then return home, thus requiring continuous replacements. Almost from the beginning, however, the rotation principle proved wrong. Many workers from abroad stayed much longer than expected and eventually had their families come and join them. These tendencies were strengthened in 1973 when, due to the economic recession, further recruitments were severely curtailed and in 1975 when bonus payments were reduced for workers whose children lived abroad. As a result, the dominant pattern is no longer a group of single male workers, but whole families from abroad.

Unemployment at home and the offer of comparatively high wages in the Federal Republic have induced workers from Mediterranean countries to migrate to West Germany. In turn, however, many of them have to put up with rather unfavorable living conditions: very poor housing, low grade jobs, disadvantages for their children at school, very dim employment prospects for this second generation, and an insecure residence status (cf. Mehrländer, Hofmann, König, & Krause, 1981). All these factors, beside others, contribute to keeping the workers from abroad and their families as a rule rather isolated from the German population. This isolation is both fostered by and conducive to clear signs of rejection and prejudices among a large number of Germans.

Over the years many surveys have confirmed that rather widespread negative attitudes towards workers and their families from abroad continue to exist in the German population (Schönbach, & Gollwitzer, Stiepel, Wagner, 1981, pp. 4-8). Most recently such negative and hostile attitudes seem to have intensified and spread even further, with foreigners being cast into the role of scapegoats for high criminality rates, unemployment and housing problems (cf. INFAS, 1982; Der Spiegel, No. 18/1982). In close parallel to American investigations (Harding, Proshansky, Kutner, & Chein, 1969), German studies consistently demonstrate a negative correlation between the educational level attained by the respondents on the one hand and the extent of their prejudices and discriminatory tendencies towards outgroups on the other (Bergler & Six, 1972; INFAS, 1982; Schönbach et al., 1981).

In the early 1960s, Schönbach (1970) studied label effects on attitudes toward workers from abroad. Two denotatively equivalent terms for this group were then in use in West Germany: *Fremdarbeiter* (foreign workers) and *Gastarbeiter* (guest workers). As hypothesized, for the major strata in the population the label *Fremdarbeiter* carried more negative connotations than the label *Gastarbeiter*, and the designation of workers from abroad as *Fremdarbeiter* stimulated more negative attitudinal reactions than designation with the label *Gastarbeiter*.

More important in the present context are some serendipitous findings from that early study and the following post facto hypotheses derived from them: stereotypical reactions elicited by the labels *Fremdarbeiter* and *Gastarbeiter* are partly mediated by association chains in which nationality labels such as Italian, Spaniard, Greek often play an important role. The more prominent this role, the more narrowly the association chains are channeled towards stereotypes of Mediterranean people. Two factors appear to partly determine the prominence of the nationality labels as mediator components in the association chains: (1) the label variation and (2) the educational status of the respondents. Both stereotypical responses on the attitudinal measure and prominence of nationality labels among pertinent associations were significantly stronger among (1) respondents who had to react to the *Fremdarbeiter* rather than to the *Gastarbeiter* label, and (2) among respondents with a low rather than a high level of formal education, regardless of the label presented to them.

Some indications in the literature, for example, Schatzmann and Strauss (1955), suggested to Schönbach (1970) further hypotheses. The rather narrow association chains among persons with a low degree of formal education may be due to a comparatively low degree of *associative flexibility* and a comparatively high degree of associative imagery. Low associative flexibility means that, on the average, the number of available associative responses to a given stimulus is small and that the probability gradient of their hierarchy is steep. Consequently, high flexibility means large numbers and flat gradients of available associative responses. *Associative imagery* is high if, on the average, a large proportion of the available associative responses to a given stimulus refer to entities that can easily and vividly be represented by mental images. Given an appropriate starter cue, low associative flexibility and/or high associative imagery may lead to and foster the dominant negative stereotypes in overt judgments about specific outgroups. These latter hypotheses formed the theoretical core of Study I, which we describe briefly below.

From the outset, two points should be made clear about out theoretical conceptualizations. Although we find it appropriate to use a stimulus–response terminology for the presentation of our original model, we do not mean to imply that this specific terminology will suffice for representing all relevant cognitive processes. (This becomes evident in our summary of Study I and in Study II.) Also, we consider neither low-level associative linkages nor cognitive processes of a higher order as sole determinants of stereotyping and prejudice. We are, of course, aware of the complex interplay of cultural traditions, public and publicized opinions, and vicarious, as well as, immediate experiences with members of an outgroup in a specific political and socioeconomic context in fostering certain prevalent attitudes towards that outgroup. It is our aim merely to contribute to the clarification of why, on the average, persons at some levels of education tend to react to such complex conditions of experience more often and more strongly with prejudices than do those at other levels of education.

Study I: An Initial Exploration of Cognitive Mediators

The theory underlying our initial investigation is represented by six hypotheses forming a nomological net (Schönbach et al., 1981, pp. 18ff.). The first hypothesis, basic to all the others, is that German respondents with lower levels of education react on the average more frequently and more strongly with negative stereotypes toward members of Mediterranean nations than do those with higher educational levels.

Several public stereotypes about workers from Mediterranean countries in the Federal Republic are both quite negative and prominent (Delgado, 1972). Following Osgood (1953), Staats (1968), and others, one may see the link between a stimulus such as "Italian" and a prominent stereotypical response such as "hot-tempered" as determined in part by covert associative mediators. If such mediators are part of a narrowly channeled association chain, then the internal associative connections and thus, also the linkage between stimulus and overt stereotypical response should be quite strong. Persons with an habitually low associative flexibility, whose association chains are generally narrow, should be prone to adopt and reproduce prominent public stereotypes. The inclination of a person to produce much imagery in his or her associations may play a similar role. Some findings in the literature suggest to us that a high proportion of imagery content might contribute to a strengthening of stereotypical response tendencies either directly or via a restrictive influence on the associative flexibility in general, or both. These speculations are represented in Hypotheses 2 through 6.

Persons with high educational status will on the average produce associations that are marked by comparatively few imagery components (Hypothesis 2) and a comparatively high degree of associative flexibility (Hypothesis 4). With educational status held constant, the probability of negative stereotypical reactions towards Mediterranean nations will be comparatively low among persons with little imagery in their associations (Hypothesis 3) and a high degree of associative flexibility (Hypothesis 5). Finally, the higher the proportion of imagery content the lower will be the associative flexibility (Hypothesis 6). A diagram of the nomological net is provided in Figure 3.1, which also depicts the degree of confirmation or disconfirmation each hypothesis received in the results of Study I.

Methods

The respondents in our first study were 305 German school children, 152 boys and 153 girls, all 14–15 years of age. These children went either to a *Hauptschule* (*n* = 149) or to a *Gymnasium* (*n* = 156). A *Hauptschule* in West Germany offers the legally required minimum of 5 to 6 years of schooling beyond the first 4 schoolyears for the age levels 6–10. A *Gymnasium* offers 9 years of education beyond the first 4 school years, education at a higher level leading to the *Abitur,* which is the main entrance qualification for the university. This dichotomy between *Hauptschule* and *Gymnasium* defined our independent variable of educational track: basic versus advanced. Data were collected in 1975.

During class time the respondents filled in four questionnaires in the following order: (1) continuous word-association test, (2) imagery test, (3) trait attributions to Italians, Turks, and Germans, and (4) sympathy–antipathy ratings of these three ethnic groups.

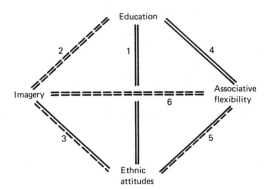

Figure 3.1. Summary of supportive (===), disconfirming (==), and contradictory or qualified (====) evidence pertinent to the network of hypotheses 1–6 of Study I. (Reproduced with permission from Schönbach *et al., Education and Intergroup Attitudes,* 1981, p. 110. Copyright: Academic Press Inc. [London] Ltd.)

The continuous word-association test was our source for various indexes of associative flexibility. This test offered 24 nouns as stimulus words and requested the respondents to write down in response to each stimulus as many words as came to mind within 25 seconds. The stimulus words were systematically varied according to degree of concreteness. (For further details, see Schönbach, 1981, pp. 30ff.)

The imagery test followed right after the word-association test. Each page of the test booklet carried 1 of the 24 stimulus words of the word association test on top of it. The students were asked to try and remember, and indicate, if he or she had had one or more images to that stimulus, and if so, whether the image(s) had been clear and vivid or unclear and hazy. One index of imagery was based on the percentage of association chains the respondent reported to be accompanied by one or more clear and vivid images. For each respondent, a sample of his or her association chains were also rated on a 7-step scale of concreteness by two independent raters. The average of these evaluations provided a second imagery index.

The trait attributions to Italians, Turks, and Germans were elicited by three identical lists of 40 adjectives. These adjectives had been selected in several pretest steps such that stereotypes of all three nationalities were included. Sixteen adjectives represented positive traits, 8, neutral, and 16, negative traits. Each adjective was accompanied by a percentage scale. The respondent had to mark on this scale his or her rough estimate of how many members of the nationality in question would possess that trait. For each respondent, we computed a separate index of negative attributions for each of the ethnic groups, the Italians, Turks, and Germans. Each index consisted of the number of negative traits attributed to 60% or more of the ethnic group in question plus the number of positive traits accorded to 20% or less of that group. For the sake of brevity, we shall not dwell on the sympathy–antipathy ratings because they yielded data patterns very similar to the trait attributions.

The social status of the respondents, middle class versus lower class, was assessed according to their fathers' occupations and the status categories of Kleining and Moore (1968). (For a critical comment on this procedure see Schönbach et al., 1981, pp. 48f). For control purposes, social class and sex of the respondents were included as blocking factors in the various analyses of variance.[2]

Results

As can be seen from Table 3.1, our basic hypothesis about the relationship between educational track and prejudice was supported. Respondents from the

---

[2]We employed analysis of variance in this study, rather than alternative path-analytic approaches because of our desire to explore several intriguing interaction effects of interest.

TABLE 3.1

Effects of Education, Sex, and Attitude Object on Negative Trait Attributions[a]

Education	Turks	Italians	Germans
Hauptschule	7.2	6.9 ——— 3.9	
Gymnasium	5.0	5.5	5.2
Boys	7.1	6.7 ——— 4.3	
Girls	5.0 ---- 5.7 ——— 4.4		

[a] ———— = p < .01; ------ = p < .05, according to Tukey-b tests. (Reproduced with permission from Schönbach *et al.*, *Education and Intergroup Attitudes*, 1981, p. 59. Copyright: Academic Press Inc. [London] Ltd.)

Hauptschule were much more negative than those from the Gymnasium in their evaluation of Turks and Italians, and correspondingly, the former group judged the Germans significantly more favorably than did the latter. A control for social class, which was highly correlated with educational track (phi = .64), did not alter this data pattern at all. Education remained the dominant factor, whereas social class did not appear as a significant independent predictor of outgroup stereotyping. The sex effect on prejudice was also significant. This factor was not included in our initial hypotheses, but respondent sex did prove to enter into a number of interaction effects discussed below.

Hypothesis 4 was also strongly corroborated. On our two main indexes of associative flexibility, the *Gymnasium* respondents definitely surpassed the *Hauptschule* group, but Hypotheses 2 and 6 were not supported by the results of the study. The degree of imagery in the association chains was neither related to educational track nor to associative flexibility. There was, however, a serendipitous finding. With concrete stimulus words, the respondents in the advanced educational track reported more imagery in their associations, and with abstract stimuli, they reported less imagery than did the respondents in the basic track. This data pattern reminds us of Lawton's (1968, p. 131) observation that better educated subjects show greater facility in code-switching between description and abstraction contexts than do working-class subjects. A steep gradient of imagery between concrete and abstract contexts may be an indicator of high associative flexibility, and a measure of this gradient was used in later analyses.

Hypothesis 3 lost some of its interest value after the failure of Hypothesis 2 because imagery could no longer seriously be considered as a mediator between educational track and stereotyping. Still, we mention in passing that although imagery as reported by respondents was not related to outgroup stereotyping, imagery as judged by external raters was significantly related to stereotyping.

Respondents whose chains were judged to be relatively concrete evaluated Turks and Italians much more unfavorably in comparison to Germans than did those respondents with low-judged imagery.

Hypothesis 5 also met with complex data, at best partially supportive. Our first index of associative flexibility (paradigmatic response tendencies) was not related to the stereotype measures. Our second flexibility index, semantic variability, was based on the number of associations representing a clear semantic step beyond the meaning of the stimulus word or any of the preceding elements in the chain. Semantic variability entered into a significant complex higher order interaction. Girls in the advanced education track and boys in the basic track, both with low semantic variability, showed relatively strong negative outgroup stereotyping as predicted. The clearest data pattern in accord with the hypothesis emerged when we used the gradient of imagery reported with concrete stimuli to imagery reported with abstract stimuli as a newly constructed measure of associative flexibility. With this measure, there was a significant main effect in that respondents with flat gradients had comparatively high prejudice scores. A significant interaction moderated this effect in that it was the boys, rather than the girls, who produced this data pattern.

Figure 3.1 summarizes the evidence pertinent to the network of our six hypotheses. Most intriguing are the complex data patterns corresponding to the hypothesized link between associative flexibility and ethnic attitudes. They are sufficiently strong and consistent to suggest that indeed some general cognitive-mediator variables are partly responsible for the association between educational track and degree of stereotyping in ethnic attitudes. On the other hand, these data imply that we either have not yet found a good measure of associative flexibility, or that our theory about the nature and functioning of associative flexibility ought to be modified, or both.

A number of alternative explanations for the correlation between educational track and prejudice are also addressed in Study I and at least tentatively disconfirmed by our data. One of these is the hypothesis that the comparatively high prejudice of respondents in the basic track is mainly due to a prevalent acquiescent response style in this group and a corresponding general tendency towards extreme responses. We could reject this explanation in that our index of negative attributions was derived from both high values for negative traits and low values for positive traits.

Another alternative hypothesis is that respondents in the advanced education track are more likely than their counterparts to give socially desirable responses in line with a democratic norm of equality and thereby hide their true negative feelings towards an outgroup. On a theoretical level one may debate whether this argument is at all relevant. One could well conceive of such normative influences either as part and parcel of the attitude in question or as a parallel determinant of behavioral intentions (Fishbein & Ajzen, 1975). At any rate, if the respondents from the *Gymnasium* had been interested only in a superficial camouflage of their true feelings about the outgroups, it would have been sufficient for them to rate all groups equally. However, in clear opposition to the *Hauptschulen*-respondents they rated the Germans significantly less favorably than the Italians on the antipathy scale. This may have been a leaning-over-backwards effect, possibly due to social desirability considerations in some cases. But the point is that one can hardly see behavioral implications related to such evaluative response dispositions that are as dangerous as intentions nourished by a stereotypical devaluation of the outgroup.

A third important alternate hypothesis relates to social-class differences. Educational track and social-class membership correlate highly. In our sample only 21% of the middle class children went to a *Hauptschule* and 79% to a *Gymnasium*. Of the lower class children, 85% went to a *Hauptschule* and only 15% to a Gymnasium. Thus, one may well hypothesize that socioeconomic conditions are mainly responsible for the stronger aversion against foreigners among the respondents in the basic track. For instance, there might be a frustration–aggression–scapegoating mechanism at work; lower class–basic education respondents may feel threatened in their occupational prospects by worker families from abroad. Also, different socialization practices, such as a more liberal and tolerant climate in middle class homes, might be considered as another social-class factor truly responsible for the attitudinal differences between the groups. As already mentioned, however, our data indicate that, with educational status controlled, respondents' social class membership (as measured by father's occupation) was not related to their prejudice scores. The same holds true in two other studies (Schönbach, 1970; Heinemann & Schönbach, 1981) in which the respondents' own occupation was used as social class indicator.

Three other alternative explanations do receive some support from the data of our Study I and the results of other studies. Groups from advanced versus basic educational tracks differ with respect to their average level of intelligence. Simpson and Yinger (1972, p. 82) and Ehrlich (1973, pp. 142ff.) summarize studies that show a negative correlation between intelligence and authoritarianism or prejudice. Whatever the causal connection between intelligence level and educational status—self selection, training effects, or both—*intelligence* might be close to the true mediator between educational status and ethnic attitudes.

Another potential mediator—related to our measure of associative flexibility—is *cognitive complexity*. Streufert and Streufert (1978) report very low correlations between conventional measures of intelligence and measures of cognitive complexity that warrants its separate consideration as a variable on which groups in advanced and basic education tracks differ and which may mediate stereotyped attitudes toward outgroups. Teaching practices in the *Gymnasium* may engender a more general disposition to reflect, weigh, and differentiate before passing judgment in many situations, including those that necessitate attitudinal reactions toward an ethnic group. It may be that this more general cognitive complexity (rather than the narrower concept of associative chains) is the critical cognitive mediator involved in the link between educational track and prejudice. Our indexes intended to measure associative flexibility may actually have been relatively poor measures of these cognitive capacities of a higher order and should therefore be replaced by better measures.

Finally, a less cognitive hypothesis holds that respondents in the *Hauptschule* react negatively towards ethnic outgroups and downgrade these groups in order to bolster their own social identity. According to Tajfel (1978), the devaluation of an outgroup serves to heighten the positive aspects of one's own group and one's own social identity connected with this group. This in turn nourishes one's self-esteem. It seems likely that in comparison to groups with an advanced education, persons with a *Hauptschulen*-education cannot, on the average, derive as much positive social identity from this fact or from present or prospective occupational groups to which they may belong. Thus, their ethnic or national membership becomes more important as a source of positive social identity. Our data are in good accord with this reasoning. On all our prejudice measures, the *Hauptschule* group rated the Germans much more favorably than they did the Turks and the Italians, and they rated the Germans much more favorably than did the Gymnasium respondents.

Our second study is designed to investigate further the role of various cognitive mediators and self-esteem factors in the differential prejudice of different educational groups.

Study II: Cognitive and Motivational Factors

Figure 3.2 presents the network of hypotheses of Study II. In this diagram an arrow with a plus sign represents a positive influence. "x —— + ——▸ y" means "An increase in x implies an increase in y." "x —— – ——▸ y" means "An increase in x implies a reduction in y."

The distribution of the respondents into middle class and lower class was again determined by the father's occupation, and we expected a partial determination of educational track by social class. Sex was included as a control variable without any specific hypothesis attached to it.

Figure 3.2. Network of hypotheses of Study II.

Data from Streufert and Streufert (1978, p. 92), Mandl and Zimmermann (1976, pp. 50ff.), and Weiss (1969, pp. 295f.) support our contention of a positive relationship between educational level (and thus, also social class) on the one hand and cognitive capacities on the other. Heeding Streufert and Streufert (1978, pp. 124f.), as we already said, we separated cognitive complexity and intelligence as potential mediators. In operationalizing these concepts we subdivided them both further. According to Schroder, Driver, and Streufert (1967) or Streufert and Streufert (1978), the degree of cognitive complexity reflects both the capacity to differentiate and integrate cognitive contents. Consequently we tried to assess these two capacities separately with our measures. Considerations concerning the relationship between language and thought (Hörmann, 1977, pp. 178ff. and 1981, pp. 171ff.) suggested to us that language-bound cognitive capacities are likely to be particularly important for the quality of judgments, including those about groups or categories of people. Therefore, we thought it advisable to include, yet distinguish, measures of both verbal and nonverbal intelligence in order to assess the role of intelligence as a potential mediator between educational status and prejudice.

It should be noted that our diagrammatic presentation of the relationships between educational track and cognitive complexity or intelligence does not necessarily mean a one-way causal path. We do, of course, assume that a more intensive education at a higher level is conducive to the development of cognitive abilities. However, our presentation also allows for those cases in which the cognitive capacities of the child determined the type of school selected for him or her. It is still appropriate, however, to present the linkage as "educational track —— + ——▶ cognitive complexity (or intelligence)" because in our hypotheses we consider these cognitive variables as the true (partial) mediators of the correlations between the educational variable and various measure of prejudice.

Self-esteem, as based on social identity, and its position in the network of hypotheses in Figure 3.2 have already been discussed. Several authors report positive correlations between educational and/or social status on the one hand and self-esteem on the other (Bachman & O'Malley, 1977; Hare, 1977; Maruyama, Rubin, & Kingsbury, 1981; Rosenberg & Pearlin, 1978).

Methods

As in Study I, students of *Hauptschulen* (n = 333) and of *Gymnasien* (n = 249), all 14–15 years of age, served as respondents in a survey carried out during class time late in 1980. The respondents had to complete a questionnaire consisting of several parts. An experimental variation was introduced by using three versions of the questionnaire that differed in the order of the measures of prejudice and the measures of self-esteem. This experimental feature was introduced for the sake of a corollary hypothesis derivable from Tajfel's (1978) theory: respondents with habitually low self-esteem (e.g., many basic education respondents) should show a rise in self-esteem if they first have had a chance to evaluate and differentiate their ingroup from an outgroup on an evaluative dimension (Oakes & Turner, 1980).

Prejudice

Because Turks currently are the largest group of worker families from abroad in West Germany, we used Turks and Germans as attitude objects. We omitted the Italians in Study II because of time limitations that had to be observed. For the same reason, the trait lists were shortened and contained those 24 adjectives that had fared best in Study I, according to test analytic criteria. Identical lists were used for the evaluation of (1) Germans and (2) Turks. In each case, and for each adjective, the respondents had to estimate whether ''almost all,'' ''most,'' ''quite a lot,'' ''not so many,'' ''only few,'' or ''practically none'' of the Turks (Germans) possess that trait. These steps were scored with due attention to the valence of the adjectives. The mean score across all adjective scales for a respondent with respect to Turks (or Germans, respectively) we call the respondent's *average range of negative attributions* to the Turks (or Germans). One measure of prejudice was the difference between the average ranges of negative attributions to the Turks and to the Germans. After the trait attributions, the respondents had to rate the Germans and the Turks by marking continuous graphic scales with their endpoints labeled ''*sehr sympathisch*'' (very likeable) and ''*weniger sympathisch*'' (not so likeable). The difference between the markings for Turks and Germans, measured in millimeters, formed the second measure of prejudice (antipathy).

Self-Esteem

Four measures were used to assess judgments about the self, three of which are relevant here. To determine the *ideal self*, the respondents had to mark, on 6-step scales, to what extent they wished to possess each of 12 traits with varying valences. Then to assess their *real self*, they had to indicate to what extent they did indeed possess these traits. The third measure was a shortened and pretested German version of Coopersmith's (1967, pp. 265f.) self-esteem questionnaire.

Cognitive Complexity

A modified German version of the Impression-Formation Test (Streufert & Driver, 1967) was used to assess the differentiative and integrative capacities of the respondents. Pretesting had shown that pupils of that age cannot readily handle six adjectives within the time limits given by Streufert & Driver. Therefore, the task was simplified. The students had to describe, within 5 minutes, a fictitious person characterized by four partly contradictory traits. These descriptions were then coded according to the instructions of Streufert & Driver (1967). The differentiation index is based on the number of contradictory traits offered in a description. The integration index represents the degree of coherence among such contradictory traits that was achieved in the description.[3]

The Use for Things Test (Guilford, 1959, p. 473) served as a measure of the creativity aspect of cognitive complexity. Within 4 minutes for each stimulus word, the respondents had to write down as many unconventional possible uses of a "brick" and a "ball" that they could think of. The numbers of such distinctive uses for both objects were added to a score of creativity.

Intelligence

The limitations of class time available for our survey necessitated our using only subtests for this part of the nomological net. For the assessment of verbal intelligence, we chose the first synonym subtest of Riegel's (1967) language achievement test. The first subtest of a culture fair intelligence test by Weiss (1971) served as a measure of nonverbal intelligence. These subtests were selected because they are rarely used in German schools, and they correlate quite highly with other tests of their domain.

Order of Questionnaire Parts

The experimental variation of questionnaire order was realized by three splits of the questionnaire. For one randomly chosen third of the students in each class, the questionnaire started with the self-esteem measures, followed by the questions about the Germans and the Turks (notation S-G-T). For the second third of each class, the questions about the Germans came first, followed by the measure of self-esteem, and then the questions about the Turks (notation G-S-T). The last third of each class responded to the self-esteem measures after they had answered the questions about Germans and Turks (notation G-T-S). For all respondents, the questionnaire then presented the Impression-Formation Test, the Use for Things Test, the verbal and the nonverbal intelligence tests, and ended, as did Study I, with questions about father's occupation, sex of respondent, and so forth. Two class periods (i.e., 1.5 hours) were available for answering the whole questionnaire and proved to be sufficient.

---

[3]A high score in integration capacities presupposes some degree of differentiation. It is necessary (not sufficient) that contradictions have been detected and mentioned. So integration capacities do not reflect a general disposition to neglect differences.

Analysis

Various statistical checks showed that no noticeable curvilinear relationships existed among the variables and that the number of interactions among two or more independent variables did not exceed the chance level. Therefore we used a general model path-analysis (Nie, Hall, Jenkins, Steinbrenner, & Bent, 1975, pp. 383ff.) as our main analytic tool, with the effects of the experimental variation of questionnaire versions always partialed out. In presenting the results of these analyses, the strength of any path to a dependent variable is represented by a standardized path-coefficient as part of a simultaneous regression to all preceding variables. Noncausal relationships, for instance, those among the cognitive capacity measures, are represented by partial correlation coefficients with all preceding variables controlled. (For details see Wagner, 1983, pp. 112ff.)

Results

Self-Esteem

Originally we had thought that a measure of self-esteem based on the discrepancy between ideal and real self might be our best index of self-esteem as a mediator between educational status and ethnic attitudes. This expectation failed; of all measures related to self-esteem in path analysis, including all cognitive and self-esteem mediators, only responses representing ideal self showed the predicted pattern of relationships, such that

$$\text{Educational status} \xrightarrow{\quad .17 \quad} \text{Ideal self} \xrightarrow{\quad -.09 \quad} \begin{array}{c}\text{Difference between ranges of}\\ \text{negative attributions to Turks}\\ \text{and Germans}\end{array}$$

$$(p < .01) \qquad\qquad (p < .10)$$

The experimental variation supported our suspicion that only ideal self was a sensitive indicator in the context of our survey. We had hypothesized that self-esteem would rise if the respondents first had a chance to make salient and stress their positive social (i.e., ethnic) identity. This proved to be the case with ideal self, and only with this index. The average values of ideal self ratings were 5.03 in condition S-G-T, 5.12 in G-S-T, and 5.18 in G-T-S. The difference between the two extreme means is significant according to a Tukey-b test. Apparently in our research setting, only expressed aspirations for the self, and not self-esteem per se, were related to the other variables of interest. We do not know why the measures of self-esteem did not conform to our expectations. Perhaps the readiness for self-disclosure was limited in the class situation where a neighbor might glance at one's answers. Under these circumstances, only the questions about one's aspirations may have been felt to be sufficiently innocuous to merit honest answers.

Our experimental variation allows for yet another assessment of the role of self-esteem as a mediator of attitudes toward ingroup and outgroups. According to Tajfel's (1978) theory, one may expect a particularly strong need for a confirmation of one's positive social identity and hence, a strengthened tendency to differentiate from the ingroup and downgrade an available outgroup in those situations in which concern with the self had just been made salient for persons with low self-esteem. Our experimental conditions S–G–T and G–S–T represent such situations in contrast to condition G–T–S. An analysis of variance with the factors, educational track, social class, sex, order of questionnaire parts, and the dependent variable of prejudice as assessed by negative attributions yielded a significant main effect of order in the predicted direction. Table 3.2 presents the corresponding means, broken by social class and educational track, that show that the order effect was produced mainly with the respondents in the basic educational track (or the lower class respondents, respectively). Note, however, that the education × order and the class × order interactions were not significant.

All in all, our hypothesis about the mediator role of self-esteem between educational status and prejudice did find some tentative support. Yet there remains the disquieting fact that direct indexes of self-esteem did not work as expected. We are presently pursuing this issue with experiments in which we manipulate the status (high or low) of the respondents' reference groups and measure both self-esteem and evaluation of an outgroup. Because of the uncertainty concerning the measures of self-esteem in Study II, we have excluded them from the following path analyses.

TABLE 3.2

Range of Negative Attributions as a Function of Social Class or Educational Track and Order of Questionnaire Parts

	Order of questionnaire parts	Negative attributions
Lower class	S-G-T	.41
	G-S-T	.41
	G-T-S	.15
Middle class	S-G-T	.02
	G-S-T	.15
	G-T-S	.03
Hauptschule	S-G-T	.46
	G-S-T	.50
	G-T-S	.19
Gymnasium	S-G-T	− .05
	G-S-T	− .00
	G-T-S	− .03

Cognitive Capacities

Table 3.3 presents the intercorrelations among our indexes and the path coefficients of two-path analyses for our two measures of prejudice (negative trait attributions and antipathy). Figure 3.3 presents the significant paths obtained from these analyses but omits the significant partial correlations among the cognitive variables.

The correlation matrix shows that sex of respondents was not significantly related to the prejudice measures in this study. As to be expected, social class and educational status were again correlated quite strongly, but, as in Study I, respondents' educational track proved to be more important than their social class membership with respect to ethnic attitudes.[4] The path analysis shows that the correlation between social class and the trait attribution measure was mediated by factors pertaining to educational status. There is, however, a direct path from social class to the antipathy measure.

The effect of educational status on ethnic attitudes seems to be mediated primarily by some of the cognitive variables. The direct paths from educational status to the trait attribution and antipathy measures of prejudice are neither strong nor significant. Among the cognitive variables, integration, creativity and verbal intelligence proved to be more important mediators than differentiation and nonverbal intelligence.

The coefficients of the paths from the cognitive mediator variables to the attitude measures are small and only marginally significant. To some extent this is due to the intercorrelations among these cognitive variables and the suppression of such collinearity by the logic of path analysis. As a partial cor-

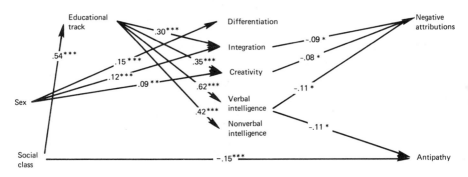

Figure 3.3. Significant paths from two path analyses with the criteria measures of prejudice. Covariations among cognitive variables are omitted. (*) = p < .10, ** = p < .05, *** = p < .01.

---

[4]The prejudice indexes presented here are difference measures, that is, negative evaluations of Turks minus negative evaluation of Germans. Parallel analyses using only the negative evaluation of Turks as prejudice indexes revealed very similar data patterns.

Intercorrelations and Results of Two Path Analyses on Prejudice Measures[a]

	1	1	2	2	3	3	3	3	4	4
$N = 474$	Sex	Class	Education	Differ-entiation	Integ-ration	Crea-tivity	Verbal intelligence	Nonverbal intelligence	Negative attributions	Antip-athy
1 Sex (1=m, 2=w)	—	-.04	.01	.15***	.13***	.10**	.04	-.02	-.01	-.05
Class (1=low, 2=middle)	-.04	—	.54***	-.03	.15***	.25***	.38***	.21***	-.17***	-.26***
2 Education (1=Hauptschule, 2=Gymnasium)	.03$_b$	.54***$_b$	—	-.06	.29***	.38***	.65***	.41***	-.27***	-.28***
3 Differentiation	.15***$_b$	.01$_b$	-.07$_b$	—	.23***	.09**	-.02	.03	-.03	-.01
Integration	.12***$_b$	-.01$_c$	.30***$_b$	.25***$_c$	—	.23***	.29***	.19***	-.19***	-.12***
Creativity	.09**$_b$	.06$_b$	.35***$_b$	.10**$_c$	.12***$_c$	—	.30***	.17***	-.19***	-.17***
Verbal intelligence	.03$_b$	.04$_b$	.62***$_b$	.01$_c$	.13***$_c$	.07$_c$	—	.40***	-.26***	-.26***
Nonverbal intelligence	-.02$_b$	-.02$_b$	.42***$_b$	.07$_c$	.09**$_c$	.01$_c$	.20***$_c$	—	-.19***	-.14***
4 Negative attributions	.01$_b$	-.03$_b$	-.10$_b$	-.01$_b$	-.09*$_b$	-.08*$_b$	-.11*$_b$	-.07$_b$	—	.52***
4 Antipathy	-.05$_b$	-.15***$_b$	-.10$_b$	-.00$_b$	-.02$_b$	-.05$_b$	-.11*$_b$	-.02$_b$	—	.11
R^2	—	—	—						.10	.11
$E = \sqrt{1 - R^2}$	—	—	—	.95	.91	.91	.74	.89	.95	.94

[a] * = $p < .10$; ** = $p < .05$; *** = $p < .01$.

Without subscript: Partial-correlation coefficients with the effect of order of questionnaire parts partialed out. Subscript b: Path coefficients/beta values produced by the simultaneous regression to all causally prior variables (indexed by lower number), controlling for the effect of order of questionnaire parts. Subscript c: Partial-correlation coefficients with the effects of all causally prior variables and the order of questionnaire parts partialed out.

R^2: Variance explained by all causally prior and equivalent variables; variance explained by the order of questionnaire parts is subtracted. R^2 and E of negative attributions and antipathy are calculated without regard to each others influence.

rection of these collinearity effects on the path coefficients, we standardized the four measures, integration, creativity, verbal intelligence, and nonverbal intelligence; and then we summed the scores for integration and creativity to form a compound index of cognitive complexity and likewise, summed the scores for verbal and nonverbal intelligence to arrive at a compound index of intelligence. New path analyses with these two compound indexes simultaneously in the mediator positions between the demographic variables and the attitude measures yielded increased and significant coefficients of the paths towards the trait attribution measure; that is:

$$\text{Education} \xrightarrow{.41} \text{complexity} \xrightarrow{-.14} \begin{array}{l}\text{negative trait}\\\text{attributions}\end{array}$$

$$p < .01 \qquad\qquad p < .01$$

$$\text{Education} \xrightarrow{.62} \text{intelligence} \xrightarrow{-.14} \begin{array}{l}\text{negative trait}\\\text{attributions}\end{array}$$

$$p < .01 \qquad\qquad p < .05$$

It is interesting to see that a differentiation capacity alone, unaccompanied by an integrative capacity, does not seem to suffice for counteracting stereotyping tendencies in forming judgments about ingroups and outgroups.[5] This reminds us of the considerations by Streufert & Streufert (1978, pp. 248ff.) that persons who are only strong in differentiation, but not integration, are still overly vulnerable to salient information features in a judgment situation open to conformity pressures. There may also be a parallel in our Study I. The associative flexibility index *semantic variability,* which is based on and may primarily reflect a differentiation capacity was of very limited predictive value with respect to stereotyped attitudes, whereas the more complex gradient index performed somewhat better as an attitude predictor.

Why is it that a mere differentiation capacity, without an integrative complement, did not have beneficial effects on ethnic attitudes? We do not know; but after the fact, the thought strikes us that such a mere differentiation capacity and disposition may be closely connected to the tendency to separate people and put them into distinct categories, that is, the very basis of ingroup–outgroup contrasts.

All in all, our hypothesis about the mediator role of cognitive capacities between educational level and prejudice in ingroup–outgroup attitudes receives some corroboration by Study II, and the data suggest valuable leads for further explorations of the nature of these mediators and their functioning. Our results

[5]Further analyses revealed evidence that this is neither due to small variance in our differentiation index nor to suppression of the coefficient by the influence of correlated cognitive measures (see simple correlation coefficients between differentiation and prejudice scores in Table 3.3).

may, for instance, be taken into consideration in approaching a basic problem posed by Streufert and Streufert (1978, p. 47). They point to the phenomenon that various measures of cognitive complexity seem to be "more or less unrelated to each other", yet "at the same time a surprisingly large degree of similarity exists in the behavior predicted by these apparently 'unrelated' measures." We think that there are essentially two possibilities:

1. Various measures of complexity do not strongly correlate because each one is loaded with a unique set of components unrelated to the other sets. However, all these measures share one basic component that is also largely responsible for the similarity of the behavioral effects (Streufert & Streufert, 1978, p. 50). It is tempting to speculate about the nature of such a common component. Could it be some sort of cognitive flexibility? Our data suggest that a low level associative flexibility concept, as we originally conceived it, is not a likely candidate for such a central position. However, considering the nature and the performance of our gradient index in Study I and the complexity index in Study II, comprising integration and creativity, we tend to think that a higher order flexibility capacity might be such an influential common component. Obviously, much work would still be necessary to approach an adequate assessment of the nature and functioning of such a capacity in general and particularly with respect to the formation and reduction of stereotyped attitudes.

2. The other possible explanation of the phenemenon observed by the Streuferts is that none of several largely unrelated variants of cognitive complexity is necessary, but that each one of those is sufficient for markedly reducing behavioral rigidities, such as the expression of prejudice (and/or corresponding actions).

Presently we cannot decide between these two hypotheses. The correlations among our three working cognitive mediators in Study II, that is, integration, creativity, and verbal intelligence, are so low that even the pair, creativity and verbal intelligence, share less than 10% of the variance (see Table 3.3). This fact is yet another demonstration of the phenomenon emphasized by the Streuferts, and it is, of course, compatible with either one of the two explanatory possibilities. The two possible modes of effect just discussed are not mutually exclusive. Obviously, however, it would be of great practical importance to learn which one carries more and how much more weight.

There are a number of dispersed studies that also furnish valuable leads, but they still lack theoretical integration. For instance, Schroder (1975) suggests *general* methods for increasing cognitive structure capacities. These methods try to maintain a close fit between the complexity demands of the learning situation and the degree of complexity already achieved by the pupils. Excessive demands are to be avoided just as much as unnecessary simplifications or the imposition of conclusions by the teacher. Several studies concentrate on the effects of various forms of complexity training on the reduction of prejudice in a kindergarten or a school setting, and all these studies report some success. Hohn (1973) trained kindergarten children in one condition with respect to perceptual awareness and role taking and in another treatment condition with respect to conservation and spatial perspective. Both treatments decreased ingroup biases. Schmitt (1979) used a strategy that combined role playing with adequate information about the attitude target. Gardiner (1972) required high school students to engage in multidimensional thinking about videotaped stimulus persons. Kraak (1968) tested the effects of a course in psychology on changes in prejudice.

These studies vividly underline the need for coordination efforts in a large-scale research program. We think that this program should take its start from the phenomenon observed by the Streuferts and its possible explanations. Our studies, as well as those just mentioned, can contribute heuristic leads, but the main task has yet to be approached: a truly systematic investigation of many modes of cognitive complexity as to their inherent qualities, the nature and degree of their overlap, and the size of their effects, separately and in various combinations, on the formation and reduction of stereotyped attitudes.

Contacts and Attitudes

So far we have not yet considered the possibility that our respondents from the *Hauptschule* may have had more and more unpleasant, contact experiences with Turkish, Italian and other Mediterranean workers and their families than the respondents from the *Gymnasium* and therefore, developed more negative attitudes towards these people. Schönbach (1970) did not find any differences between respondents who had previous contact with workers from abroad and those who had not had such contact with respect to their attitudes towards *Fremdarbeiter* or *Gastarbeiter*. Bergius, Werbik, Winter, & Schubring (1970), on the other hand, report that contacts made with persons from Mediterranean countries (Italy and Greece) *within* the Federal Republic increase the tendency of adult Germans to react with stereotyped negative judgments about these ethnic groups, whereas respondents express less prejudice towards Italians if they had contact with them in Italy. Unfortunately, Bergius *et al.* did not control for educational or social status of the respondents. Those from the better situated strata may well have been overrepresented in the group with contact experiences abroad, and at the same time, those respondents voiced little prejudice, for whatever reason. At any rate, in our case we can be quite certain that contact experiences with Turks reported by our respondents are, at most, with very few exceptions, contacts with Turkish workers and their families within the Federal Republic because Turkey is not at all a popular vacation area for Germans.

The two studies reported here furnish some data that disconfirm the hypothesis that the link between educational track and prejudice is mediated by differential contact experiences. There were practically no Turks among the students of the *Gymnasien* that participated in Study II. In the four *Hauptschulen* that took part in the study, the percentages of Turkish students ranged widely from 0.5 to 21%. If amount of contact with Turks were largely responsible for the attitudes toward this ethnic group among basic educational respondents, then we should expect the four respondent groups from those four *Hauptschulen* to differ markedly in their attitudinal reactions. However, no such differences were obtained. Study II allows for a further check. One *Gymnasium* and one *Hauptschule* were housed in the same building and shared some facilities. This *Hauptschule* had a very low percentage (2%) of Turkish students overall, and in the five classes that were interviewed, there were only two Turkish children in total. Furthermore, the students of these two schools lived in very similar, if not the same, urban regions. Thus, one may conclude that these two subgroups of *Hauptschule* and *Gymnasium* respondents had had very similar contact experiences with Turks. Nevertheless, they showed the well-known pattern of differences in their ethnic attitudes.

At least with respect to our data, frequency of contact per se may be set aside as a potential mediator of the negative relation between educational status and prejudice; but what about quality of contact? Could it be that persons in the higher educational track usually meet foreigners under more pleasant circumstances than do people from the lower education level? In Study I we asked the students if, and how much, contact they had had with Italians and Turks. Quite in accord with the objective data from Study II, the respondents from the *Hauptschulen* in Study I reported on the average much more contact with Turks than did the respondents from the *Gymnasien*. However, in their trait attributions to Turks, the respondents with some contact, especially those from the basic educational track, were rather more favorably disposed than the no-contact respondents. Contact may have engendered more favorable attitudes towards Turks, or friendly attitudes may have facilitated contact. But this uncertainty as to direction of causality is irrelevant for the question at hand. Holding the contact variable constant does not diminish the attitudinal differences between the basic and advanced education groups. If anything, these differences become even more pronounced with control of the contact factor.

Frequency and quality of contact do not seem to be important factors that could explain the comparatively strong stereotyping tendencies and hostility towards Mediterranean groups, notably the Turks, among respondents from the basic educational track. This fact, however, does not obviate the possibility that contacts in situations that minimize status differentials and furnish opportunities for cooperation in pursuing common superordinate goals may prove to be beneficial and lead to a reduction of stereotyping and prejudice (Sherif, 1979). Such common goals define new common reference groups that may diminish the salience and importance of the former ingroup–outgroup distinction. Informal observations encourage us to think that Aronson's "jigsaw puzzle" method for example (Aronson, Blaney, Stephan, Sikes, & Snapp, 1978), using interdependent cooperation for the development of mutual esteem, may be quite helpful also in German schools with ethnically mixed student populations.

Acknowlegments

Our shares of responsibility for this chapter are equal; order of authorship was decided by a flip of a coin. We are very grateful to the editors of this volume for most valuable, detailed counsel and to Ursula Schomann and Margret Ernsting for kind and efficient assistance in editing and typing drafts and the final version of this chapter.

References

Aronson, E., Blaney, N., Stephan, C., Sikes, J., & Snapp, M. *The jigsaw classroom*. Beverly Hills, CA: Sage, 1978.

Bachman, J. G., & O'Malley, P. M. Self-esteem in young men: A longitudinal analysis of the impact of education and occupational attainment. *Journal of Personality and Social Psychology*, 1977, *35*, 365–380.

Bergius, R., Werbik, H., Winter, G., & Schubring, G. Urteile deutscher Arbeitnehmer über Völker in Relation zur Zahl ihrer ausländischen Bekannten. II: Unterschiede zwischen verschiedenen Kontaktgruppen. *Psychologische Beiträge*, 1970, *12*, 485–532.

Bergler, R., & Six, B. Stereotypes und Vorurteile. In C. F. Graumann (Ed.), *Handbuch der Psychologie* (Vol. 7). Göttingen, Germany: Hogrefe, 1972.

Coopersmith, S. *The antecedents of self-esteem*. San Francisco, CA: Freeman, 1967.

Delgado, M. J. *Die "Gastarbeiter" in der Presse*. Opladen, Germany: Leske, 1972.

Ehrlich, H. J. *The social psychology of prejudice*. New York: Wiley, 1973.

Fishbein, M., & Ajzen, I. *Belief, attitude, intention, and behavior*. Reading, MA: Addison–Wesley, 1975.

Gardiner, G. S. Complexity training and prejudice reduction. *Journal of Applied Social Psychology*, 1972, *2*, 326–342.

Guilford, J. P. Three faces of intellect. *American Psychologist*, 1959, *14*, 469–479.

Harding, J., Proshansky, H., Kutner, B., & Chein, I. Prejudice and ethnic relations. In G. Lindzey & E. Aronson (Eds.), *The handbook of social psychology* (Vol. 5.). Reading, MA: Addison–Wesley, 1969.

Hare, B. R. Racial and socioeconomic variations in preadolescent area-specific and general self-esteem. *International Journal of Intercultural Relations*, 1977, *1*, 31–51.

Heinemann, W., & Schönbach, P. Cognitive and conative components of attitudes towards workers from abroad. In P. Schönbach, & P. M. Gollwitzer, G. Stiepel, U. Wagner, *Education and intergroup attitudes. European Monographs in Social Psychology* (Vol. 22). London: Academic Press, 1981, pp. 74–87.

Hohn, R. L. Perceptual training and its effect on racial preferences of kindergarten children. *Psychological Reports,* 1973, *32,* 435–441.

Hörmann, H. *Psychologie der Sprache.* Berlin: Springer, 1977.

Hörmann, H. *To mean - to understand.* Berlin: Springer, 1981.

INFAS - Institut für angewandte Sozialwissenschaft. *Meinungen und Einstellungen zu Ausländerproblemen.* Bonn: 1982.

Kleining, G., & Moore, H. Soziale Selbsteinstufung (SSE). *Kölner Zeitschrift für Soziologie und Sozialpsychologie,* 1968, *20,* 502–552.

Kraak, B. *Auswirkungen von Psychologieunterricht auf soziale und pädagogische Vorurteile.* Weinheim, Germany: Beltz, 1968.

Lawton, D. *Social class, language and education.* London: Routledge and Kegan Paul, 1968.

Mandl, H., & Zimmermann, A. *Intelligenzdifferenzierung.* Stuttgart: Kohlhammer, 1976.

Maruyama, G., Rubin, R. A., & Kingsbury, G. G. Self-esteem and educational achievement: Interdependent constructs with a common cause? *Journal of Personality and Social Psychology,* 1981, *40,* 962–975.

Mehrländer, U., Hofmann, R., König, P., & Krause, H. J. *Situation der ausländischen Arbeitnehmer und ihrer Familienangehörigen in der Bundesrepublik Deutschland.* Forschungsbericht im Auftrag des Bundesministers für Arbeit und Sozialordnung. Bonn: July 1981.

Nie, N. H., Hull, C. H., Jenkins, J. G., Steinbrenner, K., & Bent, D. H. *SPSS.* New York: McGraw–Hill, 1975.

Oakes, P. J., & Turner, J. C. Social categorization and intergroup behavior: Does minimal intergroup discrimination make social identity more positive? *European Journal of Social Psychology,* 1980, *10,* 295–301.

Osgood, C. E. *Method and theory in experimental psychology.* New York: Oxford University Press, 1953.

Riegel, K. F. *Der sprachliche Leistungstest, SASKA.* Göttingen, Germany: Hogrefe, 1967.

Rosenberg, M., & Pearlin, L. I. Social class and self-esteem among children and adults. *American Journal of Sociology,* 1978, *84,* 53–77.

Schatzmann, L., & Strauss, A. Social class and modes of communication. *American Journal of Sociology,* 1955, *60,* 329–338.

Schmitt, R. *Kinder und Ausländer. Einstellungsänderung durch Rollenspiel—Eine empirische Untersuchung.* Braunschweig, Germany: Westermann, 1979.

Schönbach, P. *Sprache und Attitüden.* Bern, Switzerland: Huber, 1970.

Schönbach, P., & Gollwitzer, P. M., Stiepel, G., Wagner, U. *Education and intergroup attitudes. European Monographs in Social Psychology* (Vol. 22). London: Academic Press, 1981.

Schroder, H. M. Die Entwicklung der Informationsverarbeitungsfähigkeit. In H. W. Krohne (Ed.), *Fortschritte der pädagogischen Psychologie.* München: Reinhardt, 1975.

Schroder, H. M., Driver, M. J., & Streufert, S. *Human information processing.* New York: Holt, Rinehart & Winston, 1967.

Sherif, M. Superordinate goals in the reduction of intergroup conflict: An experimental evaluation. In M. Schwebel (Ed.), *Behavior, science, and human survival.* Palo Alto, CA: Science and Behavior Books, 1965. (Reprinted in W. G. Austin & S. Worchel [Eds.], *The social psychology of intergroup relations.* Monterey, CA: Brooks/Cole, 1979).

Simpson, G. E., & Yinger, J. M. *Racial and cultural minorities: An analysis of prejudice and discrimination.* New York: Harper & Row, 1972.

Staats, A. W. *Learning, language, and cognition.* New York: Holt, Rinehart and Winston, 1968.

Streufert, S., & Driver, M. J. Impression formation as a measure of the complexity of conceptual structure. *Educational and Psychological Measurement*, 1967, *27*, 1025–1039.

Streufert, S. & Streufert, S. C. *Behavior in the complex environment*. New York: Winston, 1978.

Tajfel, H. *Differentiation between social groups. European Monographs in Social Psychology* (Vol. 14). London: Academic Press, 1978.

Wagner, U. *Soziale Schichtzugehörigkeit, formales Bildungsniveau und ethnische Vorurteile*. Berlin: Express Edition, 1983.

Weiss, R. Das Verhältnis von Schulleistung und Intelligenz. In H. R. Lückert (Ed.), *Begabungsforschung und Bildungsförderung als Gegenwartsaufgabe*. München: Reinhardt, 1969.

Weiss, R. *Grundintelligenztest CFT 3 Skala 3*. Braunschweig, Germany: Westermann, 1971.

4

Interethnic Relations and Education: An Israeli Perspective

Joseph Schwarzwald
and
Yehuda Amir

Historical Background

Tension between ethnic groups is a common phenomenon among heterogeneous populations. Historically, Jews have not been spared the consequences of such tensions, especially in times of mass migration or religious schisms (Ben-Sasson, 1969). In Israel today, interethnic tensions are primarily the result of the massive immigration of Jews from different cultural and national backgrounds since the creation of the Jewish state in 1948. In addition to the tensions between Israeli Jews and Arabs, tensions and cleavage exist in the religiosity of observant and nonobservant Jews and in the ethnicity of Jews from multiple cultural backgrounds. This paper focuses on the consequences of the encounter between the two major Jewish ethnic categories today. Jews of North African and Asian origin (hereafter referred to as *Middle Easterners*) and Jews of European-American origin (referred to as *Westerners*).

At the foundation of the state, Israel's population was approximately 650,000. In its first decade, this society absorbed an estimated 485,000 Middle Eastern and 321,000 Western immigrants (Bentwich, 1960). The basically modern, Western cultural patterns of the absorbing society made the adjustment in the new country easier for Western immigrants but more problematic for Middle Easterners. Indeed, for Middle Easterners coming from a conservative religious and social tradition, Western cultural patterns were often strange and, at times, even objectionable (Adler, in press; Eisenstadt, 1973; Shuval, 1963). Over time, Westerners acquired positions of high-social status, whereas Middle Easterners populated the bottom of the social ladder (Smooha & Peres, 1974). This process of ethnic and social differentiation was accompanied by alienation, prejudice, and social distance in the relations between the two ethnic groups.

These problems of interethnic tensions arose despite the national aspiration to merge the various Jewish diaspora communities into a common Israeli culture. In this regard, it was clear that in order to attain a high level of technological achievement in the critical areas of defense and economy, the new Israel would have to become even more Western-oriented in its economy, social structure, and educational system (Simon, 1957). Thus, the Israeli national leadership adopted the approach (supported also by social scientists) that Middle Easterners should become Westernized through a process of resocialization (Swirsky, 1981). It was thought that resocialization would be facilitated by such factors as common Jewish nationality, religious tradition, and the relative similarity in physical appearance. Ethnic, cultural, and economic differences were considered to be temporary and of only superficial importance.

The absorption process was often accompanied by the attitude that Middle Easterners were uncultured. Counselors, supervisors, and teachers—primarily from Western background's—hurried to teach the "primitives" new behavior patterns. Due to their attitudes of superiority and insensitivity, these official representatives of the dominant culture showed unintentional scorn for the Middle Easterners' existing cultural values.

The ignoral and devaluation of Middle Eastern culture throughout the absorption process, as well as shortages in housing, employment, and education, often generated a feeling of powerlessness and insignificance among Middle Easterners. These absorption conditions were neither conducive for facilitating the process of integration nor for attaining national unity. In fact, the interethnic encounter was occasionally accompanied by hostility and hindered the development of the Middle Easterners' local initiatives and independent activity.

Course of the Chapter

This chapter describes the role of schools in the process of integration. In the initial section, the literature documenting the unbalanced relations between Middle Eastern and Western Jews is described. Particular attention is given to the asymmetry which characterizes these relations. Whereas Westerners accept other Westerners and reject Middle Easterners, Middle Easterners tend to prefer Westerners over themselves.

As shown in subsequent sections, this same bias is reflected within schools and poses major social and educational difficulties for Middle Eastern students.

Among the difficulties reviewed here are those of preferential standing given to Western culture in the curriculum and the negative teacher-attitudes toward Middle Easterners. The deficit in academic achievement among Middle Eastern students accompanying these conditions becomes a focal concern addressed by educators and politicians alike.

Two major stages in the school system's attempt to respond to these socioeducational problems are outlined. The first of these comprised a series of sporadic enrichment programs aimed at the Middle Eastern population, its impact fell below expectations. The second and more recent attempt involves structural Reform of the school system based upon forced desegregation. The social outcomes of this latter effort are described in detail.

For the social scientist at large, Israeli implementation of integration in a school system uniquely divided into religious and secular sectors offers unusual insight into the factors influencing integrational process. Research data demonstrating the situational contingence of effective integration are discussed in depth and are summarized from a theoretical perspective. Original intervention measures developed in Israel for improved integration are also described.

In the final section, integrational efforts within the school system are placed back into the broader social and historical perspective. A theory of perceived inequality is presented and applied to current trends in interethnic relations. This theory suggests that the differential pattern of change in cultural similarity and social standing between ethnic groups is leading to more potent feelings of inequality among Middle Easterners. The resulting activism of this group, it is concluded, may lead to renewed efforts for genuine educational integration and equality.

Patterns of Acceptance and Rejection

One persisting outcome of the unfavorable encounter between Western and Middle Eastern Jews in the absorption process is a pattern of asymmetry in acceptance and rejection between these ethnic groups. Westerners tend to evaluate people of their own community positively and Middle Easterners negatively. Middle Easterners tend to reflect the attitudes of the dominant group, evaluating people from their own ethnic category less positively than Westerners. Empirical evidence for this asymmetrical relationship appears repeatedly in studies with subjects from elementary school age through adulthood, irrespective of research methodology.

At the elementary school level, pronounced asymmetry is reflected in children's judgment of ethnic features representing the typical Israeli (Rim, 1968). Western facial features are considered more Israeli than the features of Middle Easterners. Pupils of Western origin perceive figures from their own membership group as more Israeli and like them better; Middle Eastern children also tend to view Westerners as more typically Israeli and like them more than figures from their own group.

Asymmetry in acceptance and rejection is also found among high school students. Both Westerners and Middle Easterners alike give more positive evaluations to Western than to Middle Eastern members (Amir, Sharan, Ben-Ari, Bizman, & Rivner, 1978; Peres, 1976). In addition, students from both ethnic groups are more willing to engage in activities with Westerners than with Middle Easterners (Amir, Sharan, Ben-Ari, Bizman, & Rivner, 1978). Finally, with regard to marriage, most Western students tend to have reservations about the possibility of marriage to Middle Easterners, whereas only a minority among Middle Easterners express any reservation about marriage to a Westerner (Peres, 1976).

Studies carried out among adults reveal a similar trend. Among residents of a new urban neighborhood, it is found that Westerners and Middle Easterners exhibit a good deal of rejection of various Middle Eastern ethnic groups and very little rejection of various Western ethnic groups (Shuval, 1956). Moreover, when asked who were least desirable as neighbors, more than half of the Western respondents indicated Middle Easterners, whereas only a small percentage of Middle Easterners had reservations about neighbors of Western origin. In a similar vein, Amir, Bizman, and Rivner (1975) demonstrate an identical asymmetry among soldiers. Those of Western origin tend to prefer friends of their own group, whereas Middle Easterners have no special preference—indicating Westerners and Middle Easterns equally as friends.

It appears that asymmetry in acceptance and rejection on the Middle Easterner's part is not only a reflection of the preference for Westerners but also involves a process of self-depreciation. For example, Rim's (1968) study reveals that Middle Eastern pupils have difficulty in accepting their identity and suffer feelings of alienation. Self-depreciation is also a finding emphasized by Peres (1971), who notes that Middle Easterners show a need to eliminate flaws in themselves before engaging in closer interethnic relations. The apparent feeling of inferiority and a subsequent adoption of a negative self-image undoubtedly affects the motivation and initiative of Middle Easterners in both the area of involvement of adults in community and public life and of the ability of their children to cope with the demands of school. Such outcomes are typical in encounters between majority (strong) and minority (weak) groups as shown by a series of studies in the United States on relations between blacks and whites that reveals that subjects from the minority group tend to adopt the majority's evaluation of their group and consider themselves less worthy (Ashmore, 1970; Brand, Ruiz, & Padilla, 1974).[1]

[1] Recent studies in the United States show an amelioration in this tendency (Davis, 1978; Weissbach, 1977).

Limited exceptions to the general rule of asymmetry appear in situations where Middle Easterners and Westerners share equal status. For example, Middle Eastern and Western Boy Scouts of equal social status both tend to rate members of their own ethnic group as more ideal and typically Israeli than members of the other ethnic groups (Gitai, 1972).

Schwarzwald and Yinon (1977) find a similar symmetry among middle class Western and Middle Eastern vocational high school students. The Middle Easterners tend to give higher ratings to figures of Middle Easterners than of Westerners. Westerners likewise tend to give a higher rating to figures from their own membership group. Moreover, students of mixed marriages (one parent Western and the partner Middle Eastern) tend to rate all the ethnic groups positively without distinction. Close examination of the data suggests that these more symmetric results do not reflect mutual acceptance but rather indicate a more positive self-image among Middle Easterners.

In each of these studies it is assumed that equality of social standing contributes to the reduction of asymmetrical patterns of acceptance and rejection. A more direct analysis of the influence of social status is offered in studies by Amir and colleagues with students (Amir, Sharan, Rivner, Ben-Ari, & Bizman, 1979) and soldiers (Amir, Bizman, & Rivner, 1975). Among high school students of different academic levels, less asymmetry is found in classes where Middle Easterners have a scholastic standing equal to or higher than that of Westerners. When Middle Easterners have an academic standing lower than Westerners, the typical pattern of asymmetry reappears. Among soldiers in the general army, Amir (1975) and his collaborators find typical asymmetry. However, in paratrooper units, consisting of volunteers carefully selected for martial skills and qualities pertinent to army standing, relations become more balanced.

In sum, these more recent studies suggest that the asymmetrical interethnic relations that arise during the initial encounter between Western and Middle Eastern Jews reflect objective as well as apparent status differences. Where status differences are ameliorated, patterns of acceptance and rejection become more symmetrical. Yet, even where status has been analyzed within confined settings, this tendency toward more balanced relations arises more from increased self-acceptance among Middle Easterners than from heightened acceptance between groups.

Schools before Reform

The school system is one institution that might be expected to propagate mutual acceptance and social integration. A review of the record indicates that, at least at the beginning, conditions in the Israeli schools are not conducive to these goals. The content of school curricula and the character of teachers' attitudes combine to devaluate the Middle Eastern students' self-esteem and diminish their social and academic standing.

Educational authorities adopted a curriculum that, at least until very recently, emphasized solely Western culture and almost completely ignored the heritage and history of the Middle Eastern ethnic group. For example, school texts almost entirely pass over the history of Middle Eastern Jews and their contribution to the foundation of the country. Similarly, childrens' readers generally have Western authors and present Middle Eastern figures in a disparaging light (Stahl, 1976). This tendency is clearly inconsistent with the theoretical position that equal representation of the various cultures is essential for interethnic acceptance, positive self-image of minority students, and harmony between the socialization process at home and in school (Frankenstein, 1977; Miller, 1980).

It is impossible to ignore the series of studies beginning in the 1950s and continuing to the present that indicate prejudice and disparaging attitudes of teachers toward their Middle Eastern students. Although it is difficult to estimate the extent of the phenomenon because these studies are limited in scope, a few examples should be instructive. Stahl, Agmon, & Mar-Haim (1976) present anecdotal data collected through observations that indicate insulting and belittling reactions to ethnic customs, negative and arrogant attitudes towards the disadvantaged Middle Eastern population, and feelings of frustration among teachers required to teach this population. These investigators note that teachers display ignorance and lack of interest in the traditions, customs, and beliefs prevalent among various Middle Eastern communities.

Other systematic studies also report instances of discrimination and prejudice. Stahl et al. (1976) also describes a laboratory experiment revealing that teachers (both Middle Easterners and Westerners) give lower grades for a composition ostensibly written by a Middle Eastern rather than a Western student. Shuval and Teichman (1972) find that kindergarten teachers are more likely to report Western than Middle Eastern children as talented, often ignoring equally talented Middle Eastern children. In a similar vein, Babad, Mann, and Mar-Haim (1975) find that graduate education students ascribe lower IQ scores to a WISC (Weschler Intelligence Scale for Children) protocol when they think it has been given by a Middle Eastern student instead of a Westerner. These studies indicate that teachers often underestimate the potential ability of Middle Eastern children, even in the face of ostensibly standardized evaluation to the contrary.

Devaluation of Middle Eastern heritage and values is reflected in a study carried out by Schwarzwald, Shoham, Waysman, and Sterner (1979). Teachers express a greater necessity to impart desirable social, personal, and educational values to "disadvantaged" Middle Eastern students than to "advantaged"

Western students. Moreover, they believe it to be less feasible to instill desirable values to the "less socialized" Middle Eastern students. Clearly, in this case, teachers hold prejudicial and stereotypic opinions about social behavior and values for which they have no objective data.

The tendency of people to behave according to beliefs and expectations that they form about themselves, others, and their social environment, even if they have little basis in reality, may lead to self-fulfilling prophecies, perpetuating a vicious cycle (Rosenthal & Jacobson, 1968). In any case, teachers' expression of such attitudes does little to improve Middle Easterners' social standing in the classroom. Teachers' perception of Middle Easterners as inferior may be one factor inhibiting latent educational potential of these students.

The major educational difficulties facing Middle Eastern students also emphasizes their social status difference from Western students. The educational gap between students of Middle Eastern origin and Western Israelis is documented in a number of studies. The most relevant of these studies tests pupils' adaptation in the early school grades (Adiel, 1968; Feitelson, 1953; Simon, 1957; Smilansky, 1957), achievement in national placement tests given in the eighth grade, which is the final elementary school class (Litwin, 1971; Ortar, 1956, 1960, 1967; Smilansky & Yam, 1969), and achievement in matriculation examinations (Smooha & Peres, 1974). These studies clearly demonstrate that many Middle Eastern students lack the most basic educational foundations, their language skills are poor, and they are bored and uninterested in school. Consequently, Middle Eastern children tend to drop out of the formal educational framework, and each successive grade contains a smaller percentage of Middle Easterners.

Clearly Middle Easterners' learning difficulties, poor achievement, and high drop-out rate are an amalgamation of home conditions as well as the transition from a traditional Middle Eastern to a modern Western culture (Adar, 1956; Simon, 1957; S. Smilansky, 1957). The Middle Eastern student frequently comes from a disadvantaged home where parents have to struggle with inadequate housing and poverty level income. In addition, the lack of Western educational experience among the Middle Eastern parents make it difficult for them to offer help and assistance to their children. Yet, whatever the reasons are, be they home or school, the resultant educational gap magnified and emphasized the social-status differences between the groups.

Introduction of School Integration

Middle Eastern students' failure in elementary school, their comparatively small numbers continuing through high school and postsecondary school education, and their subsequent difficulty adjusting to the realities and demands of social and economic life are all a source of concern to those dealing with educational policy in Israel (Adler, 1974; Eisenstadt, 1973; Peled, 1976). Consequently, these policymakers instituted a variety of planned enrichment programs to advance Middle Eastern immigrant children. Schools populated predominantly by Middle Eastern students were given preferential allocation of funds to institute special remedial programs intended to narrow the educational gap. These programs included a longer school day (the regular school day in Israel ends at about 1:00 P.M.), auxiliary teaching, and tracking in major subjects. Guidance, counseling, nutrition, and health services were expanded, and teachers specially trained to supervise the programs were placed in these schools. An effort to solve the drop-out problem was made by not allowing children to be left back and by lowering entrance requirements in order to encourage disadvantaged students to continue high school studies (Adiel, 1970; Minkovitch, Davis, & Bashi, 1982; M. Smilansky, 1973).

Certainly these efforts had some remedial effect. Illiteracy almost disappeared (Adiel, 1968). The percentage of Middle Easterners in high school and higher education increased (Smooha & Peres, 1974). The fact that the educational gap in Israel remains constant (Lewy & Chen, 1976; Minkovich et al., 1980) is also a positive index when taken in contrast to the continuing growing gap found for ethnic minorities in the United States (Coleman, Campbell, Hobson, McPartland, Mood, Wernfield, & York, 1966).

Nonetheless, at the bottom line, the results of the enrichment programs are disappointing; preferential allocation of funds did not close the educational gap between Western and Middle Eastern students just as such enrichment programs in the United States have not succeeded (Orfield, 1978). A national evaluation study (Minkovich et al., 1980; Razael, 1978) actually revealed that preferential treatment of schools for the disadvantaged often benefits the advantaged children. By the same token, Kfir and Chen (1980) argue that these special programs for the disadvantaged children work in reverse; it labels them with the stigma of weakness and inferiority, thereby increasing social segregation.

In light of the limited success associated with these enrichment programs, a political decision was taken in 1968 to reform the educational structure and impose ethnic integration within the schools. Instead of the division into elementary and postelementary schools, regional intermediate schools (junior high schools consisting of Grades 7, 8, and 9) were established as a first stage of high school or a transitional phase from elementary to high school. This reform plan, as it was termed, sought to fulfill two basic national goals: to bring about understanding and harmony between ethnic groups, thus helping to forge a single nation out of the varied mixture of Jewish ethnic communities; and secondly, to increase the efficacy of the educational process, raising the achievement levels of all the pupils in general and closing the educational gap.

It is important to recognize that the decision to implement a policy of integration in the schools in Israel was not a response to any legal discrimination against Middle Eastern children. The Reform in the educational system was not perceived by any explicit ethnic segregation in law or in socially accepted norms. Yet, de facto forms of ethnic segregation are prevalent, due to the fact that schools drew their student bodies from local neighborhoods generally characterized by families from similar socioeconomic levels and, often, ethnic origin. Even where student bodies are drawn from different ethnic groups and dissimilar economic strata, their proportions are not representative of the general population. Thus, the Reform plan was designed more to increase interethnic contact than to create it. The new junior high schools were established to institutionalize positive interethnic relations and ensure equal opportunity for all.

Outcomes of the Educational Reform

What was the impact of Reform? The present literature does not permit clear-cut conclusions. First, the Reform program has not been completely implemented, either at the level of the system as a whole or at the level of the individual school. Second, data on the social and educational outcomes of Reform are limited, often ambivalent, and beset by methodological problems.

From the standpoint of implementation, the Reform program has never been fully attained. Program planners feared that the wide gap in basic skills and learning achievements would make teaching difficult and would have a deleterious effect on the scholastic level. Hence, they permitted junior high-school principals to weed out problematic students, to form special classes for weak students, and to teach a small number of basic subjects (such as Hebrew, mathematics and English) in tracked classes. Of these measures, tracking was the major method used. Consequently, in the majority of junior high schools, students study most subjects in heterogeneous homeroom classes, whereas major subjects are taught in homogeneous groups formed according to scholastic level. Because of the congruence of learning achievement and ethnic origin, most higher level tracks are populated by Westerners, whereas the low level tracks are made up mainly of Middle Easterners.

Tracking is an outgrowth of an individualistic educational philosophy aimed at allowing students to progress in accordance with their ability and talents. As might be expected, in the higher-level tracks learning is more rapid than in the lower tracks (Chen, Lewy, & Adler, 1978). Hence, tracking, even in this integrated framework, undermines the educational goal of closing the achievement gap and stresses academic differences associated with ethnic origin.

Educational achievements of students in the newly integrated junior high schools are compared by Chen *et al.* (1978) with the achievements of students studying in the old system. No major advantages are noted for the integrated framework. After the Reform, the gap between Middle Easterners and Westerners remains significant and is estimated to be the equivalent of 2 school years. The achievement level of Middle Eastern students in the basic skills at the end of the ninth grade is equivalent to that of Western children completing the seventh grade. This gap has remained constant over the years—the Reform did not reduce it. The negligible achievement results in the study by Chen and his colleagues are not conclusive. These data were gathered at the onset of a program when the educational potential may not have as yet been fully realized. It is possible that the current situation is more positive, but, at present, no research data are available. In this regard it is important to note the encouraging findings that under Reform, school drop-out rates were reduced by 20%. Anecdotal testimony presented to the Public Commission on Reform (Israel Ministry of Education & Culture, 1979) also indicates more positive evaluation of learning achievements.

Has integration fulfilled the hopes for improving interethnic relations? Levin and Chen (1977) investigate social relations in ethnically-mixed classes in the junior high schools by asking two sociometric questions: "Next to which three children in your class would you like to sit?" and "With which three children do you like to play during recess?" The analysis of the combined index of the two questions reveals balanced and almost completely symmetrical interethnic acceptance. Indeed, Middle Eastern students are found to be almost as popular as Western students. The researchers note a slight tendency towards ethnic cleavage shown by the subjects' preference for members of their own ethnic group.

In another study (Amir, Rich, and Ben-Ari, 1978), interviews and observations of relations between students during class and at recess are focused on more intimate social relations. Contrary to the previous study, findings are less encouraging. They point out that children are more likely to interact with classmates of similar scholastic ability. Given that congruence between scholastic ability and ethnic origin exists, ethnic cleavage remains prevalent.

The use of different methods for collecting data and the lack of definition and strength of the interethnic dimension studied makes comparison of the findings of these two studies difficult. In a more recent study conducted by Schwarzwald and Cohen (1982), a unidimensional scale was constructed to distinguish various degrees of interpersonal acceptance for classmates, ranging from casual relations demanding little social commitment to intimate relations en-

tailing very considerable social commitment. Interethnic acceptance was analyzed with and without regard to the academic track to which the classmate
belonged. When track was included as a variable, typical asymmetry in interethnic social acceptance appeared—both Middle Easterners and Westerners
showed more interpersonal acceptance for their Western classmates. When the
factor of tracking was included in the analysis, the degree of social acceptance
was positively related to the classmate's tracking level. The higher the tracking
level of a classmate, the more students were willing to accept him or her. When
tracking was held constant, neither the ethnic origin of the respondent nor the
origin of classmates had any significant effect. Thus, it appears that the asymmetry revealed by the first analysis results from the unbalanced distribution of
Middle Eastern classmates in the different tracks and not from ethnic origin per
se. These data tend to substantiate similar claims put forth by other researchers
(Amir, Sharan, Ben-Ari, Bizman, & Rivner, 1978; Hadad & Shapira, 1977).

Schwarzwald and Cohen (1982) also indicate the importance of intimacy in
the assessment of interethnic acceptance. At low levels of intimacy, no ethnic
cleavage is found, a result concurring with Levin and Chen's (1977) findings.
However, when more intimate or demanding interethnic relations are at stake,
the findings are similar to those of Amir, Rich, & Ben-Ari (1978); The students
tend to show a greater degree of social acceptance for classmates of Western
origin and less acceptance for Middle Eastern classmates.

Schwarzwald and Cohen's (1982) study raises major questions regarding the
methodology used in earlier studies assessing interethnic acceptance. The lack
of attention given to the variables of intimacy and tracking in previous work
constricts the interpretation of results regarding the degree of asymmetry prior
to Reform as well as change following integration. Yet, in any case, it seems
that Reform did not irradicate unbalanced interethnic relations.

Integration as a Situational Contingent

Social scientists postulate that successful interethnic relations and positive results of integration are contingent on a number of conditions such as: equal
status, interpersonal intimacy, social and institutional support, balanced representation of different cultures, and an atmosphere of cooperation (Amir, 1969;
Miller, 1981; St. John, 1975). In Israel, the presence of two parallel public
education systems—one secular and the other religious—provide a "living laboratory" for exploring the influence of these conditions on integration. In the
following section we describe the factors differentiating between the religious
and secular systems and explore their influence upon educational and social outcomes of integration.

Due to the Educational Law of 1953, the religious sector of public education enjoys a legal status equal to its secular counterpart. Under that law, state-supervised schools—religious in orientation, curriculum, and staffing—are made available to any parents aspiring to provide their children with a religious education. These schools open their doors to any student willing to adhere to basic behavior codes both in and out of school. Currently, about 21% of the entire Jewish school population is enrolled in the public religious schools.

One of the factors distinguishing the two sectors is the relative percentage of disadvantaged students, primarily of Middle Eastern descent. Disadvantaged students make up the majority in the religious system (63%), but comprise only a minority (36%) in the secular system (Egozi, 1979). This difference is accentuated by a second factor, namely the relative degree of deprivation. The disadvantaged students in the religious school system come from lower socio-economic strata than their disadvantaged peers in the secular school system (Algarebali, 1975; Lewy & Chen, 1976; Minkovich et al., 1980). Consequently, the gaps in basic skills and learning achievements associated with socioeconomic and ethnic background are more apparent in the religious than in the secular schools.

A third distinguishing factor is the geographical distribution of the population. Because the religious school system comprises only about a fifth of all public Jewish education, it must recruit children from a wider geographical area. This geographical dispersion increases the heterogeneity of the classmates but limits the possibilities of contact after school hours.

The central role of religion in the religious school comprises a fourth differentiating factor between the two sectors, and the influence is quite opposite to expectation. The many aspects of religious life common to Middle Easterners and Westerners might have been supposed to act as a bridge, mitigating interethnic polarization (Leacock, Deutsch, & Fishman, 1959; Parker, 1968). But just as Israeli society generally disparages the Middle Eastern heritage and esteemed Western ways, the religious school system also gives preference to Western religious traditions, disregarding the Middle Eastern religious culture to which most of its students belong. Moreover, because parents of religious students vary greatly in their religiosity, not only the form of religious tradition but also the degree of its observance has become a point of contention. Parents of students from well-to-do neighborhoods (mainly Westerners) tend to make stricter demands than those from disadvantaged neighborhoods (mainly Middle Easterners). This arouses opposition to integration from parents of Western students who fear that contact with disadvantaged students will affect not only their children's scholastic achievements, but their religious behavior as well. In sum, the religious way of life as presented in the school has often become a disruptive factor for the Middle Eastern students by rupturing the continuity between home and school.

How did these factors affect integration under Reform? In regard to implementation, it is evident that in the religious sector the principle of interethnic integration is applied only in a formal sense at the school level. At the class level, integration is only partially instituted, applying a policy of homogeneous, academic-level homeroom classes (Chen, Lewy, & Adler, 1978). It is of interest to note that this policy of partial integration is also implemented in the secular school system in those schools in which disadvantaged students make up the majority. Conclusions regarding the influence of the relative proportion of disadvantaged students on the implementation process are self-evident.

While integration is only partially implemented in the religious school system, the conditions of the encounter there are instrumental in fostering the development of negative self-concept among Middle Eastern students. This claim is supported by data from a series of studies. Using a Hebrew version of the Fitts (1965) Self-Concept Scale, Schwarzwald (1979) compares integrated schools (Middle Easterners and Westerners) versus ethnically homogeneous (predominantly Middle Easterners) schools in both the religious and secular school systems. It appears that in the secular schools there is no difference between the self-concept of Middle Eastern and Western students. By contrast, in the integrated religious schools, the self-concept of Middle Easterners is not only more negative than that of their Western classmates but even more negative than the self-concept of Middle Eastern students in ethnically homogeneous religious as well as secular schools. This pattern is also reflected in the items on the scales measuring personality adjustment.

Further evidence of differential effects of integration was obtained in a study (Schwarzwald, 1980) investigating stereotypes in integrated and ethnically homogeneous schools in the two school systems. Using a semantic differential scale, students were asked to describe four figures from Israeli society: (1) the Middle Eastern, nonreligious Israeli; (2) the Western nonreligious Israeli; (3) the Middle Eastern, religious Israeli; and (4) the Western, religious Israeli. Based on results of a factor analysis, two evaluation indexes were computed for each student—one representing ratings of success and progress and the other for interpersonal relations. Students related both factors to ethnic background. The Western Israeli (whether religious or not) was rated as more successful and upwardly mobile than his Middle Eastern (whether religious or not) counterpart, whereas on the interpersonal relation factor, the Middle Easterner was rated higher than his Western counterpart. The differential assessment of success was found to be more extreme in integrated schools in the religious system than in the secular system. Compared to students in secular schools, students in religious schools rated Middle Eastern Israelis (whether religious or not) lower on success and progress. Middle Eastern students in integrated religious schools adopted similar assessments for the Israeli of their ascriptive group, assigning lower ratings than those of Middle Eastern students in other institutions studied. Our contention is that this ascription of traits to the various types in Israeli society reflects the difference in social reality found in the composition of the two school sectors inside and outside of school.

In respect to self-concept, therefore, integration appears to have negative consequences for the self-image of Middle Eastern students in religious schools, whereas their counterparts in secular schools are relatively unscathed. These findings are not unique in Israel—studies in the United States, testing the influence of integration on self-concept when considerable interethnic scholastic-achievement differences existed, point to similar phenomena (Armor, 1972; Gerard & Miller, 1975).

Comparing religious and nonreligious schools presents interesting findings about the attitudes of parents as well. It should be noted that the aims of integration are to reduce scholastic differences and unify ethnic groups. Chen et al. (1978) point out that the importance of these two goals to parents is related to the ethnic composition and academic level of students in any given school. Parents of children from low socioeconomic strata, as well as parents who fear that integration would lower the educational level, espouse the primacy of scholastic achievements and relegate social integration to secondary importance, although parents did not publicly oppose integration. Yet, because the fear of lowering the educational standards and religious norms is greater in the religious system, parents of religious students express more opposition than parents in secular schools. Investigation of the attitudes of parents to integration in schools of varying proportions of disadvantaged students have not yet been carried out in Israel. It should be pointed out, however, that in the small number of schools in which Western parents did oppose integration, the explicit fear was that educational standards would be harmed, rather than general opposition to integration per se.

From a theoretical perspective, it is possible to attribute these findings concerning self-concept, stereotypes, and parental attitudes to situational factors in the two sectors that emphasize interethnic differences. Inherent in the formation of one's self-concept are two fundamental processes that provide individuals with the basis for evaluating their ability and their social standing: first, the appraisal of the reactions and opinions of people with whom individuals are in contact, especially those he or she respects and admires, and second, the appraisal of the results of social comparisons that individuals make between themselves and others. A positive self-concept is formed when individuals are provided with positive evaluations and when social comparison indicates sufficient ability and reasonable social standing. On the other hand, the absence of positive evaluations from others and critical social comparison results can lead to the formation of a negative self-concept. In this view, poor achievements, inferior social standing, and the rejection of one's own tradition would all contribute to the development of a negative self-concept among Middle Eastern students in the religious educational system.

Yet, it is precisely these factors that are accentuated for Middle Eastern students in the religious educational system. The increased self-depreciation among these students, as well as the negative stereotypes pertaining to their ethnic group appear to demonstrate situational contingent factors surrounding the implementation of integration. Similar arguments of situational contingency can be offered concerning parental attitudes. Integration that intensifies interethnic differences arouses parental opposition, thus polluting the essential supportive atmosphere. It makes educational achievements the major focus of attention. When such polarization exists, in many cases integration is implemented only at the institutional level and not at the class level.

Supportive Intervention

Although ethnic integration has not fulfilled the great expectations held for it, social scientists continue to profer the idea as fundamentally sound. Integration, it is argued, is not a direct outcome of the interethnic encounter per se, but rather is conditional on the more comprehensive intervention plans whose purpose is to create supportive conditions for success (Amir, 1976; Cohen, 1972; Miller, 1980; St. John, 1975). Integration in the Israeli school system has been accompanied by only limited efforts of broader intervention plans and rarely guided by scientific knowledge (as in other countries facing similar problems). Yet, in recent years a number of original attempts have been made to develop supportive intervention programs aimed at the enhancement of positive interethnic relations as well as stimulation of learning.

A detailed program for teacher guidance and training in integrated schools has been developed by Amir, Rich, Ben-Ari, and Agmon (1980). Its purpose is to assist teaching staff to cope with the distinctive psychological, educational, and social problems in integrated schools. The first stage of training, conducted outside the school, presents teachers with the theoretical and practical knowledge available in professional literature. Discussions, case studies, and a series of especially developed exercises for the program touch upon such problems as the harmful effect of stereotyping and prejudice on educational initiative, barriers in communication, tensions in the school climate, and techniques for teaching heterogeneous classes. The second stage, conducted in the school, offers assistance in the implementation of the new programs learned during training sessions and solutions to problems as they arise. The training program has elicited positive reactions from both teaching staffs and students in a number of schools where it has been implemented. However, program effectiveness has not yet been systematically investigated.

Cooperative learning—another approach that has been considered by researchers in the last decade to be promising for the improvement of scholastic achievements and interethnic relations (Slavin, 1980)—has reached Israel as well. Group Investigation, a cooperative teaching method developed in Israel, is designed for teaching the scholastically heterogeneous class (Sharan & Sharan, 1976). First, the teacher presents a general subject to the class. Then, under the teacher's supervision small heterogeneous groups (consisting of two to six students) choose one component of the general topic, collect material, assist one another, decide how the material is to be summarized, and present it to the class. Finally, the work of each group is graded by the teacher as well as by other students.

Recently, Hertz–Lazarowitz, Sapir, and Sharan (1982) compare the impact of Group Investigation, the Jigsaw technique (Aronson, 1978), and traditional frontal-lecture methods on scholastic achievement and interethnic relations. The Jigsaw method raised Middle Eastern students' achievement, but provoked a more negative peer evaluation from their Western classmates. Group Investigation, on the other hand, improved interethnic acceptance. In a different study comparing small group to frontal teaching, Ben-Yitschak, Lotan, and Sharan (1980) find that Middle Easterners prefer small group teaching more than Westerners.

Research on Mexican-American students in the United States suggests that social orientation may be operating as an intervening variable in Middle Eastern students' positive experience with cooperative learning. Studies over the last 10 years have shown that a cooperative social orientation is prominent among Mexican-American children, whereas a competitive orientation is more common among Anglo-Americans (Kagan, 1977). Correspondingly, research outcomes indicate that Mexican-Americans benefit more from cooperative learning than do Anglo-Americans (Kagan, 1976; Slavin, 1980;). The argument is that the competitive orientation of Western society (Seymour, 1981) and schools is inconsistent with cooperation and the consideration for others and thus, is mismatched with the cooperative social orientation of Mexican–American students.

Similar arguments concerning a cooperative social orientation and its educational mismatch with a competitive school is adduced for Middle Eastern students in Israel. McClintock, Bayard, and McClintock (in press) contend that social orientations evolve from family structure and relations among its members. Features such as family size, mutual dependence of family members, and the extent of autonomy given to children distinguish between Mexican–American and Anglo–American families and are analogous to the features distinguishing Middle Eastern from Western families in Israel. Consequently, a more cooperative orientation may be expected from Middle Easterners. Because the orientation of the Israeli school is essentially competitive (Rich, Amir, & Ben-Ari, 1981), it may be that there is a natural affinity to the social orientation of Western children that is in conflict with Middle Eastern students' social orientation. Of course, this hypothesis requires systematic investigation. In this connection, it should be noted that Schwarzwald's (1980) study (discussed earlier) finds that Middle Eastern Israelis are indeed rated higher on the interpersonal relations factor than the Western Israeli.

A third method of intervention developed by Ben-Ari and Amir (Ben-Ari, 1982) is based on the satisfaction of the three interactional social needs outlined by Schutz (1966)—inclusion, control, and affect. Schutz assumes that a group that fulfills these needs will attract the individual and increase positive feelings among its members. Derived from this assumption, Ben-Ari and Amir maintain that an ethnically heterogeneous group providing these basic needs would improve interethnic relations and consequently, facilitate learning. With a set of original psychological exercises devised for the program, they create an atmosphere totally different than found in regular classrooms and exclude such external goals as grades and achievement. By deemphasizing scholastic achievements and previous knowledge, the exercises permit interpersonal experience in a nonroutine context and deeper interpersonal acquaintance. Ben-Ari measured the method's effect on self-concept, class climate, and the mutual evaluations and relations among group members. Relations among students improved in comparison with control groups who did not take part in the exercises. However, self-concept and class climate were not affected.

Overall, it is difficult to say that social scientific literature is rich with techniques to ensure successful ethnic integration or that methods with promise have been utilized on a significant scale in Israel. Despite the effectiveness of work in small groups and individual attention to weaker students (Klein & Eshel, 1981), traditional, basically competitive, frontal-teaching methods continue to dominate the teaching in ethnically integrated schools in Israel (Rich et al., 1981).

A Look to the Future: A Theory of Perceived Inequality

A look to the future of interethnic relations in Israel suggests a greater need for the utilization of existing theoretical and practical knowledge concerning effective integration in the schools. In the past, planned integration was fueled primarily by policymakers' desire to bridge educational gaps and enhance positive social relations, with little involvement or pressure by Middle Easterners in the decision-making process. However, in the future it seems that this pattern will change; more pressure for genuine integration and equality of education will be exerted by Middle Easterners. The reasons for this projection are rooted in more global changes currently arising within the Israeli society.

As noted earlier, the encounter between Middle Easterners and Westerners in Israel must be understood against a background of the national aspiration for unity across different cultural orientations. Israelis seek to create a national Israeli culture. Peres (1971, 1976) finds expression of this desire among high school students, most of whom (75% of the Middle Easterners and 64% of the Westerners) support the blurring of ethnic differences. Along with this aspiration, both Western and Middle Eastern students wish to base the model of integration on a modern way of life that in actuality favors Western culture.

A down-to-earth expression of the wish for interethnic mingling is the percentage of mixed marriages, which rose from 9% in 1952 to 20% In 1981. Chen et al. (1978) evidences a different expression for mingling. Parents whose children are enrolled in integrated junior high schools generally favor integration and only a minority (15%) oppose it. Moreover, children in integrated schools currently seem to prefer classmates mainly on the basis of scholastic achievement, whereas ethnic background is of secondary importance (Amir, Sharan, Ben-Ari, Bizman, & Rivner, 1978; Hadad & Shapira, 1977; Schwarzwald & Cohen, 1982).

In the course of time, the assimilation of Middle Easterners to Western culture (Smooha, 1978) has in many respects decreased the differences between Middle Easterners and Westerners. Adoption of Western customs are evidenced by Middle Easterners having fewer children and marrying at a later age than they did in the past (Weller, Don, & Hovav, 1976). The data also show a great similarity in cultural leisure time pursuits among high school students of both Western and Middle Eastern origin (Katz & Gurevitch, 1973) and evidence of decreasing differences in language and consumer habits throughout the population as a whole.

Unfortunately, the gap in socioeconomic status has not been decreasing at the same rate as cultural differences. Peres (1982) presents evidence that the average Middle Eastern income is still appreciably less than the average Western income, although the gap has been reduced in the last decade. Similarly, because there has been an appreciable growth in Middle Eastern political representation, their number in government and political parties falls far below their proportion in the general population.

What is the social psychological significance of the increased cultural similarity on the one hand and the comparatively slow progress made in reducing the gap in socioeconomic standing on the other? Peres (1982) argues that closing the cultural gap has intensified awareness of inequality in the allocation of economic, social, and political resources and thereby, has increased the feeling of discrimination among Middle Easterners. Against the background of a tre-

mendous increase in cultural similarity between Middle Easterners and Westerners, the relatively poor improvement in the social standing of Middle
Easterners has accentuated their feelings of deprivation.

This claim is consistent with Festinger's (1954) theory of social comparison
processes that contends that only individuals with similar relevant characteristics
serve as a basis for social comparison. As long as there are significant cultural
differences, Westerners serve as a distant (and perhaps irrelevant) comparison
model for Middle Easterners. The elimination of cultural differences has made
the Westerner a relevant model for comparison. Consequently, the perception
of and objection to inequitable resource allocation has become more pronounced. The argument is graphically illustrated in Figure 4.1.

The horizontal axis in Figure 4.1 depicts the extent of cultural similarity
between Westerners and Middle Easterners in the past compared to the present;
the vertical axis represents the extent of the gap in social status. The differences
between data points for Middle Easterners in the past and present indicate that
the reduction in social-status differences is considerably smaller than that for
the cultural dimension. The slope of the diagonal in Figure 4.1 between data
points for the two ethnic groups expresses the intensity of feelings of inequality
among Middle Easterners—the steeper the slope, the stronger the feeling of
inequality expressed. Because the improvement in social standing has fallen behind the growth in cultural similarity, the slope of perceived inequality is steeper
for the present than for the past.

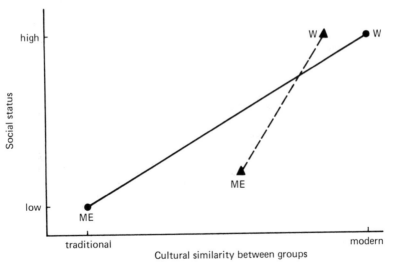

Figure 4.1. Perceived inequality among Middle Easterners (ME) (as expressed by line slope)
in past (solid line) and present (dashed line) as a contingent of cultural and economic similarity
to Westerners (W).

There have been no systematic investigations of the theory of perceived inequality to date, but there are some supportive data for the general populace as well as for schools. In the recent 1981 national election, an ethnic party whose platform called for the elimination of interethnic differences and increased cultural and social equality succeeded in electing three members to the Israeli Knesset (or parliament). This party obtained important ministerial and governmental positions for Middle Easterners. Today, more than ever, Middle Easterners are demanding prominent and influential positions within existing political parties.

With regard to schools, in an article describing the integration process in a number of schools in Israel, Halper, Shokeid, and Weingrod (in press) conclude that pressure to institute maximal integration is exerted particularly by Middle Easterners who have made social progress. In their article, they argue that upward mobility is accompanied by previously unexpressed demands for equality. Another indication of the current pressure for equality in schools is the demand of Middle Easterners to provide more time for the study of their heritage in the educational curricula (Stahl, 1976). These reflect greater sensitivity to social inequality among Middle Easterners.

If these trends persist, greater pressure for genuine integration and educational equality should face the educational and political systems. One could only speculate as to the specific outcomes in response to these pressures. In any case, it seems that social scientists will be asked to be more intensively involved.

Acknowledgments

The authors thank Michael Hoffman for his valuable comments and suggestions on the manuscript.

References

Adar, L. Toward a study of learning difficulties of the immigrants' children. *Megamot*, 1956, 7, 139–180.(H)*

Adiel, S. Reading ability of culturally deprived first graders. *Megamot*, 1968, 15, 345–356. (H)

Adiel, S. A decade of fostering the disadvantaged. In S. Adiel, G. Bergson, & A. Stahl (Eds.), *A decade of fostering the disadvantaged.* Jerusalem: Ministry of Education and Culture, 1970. (H)

Adler, C. The disadvantaged child in the formal and nonformal educational system. *Saad*, 1974, 4, 43–49. (H)

Adler, C. School integration in the context of Israel's educational system. In Y. Amir, S. Sharan & R. Ben-Ari (Eds.), *School desegregation: Cross cultural perspectives.* Hillsdale, NJ: Lawrence Erlbaum Associates, in press.

Algarebali, M. Indices for the characterization of the social composition of schools and a system

*(H) = published in Hebrew.

for allocation of budgets to schools with disadvantaged pupils. *Megamot*, 1975, *21*, 219–227. (H)

Amir, Y. Contact hypothesis in ethnic relations. *Psychological Bulletin*, 1969, *71*, 319–342.

Amir, Y. The role of intergroup contact in change of prejudice and ethnic relations. In P. A. Katz (Ed.), *Towards the elimination of racism*. New York: Pergamon Press, 1976, pp. 245–308.

Amir, Y., Bizman, A., & Rivner, M. Effects of interethnic contact on friendship choices in the military. *Megamot*, 1975, *21*, 287–294. (H)

Amir, Y., Rich, I., & Ben-Ari, R. Problems of school integration in the junior high school, gain and loss to pupils, and proposed solutions. *Studies in Education*, 1978, *18*, 15–36. (H)

Amir, Y., Rich, I., Ben-Ari, R., & Agmon, T. Social integration in the junior high school: An in-service staff training program. Ramat Gan, Israel: Center for Applied Manpower, Bar-Ilan University, 1980. (H)

Amir, Y., Sharan, S., Ben-Ari, R., Bizman, A., & Rivner, M. Asymmetry, academic status, differentiation, and the ethnic perceptions and preferences of Israeli youth. *Human Relations*, 1978, *31*, 99–116.

Amir, Y., Sharan, S., Rivner, M., Ben-Ari, R., & Bizman, A. Group status and attitude change in desegregated classrooms. *International Journal of Intercultural Relations*, 1979, *3*, 137–152.

Armor, D. J. The effects of bussing. *Public Interest*, 1972, *28*, 90–126.

Aronson, E. *The jigsaw classroom*. Beverly Hills, CA: Sage, 1978.

Ashmore, R. D. Solving the problem of prejudice. In B. E. Collins (Ed.), *Social psychology: Social influence, attitude change, group processes and prejudice*. Reading, MA: Addison-Wesley, 1970.

Babad, E. Y., Mann, M., & Mar-Haim, M. Bias in scoring the WISC subtests. *Journal of Consulting and Clinical Psychology*, 1975, *43*, 263.

Ben-Ari, R. *Satisfaction of interpersonal needs in desegregated schools and change in ethnic relations*. Unpublished doctoral dissertation, Bar-Ilan University, Israel, 1982. (H)

Ben-Sasson, H. H. *The middle ages*. Tel-Aviv: Dvir, 1969. (H)

Bentwich, J. S. *Education in Israel*. Tel-Aviv: Joshua Chachik Publishing House, 1960. (H)

Ben-Yitschak, Y., Lotan, M., & Sharan, S. *Developing equal-status interaction in groups of mixed-status Israel youth*. Report submitted to the Israel Ministry of Culture and Education. Ramat Gan, Israel: Sociological Services, 1980. (H)

Brand, E. S., Ruiz, R. A., & Padilla, A. M. Ethnic identification and preference: A review, *Psychological Bulletin*, 1974, *81*, 860–890.

Chen, M., Lewy, A., & Adler, C. *The junior high school study*. Jerusalem: Ministry of Education and Culture, 1978. (H)

Cohen, E. Interracial interaction disability. *Human Relations*, 1972, *25*, 9–24.

Coleman, J. S., Campbell, E. R., Hobson, C. J., McPartland, J., Mood, A. M., Wernfield, F. D., & York, R. L. *Equality of educational opportunities*. Washington, D.C.: U.S. Government Printing Office, 1966.

Davis, F. J. *Minority–dominant relations*. Arlington Heights, IL: AHM Publishing Corporation, 1978.

Egozi, M. *Statistical data on the Israeli educational system*. Jerusalem: Ministry of Education and Culture, 1979. (H)

Eisenstadt, S. N. *The Israeli society: Background, development and problems* (2nd ed.). Jerusalem: Magnes Press, 1973. (H)

Feitelson, D. Causes of failure in first grade pupils. *Megamot*, 1953, *4*, 123–173. (H)

Festinger, L. A theory of social comparison processes. *Human Relations*, 1954, *7*, 117–140.

Fitts, W. H. *Tennessee Self-Concept Scale*. Nashville, TN: Counselor Recordings and Tests, 1965.

Frankenstein, C. *Sincerity and equity.* Tel-Aviv: Sifriat Poalim, 1977. (H)

Gerard, H. B., & Miller, N. *School desegregation.* New York: Plenum, 1975.

Gitai, A. The youth movement as an agent of communal integration. *Megamot,* 1972, *18,* 401–418. (H)

Hadad, M., & Shapira, R. Commanding resources and social integration. *Megamot,* 1977, *23,* 161–173. (H)

Halper, T., Skokeid, M., & Weingrod, A. Communities, schools and integration: Some evidence from Israel. In Y. Amir, S. Sharan & R. Ben-Ari (Eds.), *School desegregation: Cross cultural perspectives.* Hillsdale, NJ: Lawrence Erlbaum Associates, in press.

Hertz-Lazarowitz, R., Sapir, C., & Sharan, S. *The effects of two cooperative learning methods and traditional teaching on the achievement and social relations of pupils in mixed ethnic junior high school classes.* Presented at the American Educational Research Association, New York, 1982.

Israel Ministry of Education and Culture. Public commission's report on the reform program in the Israeli educational system. Jerusalem: Ministry of Education and Culture, 1979. (H)

Kagan, S. *Resolutions of simple conflicts among Anglo–American, Mexican–American and Mexican children.* Paper presented at The Western Psychological Association meeting, Los Angeles, April 1976.

Kagan, S. Social motives and behaviors of Mexican–American and Anglo–American children. In J. L. Martinez (Ed.), *Chicano psychology.* New York: Academic Press, 1977.

Katz, E., & Gurevitch, M. *The culture of leisure in Israel.* Tel-Aviv: Am Oved, 1973. (H)

Kfir, D., & Chen, M. Desegregation and students' attitudes towards themselves and society. Unpublished manuscript, 1980.

Klein, Z., & Eshel, Y. *The other side of the street.* New York: Pergamon Press, 1981.

Leacock, E., Deutsch, M., & Fishman, J. A. The Bridgeview study: A preliminary report. *Journal of Social Issues,* 1959, *15,* 30–37.

Levin, J., & Chen, M. Sociometric choices in ethnically heterogeneous classes. *Megamot,* 1977, *23,* 189–205. (H)

Lewy, A., & Chen, M. Reducing or increasing educational achievement gaps in the primary schools. *Studies in Education Administration and Organization,* 1976, *4,* 3–52. (H)

Litwin, U. The allocation of resources in education in the "Seker" examination. *Megamot,* 1971, *18,* 166–186. (H)

McClintock, E., Bayard, M. P., & McClintock, C. G. The socialization of social motivation in Mexican–American families. In E. Garcia & M. San Vargas (Eds.), *The Mexican–American child: Language, cognition and social development.* Tempe, AZ: University of Arizona Press, in press.

Miller, N. Making school desegregation work. In W. Stephan, & J. Feagin (Eds.), *School desegregation: Past, present and future.* New York: Plenum, 1980.

Miller, N. Changing views about the effects of school desegregation: Brown then and now. In M. B. Brewer & B. E. Collins (Eds.), *Scientific inquiry and the social sciences.* San Francisco, CA: Jossey-Bass, 1981.

Minkovich, A., Davis, D., & Bashi, J. *Success and failure in Israeli elementary education.* New Brunswick, NJ: Transaction Books, 1982.

Orfield, G. Research, politics and the antibusing debate. *Law and Contemporary Problems,* 1978, *42,* 141–173.

Ortar, G. General survey of the 1955 elementary school graduates—A governmental project. *Megamot,* 1956, *7,* 77–85. (H)

Ortar, G. The predictive value of the "eighth grade survey" tests: A follow-up study. *Megamot,* 1960, *8,* 209–221. (H)

Ortar, G. Educational achievements as related to socio-cultural background of primary school graduates in Israel. *Megamot,* 1967, *15,* 220–229. (H)

Parker, J. H. The integration of Negroes and whites in an integrated church setting. *Social Forces,* 1968, *46,* 359–366.

Peled, E. *Education in Israel in the 1980's.* Jerusalem: Ministry of Education and Culture, 1976. (H)

Peres, Y. Ethnic relations in Israel. *American Journal of Sociology,* 1971, *76,* 1021–1947.

Peres, Y. *Ethnic relations in Israel.* Tel-Aviv: Sifriat Poalim, 1976. (H)

Peres, Y. *Horizontal integration and vertical differentiation among Jewish ethnicities in Israel.* Unpublished manuscript, 1982.

Razael, O. *Compensatory education and welfare for whom?* Jerusalem: Ministry of Education and Culture, 1978. (H)

Rich, Y., Amir, Y., & Ben-Ari, R. Social and emotional problems associated with integration in the Israeli junior high school. *International Journal of Intercultural Relations,* 1981, *5,* 259–275.

Rim, Y. National stereotypes in children. *Megamot,* 1968, *16,* 45–50. (H)

Rosenthal, R., & Jacobson, L. *Pygmalion in the classroom.* New York: Holt, Rinehart & Winston, 1968.

Schutz, W. *The interpersonal underworld.* Palo Alto, CA: Science and Behavioral Books, 1966.

Schwarzwald, J. The self-concept of junior high school students and its significance to religious education. *Megamot,* 1979, *24,* 580–588. (H)

Schwarzwald, J. Relatedness of ethnic origin to the stereotype of the Israeli in the eyes of junior high school students. *Megamot,* 1980, *25,* 322–340. (H)

Schwarzwald, J., & Cohen, S. The relationship between academic tracking and the degree of interethnic acceptance. *Journal of Educational Psychology,* 1982, *74,* 588–597.

Schwarzwald, J., Sholam, M., Waysman, M., & Sterner, I. Israeli teachers' outlook on the necessity and feasibility of teaching values to advantaged and disadvantaged children. *The Journal of Psychology,* 1979, *101,* 3–9.

Schwarzwald, J., & Yinon, Y. Symmetrical and asymmetrical interethnic perception in Israel. *International Journal of Intercultural Relations,* 1977, *1,* 40–47.

Seymour, S. Cooperation and competition: Some issues and problems in cross-cultural analysis. In R. H. Munroe, R. L. Munroe, & B. B. Whiting (Eds.), *Handbook of cross-cultural human development.* New York: Garland STPM Press, 1981.

Sharan, S., & Sharan, Y. *Small group teaching.* Englewood Cliffs, NJ: Educational Technology Publications, 1976.

Shuval, J. T. Patterns of intergroup tension and affinity. *UNESCO International Social Science Bulletin,* 1956, *8,* 75–123.

Shuval, J. T. *Immigrants on the threshold.* New York: Atherton Press, 1963.

Shuval, R., & Teichman, Y. Conditions for intellectual growth in gifted children from varying backgrounds. In A. Ziv (Ed.), *Psychology and counseling in education.* Tel-Aviv: Tel-Aviv University, 1972. (H)

Simon, A. On the scholastic achievements of immigrant children in the lower elementary grades. *Megamot,* 1957, *8,* 343–368. (H)

Simon, U. Education of the oriental immigrant child–parent relations. *Megamot,* 1957, *8,* 41–55. (H)

Slavin, R. E. Cooperative learning. *Review of Educational Research,* 1980, *50,* 315–342.

Smilansky, M. How does the educational system cope with the problem of disadvantaged students. In H. Ormian (Ed.), *Education in Israel.* Jerusalem: Ministry of Education and Culture, 1973. (H)

Smilansky, M., & Yam, Y. The relationship between family size, ethnic origin, father's education and students' achievement. *Megamot,* 1969, *16,* 248–273. (H)

Smilansky, S. Children who fail in the first elementary grades and their parents. *Megamot,* 1957, *8,* 430–445. (H)

Smooha, S. *Israel: Pluralism and conflict.* London: Routledge and Kegan Paul, 1978.

Smooha, S., & Peres, Y. Ethnic inequality in Israel. *Megamot,* 1974, *20,* 5-22. (H)

St. John, N. S. *Social desegregation: Outcomes for children.* New York: Wiley, 1975.

Stahl, A. *Cultural integration in Israel.* Tel-Aviv: Am Oved, 1976. (H)

Stahl, A., Agmon, T., & Mar-Haim, M. Teachers' attitudes towards the culturally disadvantaged. *Studies in Education,* 1976, *11,* 45-58. (H)

Swirsky, S. *Orientals and Ashkenazim in Israel.* Haifa, Israel: Mahbarot Lemehkar Ulvikoret, 1981. (H)

Weissbach, T. Racism and prejudice. In S. Oskamp (Ed.), *Attitudes and opinions.* Englewood Cliffs, NJ: Prentice Hall, 1977, 318-338.

Weller, L., Don, Y., & Hovav, H. The impact of education on family change. *The Israel Annals of Psychiatry and Related Disciplines,* 1976, *14,* 266-274.

5

The Desegregated School: Problems in Status Power and Interethnic Climate[*]

Elizabeth G. Cohen

Thinking about social processes in desegregated schools tends to be simplistic. For a long time it was believed that putting lower-class black children next to higher-achieving white children in a classroom would automatically confer benefits upon the academic performance of the blacks. More recently we hear that if teachers will design cooperative tasks for interracial classroom groups, all will be well.

In this chapter, I use data from three desegregated schools to highlight the operation of several social processes that have an impact on the interracial behavior of students. Many of the findings on these schools are counter-intuitive. All of this helps to illustrate my central point: unless we have more humility about the complexities of school social structure, general recommendations as to what to do in desegregated schools may do more harm that good.

Academic and Racial Status

The construction of *equal status conditions* is one of the goals of creators and consultants of desegregated schools. The traditional view is that if the groups meet each other on an equal basis, there will be diminution of prejudice, a ''getting to know'' each other and perhaps even becoming friends with each other. The difficulty has been in how to formulate what constitutes equal status

[*]This research was supported by the National Institute of Education, Grant No. OB–NIE–G–78–0212.

GROUPS IN CONTACT:
THE PSYCHOLOGY OF DESEGREGATION

conditions. This discussion uses the concept of equal-status behavior as social interaction in which the participation and influence rates are unrelated to the academic and/or racial status of the children.

Researchers consistently find in interracial and mixed academic status groups working on cooperative nonacademic tasks that high-status schoolchildren tend to be more active and influential than low-status children. The collective task in all these studies is a game called Shoot-the-Moon. In this game the group has to make decisions as a team as to which way to move on the board. Videotapes of the interaction are scored for activity and influence by counting who makes speeches relevant to the task and whose suggestions are accepted by the group for each of 14 turns.

In the earliest study whites were more active and influential than blacks in four person groups of two white and two black junior high school boys from similar social class backgrounds (Cohen, 1972). Subsequently the same pattern of dominance by high-status students was observed for ethnic-looking Chicanos and Anglos of the same sex and age group (Rosenholtz & Cohen, in press) and for mixed Indian-Anglo groups of boys and girls in Canada (Cook, 1974). Similar findings for groups mixed as to perceived reading ability were documented by Rosenholtz (in press) and Tammivaara (1982).

The underlying phenomenon was demonstrated a number of years earlier by Katz (Katz & Benjamin, 1960; Katz, Goldston, & Benjamin, 1958). More recently it has been conceptualized as a process of status organization in connection with the *Expectation States Theory* developed by Berger, Cohen, & Zelditch (1972). A body of applied research using this theory has developed simultaneously along with the formal theorizing and laboratory experimentation. Over time, the theory and its terminology have changed. The most recent formulation is the most comprehensive; from an applied perspective, it is also the most constructive (Humphreys & Berger, 1981).

How does the theory explain the operation of the phenomenon described above? Race is a prime example of what the theory calls a *diffuse status characteristic*. Technically, a status characteristic is diffuse if it has two or more states that are differentially evaluated by the society in terms of honor, esteem, and desirability. Associated with these states are general expectations for high and low competence at a wide range of important tasks. For instance, many Americans believe that whites are more intelligent than blacks. Diffuse status characteristics like race and sex are not the only characteristics capable of organizing expectations on new tasks in which there is no necessary connection between ability on the new task and the status difference. In classrooms, academic status and reading ability are examples of what theory calls *specific status characteristics*. Specific status characteristics like reading ability can also spread to new and irrelevant tasks.

The theory specifies certain conditions under which the status-organizing process will occur. These are referred to as *scope conditions*; at least under these conditions we may expect to observe status-organizing processes. More than one actor must be involved in a collective task that demands evaluation from the actors of each other's contributions. The group believes that the contributions will affect the success or failure of the outcome. Group members are distinguishable on at least one status characteristic. Under these conditions the diffuse status characteristic becomes salient and the general expectation states become connected to the task ability involved in the immediate situation.

When a racial-status characteristic becomes salient in the situation, the prestige and power order of the small group working on a collective task comes to reflect the broader social-status ranking of the races in a kind of self-fulfilling prophecy. The actors behave as if the status elements are relevant indicators of skills on the new collective task, thus putting the burden of proof on anyone who would show otherwise. (For a full description of this process, see Berger, Rosenholtz, & Zelditch, 1980.)

Reading Ability can operate in a similar fashion. If the task meets scope conditions as defined above and if some group members are known to have higher reading ability than others, actors will associate this ability with a more general problem-solving ability. Unless something intervenes, the ability will become connected to the new task, even if the task does not require reading and will become the basis for expectations for competence on the new task. As a result, those who are seen as having higher reading ability will hold higher rank on the prestige and power order on the new task than those who are low on the characteristic of Reading Ability (Rosenholtz, in press).

In the integrated school, when the low-status ethnic group is also lower in socioeconomic status, there is likely to be a strong correlation between being black or brown and being a poorer reader (although this is clearly not true for every black or brown student.) In such schools there is a double basis for expecting depressed rates of activity and influence of minority students with poorer academic skills—academic status and racial status.

Having the white students who have better reading skills dominate the discussion in an interracial group is hardly a desirable outcome; it tends to confirm preexisting racist beliefs concerning lesser intellectual competence of blacks and browns in American society. Beyond these implications for stereotyping, this phenomenon has implications for the academic goals of the desegregated setting. If students who are poor readers expect to be and are expected to be incompetent at intellectual tasks, they will withdraw, refuse to work on learning tasks, and even become what is known as a "difficult" student, regardless of the challenge or intrinsic interest of the task at hand.

The Status Equalization Project

Three schools were selected to participate in the Status Equalization Project, a 2-year study including a large scale field experiment. The project sought schools with approximately 50% minority children and a wide social class range. In many ways these three schools and their teachers who volunteered to work with us were exemplary. Teachers who are gravely dissatisfied with their teaching and principals who are defensive about their schools are unlikely to ask university teams into their halls, yards, and classrooms for lengthy observation. There was no tracking; so classrooms were academically mixed. In addition, all three schools made vigorous efforts to include the culture and history of the minority student populations as a legitimate part of the school program. Two of the schools (which we shall call Schools B and C) had been written up and were known for the excellent way in which they integrated children from different social backgrounds.

Wordsworth had a very large population (736), Grades 4–6 and 52% black students; most of the subjects of the sample were drawn from 13 fifth and sixth grade classrooms of this school. It is known for its academic orientation and has graduated many successful black students; there were a significant number of influential and effective black faculty; the PTA was predominantly black and very active; and the principal at the time of the study was Asian and the vice-principal black. There were signs of vibrant black culture everywhere in the school, ranging from pictures of black heroes to the singing of spirituals. The community context here was one of successful black political activism. About 300 children (both black and white) were bused into the school as part of a desegregation plan. There was a wide social class range with enough poor families so that the school qualified as a Title I School. The white families included some affluent and highly educated parents. The small Asian minority (7%) was also middle class.

School B, located in a large city, had 366 children with 39% whites, 16% Hispanics, 25% blacks, 17% Asian, with the remaining identifying themselves as other nonwhites. The racial composition was partly a product of a naturally integrated urban neighborhood and a product of a court-ordered desegregation plan. Both Hispanics from a poor district and white children from a wealthy area were bused into the school (50% of the student body.) Thirty-eight% of the children received free lunches.

School C had only 237 students; it was located in a middle- to upper-status suburban community. Because it was located in the one area containing relatively inexpensive housing, the school's enrollment was 50% minority. The minority population consisted of 26% blacks, 13.5% Hispanics, and 10% Asians. Up to one-third of the student population consisted of parents who chose to enroll their children; these were students from white and minority middle-class families who wanted an integrated school environment. This school was often called a model desegregated school; it had a strong multicultural program, emphasizing social studies, offered bilingual teaching, had a long-standing program of improving student self-esteem, and featured ungraded classrooms as well as many social services.

Status Effects in the Three Schools

In the three schools of this study there was abundant evidence of the strength of the status characteristic of Reading Ability. In a sample of 22 fifth and sixth grade classrooms[1] the children rank ordered classmates of their own sex and how good they were at reading. The level of agreement on ranking between children was measured by Kendall's coefficient of concordance (Kendall's W). Out of 42 class groups of rankings, 33 had a Kendall's W of over .50, with some as high as .83. The teacher's ranking showed close agreement with those of the children.

Overall, far more of the lower-ranked readers were black or Hispanic than the higher-ranked readers. Classroom observations in these classrooms revealed much academic heterogeneity. One could discover functional illiterates (mostly minorities) working beside children reading material at the high school level. There were also many children of all races working at grade level.

In the second year of the study, groups were composed of pairs of students. These pairs were selected from classrooms so as to match on social power (as measured by a sociometric question on influence) and sex. No close friends were paired. Each pair was differentiated by at least three reading ranks so that the High Reader saw the Low Reader at least three ranks below him- or herself. Twenty-eight pairs were made up of black members who were different on reading rank. Sixty-nine pairs had white High Readers and black or Hispanic Low Readers.

There were clearly effects of academic status operating in all three schools. This is quickly shown by calculating the difference in percentage of successful influence scores between the High and the Low Reader for each pair. The average influence advantage for the white High Reader in pairs in which the Low Reader was black or Hispanic was 24% (57 pairs) for Wordsworth, 30% (20 pairs) for School B, and 54% (11 pairs) for School C. For all-black pairs, the comparable figure was 14% (31 pairs) for Wordsworth. Regression of probability of successful influence on the game using several predictors revealed that if a person held the lower reading rank of the pair, his or her probability of successful influence was greatly reduced. ($B = -.511$; $F = 93.19$; $p < .01$).

[1]There were four classrooms at each of the two smaller schools and 14 at Wordsworth, the large school.

Implications of Status Effects

The game behavior of the interracial pair illustrates, in microcosm, what happens when the teacher assigns a cooperative task to mixed-ability interracial groups. On the one hand, students may frequently report that they like one another. There is a solid body of evidence indicating that the use of cooperative groups in the classroom will increase interracial friendliness (Patchen, 1982; Sharan, 1980; Slavin, 1980). On the other hand, interaction on these collective tasks will tend to confirm expectations for differential competence attached to academic status. Instead of white High Readers learning what the minority Low Readers have to offer in the way of original suggestions, they are likely to learn that Low Readers have less to say and are willing to give in to one's "superior" on academic status dimensions in the classroom. If the High is also white and the Low is black, interaction tends to confirm racist stereotypes of differential competence of blacks and whites.

The fact that academic status operated within all-black pairs is also important. It is often thought that blacks from a lower social class care less about being competent in school. If blacks thought reading was an unimportant skill, irrelevant to other situations, there would not have been such a strong effect of academic status on behavior in all-black groups.

There is no reason to accept passivity of the poor reader as an inevitable consequence of supposedly limited ability. A number of successful experiments have shown that if the expectations of all group members are altered, the result will be equal-status behavior in interracial or mixed academic status groups. (See Cohen, 1982, for a complete review of status treatments and their limitations.) The behavior of the low-status student is not a function of true incompetence; this is shown by significantly boosted participation, influence, and perceived competence of such students in treated groups (Cohen & Roper, 1972; Rosenholtz, in press).

Interpersonal influence stemming from informal social relations had a powerful impact on observed interracial behavior, quite independent of the impact of academic status. The question we used to measure social power is almost as old as the sociometric research tradition (Zander & Von Egmond, 1958). Each child in 22 fifth and sixth grade classrooms named the three classmates of their own sex who "were most able to get them to do things." However, *social power* is a difficult concept to define. In this discussion, social power means the successful exercise of interpersonal influence. The influence may stem from specific status characteristics in the informal social structure such as attractiveness or athletic ability or from status characteristics such as race or reading ability. Processes that have little to do with status can also result in successful influence; for example, influence can reflect various forms of coercion. Alternatively, influence might result from an exchange process between particular students over time so that one will comply with another in return for favors, esteem, or other valued resources. Thus when students say that certain individuals are able to get them to do things, they are reporting on the successful influence that is the net result of any or all of the following: a status organizing process, the operation of coercion (or threat of coercion), or an exchange process.

Black Power Index

To capture the concept of social power attributed to blacks by whites, a simple statistic of the proportion of white choices given to black students as socially influential was calculated. This statistic does not take into account the number of blacks in the classroom but is allowed to reflect black dominance, whether it comes about through sheer numbers of blacks or through other means. This Black Power Index represents a purely contextual measure of the extent to which blacks are seen as influential by whites in the classroom.

During the 2 years of the Status Equalization study, the project staff spent much time in the three schools, particularly in Wordsworth. Experienced classroom teachers who served as research assistants, in-service staff, and observers came home from the field every day murmuring that they had never seen such active children. They were usually talking about black children. These staff members admired the skill of the teachers in managing such "dynamos" and maintaining the process of instruction in large classes. Certain black children could be seen leading in games on the playground, organizing other people's behavior, and negotiating with white and black students inside and outside the classroom. There was little voluntary social segregation characteristic of other integrated settings. In the classroom a trail of black students, clamoring for academic attention, followed the teacher as he or she supervised small groups or seatwork. These children came up to the observers to find out their names, check on what they were doing, and make friends. At Wordsworth, the observers concluded they were visiting what is called in the vernacular "Black Turf."

These observations in Wordsworth were confirmed by analysis of the Black Power Index. Wordsworth, with its larger percentage of blacks, had the highest average classroom score on black power. In this school 50.6% of white choices on the social power question went to blacks; in school B, 39.4% of white choices went to blacks; and in School C, the comparable figure was 27%. For the girls, the value of the Black Power Index was closely related in all three schools to the number of black girls in the classroom ($r = .70$). The same was not true for boys in that there was much less of a relationship between the actual number of black boys in a classroom and the proportion of white choices given to blacks ($r = .22$). There were several classrooms in School B where blacks constituted only 25% of the males but 47 and 78% of white choices on the social influence question went to black males.

Attributed Power

We also examined the influence attributed to each individual by classmates. The Attributed Power score was calculated for the individual by adding up the number of choices received as most influential and subtracting the number of choices as least influential; this figure was divided by the total number of choices and multiplied by 100.

An analysis of variance of attributed power scores of blacks and whites showed significant main effects for race ($F = 24.99$; $p = 0$), almost significant effects for school ($F = 2.47$; $p < .086$), but not for sex. (It should be noted that boys and girls were constrained by the question to selections within their own sex.) Examination of mean scores for blacks and whites within each school showed that blacks had significantly higher average scores than whites in each setting. The highest average Attributed Power score was in School C, the school with the smallest representation of blacks.

In studies of classrooms, academic status and social influence are often positively related. In this population, the two dimensions were essentially independent of one another. At the classroom level, only 5 out of 44 sex-class cohorts had statistically significant positive correlations between the Average Reading Rank and the Attributed Power score. There were four with a significant negative relationship, meaning that better readers had lower scores on Attributed Power than lower ranking readers. There were clearly many socially powerful students who received a low rank on reading from peers.

Because Attributed Power and reading status were rarely positively related (and were sometimes negatively related), many of the Low Readers in the pairs of children who played the game had higher scores on attributed social power than the High Readers. This occurred despite the fact that we had matched the pair on whether they had chosen each other on the items concerning influence. Out of 96 pairs, 48 contained Lows who had the same or higher scores on Attributed Power than the Highs. For these 48 pairs, the average difference in influence between members of the pair was close to zero. In other words, the influence measure showed what looked like equal-status behavior as a result of these two variables working in opposing directions.

The data on the game from Wordsworth were greatly affected by the occurrence of Low Readers who were socially powerful blacks. Of the 57 pairs with white High Readers and black Low Readers at this school, 49% had Low Readers with higher scores on Attributed Power than the High Readers. Even among the 31 all-black pairs, 54.8% had Low Readers with higher scores on Attributed Power than High Readers. The equivalent percentages at school B were 23.5% of 17 mixed-race pairs and 27.2% of 11 mixed pairs at School C.

The high frequency of such pairs at Wordsworth accounts for the lower average expectancy advantage of High Readers as compared to the other two schools.

Influential Low Readers were often seen as intellectually competent. On a questionnaire given after the game, each subject chose the member of the pair who had better ideas. In the half of the sample in which the Low Reader had the same or higher Attributed Power than the High Reader, Lows were just as likely to be seen as having the better ideas as the Highs.

When the Low Reader was lower in Attributed Power than the High Reader, there were a number of statistically significant predictors of the probability that the Low Reader would make unique suggestions as to which way to proceed on the game board. Table 5.1 shows these predictors in a regression in which the dependent variable is the percentage of unique suggestions made by the Low Readers.

First there was a strong effect of Attributed Power in this half of the sample; Attributed Power of both the Highs and Lows had independent effects on the activity rate of the Lows. Lows' own Attributed Power had a positive effect and the Highs' Attributed Power had a negative effect. Secondly, academic status had a statistically significant beta weight. The higher the reading rank attributed to the High (by the Low), the more depressed was the activity rate of the Low Reader. Finally, there was a positive effect of the Black Power Index; the activity rate of the Low was higher if his or her classroom had a higher score on the Black Power Index. All these standardized regression coefficients had statistically significant F values.

The opposing effects of academic status and Attributed Power were clearly illustrated in this analysis. Being a Low Reader depressed attempts at influence (as measured by the rate of unique suggestions); having higher Attributed Power boosted influence attempts. What made the effect of Attributed Power rather remarkable was the fact that these pairs were matched on their perceptions of each other's social influence. Nevertheless, the reputation each member of the

TABLE 5.1

Regression of Percentage of Unique Suggestions by Low Reader on Attributed Power, Black Power, and Reading Rank[a]

Predictors	Beta	F
Attributed Power, Low Reader	.509	13.838*
Attributed Power, High Reader	−.353	6.234*
Reading Rank, High Reader[b]	−.342	6.370*
Black Power Index	.331	7.317*
Average Reading Rank, Low Reader	−.074	.293

[a]For those pairs in which attributed power of Low Reader ≤ High Reader; $R^2 = .38$.
[b]Reading Rank given to High Reader by Low Reader.
*$p < .01$.

pair held in the class as a whole had a strong and independent effect on the individual's rate of attempted influence on the game.

The ability of the Black Power Index to predict behavior of the Low Reader who was interacting with a more socially powerful High Reader was especially provocative. Independent of interpersonal perceptions of the pair and the general reputation for influence held by self and others, there appeared to be a "booster" effect on speaking up; this effect was related to having a classroom in which one's own race was seen as influential by whites. In the language of Expectation States Theory, this effect would be expected as a consequence of having *referent actors* (who are the same on status characteristics, such as race and Reading Ability) but who are seen as high on some other characteristic. Referent actors are in the situation but not involved in the collective task. In the case of the all-black pairs the presence of other black classmates who were also lower in reading ability but seen as competent on other dimensions would theoretically boost the expectations for competence of black Low Readers just as the fact that blacks were seen as influential in general would boost the expectations of blacks in mixed-race pairs (Humphreys & Berger, 1981; Cohen, 1982).

Black Power as a Natural Treatment

In addition to documenting the operation of an academic status order, these data suggest the operation of alternative-status characteristics in which minority children who are poor readers can rank highly among their peers. The presence of classrooms with high scores on the Black Power Index, especially at Wordsworth, suggests the operation of influential, high-status minority students.

The index of Attributed Power may be seen as a partial reflection of alternative bases of status to academic status. Low Readers who were high in Attributed Power were often seen as having the best ideas by their partner who had better reading skills. In addition, Attributed Power correlated with sociometric status among black students. Thirty-one percent of High Power blacks were frequently choses as friends; only 14% of the Low Power blacks were as frequently chosen. Students who are so highly chosen by their classmates must be very attractive to their classmates, socially and/or physically. In a review of relevant studies, Webster and Driskell conclude that attractiveness, as a physical characteristic, appears to function as a specific status characteristic with more attractive individuals seen as more desirable, competent and influential (1980). We may speculate that some of the competence and influence correlated with high scores on Attributed Power is due to the attractiveness–popularity of individuals rather than their academic status.

The effects of social power on interracial behavior suggests a treatment for academic status problems. Insofar as a "low status" group becomes socially influential in the context of the desegregated situation, those who have low academic status will be more likely to participate and be influential in classroom groups with mixed academic levels. If the teacher assigns cooperative tasks to mixed-ability groups, both power and academic status processes will affect participation rates. Those minority students who are poor readers but who are seen as socially powerful by classmates, will be just as active and influential as majority students who are better readers.

Poor readers with high and low scores on Attributed Power represent very different kinds of students; they occupy different places in the social structure of the classroom. The poor reader who is high on some alternative status characteristic may only require the opportunity to work in small groups on school-related tasks to be drawn into more successful, active efforts at learning. In contrast, poor readers who are also powerless may have to experience an opportunity to be influential with peers, possibly in classroom leadership roles, so as to change their power position. Although the powerless student will be more active in classrooms in which there are many influential students of his own race, special interventions are necessary in order to achieve equal-status behavior. The students themselves and their peers all need to acquire changed expectations for intellectual competence of powerless students of low academic status.

Using small group tasks for academic assignments and permitting the exercise of social influence by socially powerful minority students appears to be an exciting natural treatment; educators can take advantage of it if they understand its potential. In classrooms in which the "weaker students" have informal and alternative sources of influence, teachers are often concerned lest the classroom authority system be undermined. Therefore they try to maintain strict controls with close supervision of large group instruction or individual seatwork. In so doing they deprive these students of an opportunity to participate in the academic sphere, probably encouraging them to turn more and more to the rewards of their peers.

It was our experience in an in-service program in Wordsworth that if the class were trained in how to work in small groups, control problems could be managed. If the task involved interaction, influential black students who were poor readers plunged in with great enthusiasm. Even in academic tasks they were highly active in a context of peers (Gamero-Flores, 1981).

Interracial Conflict

Of the three schools, Wordsworth had the highest level of physical conflict, reported by the children. Using the Multicultural Social Climate Scale created by James Deslonde (Cohen & Perez, 1980), we asked the children to report how frequently they saw aggressive behavior ranging from pushing, name calling, to stealing and extortion. There were two indexes created from the items on conflict. One called the Generalized Conflict Index (7 items) included items dealing with aggressive behavior with no specific interracial overtones. The value of Cronbach's alpha for this scale was .84. A second index called the Intergroup Conflict Index (5 items) had distinct implications of racial or religious conflict (Cronbach alpha = .775). For example, items on frequency of "making jokes about skin color," "joking about the way someone talks," or "messing in someone's hair" were part of the Intergroup Conflict Index. In contrast, frequency of "being pushed around," "using someone's belongings without permission," or "name calling" were items of the Generalized Conflict Index. Average scores showed that one school (School C) had the lowest level of reported conflict on either index—an average score of 10.7 on the Intergroup Conflict Index and an average score of 18.9 on the General Conflict Index. In contrast, Wordsworth clearly had the highest level of reported conflict on either index; a score of 14.5 on Intergroup Conflict and a score of 25.3 on General Conflict. The other of the three schools was intermediate on the two indexes—13.0 on the Intergroup Conflict Index and 23.4 on the General Conflict Index. Children reporting on conflict within a given school showed less variability in their responses than children in different schools (For the General Conflict Index, $F = 31.9$, $p < .01$; for the Intergroup Conflict $F = 7.95$, $p < .01$.) This "school effect" suggests that there were climate differences that children consistently noted. There was a strong correlation between scores on the two conflict indexes in all schools (in Wordsworth, $r = .63$). One could have merged the two indexes to study conflict in general, but they were separated in order to examine intergroup conflict.

Wordsworth had a generally aggressive environment both within and between races. Interracial aggression was part of a pattern of the generally undesirable way people treated each other. There was no firmly enforced general policy on how people should treat each other outside classrooms. In the classrooms the teachers maintained a safe and reasonably well-ordered environment. The pattern of conflict was not specifically interracial.

In School C, in which there was a lower level of reported conflict in 1977, the principal had carried on a long and skilled campaign working closely with his staff. Norms of humane treatment of one another appeared on a mural at the entrance of the school. Considerate behaviors were modeled by the faculty and were practiced in special exercises in the classrooms. The same school was thrown into turmoil by conflict over its closure in 1978. Coincidentally, the General Conflict average score rose from 18 to 22; the schools' conflict levels were no longer distinctive in 1978.

In all three schools a relatively high proportion of white friendship choices went to blacks. If this proportion is compared to the proportion of blacks in each school population, white friendship for blacks was 15.4% less than what would be expected from complete social integration in Wordsworth. The comparable figures for Schools B and C were 10.6 and 8% respectively. In a recent study of desegregated schools in Indianapolis, Patchen found no relationship between friendly and unfriendly contact between races (1982), suggesting that friendliness and unfriendliness are not two ends of the same dimension; they are different dimensions. This may be partly because opportunities to make friends occur in the classroom and in extracurricular activites (Patchen, 1982), which are domains under the teacher's control, but conflict occurs in the corridors and yards, areas more subject to the principal's control.

Unfriendly contact was also a function of the proportion of minority students in a school. When minorities represented a very small proportion, the probability of unfriendly contact was low. It rose with proportion minority to a peak in the 49–50% range and thereafter fell off once again (Patchen, 1982, p. 143). Unfriendly contact may be partly a function of turf issues. When there is an open question of which group is to dominate the informal social structure of the school, unfriendly interracial contact is very likely to occur. When that issue is settled because of sheer numbers, the consequences of aggressive behavior towards members of the dominant group may be too dangerous; and normally aggressive individuals will desist.

Issues of human relations in the desegregated setting do not appear to have the same roots as issues of academic status. The school in our study with such an excellent climate for human relations aptly illustrates this point; there were severe problems of academic status observable in the interaction of white High Readers and black and brown Low Readers despite the considerate way they interacted inside and outside classrooms (an average expectancy advantage for High Readers of 54%). Consistent with this finding, Patchen (1982) found that friendly or unfriendly contact was quite unrelated to academic and social-status differences between the races in a school.

Human relations in a desegregated school is an important issue. However aggressive conflict may not be a symptom of poor race relations. Very often, in desegregated schools, faculty interpret every aggressive incident involving different races as race conflict. In some schools that may well be true; in the three schools described here it was probably not true. It seemed more a product of the social class and racial composition of the school and was affected by whether or not the administration chose to do something to enforce and teach prosocial behavior throughout the school. In addition the experience over the two years in School C suggests that conflict in the school can be affected by conflict among the adults in the environment.

The Teacher as a Factor in Classroom Status

Where does the teacher fit into this picture of the operation of status orders and interpersonal power? The teacher affects these processes through the methods of instruction and evaluation techniques. In turn, the teacher is affected by the status and power position of individual students.

Teacher Evaluation Practices

The teacher's evaluation system can be shown to have an important impact on the student's evaluation of his or her academic abilities relative to that of classmates. To the extent that teachers used varied and specific forms of feedback to their students in our three project schools, minority students were likely to have higher self-evaluations on academic tasks (Macias-Sanchez, 1982). Teachers high on the varied and specific feedback index used a combination of marking and grading with individual conferences with students in which they told them what they were doing well, what they needed to work on, and what kind of progress they were making (Oren, 1979). The use of varied and specific feedback also predicted minority students' report of more academic participation in both years of the study (Gorrez, 1979; Macias-Sanchez, 1982).

These findings suggest that evaluation practices are of central importance for the formation and maintenance of academic status systems. Insofar as students who are not high scorers on tests of academic achievement receive consistent, negative feedback, they will have lowered expectations for competence in all academic areas and will show lower participation rates. Insofar as they receive mixed evaluations, understanding clearly where they are weak and where they have made good progress and show some strengths, they will have somewhat higher expectations for competence on new tasks and are likely to participate more frequently.

Agreement between teacher ranking on reading and student ranking suggests that children respond to evaluations that teachers make of reading skill. The average rating given by classmates to each student was correlated with the rating given by teachers. In the three project schools the result was an r of .79 for boys and .80 for girls (Wilson, 1979).

In an earlier study Rosenholtz and Wilson found that teachers who used competitive evaluation procedures and traditional large-group instruction with standardized tasks had classes in which there was more agreement on reading rank than teachers who used alternative task and evaluation structures (1980). Wilson (1979) failed to find a relationship between instructional practices and agreement on reading rank in data from the Status Equalization Project. The level of agreement on reading rank was lower than in the previous Rosenholtz and Wilson study; there were major differences between the level of agreement on reading rank for boys and girls in the same classroom. Subsequent analyses of these and other data suggest that in classrooms in which there is no relationship (or a negative relationship) between social power and academic status, student ranking of their classmates on reading will be affected by the inconsistency in status position of individuals. For example, a student who is a poor reader, but who is influential on other grounds, will be given a higher rank by some classmates than would be predicted from teacher's rating or from a test score. Other students in the classroom will, however, rank such an individual low in reading. The net result is a lower level of agreement between rankers than in classrooms where social power and academic status are highly correlated. In classrooms with such inconsistencies in status dimensions, it is impossible to use agreement on reading rank as a measure of the effect of teacher's instructional practices.

Student-Teacher Interaction

Systematic scoring of the frequency with which teachers interacted with children of different racial groups was carried out during repeated classroom visits in the first year of Status Equalization Project. Minority children were receiving slightly more interaction from the teacher on academic matters than would be expected by chance. White children were receiving about what would be expected by chance, or in some classrooms, quite a bit less. Teachers were more likely to exhibit warm, friendly, behavior on nonacademic matters with minority children than with majority children (Lujan, 1980). He interpreted this as a product of the necessity of co-opting active, low-achieving children, thereby making them conforming and pliable in classroom activities.

The children themselves reported how frequently they received teacher's assistance of various kinds in Deslonde's Multi-Cultural Climate Scale. An analysis of variance conducted on the Teacher Assistance Scale indicated that race had a strong main effect on reported teacher assistance ($F = 6.81$; $p < .01$). Table 5.2 presents the proportions of children who had high scores (7 or more) on this index by race, sex, and social power. Blacks were more likely to report assistance from their teachers than whites; boys were more likely to have high scores than girls. Furthermore, this table shows that the subgroup most likely to have high scores on Teacher Assistance was Low Power black boys (35%).

To some extent the teachers were responding to the lively behavior presented by certain youngsters and to the organizational imperative of keeping everyone on task. Certain children were undoubtedly co-opting the teacher just as the teacher was co-opting them. For example, the Low Power black boys, "nobodies" in the world of their peers, might have been the boys we saw following

TABLE 5.2

Percentage Reporting High Teacher Assistance
by Race, Sex, and Attributed Social Power

Sex	Race	Social power	High teacher assistance (%)	N
Boys	Black	Low	35.7	28
		Medium	28.0	50
		High	21.0	42
	White	Low	9.4	32
		Medium	25.6	43
		High	17.9	28
Girls	Black	Low	23.1	26
		Medium	28.6	42
		High	25.5	47
	White	Low	9.8	51
		Medium	6.1	33
		High	21.7	23

the teacher around clamoring for attention. Boys with higher social power may have felt little need for the teacher; they were functioning well in the world of peers. The white girls who reported so little teacher assistance might have been the best students who appeared to require little attention or they may merely have been docile and overlooked amidst these active classrooms.

Origins of Minority Group Influence

The picture drawn here is purposely intricate. Throughout runs a theme of influence and activity of black students, particularly in Wordsworth in which they were over half the student body. Where did it come from? Many educational sociologists see the school as a faithful reproduction of the economic dominance relations of the outer society. Wordsworth, in which blacks were the most influential and active, was not in a community dominated by black economic interests although blacks held many important political offices.

There were several important features of the organizational context particularly in Wordsworth that communicated to all concerned that black people were competent and that black culture and dialect were a valuable and legitimate part of American society. There were important black adults who administered and taught in the school; the children saw black authorities tell white authorities what to do.

Over the course of the applied research program on status characteristics in schools, it has become increasingly clear that something about the school itself is a source of alternative-status characteristics that will affect interracial inter-action. In future analyses of status effects, it is desirable to include enough subjects within each school so that analysis can take place, holding school or-ganizational context constant. In the Status Equalization Project the bulk of the pairs observed came from Wordsworth.

In a sample of desegregated schools, Iadicola (1979) finds several important variables that predict the extent to which majority children dominate minority children in interaction on a collective task. In schools in which the minority population is larger, there are more minority faculty, and there are multicultural curricula, minority children are much more likely to be active and influential in small groups. These school characteristics are so intercorrelated that Iadicola could not analyze their effects separately.

The nature of the process by which organizational authority and resources in the hands of low-status persons leads to the creation of alternative status characteristics on which low-status students hold high ranks is not well under-stood. However once these status characteristics are created in a school like Wordsworth, influential black peers may be conceptualized as referent actors who increase black expectations for competence in mixed-race interactions.

Conclusions

This chapter has presented data from three exemplary integrated schools—schools that carry out many practices currently recommended for successful integration. Yet an academic status characteristic is producing problems for interracial interaction. Even in purely cooperative interracial groups there is a strong probability that white students who are seen as better readers dominate minority students who are seen as poorer readers. This occurs with a task that does not require reading or other conventional academic skills. The effect of the reading-status characteristic is visible within all-black groups as well.

Independent of the operation of an academic status characteristic, minority students who are low in academic status may become socially powerful and are seen as smart, likeable, and influential. These children will not show a depressed rate of interaction when working with majority children who have higher ac-ademic status. We have speculated that such a phenomenon is more likely to take place where minorities are a larger percentage of the student body and there are powerful adults in authority who are minority group members.

In such desegregated schools student social power can become an effective treatment for problems stemming from academic status distinctions. However this natural treatment will not lead to academic improvement for minority stu-dents unless they are given a chance to participate in challenging, intellectual and academic tasks in the social context of group interaction. Under present circumstances, teachers are not likely to allow this to happen. They are concerned lest the alternative social system of the students take over the authority system of the classroom and so are very timid about using such techniques. The teachers will need assistance and organizational support in introducing strong new norms for classroom behavior to govern this radically different method of instruction.

If the desegregated school does not have adults of minority background in positions of authority, if the proportion of minority students is small and socially powerless, and if the minority students are likely to be weaker in academic skills because of their socioeconomic background, the stage is set for the unchecked operation of an academic status characteristic. Even though skilled professionals may be able to produce intergroup feeling and friendliness through such interventions as cooperative grouping, students who are low on academic status characteristics will exhibit depressed rates of interaction on academic tasks. Lowered rates of task-related peer interaction has, in turn, been shown to affect learning outcomes negatively (Cohen & Anthony, 1982).

A complete redesign of the task and evaluation structure of the classroom seems necessary to alter the status of those who are low in academic status and in social power. If the goal is to improve academic performance as well as to achieve social integration, then the curriculum materials will have to be changed to provide appropriate and challenging learning experiences for classrooms with such a wide range of academic achievement. These changes should be seen as supplementary to the introduction of cooperative task groups that have demonstrated a positive effect on intergroup relations (Patchen, 1982; Sharan, Kussell, Bejarano, Raviv, Hertz-Lazarowitz, & Brosh, 1982; Slavin, 1980).

In the literature on desegregation there is no area more in need of conceptual clarification than the issues of interracial conflict, interracial friendliness, and equal-status behavior. They are often treated as a set of three indicators of one underlying phenomenon: social integration in the desegregated school. However the evidence suggests that they are different phenomena stemming from different sources and may well vary quite independently within the desegregated situation.

Problems of academic status are by no means the same thing as human relations problems in the environment. Human relations have to do with norms, administrative policies, and the social situations in which the interracial contact occurs. Status problems have to do with the perceptions of competence in intellectually important situations.

In conclusion, there is so much more that needs to be done in the way of intervention at all levels—even in these exemplary schools. There is no way that teacher workshops, the introduction of cooperative groupwork techniques, or any of the other techniques now recommended as general, all-purpose solutions will produce the desired results for integrated schools. These desired results are, in my opinion, attainable. But if we do not start facing the complexity of the social structure of the school in which recommended changes must operate, I am afraid we will never see many of the results we are seeking.

References

Berger, J. Cohen, B. P., & Zelditch, M., Jr., Status characteristics and social interaction. *American Sociological Review*, 1972, *37*, 241–255.

Berger, J., Rosenholtz, S. J., & Zelditch, M. Jr. Status organizing processes. *Annual Review of Sociology*, 1980, *6*, 479–508.

Cohen, E. G. Expectation states and interracial interaction in school settings. *Annual Review of Sociology*, 1982, *8*, 209–235.

Cohen, E. G., & Anthony, B. *Expectation states theory and classroom learning.* Paper presented at the annual meeting of the American Educational Research Association, New York, April 1982.

Cohen, E. G., & Perez, T. R. L. Status Equalization Project: Changing expectations in the integrated classroom. *Final Report,* NIE Grant OB-NIE-78-0212 (p-4) Stanford University: June, 1980.

Cohen, E. G., & Roper, S. S. Modification of interracial interaction disability. *American Sociological Review,* 1972, *37,* 648–655.

Cook, T. *Producing equal status interaction between Indian and white boys in British Columbia: An application of expectation training.* Unpublished doctoral dissertation, Stanford University, 1974.

Gamero-Flores, D. C. *Evaluation of a small group curriculum.* Unpublished doctoral dissertation, Stanford University, 1981.

Gorrez, L. *Variations in individualized instruction and student involvement in learning.* Unpublished doctoral dissertation, Stanford University, 1979.

Humphreys, P., & Berger, J. Theoretical consequences of the status characteristic formulation. *American Journal of Sociology,* 1981, *86,* 953–983.

Iadicola, P. *Schooling and social power: A presentation of a Weberian conflict model of the school.* Unpublished doctoral dissertation, University of California at Riverside, 1979.

Katz, I., & Benjamin L. Effects of authoritarianism in biracial work groups. *Journal of Abnormal and Social Psychology,* 1960, *61,* 448–556.

Katz, I., Goldston, J., & Benjamin, L. Behavior and productivity in biracial work groups. *Human Relations,* 1958, *11,* 123–141.

Lujan, J. *Teacher warmth and student effort for high and low status students.* Unpublished doctoral dissertation, Stanford University, 1980.

Macias-Sanchez, M. *Instructional organization and academic self concept.* Unpublished doctoral dissertation, Stanford University, 1982.

Oren, D. *Classroom structure and attributions: The effects of structural characteristics on attributional tendencies.* Unpublished doctoral dissertation, Stanford University, 1979.

Patchen, M. *Black–white contact in schools: Its social and academic effects.* West Lafayette, Indiana: Purdue University Press, 1982.

Rosenholtz, S. J. Treating problems of academic status. In J. Berger & M. Zelditch, Jr. (Eds.), *Status, attributions and justice.* San Francisco, CA: Jossey Bass, in press.

Rosenholtz, S. J., & Cohen, E. G. Status in the eye of the beholder. In J. Berger & M. Zelditch, Jr. (Eds., *Status attributions and justice,* San Francisco, CA: Jossey Bass, in press.

Rosenholtz, S. J., & Wilson, B. The effects of classroom structure on shared perceptions of ability. *American Educational Research Journal*, 1980. *17*, 175–182.

Sharan, S. Cooperative learning in small groups: Recent methods and effects on achievement, attitudes and ethnic relations. *Review of Educational Research*, 1980, *50*, 241–271.

Sharan, S., Kussel, P., Bejerano, Y., Raviv, S., Hertz-Lazarowitz, R., & Brosh, T. *Cooperative Learning, whole-class instruction and the academic achievement and social relations of pupils in ethnically-mixed junior schools in Israel*. Final Report to the Ford Foundation, Tel Aviv University, Tel Aviv, Israel, 1982.

Slavin, R. Cooperative Learning. *Review of Educational Research*, 1980, *50*, 315–342.

Tammivaara, J. S. The effects of task structure on beliefs about competence and participation in small groups. *Sociology of Education*, 1982, *55*, 212–222.

Webster, M., Jr., & Driskell, J. E., Jr. *Attractiveness and Status*. Paper presented at the annual meeting of the American Sociological Association, New York, 1980.

Wilson, B. L. *Classroom Instructional Features and Conceptions of Academic Ability: An Application of Source Theory*. Unpublished doctoral dissertation, Stanford University, 1979.

Zander, A., & Van Egmond, E. Relationship of intelligence and social power to the interpersonal behavior of children. *Journal of Educational Psychology*, 1958, *49*, 257–268.

6

Desegregation of Suburban Neighborhoods*

David L. Hamilton
Sandra Carpenter
and
George D. Bishop

Introduction

In 1968 the Kerner Commission Report stated that "our nation is moving toward two societies, one black, one white—separate and unequal" (U.S. National Advisory Commission on Civil Disorders, 1969, p. 1). The accuracy of this statement for housing patterns is obvious when one looks at a map showing the distribution of the black and white populations in virtually any metropolitan area. Impressive documentation of the degree of residential segregation in the United States has been reported by Taeuber and Taeuber (1965). Using 1960 census data, they calculated a residential segregation index that indicated the percentage of blacks who would have to move from their current location to another block in order to fully desegregate the city in which they lived. The average value of this index for 207 of the largest United States cities in 1960 was 86.2. That is, an average of 86% of all blacks would have to change residence in order to create a population distribution that was undifferentiated by race.

The civil rights movement of the 1960s brought about numerous gains for

*The research reported here and preparation of this chapter were supported in part by a Grant-in-Aid from the Society for the Psychological Study of Social Issues.

blacks in America, including antipoverty programs, protection of voting rights, and access to better jobs and educational opportunities. As a result, increased racial balance was achieved in several domains, including schools and work settings. However, comparable gains were not achieved in residential integration. Recent analyses comparing 1960 and 1970 census data indicate little, if any, overall decrease in residential segregation in the major metropolitan areas of the United States (Schnare, 1980; Van Valey, Roof, & Wilcox, 1977). It appears then that the segregation of housing patterns has been more resistant to change than other, more institutionalized aspects of society.

In this chapter we are concerned specifically with desegregation in *suburban* neighborhoods, and here too the picture is much the same. Blacks are grossly underrepresented in suburban areas; in fact the degree of racial segregation is greater in the suburbs than in the cities (Farley, 1976). It is true that the number of blacks living in the suburban portions of metropolitan areas has increased dramatically in the past 20 years (Connolly, 1973; Farley, 1976), rising from 2.7 million in 1960 to 3.4 million in 1970 and 4.6 million in 1977 (Clark, 1981). However, because the movement of whites into the suburbs has occurred at the same or greater pace (Frey, 1978; Pendleton, 1973; Schnore, André, & Sharp, 1976), blacks are still proportionally underrepresented among suburban residents. Whereas over 40% of the national white population lives in suburban communities, only 18.8% of blacks live in these areas (Clark, 1981). By 1974 only 5% of all suburban residents were black (Guest, 1978).

What the larger number of blacks moving into the suburbs does mean, however, is that an increasing number of white suburban residents are experiencing the initial desegregation of their previously all-white neighborhoods (Schnare, 1980). Historically the arrival of the first black family in the neighborhood has been, for many whites, a highly significant event. It is this situation that is the primary focus of this chapter. It is a situation that generates numerous questions of social psychological interest. What effect does this first black family have on the neighborhood in which they live? What are the white residents' feelings, concerns, and reactions to the black family's presence in their neighborhood? Does this desegregation of a residential area influence the attitudes of the white neighbors? What changes occur with the passage of time? Is the entrance of one black family in a neighborhood followed by the inmigration of others? Does the presence of a black family in a neighborhood influence the property values of nearby homes?

In this chapter we report the findings of an investigation aimed at addressing these questions. Before presenting our research, however, it will be useful to consider several issues that are important for understanding both the nature of suburban housing patterns and the research literature pertinent to this topic.

Segregation in Suburbia: Context and Issues

It has often been argued that the segregated nature of housing patterns in America is largely a consequence of differences in economic status: blacks typically have poorer jobs, therefore have lower incomes, and consequently cannot afford the same quality of housing that whites can. Whereas it is certainly true that the average income of blacks is still lower than that of whites (though the gap has closed considerably in the last two decades; see Freeman, 1978; Smith, 1978), economic factors alone cannot account for existing levels of residential segregation. There is considerable overlap in the income distributions of the racial groups, yet blacks and whites of comparable economic status still live in racially segregated areas that are of differential quality. Statistically controlling these economic factors does not come close to eliminating the degree of residential segregation evidenced in census data. Blacks and whites of comparable education, occupation, and family income continue to live in highly segregated areas (Bianchi, Farley, & Spain, 1982; Farley, 1975, 1976; Hermalin & Farley, 1973; Taeuber & Taeuber, 1965; Wilson & Taeuber, 1978). As Taeuber (1969, p. 186) has noted, "It would be a major accomplishment indeed to reduce racial housing segregation to the level of socioeconomic segregation."

Thus the economic gains achieved by blacks have and will continue to increase their ability to compete in the housing market, but will not entirely solve the existing conditions of residential segregation. "To a large extent the locus of the problem is in the racial prejudice of the white population. One path to solution might be sought in principles of social psychology, entailing analyses not merely of prejudice in general but of how it relates to views of home, house, and neighborhood" (Taeuber, 1969, p. 184). This statement reflects well the focus of the research reported in this chapter.

Residential segregation is important not only in and of itself but also because of its concomitants (Farley, 1975; Wilson & Taeuber, 1978). People tend to work, attend schools, attend church, shop in stores, play in parks, and so forth, in places where they live. Housing segregation thus provides the basis for segregated experiences in numerous other aspects of everyday life. For example, the policy of busing school children to achieve racially balanced schools can be viewed as a policy necessitated by the white majority's resistance to the residential integration of their neighborhoods. Reduction of the current degree of residential segregation would thus, of necessity, result in simultaneous reductions in other forms of segregation.

Survey research findings point to the prejudicial attitudes of the white majority as a major factor in the resistance to residential integration. Although white attitudes toward interracial housing became progressively more tolerant during the 1950s and 1960s (Pettigrew, 1973), whites continue to have strong reservations about the integration of their neighborhoods. In surveys conducted in the 1960s—at the height of the civil rights movement—Campbell (1971, p. 4) found that whites were about evenly divided on the issues of whether they would object to having a black family with the same income and education living next door and of whether or not they oppose laws to prevent racial discrimination in housing. Similarly, at about the same time, Bradburn, Sudman, and Gockel (1971, p. 121) found that only 36% of white residents disagreed with the view that "white people have a right to keep Negroes out of their neighborhood." More recent evidence (Farley, Schuman, Bianchi, Colasanto, & Hatchett, 1978; Lake, 1981) indicates that whites continue to have a strong preference for living in all-white or predominantly white neighborhoods. (Blacks, in contrast, expressed an even stronger preference for racially mixed neighborhoods in both studies.) Significant for our concern with the segregated nature of white suburban neighborhoods is the consistent finding that these discriminatory white attitudes are more strongly evidenced among residents in all-white or minimally integrated neighborhoods than among whites living in integrated areas (Bradburn et al., 1971; Lake, 1981).

Historically these attitudes have produced a self-fulfilling prophecy known as the "invasion–succession sequence" (Wolf, 1957). In this process the purchase of a house by a black family in a previously all-white neighborhood was followed by "panic selling" by white residents, often eagerly encouraged by enterprising real estate brokers (Fishman, 1961; Helper, 1969). The consequence typically was a rapid change of the neighborhood from all white to all black. Such "block busting" and resulting rapid turnover was particularly frequent in the 1950s and occurred primarily in neighborhoods bordering on the predominantly black areas of a city. Although this invasion–succession sequence is less common today (due in part to legal constraints placed on the facilitating role of real estate agents), relatively quick changes in the racial composition of neighborhoods still occur (Connelly, 1973; Mullendore & Cooper, 1972; Rent & Lord, 1978), primarily as a result of "spillover" from a predominantly black area into white neighborhoods.

An important component of this change sequence, in addition to racial prejudice, is the widely held belief that the entrance of blacks into a previously white area has a detrimental effect on property values in that neighborhood (Farley, et al., 1978). This belief persists despite a notable lack of supporting evidence in the social science literature. The most extensive and widely cited analyses of this issue (Laurenti, 1960) found no evidence of decreased resale values in integrated as compared to comparable unintegrated neighborhoods. Other studies, conducted mostly in the 1950s and 1960s, found similar results (Hunt, 1959; Ladd, 1962; Marcus, 1968; Palmore & Howe, 1962), although evidence that integration can have both positive (Mullendore & Cooper, 1972) and detrimental (Rent & Lord, 1978) effects on housing prices is available in the literature.

Much of the literature we have referred to on residential segregation and on the nature and consequences of the integration process is limited by a number of characteristics. This literature is scattered and diverse: we have cited works by psychologists, sociologists, demographers, geographers, and urban economists who often differ in their research foci, levels of analysis, and methodologies. These differences make it difficult to compare different analyses of the same issue and generalize across studies. In the literature we have cited, there are two major classes of studies. In one type of research the investigator analyzes data from numerous communities in large metropolitan areas, typically encompassing the non-central-city portions of the Standard Metropolitan Statistical Areas (SMSAs) defined by the U.S. Bureau of the Census. These analyses are extremely useful for detecting overall trends, particularly changes over time (e.g., from one census to another), as well as for identifying regional differences in residential segregation. However, because they rely on aggregate data from such large areas, these analyses ignore the variations among types of neighborhoods that exist in the suburban rings surrounding metropolitan centers and hence fail to recognize the possibility that residential integration may take different forms and have differing effects in neighborhoods that vary in important respects. The second type of research, in contrast, focuses on a single neighborhood or community (and perhaps—but not always—a comparison neighborhood or community) and typically investigates the concomitants and consequences of the residential integration process as it occurs in a particular area. These studies are often useful in providing information about the nature and course of integration as it occurs in the community under investigation and about the factors that influence the outcomes observed in that particular case. The problem with this approach, of course, is that the findings from any one community may not generalize to other areas, particularly to areas consisting of different types of suburban neighborhoods. Typically one has no way of determining the extent to which this problem imposes limitations on the conclusions to be drawn from the research.

The problems posed by these different research strategies are particularly acute when one's focus of interest is on suburban neighborhoods. As Lake (1981) points out, there are several different types of suburban residential areas. For example, he differentiates between densely populated "central-city spillover" areas in which neighborhoods become integrated because they are adjacent to an urban black area, "dormitory" neighborhoods that are predominantly residential and characterized by a high rate of private home ownership, "metropolitan–rural" areas that are near a city but rural in character and land use, and "outer–industrial" areas that are outside of a city but include business and industrial development. These different types of areas vary in wealth, population density, degree of integration, and migration patterns (Lake, 1981), and, as a consequence, people residing in these areas experience quite different living conditions. Much of the literature on racial residential patterns in suburban communities ignores these differences (e.g., all of them would be included in the suburban portions of SMSAs), yet it would be surprising if findings regarding racial integration generalized across all of them.

In our research we have concentrated on one particular type of neighborhood—what Lake (1981) referred to as *dormitory* neighborhoods. Because our initial interests were in social psychological questions relating to the process and consequences of desegregation, we focused on specific neighborhoods and the residents living in them and conducted our investigation in several neighborhoods in the same metropolitan area. Thus our research combined a telescopic approach to investigating the desegregation process at the level of specific neighborhoods with a concern for the consistency of our findings for a number of comparable neighborhoods.

The research project consisted of two phases. The first phase investigated the reactions of white residents to the arrival of the first black family in their neighborhoods. This phase was completed several years ago and was reported by Hamilton and Bishop (1976). Therefore that aspect of the research is briefly summarized in the next section. The second phase sought to determine if this initial desegregation of neighborhoods had long-term effects on the racial composition of the neighborhoods and the property values of the homes included in them. This recently completed phase of the project is described in the subsequent section.

Desegregation of Suburban Neighborhoods: Initial Response to Black Neighbors

Our research on the processes and consequences of residential desegregation in suburban communities was initiated a decade ago. In 1972–1973 Hamilton and Bishop (1976) investigated the response of white suburban homeowners to the initial desegregation of their previously all-white neighborhoods. Specifically, the research focused on the following question: When a family moves into a white neighborhood, what differences occur in the residents' response to their new neighbors as a function of the new family's race? To examine this question, interviews were conducted with residents in 18 white suburban neighborhoods, selected from four towns surrounding (but not including) New Haven, Connecticut. In eight of those neighborhoods, a black family had just purchased a home; in the other 10, a white family had just moved in. This defined the two major conditions of Hamilton and Bishop's (1976) investigation, which will be referred to as *desegregated* and *segregated* neighborhoods.

It is important to note that in its usage in describing this research the term *desegregated* refers to the *initial* entry of a black family into an area—in 1972 one black family moved into a previously all-white neighborhood. Similarly, *segregated* neighborhoods are those in which a white family purchased a house in 1972, maintaining the unintegregated nature of those neighborhoods at that time.

The 18 neighborhoods included in this study were highly comparable in most important respects. All were pleasant, middle-class residential neighborhoods consisting entirely of privately owned single-family dwellings. In most cases the neighborhoods were well-established, such that new construction in the areas was rare. None of the neighborhoods bordered on areas heavily populated by blacks. Respondents interviewed in the segregated and desegregated neighborhoods were highly comparable with regard to a variety of social and demographic characteristics, including age, socioeconomic status, highest level of education, religious preference, political party affiliation, years lived in present home, number of children living at home, and liberalism–conservatism in general political attitudes. For the sample as a whole, almost half of the husbands in the households interviewed had at least some college education, approximately 70% held white-collar jobs, and many of them commuted into New Haven for work. In sum, Lake's (1981) term *dormitory neighborhood* provides an apt characterization of the neighborhoods studied in this research.

For each of the 18 target (new family) homes, Hamilton and Bishop (1976) defined a *microneighborhood* consisting of a number of houses (ranging from 10 to 16) immediately surrounding or near to the target house purchased by the new family. Interviews were conducted with the (white) residents living in these microneighborhoods and assessed a variety of behavioral and attitudinal indicators of the residents' reactions to their new neighbors. These interviews used indirect assessment procedures, such that the respondents were unaware that the investigation was concerned with either race-related issues or responses to new neighbors. This was accomplished by introducing the study as a survey of "the most important ways that neighborhoods differ from each other, and how these differences influence people's satisfaction or dissatisfaction with the places in which they live." The investigators' interest in race and their knowledge that the respondent had a new neighbor were never mentioned. The interview schedule assessed family background information, the respondents' interactions with neighbors, their perceptions of their neighborhoods, and their knowledge of information about other families living nearby, always including the new family. In addition, an attitude questionnaire that included several items indirectly assessing racial attitudes was administered.

The interviews were conducted at various times over a 1-year period. In some neighborhoods it was possible to interview residents one month before the new family moved in, permitting determination that the residents in the two categories of neighborhoods were in fact comparable. Interviews were conducted in all neighborhoods either 1 or 3 months after the new family's arrival and in most cases again after they had lived there for 1 year. Thus the scheduling of interviews permitted not only comparisons between residents in newly desegregated and still-segregated neighborhoods but also an evaluation of how responses to the black and white target families changed over time.

Analyses using the various indicators coded from these interviews yielded a number of significant and meaningful findings that can be summarized as follows:

1. *Salience of a black family in a white neighborhood.* Whereas the presence of a new white family in a neighborhood was noticed and reported only in the period immediately after their arrival, the entrance of a black family into a white area was a much more salient event, the perceived importance of which continued for a much longer period of time. Interviewers asked the seemingly innocuous question, "Have there been any changes in the nature of the neighborhood in the last year or so?" Responses to this question were coded as to whether or not the interviewee mentioned the new family. During the first month or so, respondents mentioned the arrival of a new family, regardless of race, in answering this question. After 3 months the frequency with which a new white family was cited dropped considerably. In contrast, the salience of a black family took longer to dissipate, such that even after a black family had lived in a neighborhood for a full year, their arrival was still cited rather frequently as a change in the nature of the neighborhood.

2. *Evaluative reactions to a black family.* The initial response of the white neighbors to the black family's presence was unfavorable. Although no overt acts of hostility were reported, the respondents' comments clearly indicated disapproval of the fact that blacks now lived in their neighborhood. A year later, however, evidence of these negative feelings had reduced considerably and favorable comments about the black neighbors were frequently made. There was, then, a noticeable change in the affective response of the residents to the presence of a black family in their neighborhood.

3. *Concern about property values.* One prominent basis for the white residents' initial negative reaction was a concern that the presence of a black family would have an adverse effect on property values in the neighborhood. Again, however, evidence of this concern had disappeared after a 1-year interval.

4. *Interactions with and knowledge about new neighbors.* The extent and nature of the residents' interaction with a new family—black or white—was quite limited. Even after a 1-year interval, over half of the respondents reported that they had never interacted with their new neighbors, a finding that was unrelated to the race of the target family. There were, however, differences in what the residents learned about the new family. Interviewees were asked a series of basic information questions about the target family—names of family members, number of children, husband's and wife's occupations, religious affiliation, and where they had moved from. Respondents' ability to answer these questions indicated that what and how much was learned depended to some extent on the race of the new family, suggesting that residents sought somewhat different information about black and white new neighbors. For example, after 1 month, respondents could answer the same *number* of questions regardless of the new family's race but there was a large difference in their knowledge of the most basic information—the family's last name. Only 11% of the interviewees knew the last name of the new black neighbors, whereas 60% knew the name of a new white family. This pattern of findings suggests that when a black family moves into a previously all-white neighborhood, the residents are less concerned about who they are than about what they are like. In contrast, one of the first things residents learn about new white neighbors is their name, despite the fact that they interact with them no more than with a new black neighbor.

5. *Effects on racial attitudes.* We found that the experience of having black neighbors had an effect on racial attitudes. Residents in the segregated and desegregated neighborhoods were highly comparable in their racial attitudes both before and soon after the new families moved into their neighborhoods. However, after a 1-year interval residents living in the desegregated neighborhoods expressed significantly less racism than did their counterparts in still-segregated neighborhoods. Moreover, this difference in racial attitudes evident after 1-year was not a function of interaction with the new family—residents in desegregated neighborhoods had significantly lower racism scores, regardless of whether or not they had interacted with their black neighbors. Because of these results (as well as the minimal overall extent of interaction), interracial contact cannot be seriously considered as an important mediator of the changes that were observed in the white residents' feelings and attitudes over this 1-year period.

In interpreting this pattern of findings, Hamilton and Bishop (1976) emphasized the role of the disconfirmation of expectancies in bringing about the changes over time that were evident in their results. From the interviews conducted soon after the black family's arrival, it was clear that the white residents had a number of fears and apprehensions about the consequences that would follow from the integration of their neighborhoods. During the first year of the black family's residence, these fears and apprehensions had not been confirmed. This disconfirmation of expectancies resulted in systematic changes in the residents' feelings and attitudes evidenced in the findings we have summarized.

Desegregation of Suburban Neighborhoods: Long-Term Effects[1]

The second phase of our research was conducted in 1981–1982, almost a decade after the target families had moved into their new homes. This phase consisted of a series of analyses aimed at investigating three issues that historically have been of central importance in the beliefs of white residents concerning the consequences of residential integration. Specifically, white residents believe that when a black family moves into a white neighborhood the following succession of events is likely to occur:

1. Some portion of the white residents will sell their houses and move out of the area, and "white flight" may follow. This would be reflected in a high turnover rate in the neighborhood.
2. At least some, and perhaps an increasing portion, of these white residents will be replaced by other black families. As a consequence, the racial composition of the neighborhood will undergo considerable change over time.
3. The fact that the neighborhood is integrated with have an adverse effect on property values. This will hurt the resale value of houses located near the black family's residence.

The analyses we have conducted evaluate the extent to which these changes have occurred over a period of several years in the 18 neighborhoods we studied in 1972. Specifically, we have utilized information available in public records to determine answers to the following questions: (1) To what extent does the initial desegregation of a suburban residential neighborhood act as a catalyst for an increased rate of sale of homes located near the black family's residence? Does it result in a higher rate of turnover than in highly comparable neighborhoods that have not yet become integrated? (2) Does the turnover that does occur following desegregation alter the racial composition of the neighborhood? Over time, does the percentage of black residents in these neighborhoods increase in relation to comparable neighborhoods that were still all-white in 1972? (3) What effect does the initial desegregation of a neighborhood have on the

[1]The authors express their deep appreciation to David L. Hall and Bruce Lewellyn for their assistance in obtaining the data on which the analyses reported in this section are based.

residents' financial investment of owning a home in that neighborhood? Specifically, does the presence of a black family in the neighborhood have a dampening effect on the value of nearby homes? The results of our analyses will be described in the following sections.

Effects on Turnover Rates

When a residence changes ownership from one party to another, the transfer of the deed is recorded in the land records office located in the city or town hall where the property is located. For each of the 203 residences (excluding target houses) included in the 18 microneighborhoods defined by Hamilton and Bishop (1976), we determined from these land records the number of times the residence changed ownership from 1972 through 1981 and the dates on which those transfers of ownership occurred. From these data we were able to compare the segregated and desegregated neighborhoods with regard to the frequency with which houses in these neighborhoods were sold, on a year-by-year basis, for the 10-year period covered by this analysis.

Of these 203 residences, 62 (30.5%) changed ownership at least once. For the period 1972–1981, an average of 7.7 (3.8%) of the houses were sold per year. Given these overall rates of turnover, is there any evidence of differential selling in neighborhoods that were and were not desegregated in 1972? Figure 6.1 shows the percentage of homes sold each year over the 10-year period for the two sets of neighborhoods. There is little—if any—evidence that the arrival of the first black family in the desegregated neighborhoods had any detectable effect on the sale of homes in these neighborhoods, compared to similar neighborhoods without black residents. The turnover rates for both sets of neighborhoods tended to increase and decrease together across years, perhaps reflecting variations in market conditions and other factors. A pairwise t-test comparing the two distributions shown in Figure 6.1 indicated that the two categories of neighborhood did not differ significantly in the percentage of homes sold per year, $t(18) = 0.12$, n.s.

There is, however, one hint of a race-related effect in these data. In 1973—the first full year after the target families' arrival—the lines diverge: sales in the newly desegregated neighborhoods increased somewhat, whereas they declined slightly in the still-segregated neighborhoods. This divergence might be viewed as differential turnover in response to neighborhood integration. However, we are skeptical that such an interpretation is warranted, for several reasons. First, both the absolute percentages and the difference between them are small. Second, this difference disappears immediately and then reverses in the succeeding years. And third, across this 10-year period, the turnover rate was higher in each type of neighborhood exactly half of the time (five of the years),

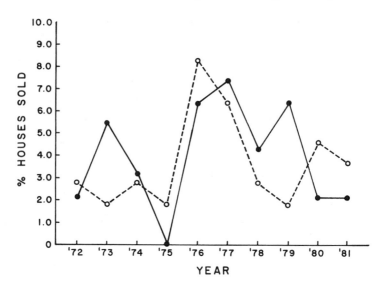

Figure 6.1. Percentage of houses sold in segregated (dashed line) and desegregated (solid line) neighborhoods, 1972–1981.

with no indication of systematic trends across multiyear periods. These aspects of the data suggest that the occasional divergences of these lines probably reflect random fluctuations. Thus, although the 1973 data alone may appear to reflect a reaction of white residents to the desegregation of their neighborhoods, other aspects of the findings indicate the need for caution in making such an interpretation.

This conclusion is strengthened by other evidence of the high degree of stability of these neighborhoods. We determined the percentage of continuous residents for the 1972–1981 period, that is, homes that did not change ownership at all during this 10-year interval. These percentages for the desegregated and segregated neighborhoods were 68.1 and 70.6%, respectively. In both cases, then, slightly more than two-thirds of the target family's neighbors lived continuously in the same home for the decade following the new family's arrival.

Taken together, these data indicate considerable comparability in the rate of turnover in neighborhoods that were or were not desegregated by a new family's arrival in 1972. They also reveal a high degree of stability in both sets of neighborhoods. The race of the target family had little effect on the tendency of other residents to move out of the neighborhood. These data hardly resemble the pattern of findings one would expect if the entrance of a black family into a previously all-white neighborhood were the catalyst for white flight, or even for the beginnings of a more gradual invasion–succession sequence in which the nature of the neighborhood changes over a more extended period of time.

Effects on Replacement

Whereas the arrival of the first black family in these neighborhoods did not produce white flight, it may nevertheless have had an influence on the replacement process. That is, when houses in the desegregated neighborhoods were sold, it may be that they were more likely to be purchased by other black families than was true in neighborhoods that still had no black residents. If so, then over a period of years a gradual change would take place in which the proportion of black residents living in the initially-desegregated neighborhoods would increase, relative to the comparison neighborhoods. Thus our second analysis was concerned with the current racial composition of these neighborhoods.

To evaluate this question, we made use of data from in the 1980 population census. The Census Bureau has available block-by-block statistics for each block in each community of major metropolitan areas. Included in the block data is information regarding the number of residents of various racial groups (white, black, Asian, etc.) living on a block. These data were used to determine whether the segregated and desegregated neighborhoods differed in racial composition in 1980, some 8 years after the target families had moved in. Because in 1972, prior to the target families' arrival, all of these neighborhoods were unintegrated, any differences in racial composition after a several year interval could be viewed as at least partly attributable to the initial desegregation that occurred in 1972.

In establishing their interview procedures, Hamilton and Bishop (1976) defined a microneighborhood for each area they studied. The microneighborhood consisted of those houses (ranging from 10 to 16) in which the residents were considered most likely to be cognizant of and influenced by the change of ownership of the target house. Typically the microneighborhood consisted of several houses on either side of the target house, several houses on the other side of the street, and a few houses behind the target house. In sampling from the block statistics, we included the data from any block that contained at least one house included in Hamilton and Bishop's microneighborhoods. Because of this, the area represented in the block statistics is somewhat larger than the microneighborhoods defined in the earlier study. However, this is not viewed as problematic. In fact, in assessing whether the racial composition of a neighborhood changes as a result of initial desegregation, it seems appropriate to include an area that extends beyond the houses immediately surrounding the target residence.

The percentage of white and black residents in each of the 18 neighborhoods in 1980 are shown in Table 6.1. It is obvious that over this 8-year period these neighborhoods have remained predominantly, and in some cases exclusively,

TABLE 6.1

Percentage of White and Black Residents in Neighborhoods in 1980

Neighborhood	Percentage white	Percentage black	Percentage other
Desegregated			
1	100.00	0.00	0.00
2	92.05	7.32	0.63
3	97.12	2.88	0.00
4	99.28	0.00	0.72
5	94.25	5.06	0.69
6	96.47	2.35	1.18
7	97.12	2.00	0.88
8	96.30	3.70	0.00
Mean	96.57	2.91	0.51
Segregated			
1	96.99	3.01	0.00
2	100.00	0.00	0.00
3	99.65	0.00	0.35
4	100.00	0.00	0.00
5	97.69	0.29	2.02
6	97.40	2.38	0.22
7	96.25	3.75	0.00
8	98.03	0.00	1.97
9	93.02	6.98	0.00
10	96.76	3.24	0.00
Mean	97.58	1.97	0.45

white. Using arcsine transformations of these percentages, t tests were conducted to determine whether the two types of neighborhoods differed in the percentage of white residents and the percentage of black residents in 1980. In neither case was the difference significant (for percentage of whites: $t(16) = 0.86$, n.s.; for percentage of blacks, $t(16) = 0.83$, n.s.).

In sum, these findings indicate that the initial desegregation of these previously all white neighborhoods has not resulted in any substantial increase of black residents in the area over an 8-year period.

Effects on Property Values

The third issue we wanted to address was the widespread belief that the desegregation of suburban neighborhoods has an adverse influence on property values. To evaluate this issue, we conducted analyses using two different kinds of data. First, we determined the assessed values of all residences included in the microneighborhoods studied by Hamilton and Bishop (1976) and compared the segregated and desegregated neighborhoods for any differential increase in these assessed values. Second, we determined the actual purchase price of any residence in these neighborhoods that changed ownership between 1972 and 1981 and compared the two types of neighborhoods for any differential increase in these resale values.

Assessed Values

For purposes of determining property taxes, each town periodically determines an assessed value of each piece of property and taxes the owner at some percentage of that value. In Connecticut these assessments are conducted approximately once each decade. From records available in the town halls, we determined the assessed property values of all residences in the 18 microneighborhoods identified by Hamilton and Bishop (1976) at two points in time: the most recent assessment before 1972 and the first assessment after 1972. For the four towns represented in these neighborhoods, the prior assessments were conducted in 1966, 1969, 1970, and 1971, and the later ones were conducted in 1979, 1980, and 1981. (For three of the towns, there was a 10-year period between assessments; for one town, there was a 13-year interval). Because the towns differ in the percentage of the property's assessed market value on which taxation is based, the assessment figures were adjusted in all cases to correspond to assessed market values.

The first column of Table 6.2 presents the average assessed value of the homes in each of the 18 neighborhoods for the prior assessment (conducted between 1966 and 1971). As one would expect, there is some degree of variation among neighborhoods in the average value of homes in these areas. However it is evident that, on the average, the assessed values of homes in the segregated and desegregated neighborhoods were highly comparable prior to 1972. A t test comparing these mean assessed values was nonsignificant, $t(16) = 0.56$. n.s.). These data substantiate that the two types of neighborhoods studied by Hamilton and Bishop (1976) were quite similar prior to their investigation.

The second column of Table 6.2 presents the average assessed value for each neighborhood from the later assessments (conducted between 1979 and 1981). It can be seen that, on the average, the assessed values of homes in the two sets of neighborhoods have remained highly similar. Again, a t test comparing these mean assessed values for the two categories of neighborhoods was nonsignificant, $t(16) = 0.28$, n.s.

The number of years between assessments differed somewhat among the four towns. Therefore we calculated for each neighborhood the difference between the two mean assessed values and divided that difference by the number of years between assessments. This procedure yielded, for each neighborhood, the average annual increase in assessed property value for houses in that neighborhood.

TABLE 6.2

Mean Assessed Values of Homes prior to and after Integration
(in Thousands of Dollars)

Neighborhood	Prior assessed value	Later assessed value	Average annual increase
Desegregated			
1[a]	23.36	45.26	1.89
2[b]	28.70	72.25	4.36
3[c]	25.49	60.51	3.50
4[d]	35.39	84.11	3.75
5[d]	21.44	54.23	2.52
6[d]	18.37	52.10	2.59
7[d]	21.85	57.13	2.71
8[d]	16.59	42.13	1.96
Mean	23.90	58.49	2.91
Segregated			
1[a]	22.69	48.49	2.58
2[b]	29.37	72.37	4.30
3[b]	27.18	66.96	3.98
4[d]	18.69	52.37	2.59
5[d]	25.81	63.01	2.86
6[d]	20.55	51.92	2.42
7[d]	17.82	46.68	2.22
8[d]	17.09	44.13	2.08
9[d]	23.22	64.83	3.20
10[d]	23.20	58.79	2.74
Mean	22.56	56.96	2.90

[a]Assessments conducted in 1969 and 1979.
[b]Assessments conducted in 1971 and 1981.
[c]Assessments conducted in 1970 and 1980.
[d]Assessments conducted in 1966 and 1979.

These values are shown in the third column of Table 6.2. The average increment in assessed value was almost identical for the segregated and desegregated neighborhoods. Once again, a t test comparing neighborhood conditions was nonsignificant, $t(16) = 0.03$, n.s.

Clearly these analyses of assessed property values provide no evidence that the move of the black families into certain neighborhoods in 1972 has had a detrimental effect on the value of owning a home in those neighborhoods. In terms of this index, the two groups of neighborhoods were highly similar before the integration occurred, were highly similar some 7–9 years later, and on average, these residences increased in value at a nearly identical rate.

It may be, however, that these assessment values are an imperfect measure for detecting the effects of desegregation on property values. For one thing, it isn't clear exactly what these assessment values are based on. Also the criteria used in making these assessments may vary somewhat from town to town. Finally, these assessments may not be sensitive to the effects of the minimal degree of integration that has occurred in these neighborhoods. For the white resident troubled by the fact that a black family lives a few houses away, the more immediate concern is whether or not that family's presence in the neighborhood will influence the price he can get if he decides to sell his house. For this reason, we obtained and analyzed data more directly relevant to this concern.

Resale Values

We reported earlier that approximately two-thirds of the houses in the neighborhoods studied by Hamilton and Bishop maintained continuous ownership during the 10-year period from 1972 through 1981. Nevertheless, there were enough transactions during this period to permit a comparison of the segregated and desegregated neighborhoods in terms of the economic gain experienced by an owner at the time a house was sold. These data are useful in determining more directly whether or not the presence of a black family in a neighborhood has an effect on resale values.

When the ownership of a residence is transferred from one person to another, a conveyance tax is paid on that transaction. The value of this conveyance tax, which is recorded on the land records mentioned earlier, is directly related to the purchase price of the house. From these records, we were able to determine the price paid by the new owner for each house sold in each neighborhood for the years 1972–1981. To test the effect of neighborhood desegregation on resale values, we performed a regression analysis in which we attempted to estimate the purchase price of a house from three predictor variables: (1) the prior assessed value of the residence, (2) the number of years between that assessment and the sale of the house, and (3) a dummy variable representing the race of the family that moved into that house's neighborhood in 1972. The results of this analysis are shown in Table 6.3. Overall predictability was high—the multiple R was .90. Analysis of the regression coefficients indicated that both the prior assessed value of the house and the number of years since that assessment were important predictors of subsequent sale prices. However, of primary concern for our analysis, the regression coefficient for the race of the target family was trivial in magnitude and statistically nonsignificant. In other words, knowing the prior assessed value of a home and the year in which it was sold, we could predict quite well the price paid for the house. Knowing whether or not the neighborhood had been desegregated in 1972 made no difference at all.

To examine further the relationship between neighborhood desegregation and

TABLE 6.3

Multiple Regression Relating Prior Assessments, Years since Assessments,
and Race of Target Family to Selling Prices of Homes Sold, 1972–1981

Variable	Regression coefficient	Standardized coefficient	t
Prior assessment	1.40	.52	10.89**
Years since assessment	2.53	.68	15.26**
Race of target family	0.61	.02	0.34

**$p < .01$

resale values, we carried out a second analysis. As we reported earlier, our analysis of the census data showed that in 1980 our two categories of neighborhoods were highly similar in racial composition. Although the percentages of black residents living in these neighborhoods were low, there was nevertheless some variation among neighborhoods in this percentage, and this was true both for neighborhoods that had and had not been desegregated by the target family's arrival in 1972 (see Table 6.1). The percentage of black residents in a neighborhood in 1980 indicates the extent to which that neighborhood had been desegregated during the last decade. If residential desegregation influences resale values, perhaps these percentages would be predictive of purchase prices (regardless of the race of the target family in 1972). To evaluate this possibility, a regression analysis was performed in which the purchase price of a house was predicted from (1) the prior assessed value of the property, (2) the number of years between that assessment and the sale, and (3) the percentage of black residents living in that neighborhood in 1980 (i.e., the extent to which desegregation was occurring in the neighborhoods during the period when the houses were sold).

The results of this analysis are shown in Table 6.4. Again, the regression

TABLE 6.4

Multiple Regression Relating Prior Assessments, Years since Assessments,
and Percentage Black in 1980 to Selling Prices of Homes Sold, 1972–1981

Variable	Regression coefficient	Standardized coefficient	t
Prior assessment	1.49	.55	10.02**
Years since assessment	2.54	.68	15.33**
Percentage black in 1980	−0.29	−.05	−0.81

**$p < .01$

equation was quite effective in estimating purchase prices ($R = .90$), and as in the previous analysis, the first two predictor variables were important contributors to this predictability. In contrast, the regression coefficient for the percentage of black residents was small and nonsignificant.

In sum, then, whether we base our analysis on the assessed values of all homes in these neighborhoods or on the sales prices of those houses that sold since 1972, we come to the same conclusion—the entrance of black families into these neighborhoods had no effect whatsoever on the property values of nearby homes. Although this conclusion contradicts a widely-held belief among white home-owners, it is entirely consistent with the findings of previous research on this topic (Ladd, 1962; Laurenti, 1960; Marcus, 1968; Palmore & Howe, 1962).

Target Families

Although the purpose of this second phase of our research was to investigate changes at the neighborhood level, questions naturally arise about the target families. What has happened to them? How many of them are still living in these neighborhoods? What has been the nature of their experience? Because our analyses of this phase have been based on data obtained from archival records, we are limited in our ability to answer such questions. Nevertheless we can address some points of interest regarding these families.

It has been suggested by some that, when buying a house in a residential neighborhood, a black family has to pay a higher price than does a white buyer for a comparable home. The reasoning behind this notion is that, because white residents prefer to "keep the blacks out" of their area, a white seller will negotiate less and lower the asking price to a lesser extent for a potential black buyer than for a potential white buyer. The data available from the present study provide no support for this belief. The average purchase price of the homes bought by the 8 black target families in 1972 ($33,250) was virtually identical to that for the 10 white target families ($33,230). Because these 18 homes were all purchased within the same 6-month period and because we know (from analyses reported earlier) that the two sets of neighborhoods were highly comparable in value prior to 1972, it seems safe to conclude that the race of the target family had no differential impact on the purchase price they paid for their home in 1972.

From the data obtained in 1981 we can report suggestive evidence on two other points, although the number of cases is so small that no firm conclusions can be drawn. First, in the 9 years since their arrival, four of the black families had sold their homes and moved elsewhere (after 4, 6, and 9 years of residence), whereas three of the white target families had since relocated (after 3, 5, and 7 years of residence). These data do not suggest any dramatic difference in the likelihood of reselling or in the length of one's residence in a neighborhood. Given the variety of factors that can lead a family to relocate, these data seem to reflect normal rates of turnover. Second, for the seven families who did relocate during this period, we determined the price for which they sold their house, subtracted from it the price they paid for it in 1972, and divided that difference by the number of years they lived in it. The average values of this index for the four black and three white target families were quite comparable, suggesting that there was no racial difference in the relative economic gain experienced by these families as a result of living in these neighborhoods.

It must again be stressed that this research was not focused on evaluating the experiences of the target families, and the number of cases available prevent a thorough analysis of these issues. Nevertheless, in the limited data we have examined, we find no indication of differential turnover or differential financial gain associated with the race of the target family.

Discussion

The findings from this research project are quite informative regarding the process and consequences of desegregation resulting from the initial black entry into a white suburban neighborhood. We found that the arrival of a black family in a previously unintegrated area was met wtih negative reactions and increased concerns of the white residents about their neighborhood, but that these feelings and concerns dissipated during the first year of the black family's residence. Moreover, the experience of having black neighbors had a positive effect on the white residents' racial attitudes during that initial year of desegregated living. Finally, our analyses of long-term consequences revealed no evidence that the entry of a black family into a white neighborhood had significant effect on turnover rates, the replacement process, or the financial investment of owning a home in these neighborhoods.

Much of the social psychological research on desegregation has been conducted in the framework of the *contact hypothesis* (Allport, 1954; Amir, 1976). In its simplest form, this hypothesis states that bringing members of different groups together will have beneficial effects on intergroup attitudes and lead to a reduction of prejudice. The accumulated research clearly indicates that this simplistic view is not tenable and such attitude change is likely to occur only under certain facilitating conditions, for example, when the contact consists of meaningful interactions between equal-status participants in the context of shared goals (Amir, 1976; Rose, 1981). These conditions are unlikely to exist in residential neighborhoods that are undergoing desegregation. Though the black and white residents of a neighborhood are likely to be of comparable socioeconomic status, the interaction that occurs among neighbors is typically better characterized as minimal than meaningful (Bradburn, et al., 1971; Cagle, 1973; Hamilton & Bishop, 1976) and rarely would the residents be working together toward achieving some common objective. Because of this, Cagle (1973) has questioned the extent to which some of the early studies of desegregated housing projects (Deutsch & Collins, 1951; Wilner, Walkley, & Cook, 1952) demonstrate the ameliorating effects of intergroup contact. Similarly, both our results (Hamilton & Bishop, 1976) and those of others (Hunt, 1959; Zeul & Humphrey, 1971) who have studied residential integration provide evidence of attitude change in the absence of, or independent of, meaningful intergroup contact. In view of these findings, some alternative explanatory mechanism is necessary.

There is abundant evidence that white residents have richly developed beliefs about the undesirable consequences that are likely to follow the arrival of a black family in their neighborhood. Many of these expectations are stereotypic in nature—that blacks will not take care of their property, that they pose a threat to personal safety, that their children will be rough, that their presence will lead to racial incidents, and that property values in the area will be adversely influenced. Over time, the white residents encounter little evidence to support any of these beliefs—the neighborhood looks the same as it always did, it is no less safe than previously, racial incidents have not occurred, and property values continue to rise as in similar neighborhoods. Faced with these realities, the racial attitudes of the white residents are likely to undergo some revision, resulting in a reduction in prejudice. In our view, then, the beneficial effects of desegregated living on attitude change can be understood not in terms of intergroup contact but as resulting from the disconfirmation of expectancies.

The results of the second phase of our research also raises issues that have been prominent both in the beliefs of white residents and in the social science literature. As we noted earlier, a widely held belief among white home owners is that the entry of a black family into a white neighborhood will soon be followed by the departure of some of the white residents, who will be replaced by other black families, producing over time a change in the racial composition of the neighborhood. Among social scientists there has been considerable discussion as to whether such "white flight" occurs, or whether neighborhood change is a result of normal processes of neighborhood transition unrelated to racial factors (Giles, Cataldo, & Gatlin, 1975; Stinchcombe, McDill, & Walker, 1969; Wurdock, 1981). A more specific issue concerns whether or not there is a "tipping point" in neighborhood change—a point at which the percentage of black residents becomes high enough to instigate white flight, but below which white residents will remain in the neighborhood (Farley et al., 1978; Giles et al., 1975; Mayer, 1960; Schelling, 1972; Stinchcombe et al., 1969). Whether or not such a tipping point exists, it is clear that this point was not reached in the 10-year period covered by our analysis. Equally important, it is clear from our results that the invasion–succession sequence implied by these concepts is not a necessary consequence of the initial desegregation of white suburban neighborhoods. Compared to highly comparable neighborhoods that were not desegregated in 1972, there is no evidence in our data of increased turnover rates or further inmigration of other blacks as a result of the arrival of the black target families. Moreover, the presence of blacks in these neighborhoods had no detectable effect on the property values and resale values of nearby homes. Thus in the neighborhoods we studied the self-fulfilling prophecy failed to materialize.

As in any research, the conclusions to be drawn from our investigation are limited by the constraints imposed by the data we were able to obtain and the sample from which they were obtained. In the neighborhoods we studied we found no evidence that the initial desegregation had any effect on the variables we have studied. But obviously some neighborhoods do change: whites do move out and are replaced by blacks, changing the racial composition of an area. It becomes important, then, to consider when these changes are likely to occur and when, as in the neighborhoods investigated here, they are not likely to occur.

In this regard it is worthwhile to note again the type of neighborhoods we studied. They were all stable, middle-class residential areas, consisting of single-family homes on tree lined streets. They were, and still are, reasonably desirable places to live. In other types of neighborhoods the picture may be quite different. Consider, for example, what Lake (1981) has called ''spillover'' neighborhoods—white neighborhoods that border on an area heavily populated by blacks. These areas typically consist of older, less expensive housing more affordable by larger numbers of black families. These neighborhoods might then be expected to undergo more change in racial composition. Also, integration of these neighborhoods over time may simply represent expansion of an area already populated by blacks, and hence this type of change may simply reflect the continuation of a migration pattern that had started some time earlier. Similarly, Logan and Stearns (1981) report differences between working class and more affluent suburban neighborhoods in the course of racial integration over time. The important point is that it may be naive to assume that the process and consequences of neighborhood desegregation will be the same for all of the diverse types of living conditions represented in suburban communities. If we are to fully understand the course of residential integration, it will be important to recognize and differentiate among the varieties of neighborhoods in which that integration can occur.

This point is important for another reason. Twenty-five years ago, most residential integration in suburban neighborhoods was of the spillover variety. Now, as more and more black families achieve the financial capability of buying a home in a more "desirable" neighborhood, the situation we have studied is likely to occur with increasing frequency. Our findings indicate that under these conditions neighborhood desegregation can occur peaceably, resulting in changed feelings and attitudes of the white neighbors, without leading to the long-term consequences that white homeowners traditionally have feared would follow the integration of their neighborhoods.

There is, however, another perspective from which these findings can be viewed. Whereas the rapid change of dormitory neighborhoods from all white to mostly black may be unlikely, one might expect that the initial entry of black families would "open up" these neighborhoods to some further, albeit still modest, degree of integration. If so, then the target families could in effect be viewed as agents of social change. It is clear, however, that such change has not occurred in these neighborhoods. Unlike schools and work settings, neighborhood integration is not under institutional control or influence, and hence progress in this domain is dependent upon other factors. With respect to the process of social change, then, the gradual integration of suburban neighborhoods is probably best viewed as a consequence of changes in other spheres, rather than as a mechanism for bringing about such change.

Acknowledgments

The authors express their appreciation to Marilynn B. Brewer, James M. Jones, Patricia W. Linville, and Norman Miller for their comments on a previous version of this chapter.

References

Allport, G. W. *The nature of prejudice.* Reading, MA: Addison–Wesley, 1954.

Amir, Y. The role of intergroup contact in change of prejudice and ethnic relations. In P. A. Katz (Ed.), *Towards the elimination of racism.* New York: Pergamon Press, 1976.

Bianchi, S. M., Farley, R., & Spain, D. Racial inequalities in housing: An examination of recent trends. *Demography,* 1982, *19,* 37–51.

Bradburn, N. M., Sudman, S., & Gockel, G. L. *Side by side: Integrated neighborhoods in America.* Chicago, IL: Quadrangle Books, 1971.

Cagle, L. T. Interracial housing: A reassessment of the equal-status contact hypothesis. *Sociology and Social Research,* 1973, *57,* 342–355.

Campbell, A. *White attitudes toward black people.* Ann Arbor, MI: Institute for Social Research, 1971.

Clark, T. A. National trends in black suburbanization. In R. W. Lake, *The new suburbanites: Race and housing in the suburbs.* New Brunswick, NJ: Center for the Urban Policy Research, 1981.

Connolly, H. X. Black movement into the suburbs. *Urban Affairs Quarterly,* 1973, *9,* 91–111.

Deutsch, M., & Collins, M. E. *Interracial housing: A psychological evaluation of a social experiment.* Minneapolis, MN: University of Minnesota Press, 1951.

Farley, R. Residential segregation and its implications for school desegregation. *Law and Contemporary Problems*, 1975, *39*,(1), 164–193.

Farley, R. Components of suburban population growth. In B. Schwartz (Ed.), *The changing face of the suburbs*. Chicago, IL: University of Chicago Press, 1976.

Farley, R., Schuman, H., Bianchi, S., Colasanto, D., & Hatchett, S. "Chocolate city, vanilla suburbs": Will the trend toward racially separate communities continue? *Social Science Research*, 1978, *7*, 319–344.

Fishman, J. A. Some social and psychological determinants of intergroup relations in changing neighborhoods: An introduction to the Bridgeview study. *Social Forces*, 1961, *40*, 42–51.

Freeman, R. Black economic progress since 1964. *The Public Interest*, 1978, *52*, 52–69.

Frey, W. H. Black movement to the suburbs: Potentials and prospects for metropolitan-wide integration. In F. D. Bean & W. P. Frisbie (Eds.), *The demography of racial and ethnic groups*. New York: Academic Press, 1978.

Giles, M. W., Cataldo, E. F., & Gatlin, D. S. White flight and percent black: The tipping point re-examined. *Social Science Quarterly*, 1975, *56*, 85–92.

Guest, A. M. The changing racial composition of suburbs: 1950–1970. *Urban Affairs Quarterly*, 1978, *14*, 195–206.

Hamilton, D. L., & Bishop, G. D. Attitudinal and behavioral effects of initial integration of white suburban neighborhoods. *Journal of Social Issues*, 1976, *32*(2), 47–67.

Helper, R. *Racial policies and practices of real estate brokers*. Minneapolis, MN: University of Minnesota Press, 1969.

Hermalin, A. I., & Farley, R. The potential for residential integration in cities and suburbs: Implications for the busing controversy. *American Sociological Review*, 1973, *38*, 595–610.

Hunt, C. L. Private integrated housing in a medium size northern city. *Social Problems*, 1959, *7*, 195–209.

Ladd, W. W. Effect of integration on property values. *American Economic Review*, 1962, *52*, 801–808.

Lake, R. W. *The new suburbanites: Race and housing in the suburbs*. New Brunswick, NJ: Center for Urban Policy Research, 1981.

Laurenti, L. *Property values and race*. Berkeley, CA: University of California Press, 1960.

Logan, J. R., & Stearns, L. B. Suburban racial segregation as a nonecological process. *Social Forces*, 1981, *60*, 61–73.

Marcus, M. Racial composition and home price changes: A case study. *Journal of the American Institute of Planners*, 1968, *34*, 334–338.

Mayer, A. J. Russell Woods: Change without conflict. In N. Glazer & D. McEntire (Eds.), *Studies in housing and minority groups*. Berkeley, CA: University of California Press, 1960.

Mullendore, W. E., & Cooper, K. M. Effects of race on property values: The case of Dallas. *Annals of Regional Science*, 1972, *6*(2), 61–72.

Palmore, E., & Howe, J. Residential integration and property values. *Social Problems*, 1962, *10*, 52–55.

Pendleton, W. W. Blacks in suburbs. In L. H. Masotti & J. K. Hadden (Eds.), *The urbanization of the suburbs*. Beverly Hills, CA: Sage, 1973.

Pettigrew, T. F. Attitudes on race and housing: A social-psychological view. In A. H. Hawley & V. P. Rock (Eds.), *Segregation in residential areas*. Washington, D.C.: National Academy of Sciences, 1973.

Rent, G. S., & Lord, J. D. Neighborhood racial transition and property value trends in a southern community. *Social Science Quarterly*, 1978, *59*, 51–59.

Rose, T. L. Cognitive and dyadic processes in intergroup contact. In D. L. Hamilton (Ed.), *Cognitive processes in stereotyping and intergroup behavior*. Hillsdale, NJ: Lawrence Erlbaum Associates, 1981.

Schelling, T. C. A process of residential segregation: Neighborhood tipping. In A. H. Pascal (Ed.), *Racial discrimination in economic life.* Lexington, MA: D. C. Heath & Co., 1972.

Schnare, A. B. Trends in residential segregation by race: 1960–1970. *Journal of Urban Economics,* 1980, *7,* 293–301.

Schnore, L. F., André, C. D., & Sharp, H. Black suburbanization, 1930–1970. In B. Schwartz (Ed.), *The changing face of the suburbs.* Chicago, IL: University of Chicago Press, 1976.

Smith, J. P. The improving economic status of black Americans. *American Economic Review,* 1978, *68,* 171–178.

Stinchcombe, A. L., McDill, M., & Walker, D. Is there a racial tipping point in changing schools? *Journal of Social Issues,* 1969, *25,* (1), 127–136.

Taeuber, K. E. Negro population and housing: Demographic aspects of a social accounting scheme. In I. Katz & P. Gurin (Eds.), *Race and the social sciences.* New York: Basic Books, 1969.

Taeuber, K. E., & Taeuber, A. F. *Negroes in cities.* Chicago, IL: Aldine, 1965.

U.S. National Advisory Commission on Civil Disorders. *Report of the National Advisory Commission on Civil Disorders.* Washington, D.C.: Government Printing Office, 1969.

Van Valey, T. L., Roof, W. C., & Wilcox, J. E. Trends in residential segregation: 1960–1970. *American Journal of Sociology,* 1977, *82,* 826–844.

Wilner, D. M., Walkley, R. P., & Cook, S. W. Residential proximity and intergroup relations in public projects. *Journal of Social Issues,* 1952, *8,* 45–69.

Wilson, F. D., & Taeuber, K. E. Residential and school desegregation: Some tests of their association. In F. D. Bean & W. P. Frisbie (Eds.). *The demography of racial and ethnic groups.* New York: Academic Press, 1978.

Wolf, E. P., The invasion-succession sequence as a self-fulfilling prophecy. *Journal of Social Issues,* 1957, *13*(4), 7–20.

Wurdock, C. J. Neighborhood racial transition: A study of the role of white flight. *Urban Affairs Quarterly,* 1981, *17,* 75–89.

Zeul, C. R., & Humphrey, C. R. The integration of black residents in suburban neighborhoods: A reexamination of the contact hypothesis. *Social Problems,* 1971, *18,* 462–474.

7

The Trajectory of Local Desegregation Controversies and Whites' Opposition to Busing

David O. Sears
and
Harris M. Allen, Jr.

Why are white Americans so opposed to busing schoolchildren as a mechanism for racially integrating the public schools? That opposition is surprising partly because they have clearly exhibited a long-term trend toward support for extending full equality to black Americans. One could note the remarkable lowering of formal barriers to equality, such as the abolition of slavery or desegregation of professional sports. More recently one could point to the increased racial egalitarianism expressed in time-series surveys of whites' opinions; for example, in the General Social Survey (Taylor, Sheatsley, & Greeley, 1978). This increased support for racial equality is focused upon the public schools just as much as it has been upon any other institution. For example, the General Social Survey consistently found throughout the 1970s that over 85% felt that white and black students should go to the same rather than to separate schools (Condran, 1979).

Yet whites equally overwhelmingly oppose the major policy for desegregating the schools, *busing*. Gallup polls and surveys by the National Opinion Research Center (NORC) and The National Election Studies (NES) in the past decade have rarely found much over 15% of the white population supporting busing. What accounts for this high level of support for the general principle for school integration and equally massive opposition to the major technique for bringing it about?

GROUPS IN CONTACT:
THE PSYCHOLOGY OF DESEGREGATION

Models of Opposition to Busing

Let us start by considering briefly the most popular general theories for the origins of policy preferences in general, and antibusing sentiments in particular. Even on as hotly emotional an issue as busing, almost all analysts would recognize the operation of a variety of causes. Nevertheless important differences in emphasis exist that lead to quite different predictions. Figure 7.1 depicts simplified versions of the five most common views, with the following specific components.

Cost–Benefit Analysis

One class of theories includes various versions of a 3-step *cost–benefit analysis*. They assert that people develop (1) interests of various kinds (self-interest, group interest, or societal interest) in a particular policy issue due to a combination of their own social location and the realities of the issue; that (2) these interests generate reasonably accurate perceptions of the costs and benefits associated with possible policy alternatives; and that (3) these perceptions of costs and benefits therefore generate, through some process of rational choice, an appropriate policy preference.[1]

Self-Interest

The self-interest version of cost–benefit analyses (Model 1 in Figure 7.1) assumes egocentricity: aspects of an issue that actually or potentially influence the

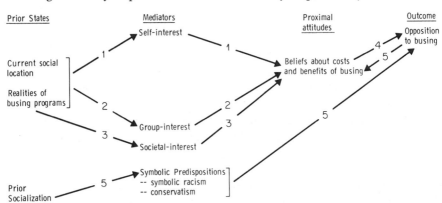

Figure 7.1. Five alternative models of opposition to busing. Cost–benefit analyses include: (1) self-interest model, (2) group-interest model, (3) sociotropic-judgments model, and (4) rational-choice model. Symbolic politics includes (5) symbolic-predispositions model.

[1]Some versions go on to predict that voting behavior will follow in an equally logical manner.

individual's personal life weigh more heavily than do others. For example, the personal costs of a busing program might include added school expenditures and hence higher taxes, lengthy and possibly dangerous bus rides for one's own children, or harm to the quality of their education, physical dangers to them, and so forth.

Group-Interest

People may have some stake in promoting or defending the interests of social groups to which they belong, whether or not such actions benefit them personally. The group-interest version of cost–benefit analyses is depicted as Model 2 in Figure 7.1. In the case of busing, whites may have some interest in maintaining the superior status of their own racial groups. Demands for radical changes in the status quo may threaten this status. Hence the threat posed by busing may be more to the superior status and "earned" privileges of whites as a group than to any specific white individual's well-being. Collective or group interests, rather than individuals' interests, are threatened. For example, Vanneman and Pettigrew (1972) interpreted whites' voting against black mayoral candidates during the late 1960s as due to fraternal deprivation, that is, to a sense that blacks are unfairly gaining, relative to whites (see also Guimond & Dubé-Sinard, 1983). Similarly, threats to the status of one's own group ("status anxiety") was thought to generate radical right activism in the 1950s (Bell, 1963) and such antibusing attitudes as those expressed in the Irish-American community of South Boston about busing black students into South Boston High School (see also Caditz, 1976; Miller, 1981).

Societal-Interest

Still other costs and benefits are perceived as being general or societal rather than personal. Meehl (1977) and Kinder and Kiewiet (1979) type this kind of thinking as *sociotropic* because it is oriented toward the welfare of the society as a whole rather than toward any individual or group. This is shown as Model 3 in Figure 7.1. The specific costs and benefits might be identical to those cited above as part of self-interest; the difference is that the crucial impact is not upon the respondent but upon society. Hence even nonparents can worry about busing endangering white children. Other sociotropic beliefs could focus on the performance of government, such as on whether the federal courts and executive branch are justified in intervening in local matters (Gatlin, Giles & Cataldo, 1978; Stinchcombe & Taylor, 1980).

Rational Choice

The final step of all these versions of cost–benefit analysis involves deducing a policy preference from the perceived costs and benefits of alternative policies.

Many theorists in economics, political science, and social psychology have argued that individuals arrive at reasonable policy preferences based on their beliefs about the above-mentioned considerations. In social psychology, expectancy-value decision theory (Edwards, 1954), attribution theory (Kelley, 1967), cognitive response theory (Petty & Cacioppo, 1981), and the "theory of reasoned action" (Ajzen & Fishbein, 1980) share these assumptions. In the political behavior area, Downs' (1957) theory of proximity, rational choice theory (Riker & Ordeshook, 1973), and retrospective voting theories (Fiorina, 1981) do, as well. The common elements of all such theories can be summarized as a "rational choice" theory, and is shown as Model 4 in Figure 7.1. As applied to the question of busing, this theory would assert that whites indeed form preferences based on some rational calculus about the relative magnitudes of cost and benefits (Armor, 1980; Stinchcombe & Taylor, 1980; Rothbart, 1976).

Symbolic Politics

Contrasting with all these cost–benefit analyses is a *symbolic politics* perspective. It asserts that symbolic predispositions are acquired relatively early in life (though not necessarily in childhood; the timing of this early acquisition remains open to debate); this early socialization leaves strong affective residues conditioned to particular attitude objects; and these affective responses, which might be described as symbolic predispositions, can be evoked by symbols cognitively similar to the original attitude objects. They also have considerable power to generate rationalizing beliefs about some new attitude object. For this general reasoning, see especially Kinder and Sears (1981), Sears and Citrin (1982), and Sears, Lau, Tyler, & Allen (1980).

In the case of busing a symbolic politics perspective would suggest that white children acquire basic racial prejudices and traditional social values quite early in life, though these may be modifiable should the person later move into a resocializing environment (Jennings & Niemi, 1981; Miller & Sears, 1983). We have described this combination of prejudice and traditional values as "symbolic racism" (Kinder & Sears, 1981), which (along with general political conservatism) in turn has been shown to generate opposition to busing (Sears, Hensler & Speer, 1979, Sears et al., 1980). The negative affect thus attached to the symbol "busing" then is rationalized in terms of a wide variety of beliefs about the negative effects of busing, such as its consequences for pupil safety, quality of education, school district budgets, and so on.

In short, prior socialization produces symbolic predispositions; these in turn generate affective responses to policy issues (such as busing) symbolically linked to the predispositions; and these new symbolic attitudes about policy issues (such as opposition to busing) in turn generate a series of cognitive rationalizations that provide socially desirable justifications for the policy preferences.

The Problem of Causality

The model implicit in each of these viewpoints involves several *causal* steps. Because almost all of the relevant data come from cross-sectional surveys, testing such causal models involves some additional assumptions about causal order. In the case of the symbolic politics model, these seem quite supportable. Variables indexing current social location cannot be influenced to any great extent by the variables that follow them in the model. Moreover, given the stability over time of such symbolic predispositions as racial prejudice and conservatism (Converse & Markus, 1979; Feldman, 1983; Sears & Gahart, 1980; Levitin & Miller, 1979), it is unlikely that they are strongly influenced by variables that follow them in the model.

What about the cost–benefit theories? The first two steps of the self-interest theory seem relatively impregnable. The self-interest variables are unlikely to influence current social location. Moreover the self-interest measures themselves are presumably reasonably nonreactive because most describe the objective circumstances of people's lives (e.g., being a parent). Hence they could not be influenced very much by attitudes toward busing (with the possible exception of white flight, as is discussed later). We have found no instances in which significant relationships exist between such self-interest variables and symbolic predispositions (Sears et al., 1980), so it is unlikely that either is influenced to any great extent by the other. Hence it seems legitimate to treat at least self-interest and symbolic predispositions as independent causal factors potentially determining opposition to busing.

The main problems of establishing causality within the cost-benefit theories occur with the rational-choice stage in the assumption that beliefs about the costs and benefits of busing determine overall attitudes toward it. It is plausible enough that people arrive at perceptions about the costs and benefits of busing programs and then derive an overall evaluation of busing as a consequence, as the numerous theories cited above maintain. Most people would probably explain their own attitude formation in just this way. However the symbolic politics perspective is equally plausible a priori—that people form attitudes toward highly charged symbols such as "busing" on the basis of their predispositions without much detailed information about or consideration of the program's potential costs and benefits, and then those attitudes toward the symbol "busing" in turn generate perceptions of costs and benefits that help rationalize and justify the overall policy preference. In this case the policy preference would generate cost-benefit assessments, rather than vice versa. Therefore the rational choice and symbolic politics perspective represent two opposed explanations for any observed consistency between cost–benefit judgments and overall attitudes toward busing. It is unlikely that current statistical technology can definitively settle this ambiguity of causal direction.

Testing all five theories would be beyond the scope of this chapter, and indeed beyond the capability of any data base currently in existence. Moreover, as a strategic matter we would opt for testing those associations whose causality can be interpreted unambiguously. Hence we treat here only the self-interest and symbolic politics models, both of which can readily be tested with available data and pose relatively few problems of causal inference. In particular, given the relative weakness of self-interest in past studies, we attempt to determine if there are particular moments in desegregation controversies that are most likely to elicit self-interested attitudes about busing.

Self-Interest

The *self-interest* perspective is a common one in economic theorizing. It simply asserts that past or potential outcomes of government policy that impact upon one's own material well-being have, for that reason, greater weight in the development of one's policy preferences. This defines self-interest rather narrowly, limiting it to material gains in the short-to-medium term. We do so in this, as in other studies (Sears *et al.*, 1980), to differentiate self-interest from the many other conceivable utilities a policy might serve (such as fueling an individual's feeling of moral righteousness). This strategy has the advantages of yielding a falsifiable set of hypotheses about self-interest and aligning its definition with what ordinary people normally mean by selfishness.[2] Whereas self-interest defined in this manner has usually proved empirically not to have a major influence over American's policy preferences (Sears, 1980), it does upon occasion, and its importance is widely assumed, so its role must always be considered quite seriously.

Numerous researchers have tested the self-interest hypothesis that whites whose private lives are most interfered with by busing are its strongest opponents. Such interference would occur most obviously if the respondent has a child that might be bused and secondarily, if desegregating neighborhood schools depreciates the desirability of the neighborhood. Following this reasoning, the most commonly used self-interest items cluster into four categories: (1) parents: individuals with school-age children, especially in the public schools; (2) proximity to busing: having children currently bused for racial integration;

---

[2]Note, however, that egocentricity may also be involved with nonmaterial values, such as status or coping with neurotic anxiety (Bell, 1963; Lane, 1962; Sears & Lau, 1983).

the distance one's child is bused; living in a school district with busing happening or threatened; having two-way, as opposed to one-way, busing; (3)
racial composition: the racial composition of neighborhood schools, of schools
to which one's child is being bused, and of the respondent's residential neighborhood; and (4) attachment to the neighborhood: homeownership, liking for
neighbors, wanting not to move, and so forth.

To make a long story short, most past analyses have not found self-interest
to have a significant effect upon whites' opposition to busing. This was the
case in analyses of national surveys by Kelley (1974), Kinder and Rhodebeck
(1982), Sears et al., (1979, 1980) and Weidman (1975). With an occasional
exception, this has also been the case in local studies in Los Angeles (Caditz,
1975, 1976; Kinder & Sears, 1981; Miller, 1981; and Allen & Sears, 1978);
Milwaukee (Jacobson, 1978); Akron (McClendon & Pestello, 1982); Louisville
(McConahay, 1982a, 1982b); Florida (Gatlin, et al., 1978). However there is
some evidence that the effect of self-interest varies across different stages of local
busing controversies. It is that question with which the rest of this paper is
most centrally concerned.

The Trajectory of Local Desegregation Controversies

The standard cycle of implementing court-ordered busing usually involves
four different stages: (1) the quiescent period prior to any court action; (2) the
period in the midst of litigation, during which a trial is being conducted, normally without much publicity; (3) the period between court order and implementation, when it is apparent that desegregation will occur, but before it is
implemented; and finally the (4) postimplementation phase that occurs after a
busing plan has been placed into operation.

The first two stages would seem least likely to provoke self-interested opposition to busing because there is usually so little information about desegregation plans that the subjective probability of busing continues to be rather
low. We might speculate that the third and fourth of these stages would yield
the strongest self-interest effects. The post-court-order, preimplementation
stage, normally rather lengthy, involves great ambiguity about the ultimate
outcome, as appeals are made and different plans are offered and rejected and
disputed by courts, school boards, special committees or commissions, plaintiffs,
and so on. This stage is marked by wild rumors and threats and a great deal
of anxiety about what might actually ensue. It is also marked by much uncertainty about the exact nature of the plan—but many parents of children in the district know that they may be affected. It is easy to imagine that the combination
of high ego-involvement, uncertainty, and threat would be unusually motivating toward resistance. Similarly the post implementation phase might pro-

duce a high level of self-interested opposition to busing. On the other hand, it might produce dissonance-reducing acceptance of busing among parents who feel they could have pulled their children out of the schools but did not. Moreover, the actual experience of desegregation may in fact not be as aversive as preimplementation fears would suggest. For these reasons, self-interested opposition to busing may actually drop off following implementation.

These considerations suggest that the strength of self-interest effects may well differ across the various stages of local desegregation controversies. What evidence exists on this point in the extant literature? Let us start with people in the first stage, those living in districts unaffected by busing. Using the National Election Studies' 1972 and 1976 national surveys, Sears et al. (1979, 1980) conducted regression analyses on respondents living in areas unaffected by busing, with controls on demographic variables, racial prejudice, and political conservatism; none of the self-interest terms attained statistical significance. Weidman (1975) and Kelley (1974) obtained similar findings with the 1972 and 1974 national General Social Surveys, using as a self-interest variable, having a school-age child at home (the great majority of such respondents—about two-thirds—should have been living in districts with no current or threatened busing, according to the 1976 NES survey). In these several national surveys, self-interest had no demonstrable effect on opposition to busing in communities with no ongoing or threatened busing.[3]

Only local studies are available on respondents in the second stage, those living in communities in the midst of litigation. Caditz (1975, 1976) interviewed members of a liberal political organization living in Los Angeles in 1969, 8 years before a final busing decision was made by the courts, and Kinder and Sears (1981) report on interviews with adults in Los Angeles in 1973. Self-interest consisted in having children in elementary and/or high school, and estimating in-busing of minorities or out-busing of Anglo children as likely. Kinder and Sears report that none of the main effects or the two-way interactions of the parenthood and likelihood items was significant in the expected direction. In Caditz's 1969 study being a parent had a weak but significant bivariate effect ($z = 2.0$, $p < .05$), but it disappeared with demographics controlled (Caditz, 1975, 1976). Jacobson (1978) and McClendon and Pestello (1982) report on surveys done in the midst of desegregation trials in Milwaukee and Akron, respectively, in 1975 and 1978. Only one of the numerous comparisons in these two studies yields a significant effect of having children in the public schools. The four studies conducted in the midst of litigation, then, do not yield reliable self-interest effects either.

Self-interest yields somewhat stronger effects in studies interviewing respondents in the third stage, between initial court order and implementation. Some

[3]Self-interest is more potential than actual in these cases, of course.

such respondents were the nearly 10% in the 1972 and 1976 National Election Studies who had "heard" that busing "might happen in the future" in their area. Presumably these people were in communities with ongoing litigation or with preliminary court orders because publicity about busing usually begins only after the matter goes to court and usually peaks when it comes out of court; the schemes of potential plaintiffs' lawyers rarely get much publicity. In neither 1972 nor 1976 did having a child in public school or having all-white neighborhood schools significantly influence opposition to busing in this group of respondents. Still, a little something shows up here; in 1976 the former yielded an effect of marginal significance and in 1972 the latter yielded a relatively large beta, though it was nonsignificant, given a small number of cases. Nevertheless Kinder and Rhodebeck (1982), analyzing the same data from another perspective, find that the likelihood of busing in the respondent's community in 1976 did not significantly affect changes in opposition to busing from 1972 to 1976.

Turning to local studies, Allen and Sears (1978) report on a survey done of Los Angeles County in 1976, not long after the State Supreme Court had finally ruled that the Los Angeles Unified School District (LAUSD) had to be desegregated. They found that having children in the target age range for the Los Angeles busing plan and living within the LAUSD contributed significantly to opposition to busing with symbolic attitudes and demographic variables controlled. However Jacobson (1978) again found a lack of self-interested opposition to busing in a survey done in Milwaukee in 1976, a week after the court decided that the school system was illegally segregated and had appointed a special master to oversee the formation and implementation of that decision. Nevertheless there are traces of positive self-interest effects in these studies done between court order and implementation.

Two national studies have been done of respondents in the fourth stage, those living in communities with implemented busing plans. Sears and colleagues (1979, 1980) analyze the approximately 25% of the NES respondents who said busing was happening in their community. In neither the 1972 nor the 1976 survey did having a child in the public school or having all-white neighborhood schools significantly affect attitudes toward busing within this group. Gatlin et al. (1978) report on surveys of parents done in seven school districts in Florida in 1973 after desegregation plans had been implemented. Most of the relevant zero-order correlations were weak but significant, but only one (of three) remained significant with other various relevant controls added.

Turning to local postimplementation studies, Miller (1981) conducted a survey of residents of the San Fernando Valley in Los Angeles in May 1979, near the end of the first year of implementation of a limited mandatory busing program. He found the most self-interested respondents (those with children either in the LAUSD target Grades 1–8 or had been in private schools for less than

2 years) did not oppose busing any more than other respondents. The most detailed local studies of postimplementation attitudes are those of McConahay in Louisville (1982a, 1982b). Two surveys were done: in the spring of the first year of busing (1976) and then again a year later. Some of the self-interest items had significant bivariate correlations with opposition to busing, but almost none had significant betas in full regression equations (nor did a composite self-interest index adding the several items), and the variance accounted for was trivial. (The unique R^2 contributed by self-interest was 0.4 and 1.1% using the composite index of self-interest.) In general it seems evident that self-interest has had at most a trivial effect in studies done during the postimplementation phase.

So-called white flight presents one possible methodological problem with these postimplementation studies. Some parents flee districts that are on the verge of desegregating or avoid moving into them, with the result that a drop in white enrollments takes place at the onset of busing (Armor, 1980). There is also reason to believe that white flight takes place particularly among those most opposed to busing. If the most antibusing parents have fled or avoided the schools, the remaining self-interested persons would necessarily be comparatively supportive of busing, artifactually deflating the effect of self-interest. However it seems doubtful that white flight explains the absence of self-interest effects. Parents whose children have moved from the public schools to private schools would be included as self-interested in the "parent" variable used by McConahay (1982a, 1982b) and Miller (1981), and it had no major effect. Antibusing parents who moved out of the district or declined to move in are of course not included in these surveys. But in 1976 only 12% of the whites in Louisville had moved within the prior year (i.e., since the court order); most of the moving was within the school district; only 9% said they would definitely move during the next year; and less than 2% said there was at least some chance they would move and cited desegregation explicitly as a reason for doing so. Hence it seems doubtful that enough moving occurred specifically because of school desegregation to influence these results significantly.

For the most part, then, self-interest has had little impact, though its role may be heightened in the third stage of desegregation controversies that occurs between court order and actual implementation.

Symbolic Racism

The symbolic politics model centers on the role of racial intolerance. We have elsewhere argued that what has been called *symbolic* (or *modern* or *contemporary*) *racism* has largely replaced *old-fashioned racism* (or *redneck racism*, the inverse of *generalized egalitarianism*) as the politically consequential form of racism today (Kinder & Sears, 1981; McConahay, 1982a; McConahay, Hardee, & Batts, 1981; McConahay & Hough, 1976; Miller, 1981; Sears & Kinder, 1971; Sears & McConahay, 1973). One reason for this contention is that the content of the most common antiblack opinions has clearly changed. McConahay (1982a) has described old-fashioned racism as involving "open bigotry of the sort frequently associated with working and lower-class (Southern) whites . . . negative stereotypes and support for social distancing, discrimination and segregation" (p. 705). Hence it revolved around three contents in particular: (1) pre–Civil War racial stereotypes, (2) restrictions on interracial social contacts, and (3) opposition to equal access or equal opportunity for persons of all races.

The content of symbolic racism, on the other hand, falls into three categories: (1) a denial that discrimination continues against blacks, such as in jobs or housing; (2) resentment about special favors for blacks, such as in "reverse discrimination," racial quotas in jobs or education, excessive access to welfare, special treatment by government, or unfair and excessive economic gains by blacks; and (3) antagonism toward blacks' "pushing too hard" and moving too fast, especially (though not exclusively) through the use of violence.

Symbolic racism has been conceptualized as a "blend of antiblack affect and the kind of traditional American moral values embodied in the Protestant ethic . . . a form of resistance to change in the racial status quo based on moral feelings that blacks violate such traditional American values as individualism and self-reliance, the work ethic, obedience, and discipline" (Kinder & Sears, 1981, p. 416). Similarly, modern racism is defined as "the expression in terms of abstract, ideological symbols and symbolic behaviors of the feeling that blacks are violating cherished values or making illegitimate demands for changes in the racial status quo" (McConahay & Hough, 1976, p. 38). "The tenets of modern racism are that discrimination is a thing of the past, blacks are pushing too hard, they are getting too much attention and sympathy from the nation's elites and that blacks' gains and demands are no longer justified" (McConahay, 1982a, p. 707).[4]

Various versions of racism have been consistent contributors to opposition

---

[4]The point of the term symbolic racism is to emphasize the fact that it centers on symbols rather than on the concrete realities of life, especially of the individual's own personal life. As McConahay (1982a, p. 705) points out, items with personal referents (e.g., "Over the past few years blacks have done better than I have") do not load on symbolic or modern racism factors, whereas the more abstract items (e.g., "Over the past few years blacks have gotten more economically than they deserve") do. However as he also has pointed out, the focus upon symbolic content does not distinguish symbolic racism from old-fashioned racism because the latter also focuses on symbols (e.g., "beliefs and stereotypes rooted in socialization and not in personal experience"; McConahay, 1982a, p. 705).

to busing. Kinder and Sears (1981), in a study of white suburbanites in Los Angeles, report correlations of .33 and .39 between expressive racism and opposition to busing in the two years they studied. Gatlin et al. (1978) also find a strong correlation between racial prejudice and opposition to local handling of desegregation (r = .35) in their study of Florida districts.[5] Sears et al. (1979, 1980) using the 1972 and 1976 CPS/NES national surveys, also found highly significant effects of similar magnitude of an omnibus scale of racial intolerance on opposition to busing in regression equations that included demographics, self-interest, and political conservatism. McConahay (1982a, 1982b) report similarly strong effects of modern racism in his studies in Louisville.

Some nonsignificant findings have been reported, but, consistent with the theory of symbolic racism, they involve associations between old-fashioned racism and opposition to busing in non-Southern locales during the 1970s (Armor, 1980; Kelley, 1974; McClendon & Pestello, 1982; Stinchcombe & Taylor, 1980; Weidman, 1975). In the South even old-fashioned racism continues to predict opposition to busing quite strongly, though not as strongly as symbolic or modern racism (Gatlin et al., 1978; McConahay, 1982a; 1982b). Hence there is considerable evidence for the role of symbolic racism in generating opposition to busing.

An Over-Time Analysis

Available evidence therefore suggests support for the symbolic politics, but not the self-interest model of opposition to busing. However there is some question about the third phase of desegregation controversies, post-court-order and preimplementation, that may induce stronger self-interest effects. Hence in the remainder of this chapter we test these two models more systematically at each of the various phases of busing controversies. First we consider them at the most general level, using national and statewide data. Then we turn to more specific studies of the impact of busing in Los Angeles during the 1970s. The Los Angeles case is particularly useful for this purpose because it was such a heated case and because reasonably good data are available for virtually every stage of the controversy.

National and Statewide Studies

Four of the samples we used were national or statewide: (1) National 1964: the 1964 National Election Study by the Survey Research Center, University

---

[5]The effect drops out in a regression equation that also includes support for school integration in general as a predictor (which is correlated with both prejudice and opposition to local desegregation policy; r = .57 and .50, respectively).

of Michigan. The population sampled from is all noninstitutionalized adults of voting age in the continental USA. (2) and (3) National 1972 and 1976: the National Election Studies done by the Center for Political Studies, University of Michigan. (4) California 1979; the California Tax Revolt Survey, a statewide telephone survey of California adults done by the Survey Research Center, University of California, Berkeley, following a special statewide referendum election in November 1979 (Sears & Citrin, 1982).

The general analytic strategy is to consider self-interest and racial attitudes jointly as predictors of attitudes toward busing. Self-interest is indexed by five types of variables: (1) having school-age children or children in the public schools, (2) having busing actually occurring in the district, as indicated by a subjective feeling that busing is happening, (3) having busing not happening in their area but having heard that it might occur in the future, (4) having an all-white neighborhood, and (5) having all-white neighborhood schools. In the analyses that follow, these several items are organized into composite self-interest scales in a somewhat different manner for each separate study, given that their availability varies across studies. The frequencies of self-interest are shown in Table 7.1.

To maintain comparability across studies, we employed only one symbolic racism item in each study. The usual item concerned whether the civil rights movement was moving ahead too fast or not. In the California 1979 study, however, we used a standard "aid to minorities" item (Sears & Citrin, 1982). The decision to use just one item reduced the power of racism considerably, of course, but it maximized comparability over time, which was our main goal here.

Finally, the dependent variables measured opposition variously to (1) school integration in the abstract (referred to in Tables 7.2 and 7.3 as *integration*), (2) federal government intervention in local desegregation disputes (*intervention*), (3) busing as a general policy (*busing*), and/or (4) local busing plans (*local busing*). The level of support whites give desegregation typically varies greatly across these several types of items, of course, with great support for school integration in the abstract but great opposition to busing as a general policy. However in our data predictors of support for or opposition to desegregation are quite similar across these types of dependent variables (as may be seen in Table 7.3), so nothing further will be said about these distinctions.

Self-Interest

For a first crack at the effects of self-interest, we simply trichotomized respondents into: (1) postimplementation (Stage 4) self-interested: parents in districts with busing happening; (2) preimplementation (Stages 2 and 3) self-interested: parents in districts with busing heard but not happening; and (3) non-self-interested: all other respondents. A first finding is that very few whites

TABLE 7.1

Frequencies of Self-Interest

	Survey	Self-Interested (%)
Children in public schools		
Some children under 18 in school in local community		
	National 1964	42
Some children attending public schools		
	National 1972	33
	National 1976	30
	California 1979	24
	Los Angeles 1976	28
	West Los Angeles 1978	19
	(youngest child only)	
	West Los Angeles 1979	14
Busing happening		
Has (court-ordered integration) (busing) happened around here?		
	National 1964	19
	National 1972	22
	National 1976	24
	California 1979	24
Are (minority) students being bused into the schools in your neighborhood now?		
	Los Angeles 1976	25
Busing threatened		
(If not) Have you heard that it might?		
	National 1964	6
	National 1972	10
	National 1976	8
	California 1979	16
(Has) heard of the California Supreme Court decision that requires the LAUSD to integrate and lives in LAUSD and does not think minorities being bused in.		
	Los Angeles 1976	23
Have you heard about the LA School Board's plan to desegregate the public schools?		
	West LA 1978	80
Racial composition of neighborhood		
(all-white)	National 1964	80
	National 1972	66
	National 1976	62
Racial composition of neighborhood schools		
(all-white)	National 1964	42
	National 1972	41
	National 1976 (grade school)	37

TABLE 7.2

Effects of Self-Interest on Opposition to Busing[a]

| | Child in school | | | Effect of: | | | |
	Busing happening (1)	Busing heard (2)	Other (3)	Happening (1–3)	Heard (2–3)	Self-interested (%)	Dependent variable
National/Statewide							
National 1964	51(104)	64 (31)	47(1051)	+4	+17*	11	Intervention
National 1972	71 (72)	58 (52)	55 (911)	+16*	+3	12	Intervention
National 1972	85 (73)	82 (54)	80 (964)	+5	+2	12	Busing
National 1976	60(115)	78 (41)	60(1199)	0	+18*	12	Intervention
National 1976	74(131)	80 (45)	73(1547)	+1	+7	10	Busing
California 1979	88 (59)	93 (74)	86(1146)	+2	+7	10	Busing
Average				+5	+9	11	
Los Angeles							
Between court order and implementation							
Los Angeles County 1976	70 (93)	74 (42)	58 (577)	+12*	+16*	19	Local busing
Los Angeles County 1976	86 (91)	88 (40)	76 (577)	+10*	+12*	19	Busing
Los Angeles County 1976	56 (86)	68 (41)	49 (580)	+7	+19*	18	Local busing
West Los Angeles 1978	—	42(101)	23 (458)	—	+19*	18	Integration
West Los Angeles 1978	—	60(102)	28 (450)	—	+32*	18	Local busing
Postimplementation							
West Los Angeles 1979	67 (48)	—	58 (432)	+9	—	10	Busing
West Los Angeles 1979	72 (47)	—	63 (426)	+9	—	10	Local busing
Los Angeles County 1979	88 (25)	82 (22)	87 (298)	+1	-5	14	Busing
Average				+8	+16	16	

[a]Entry in Columns 1–3 is the percentage opposed, or strongly opposed, to busing of those with an opinion. The base for the percentage is shown in parentheses.
*$p < .05$

are directly affected by busing. The percentage varies somewhat across studies, but generally is around 11% nationally, as shown in Table 7.2 (Column 6). This fact alone reinforces our earlier skepticism about the role of self-interest in generating massive opposition to busing.

In 11 of the 12 comparisons in national or statewide studies, the self-interested were as a group more opposed to busing than were the disinterested. Nevertheless the magnitude of the effect is rarely impressive. Only 3 of the 12 differences are themselves statistically significant. The self-interested were on the average 7% more likely to oppose busing than were the disinterested. These

TABLE 7.3

Opposition to Busing: Regression Equations[a]

| | Self-interest | | | | | Interactions | | | Demographics | | | | |
| | Main effects | | | Racial Composition | | | | Symbolic racism | | | | | Dependent |
	Child in school (1)	Happened (2)	Heard (3)	neighborhood (4)	School (5)	(1)×(2) (6)	(1)×(3) (7)	(8)	Education (9)	Region (10)	N	R²	variable
National/Statewide													
National 1964	-.05	.08*	.08*	-.02	.07	.04	.05	.26***	-.11***	.21***	817	.19	Intervention
National 1972	.00	.07	.06	.10*	-.06	.03	.05	.26***	.07*	.10*	723	.12	Intervention
National 1972	.05	-.04	.00	.08*	-.04	-.01	.00	.27***	-.13***	.08*	768	.13	Busing
National 1976	.04	-.04	.04	.09*	-.08*	.00	.07*	.23***	-.02	.05	1045	.08	Intervention
National 1976	-.07**	-.02	.03	.06	-.02	.02	.04	.27***	-.12***	.04	1325	.11	Busing
California 1979	.08**	-.01	.05	na	na	.02	.04	.15***	-.10***	na	1116	.05	Busing
Los Angeles													
Between court order													
and implementation													
Los Angeles County 1976	.11**	-.01	.01	na	-.07/-.02	.06	.08*	.34***	-.06	na	643	.14	Local busing
Los Angeles County 1976	.11**	.00	.04	na	-.07/-.02	.03	.08*	.30***	-.07	na	638	.11	Busing
Los Angeles County 1976	.13***	-.10*	.03	na	-.05/-.02	.02	.11*	.36***	-.04	na	639	.15	Local busing
West Los Angeles 1978	.12**	na	-.02	na	na	na	.11**	.31***	-.03	na	512	.12	Integration
West Los Angeles 1978	.21***	na	.05	na	na	na	.22***	.24***	-.08	na	506	.13	Local busing
Postimplementation													
West Los Angeles 1979	.08	na	na	na	na	na	na	na	-.19***	na	479	.04	Busing
West Los Angeles 1979	.09*	na	na	na	na	na	na	na	-.17***	na	473	.03	Local busing
Los Angeles County 1979	.01	.06	.05	na	na	.03	-.01	.18**	-.18**	na	291	.08	Busing

[a] Each row depicts a single regression equation, except that the two interaction terms are taken from regression equations in which the interaction effects specified were substituted for the self-interest main effects. The entries are betas. na = not available. The two terms for racial composition of schools in the Los Angeles County 1976 study refer to black and Hispanic composition, respectively. na = not available.

* $p < .05$.
** $p < .01$.

figures closely resemble the quite modest prevalence and strength of self-interest effects that we have obtained on other political issues (Sears, 1980).

These cross-tabulations suffer from the lack of control over other relevant variables, of course. Hence we present in Table 7.3 multiple regression equations on the same dependent variables. Columns 1–5 and 8–10 show equations including main effects of the basic self-interest variables that most of these studies had in common and the rudimentary measure of symbolic racism described earlier. In addition, we included the two demographic variables, education and region, that in past studies have proven most predictive of racial attitudes. As will be seen, spurious effects of both self-interest and symbolic racism emerge if these two demographic factors are not held constant.

Again self-interest is not an important factor in whites' opposition to busing, as assessed in the most general (national or statewide) surveys. Most of the terms are positive (17 are positive, 9 are negative), but relatively few are statistically significant (7 of 28 in the expected direction, and 1 in the wrong direction, for a net of 6 or 22%). Even those are of small absolute magnitude; the largest beta for a self-interest effect is $+.10$, and the median, $+.04$.

However, the most theoretically appropriate tests of self-interest are interactions between the parental and happened–heard variables that ask whether parents with children in districts in which busing is happening or threatened are more opposed to busing than unaffected respondents (other parents, or nonparents). To test these hypotheses, the same regression equations were redone, substituting these two interaction terms for the three self-interest main effects.[6] Columns 6 and 7 of Table 7.3 only show the betas for the interaction terms because the other terms in the regressions are about the same as they had been with the simple self-interest main effects included. However, as can be seen, all these interaction terms are very small. The general conclusion is that self-interest has little effect in these national and statewide surveys.

Despite the overall weakness of self-interest, it should be noted that having heard that busing might occur in one's own area yields slightly greater parental opposition to it than do other conditions. On the average, as shown in Table 7.2, being a parent contributes most to opposition when busing is "heard of," and Table 7.3 shows that the only significant self-interest interaction occurs between parenthood and "heard" in the 1976 national CPS/NES survey. Although these are not strong effects, they do reinforce the data discussed earlier suggesting that the third stage of desegregation controversies, between court order and actual implementation, might produce the most self-interested opposition to busing.

---

[6]This procedure is used to maximize the chances of obtaining significant interaction effects by concentrating as much self-interest variance as possible in the interaction effects rather than distributing it between main effects and interactions.

Busing Moves North

Did opposition to busing seemingly become so massive during the 1970s because at that time busing programs began to be applied throughout the nation, rather than just in the South? Table 7.3 shows that region was a major predictor of antibusing sentiment in 1964 but its effects were about gone by 1976. In 1964, of course, court-ordered desegregation was almost exclusively confined to the South. During the early 1970s, however, it began to move north. This analysis confirms that opposition to busing moved north along with its implementation. However, it yields the additional result that opposition moved north not, as is usually assumed, because of the personal impact of busing in the North. Rather, self-interest remained a minor factor, as can be seen in the generally nonsignificant self-interest effects in the National 1972 and 1976 and the California 1979 studies. Hence the seeming racial backlash often noted in the North during this period was not, as often alleged, because white Northern parents suddenly started worrying about their own children; such parents remained little more opposed to busing than anyone else.

Rather, the effect of introducing busing plans in the North, as well as in the South, was to change the symbolic basis for opposition to it. In the 1960s opposition seems to have been focused particularly upon federal intervention, but by the mid 1970s it had shifted to "busing." This can be seen by comparing earlier with later studies in this period of change. In our earliest national studies (1964 and 1972), having busing in one's own community contributed significantly and substantially to opposition, whether or not the respondents had children themselves. Nonparents living in communities with busing were 18% and 14% more opposed to the federal government's intervention in local school desegregation disputes than were nonparents in locales untouched by busing. However such differences emerged only on the item measuring opposition to federal intervention, not on the item measuring opposition to busing per se. And in the comparable later studies (National 1976 and California 1979), living in affected communities contributed to no such special opposition to busing among nonparents.

The implication of these findings is that the change in public opinion that occurred when busing moved north was a symbolic change, not a result of an expansion of self-interest. In the late 1960s, the federal government's desegregation efforts in the South seem to have engendered some special resentment in affected communities against federal intervention, among parents and nonparents alike. The regional base of this resentment is suggested by the fact that the differences cited just above nearly disappear with region controlled, as shown in Table 7.3 (see the top two entries in Column 2). In short, the effect on whites of moving buses north was some shift from resentment of federal intervention in affected Southern communities to antagonism toward "busing" in all regions. But in neither case was the personal impact of busing a strong determinant of opposition to it.

The Los Angeles Case

The other seven samples were from all or part of Los Angeles County. The Los Angeles Unified School District includes the entire city of Los Angeles, but less than half the population of Los Angeles County. Whites represent a majority of the adult population of the District, and the voting population is even more strongly dominated by whites. As a whole, the district's pupils were over 60% white early in the 1960s. The 1970s saw a rapid increase in the number of Hispanics until 1980, when they had nearly achieved a majority and had in fact achieved a majority in the lower grades. Throughout this period there was a reasonably stable black enrollment of slightly over 20%.

The greatest opposition came from the San Fernando Valley, a large suburban area that remained almost all-white (though with an increasing minority of Hispanics) throughout the period. The affluent West Los Angeles area, also mainly white, seemed to generate less organized opposition, partly perhaps because the plan as implemented left the area much less involved in mandatory busing.

The Trajectory of the Los Angeles Case

The Los Angeles case began when suit was filed in August 1963 to desegregate the schools. We have no surveys from the first, prelitigation phase.

The second stage of desegregation controversies, which we have described as in the midst of litigation, began with a trial in local court, *Crawford v. Los Angeles School Board* in October 1968. This was settled in February 1970 by Judge Gitelson's decision mandating that any given school deviate in minority enrollment by no more than 15% from the aggregate minority percentage in the district as a whole. The phase continued for 6 more years, however, with a seemingly interminable set of legal delays and appeals, none of which received much publicity. As far as the general public was concerned, the case had just about disappeared. We have access to two surveys collected during this phase: (1) ACLU (American Civil Liberties Union) 1969: interviews conducted with members of the ACLU in West Los Angeles by Caditz (1975, 1976). These data are cited but not analyzed below. (2) Valley 1973: a survey of adults in the northernmost two councilmanic districts in the San Fernando Valley (i.e., the northern half of the Valley). These data are cited but not analyzed below (Kinder & Sears, 1981).

The third stage, between court order and implementation, suddenly began in June 1976 with a state Supreme Court decision upholding Gitelson's decision mandating desegregation. However the Supreme Court did not specify any details of a busing plan or indeed even mention transportation of pupils as a solution to the problem of segregated schools. Instead it remanded the case to the local courts to settle all specifics. Judge Paul Egly was assigned to the case. A limited mandatory desegregation plan was accepted by the school board and judge in September 1977, though it was heatedly debated and continuously modified without being implemented for a full year thereafter. This phase thus lasted for over 2 years. It was a period of constant uncertainty, constant radical changes in plans, and great emotionality in the community, including much publicity, and some protest and threats of boycotts. We have analyzed two surveys done in this third phase: (3) Los Angeles County 1976: a telephone survey of adults in Los Angeles County, conducted in December 1976 (see Allen & Sears, 1978; Miller, 1981; for earlier analyses). (4) West Los Angeles 1978: a telephone survey conducted in West Los Angeles in the Spring of 1978. The sample area was defined by the West Los Angeles telephone directory and bounded approximately by Los Angeles International Airport on the south, the eastern boundary of Beverly Hills on the east, Mulholland Boulevard (the ridge of the Santa Monica Mountains) on the north, and the Pacific Ocean.

The fourth, postimplementation, phase began when about 7000 pupils were placed in a mandatory busing procedure in September 1978. The school board president, Howard Miller, was recalled in a special election in May 1979 for his participation in formulating the plan, and a constitutional amendment to abolish busing (Proposition 1: the Robbins Amendment) was passed in a special statewide election in November 1979. When this proposition was finally found constitutional, the mandatory busing plan was ended in the spring of 1981 (Miller, 1981). We have access to three surveys done in this postimplementation phase: (5) West Los Angeles 1979: a survey similar to (4) conducted in the spring of 1979 in the same sample area. This was the only one of these surveys that failed to screen out nonwhites, although in this area that was not a large number. (6) Valley 1979: a telephone survey conducted in the San Fernando Valley by Miller (1981). These data are cited but not analyzed below. (7) Los Angeles County 1979: the California 1979 survey yielded a large enough number of respondents in Los Angeles County to permit us to use it in the Los Angeles comparisons.

In the analyses that follow, we will treat all these surveys as if they were repeated measures of the same sample area using the same methodology. The argument for comparability is that the sample areas are similar, concentrated in middle class, suburban, and predominantly white areas, and that there is little evidence that minor differences in wording of self-interest items or indicators of opposition to busing make much difference in the strength of the obtained associations between the two sets of variables (though they considerably affected marginal frequencies, of course). But the surveys all did differ somewhat in these respects, so the cross-survey comparisons must remain somewhat speculative.

Self-Interest

How do the Los Angeles findings square with our speculation that self-interest may affect opposition to busing only in the ambiguous and anxiety-arousing stage of desegregation controversies between court order and implementation? Quite well, in fact. Two studies were conducted in Stage 2, the *in the midst of litigation* phase. Caditz' (1976) survey of members of a primarily West Los Angeles liberal political organization was conducted during the original trial and found at best a marginally significant effect of parental self-interest, as indicated earlier. Kinder and Sears (1981) analyzed a survey done in the San Fernando Valley in 1973 in the midst of the almost surreptitious appeals period and found no trace of any self-interest effects.

The two studies obtaining significant self-interest effects were done in the third phase, between court order and implementation. First of all, in both the Los Angeles County 1976 and West Los Angeles, 1978 surveys, having a child in the public schools consistently led to greater opposition to busing. This can be seen in the significant Child in School effects in Table 7.3 (Column 2, Rows 7–11). Second, these parental effects were greatest for those who had heard of some impending busing plan. This can be seen in the cross-tabulations in the Heard column of Table 7.2 (Column 5) and in the significant interaction terms for Child-in-School × Heard in Table 7.3 (Column 7). That is, respondents in these two surveys who both had children in the public schools and had heard of the busing court order were the most opposed to busing.

Finally, we reviewed three surveys done during the fourth, postimplementation, phase that lasted from September 1978 through March 1981. Tables 7.2 and 7.3 reveal generally nonsignificant self-interest main effects and interactions in the West Los Angeles survey in the spring of 1979 and the Los Angeles County survey in the fall of 1979. Miller (1981) reports only trivial differences in his May 1979 survey in the San Fernando Valley, as indicated earlier. Hence the distinctively antibusing stance of parents, and especially parents who had heard of impending busing in the L.A. County 1976 and West L.A. 1978 surveys stand up as the only reliable effects of self-interest to emerge from all the earlier findings reviewed in this chapter, the analyses shown in Tables 7.2 and 7.3, and the only ones to emerge from our broader consideration of the Los Angeles case. In short, only the third phase, between court order and implementation, yielded significant self-interest effects.

Symbolic Racism

Consistent with all past studies, our indicators of symbolic racism had much stronger effects than did self-interest in every one of these surveys, nationally and in Los Angeles, alike. Symbolic racism generated a strongly significant effect in every survey, in contrast to the usually weak effects of self-interest (see Table 7.3, Column 8). This is especially impressive given the very limited measure of racism used in these analyses—just one item in each case.[7]

Self-Interest in Special Populations

In a final effort to find self-interest effects, we examined interactions between self-interest and the other variables included in our regression equations. There are good reasons to expect such interactions. Concern about the quality of education is often thought to be most concentrated in the better-educated parents, so perhaps busing would threaten them the most, promoting an interaction of educational level with self-interest. Parents who live in all-white neighborhoods or whose children attend all-white public schools presumably have the most to lose from busing, so perhaps parenthood and racial composition would interact. As opposition to school desegregation spread to the nation as a whole rather than being concentrated in the South, it was widely speculated that Northern liberal parents were becoming particularly hostile to it because their own children would now be threatened. This would suggest that both racial prejudice and region would interact with self-interest.

In testing these interactions we defined self-interest in two ways. In the national (1964, 1972, and 1976) and statewide (1979) studies, we defined self-interest as being a parent in a district with Stage 4 (ongoing) busing, because insufficient numbers of parents existed in districts in Stage 3, with busing merely threatened. In the two studies in which we had already found significant self-interest effects (Los Angeles 1976 and West Los Angeles 1978), both conducted in the third, post-court-order, preimplementation phase of the controversy, we defined the self-interested as parents who had heard of forthcoming busing. Then the effect of self-interest on opposition to busing was compared for (1) high-versus low-educated respondents, (2) those in all-white versus racially mixed neighborhoods or with all-white versus mixed-neighborhood schools, (3) Northern versus Southern and (4) low versus high in racial prejudice.

However no significant interactions emerge in any of these studies. Nor do any systematic but nonsignificant interactions emerge. Thus we have not pre-

---

[7]Indeed the self-interest measures are probably more reliable than the racism item, because measures of such objective conditions as having a school-age child in the household are presumably more reliable than measures of subjective feelings such as opposing an accelerated civil rights movement. However it might be tempting to conclude that some response artifact contributes to a stronger effect of symbolic racism than of self-interest because the racism measure and the dependent variable, opposition to busing, are both subjective preferences while self-interest is an objective condition. This seems unlikely because none of the usual method-variance response artifacts (like acquiescence response sets) would seem to imply—the response scales for the three sets of variables are all quite different.

sented any of these data. There is no evidence that any special self-interested backlash against school desegregation arose either nationally or in Los Angeles as previously all-white environments were threatened, among liberals or the well educated, or in the North.

Discussion

We began by presenting a taxonomy of the main factors thought to influence whites' attitudes toward busing. However our primary focus is upon just one of these, self-interest, in an attempt to isolate conditions under which it significantly affects such attitudes.

Self-Interest: Uncertain Threats, Certain Remedies

Opposition to busing has not generally been strongly influenced by self-interest; that is, the main opponents of busing have not been drawn disproportionately from those who are actually or potentially affected by it personally. Only a small minority of whites have been directly affected by busing in any study we have reviewed. While the self-interested have been slightly more opposed to busing than the disinterested in most studies, the effect has generally been of very small magnitude and only occasionally statistically significant. Nor does self-interest show up as a significant factor in interaction with other variables. This generally weak impact of self-interest upon opposition to busing is of the same rough order of magnitude that we have discussed in studies of its effects on other policy preferences (Sears, 1980).[8]

Nevertheless, we did find some statistically significant effects of self-interest under one set of circumstances: during the third phase of local busing controversies, between final court orders to begin desegregation and actual implementation of mandatory busing. The clearest evidence for this point came from our case study of Los Angeles, but it was also suggested in our analysis of national surveys and from earlier published studies. This third stage, then, between court order and implementation, may be the time when self-interest is most likely to play a significant motivational role in generating antibusing sentiments. We might note that maximum white flight occurs during this phase as well. Armor has shown that white flight in Northern cities is typically at a maximum in the first year of desegregation (1980, p. 202). This suggests that

[8]We must add the caveat that our studies are concerned only with the mass public and with attitudinal opposition to busing. It is quite possible that active participants in antibusing protest movements are drawn disproportionately from the self-interested, as some have suggested (Weatherford, 1978).

the greatest rate of withdrawal occurs just prior to the actual implementation of busing, since this presumably mainly reflects failure to enroll children in the Fall of the first year of desegregation.

How should we interpret this finding? In the absence of any further direct data, all we can do is speculate. This period certainly maximizes uncertainty and anxiety about the nature of a busing program and hence about its potential personal effects. Lurid rumors and fantasies abound, both about the scope of the program and about what life would be like for children under it. We suspect that perceptions of threat peak during this period as well. Certainly the range of imagined threats seems to peak then, and it may be that the average level of white parents' feelings of realistic probable threat is highest' at this time as well.

Total and certain political remedies, rather than partial and uncertain remedies, also seem to be advocated most intensely in this period. Busing opponents tend to advocate total resistance, boycotts, or other means of eliminating any possibility of mandatory busing. Alternative private schools also seem to open most frequently in this phase. All these remedies are extreme, to be sure, but their most telling characteristic is that they would remove all danger to white parents, not just ameliorate their fears.

We would speculate that uncertain but possibly serious personal threats, combined with the availability of total remedies, may offer the most favorable conditions for self-interested political behavior on the part of the mass public. This would be consistent with much of the research on fear-arousing communications, that suggests that both fear and an available remedy are prerequisites for attitude change (Janis, 1967; Leventhal, 1970). It would also be consistent with findings on radical tax limitation referenda, which drew strongly self-interested support from property tax payers in the late 1970s (Lau, Coulam, & Sears, 1983; Sears & Citrin, 1982). In a period of inflation-driven rapid escalation in property taxes, it was possible to imagine that the threat would not end until homeowners had been taxed out of their homes or were paying half their incomes in property taxes. Ballot propositions, such as California's Proposition 13 or Massachusetts' Proposition 2½, were certain remedies, clamping lids on both reassessment and tax rate. This combination of sudden and seemingly endless inflationary rises in property taxes, and the promise of a certain lid on the tax offered by such ballot propositions may resemble the combination of threat and total remedies that produce self-interested policy preferences in the post-court-order preimplementation phase of busing controversies.

This reasoning would suggest that the crucial aspect of personal threat, as far as motivating political action in concerned, is that it be uncertain with very severe downside possibilities. It does appear that clear and certain personal problems (which are analogous to the final, postimplementation, phase of desegregation controversies) rarely lead to self-interested politics. Good examples would be unemployment (Schlozman & Verba, 1979) and postimplementation busing, as indicated above. People seem to accommodate to unpleasant but known realities, whether because of dissonance–reduction (Festinger, 1957; Jacobson, 1978), the feeling that the status quo cannot be changed (Tyler & Sears, 1977), or simple familiarity with realities that turn out not be so unpleasant after all (Deutsch & Collins, 1951). Uncertain remedies seem not to lead to self-interested politics either. For example, inflation is a very uncertain and quite personal threat but one for which there has been no very clear solution, and inflation by itself has not been found to generate much self-interested political thinking (Sears & Citrin, 1982; Sears & Lau, 1983).

Toward a More Complete Model

We have opted here for addressing the problem of self-interest rather than testing a more complete model of opposition to busing. Nevertheless, in all these surveys the most important factor in determining antibusing attitudes is racism, at least of those factors we have considered in this study. Our literature review suggested that symbolic or modern racism, rather than the old-fashioned racism typical in the South during the century following the Civil War, was the most powerful content in this respect.

A second deliberate choice here is to limit ourselves to testing models that allow for unambiguous causal inferences from cross-sectional surveys. Among other things, therefore, we did not attempt to test the rational-choice notion that the perceived costs and benefits of busing determine policy attitudes toward it (Model 4 in Figure 7.1). In general, beliefs about the effects of busing certainly are strongly correlated with both general opposition to busing and racism (Armor, 1980; Gatlin et al., 1978; McClendon & Pestello, 1982; McConahay & Hawley, 1978). The association between racism and opposition to busing frequently has diminished rather sharply with such beliefs controlled. For example, Gatlin et al. (1978) report that a raw correlation of .35 is reduced to .04 by such a procedure. Armor (1980) finds that prejudice has almost no residual effect with controls on beliefs about the benefits or harms of desegregation. Stinchcombe and Taylor (1980), McClendon and Pestello (1982), and Miller (1981) report similar data, though the latter finds that racism remains a strong predictor.

Cost–benefit theorists interpret such findings as indicating that policy preferences emerge from an assessment of possible policy effects. But a symbolic politics interpretation would be that these reflect rationalizations for opposition to busing arrived at for predispositional reasons. The fact that opponents of busing seem so unanimous that busing has negative effects on virtually every possible dimension (McConahay & Hawley, 1978; Miller, 1981) leads us to suspect they are applying a blanket condemnatory rationalization rather than articulating the particular mix of beliefs that lead them to oppose busing. But it is not currently possible to determine the causal status of such beliefs either from the data analyses presented or from additional side information. Even laboratory experimentation has not succeeded in unravelling the causal ordering of such tightly linked affective and cognitive components of an attitude (Tetlock & Levi, 1982). Despite these obstacles to providing a clear test between certain aspects of the rational choice and symbolic politics models, some differential predictions can be tested, as this chapter indicates. Future work may also usefully explore the implications of a group interest model, as in the provocative work of Vanneman and Pettigrew (1972). Some of the same causal ambiguities may arise, but the limits they impose have not so far been approached.[9]

Historical Change

We have noted the puzzling general finding that in the early 1960s there appeared to be a broad national consensus among whites outside of the South that school desegregation was undesirable and must be ended, yet throughout the 1970s the majority of whites appeared to be equally strongly opposed to busing, which was the main practical mechanism for accomplishing that goal. Perhaps the most common explanation for this seeming reversal is that it was easy for Northern whites to oppose the far-distant and obviously inequitable de jure system of school segregation in the South, but once the courts began to rule against segregation in the North and their own lives began to be threatened, Northern whites began to resist. The ominous implication was that Northern whites' support for school desegregation in the 1960s was illusory because it depended upon civil rights progress not interfering at all with their own lives.

Our over-time data do in fact document the fact that Southern whites were the main opponents of school desegregation in the mid-1960s and that regional differences were no longer very great during the 1970s. Nevertheless, the white consensus in favor of the general principle of integrated schooling scarcely flagged at all throughout the 1970s but persisted alongside equally strong opposition to busing. Nor do we find any evidence that self-interest became an important determinant of opposition to busing in the 1970s, as this theory

---

[9]We might also mention that the need for approximate comparability of measurement across surveys led us to limit ourselves to minimal measures of variables other than self-interest. Consequently the R^2 is lower than could readily be achieved by "massaging" the data available. For example, Sears et al. (1979), using some appropriate statistical corrections and more elaborate equations, obtained an R^2 of 29% on the National 1972 survey, rather than the 13% obtained here on exactly the same data.

would suggest. Therefore it seems unlikely that the strong opposition to busing among Northern whites in the 1970s is due to the newly arrived threats to their own personal lives. Rather we would suggest that whites' massive opposition to busing, even in the presence of great support for school desegregation in the abstract, is due at least in part to its evoking a relatively new and potent form of racism, rather than a resurgence of old-fashioned segregationism. The evidence presented here suggests that "busing" functions as a symbol evoking symbolic racism no matter what phase of busing controversies the individual is in—or indeed if he or she is many miles and/or years away from direct contact with its realities.

Acknowledgments

We thank Steven D. Miller for his many helpful comments before, during, and after preparation of this chapter; Marilynn Brewer and James Jones for their helpful comments on this chapter; and Gerald Shure for making data available to us. Computer assistance was provided by the Office of Academic Computing, UCLA.

References

Ajzen, I., & Fishbein, M. *Understanding attitudes and predicting social behavior.* Englewood Cliffs, NJ: Prentice-Hall, 1980.

Allen, H. M., Jr., & Sears, D. O. *White opposition to busing in Los Angeles: Is self-interest rejuvenated?* Paper presented at the annual meeting of the American Psychological Association, Toronto, 1978.

Armor, D. J. White flight and the future of school desegregation. In W. G. Stephan & J. R. Feagin (Eds.), *School desegregation: Past, present, and future.* New York: Plenum Press, 1980.

Bell, D. (Ed.). *The radical right: The new American right.* Garden City, New York: Doubleday, 1963.

Caditz, J. Dilemmas over racial integration: Status consciousness vs. direct threat. *Sociological Inquiry*, 1975, *45*, 51–58.

Caditz, J. *White liberals in transition.* New York: Spectrum Press, 1976.

Condran, J. G. Changes in white attitudes towards blacks: 1963–1977. *Public Opinion Quarterly*, 1979, *43*, 463–476.

Converse, P. E., & Markus, G. B. Plus ça change . . .: The new CPS election study panel. *American Political Science Review*, 1979, *73*, 32–49.

Deutsch, M. & Collins, M. E. *Interracial housing: A psychological evaluation of a social experiment.* Minneapolis, MN: University of Minnesota Press, 1951.

Downs, A. *An economic theory of democracy.* New York: Harper-Row, 1957.

Edwards, W. The theory of decision-making. *Psychological Bulletin*, 1954, *51*, 380–417.

Feldman, S. Economic individualism and American public opinion. *American Politics Quarterly*, 1983, *11*, 3–30.

Festinger, L. *A theory of cognitive dissonance.* Evanston, IL: Row, Peterson, 1957.

150   David O. Sears and Harris M. Allen, Jr.

Fiorina, M. P. *Retrospective voting in American national elections.* New Haven, CT: Yale University Press, 1981.

Gatlin, D. S., Giles, M. W., & Cataldo, E. F. Policy support within a target group: The case of school desegregation. *American Political Science Review,* 1978, *72,* 985–995.

Guimond, S. & Dubé-Simard, L. Relative deprivation theory and the Quebec nationalist movement: The cognition-emotion distinction and the personal-group deprivation issue. *Journal of Personality and Social Psychology,* 1983, *44,* 526–535.

Jackman, M. R. General and applied tolerance: Does education increase commitment to racial integration? *American Journal of Political Science,* 1978, *22,* 302–324.

Jacobson, C. K. Desegregation rulings and public attitude changes: White resistance or resignation? *American Journal of Sociology,* 1978, *84,* 698–705.

Janis, I. L. Effects of fear arousal on attitude change. Recent developments in theory and experimental research. In L. Berkowitz (Ed.), *Advances in experimental social psychology* (Vol. 3). New York: Academic Press, 1967. pp. 166–224.

Jennings, M. K., & Niemi, R. G. *Generations and politics.* Princeton, NJ: Princeton University Press, 1981.

Kelley, H. H. Attribution theory in social psychology. In D. Levine (Ed.), *Nebraska symposium on motivation.* Lincoln, NE: University of Nebraska Press, 1967, pp. 192–238.

Kelley, J. The politics of school busing. *Public Opinion Quarterly,* 1974, *38,* 23–39.

Kinder, D. R., & Kiewiet, D. R. Economic discontent and political behavior: The role of personal grievances and collective economic judgments in congressional voting. *American Journal of Political Science,* 1979, *23,* 495–527.

Kinder, D. R., & Rhodebeck, L. A. Continuities in support for racial equality, 1972 to 1976. *Public Opinion Quarterly,* 1982, *46,* 195–215.

Kinder, D. R., & Sears, D. O. Prejudice and politics: Symbolic racism versus racial threats to the good life. *Journal of Personality and Social Psychology,* 1981, *40,* 414–431.

Lane, R. E. *Political ideology: Why the American common man believes what he does.* Glencoe, IL: Free Press, 1962.

Lau, R. R., Coulam, R. F., & Sears, D. O. *Proposition 2½ in Massachusetts: Self-interest, anti-government attitudes, and political schemas.* Paper presented at the annual meeting of the Midwest Political Science Association, Chicago, 1983.

Leventhal, H. Findings and theory in the study of fear communications. In L. Berkowitz (Ed.), *Advances in experimental social psychology,* Vol. 5. New York: Academic Press, 1970, pp. 120–186.

Levitin, T. E., & Miller, W. E. Ideological interpretations of presidential elections. *American Political Science Review,* 1979, *73,* 751–771.

McClendon, M. J., & Pestello, F. P. White opposition: To busing or to desegregation? *Social Science Quarterly,* 1982, *63,* 70–81.

McConahay, J. B. Self-interest versus racial attitudes as correlates of anti-busing attitudes in Louisville: Is it the buses or the blacks? *Journal of Politics,* 1982, *44,* 692–720. (a)

McConahay, J. B. *It's still the blacks and not the buses: Self-interest vs racial attitudes as correlates of opposition to busing in Louisville, a replication.* Unpublished manuscript, Duke University, 1982. (b)

McConahay, J. B., Hardee, B. B., & Batts, V. Has racism declined in America? *Journal of Conflict Resolution,* 1981, *25,* 563–579.

McConahay, J. B., & Hawley, W. D. *Reactions to busing in Louisville: Summary of adult opinions in 1976 and 1977.* Working paper, Center for Policy Analysis, Institute of Policy Sciences and Public Affairs, Duke University, 1978.

McConahay, J. B., & Hough, J. C., Jr. Symbolic racism. *Journal of Social Issues,* 1976, *32,*(2), 23–45.

Meehl, P. E. The selfish voter paradox and the thrown-away vote argument. *American Political Science Review*, 1977, *77*, 11–30.

Miller, S. *Contemporary racial conflict: The nature of white opposition to mandatory busing.* Unpublished doctoral dissertation, University of California, Los Angeles, 1981.

Miller, S., & Sears, D. O. *Stability and change in social tolerance: A test of the persistence hypothesis.* Unpublished manuscript, University of California, Los Angeles, 1983.

Petty, R. E., & Cacioppo, J. T. *Attitudes and persuasion: Classic and contemporary approaches.* Dubuque, IA: William C. Brown Co., 1981.

Riker, W. H., & Ordeshook, P. C. *An introduction to positive political theory.* Englewood Cliffs, NJ: Prentice-Hall, 1973.

Rothbart, M. Achieving racial equality: An analysis of resistance to social reform. In P. A. Katz (Ed.), *Towards the elimination of racism.* New York: Pergamon Press, 1976.

Schlozman, K. L., & Verba, S. *Injury to insult: Unemployment, class, and political response.* Cambridge, MA: Harvard University Press, 1979.

Sears, D. O. *Public opinion and the personal impact of policy issues.* Paper presented at the annual meeting of the American Psychological Association, Montreal, Canada, 1980.

Sears, D. O., & Citrin, J. *Tax revolt: Something for nothing in California.* Cambridge, MA: Harvard University Press, 1982.

Sears, D. O., & Gahart, M. T. *The stability of racial prejudice and other symbolic attitudes.* Paper presented at the annual meeting of the American Psychological Association, Montreal, Canada, 1980.

Sears, D. O., Hensler, C. P., & Speer, L. K. Whites' opposition to "busing": Self-interest or symbolic politics? *American Political Science Review*, 1979, *73*, 369–384.

Sears, D. O., & Kinder, D. R. Racial tensions and voting in Los Angeles. In Werner Z. Hirsch (Ed.), *Los Angeles: Viability and prospects for metropolitan leadership.* New York: Praeger, 1971, pp. 51–88.

Sears, D. O., & Lau, R. R. Inducing apparently self-interested political preferences. *American Journal of Political Science*, 1983, *27*, 223–252.

Sears, D. O., Lau, R. R., Tyler, T. R., & Allen, H. M., Jr. Self-interest vs. symbolic politics in policy attitudes and presidential voting. *American Political Science Review*, 1980, *74*, 670–684.

Sears, D. O., & McConahay, J. B. *The politics of violence: The new urban blacks and the Watts riot.* Boston: Houghton-Mifflin, 1973, (Reprinted by University Press of America, 1981).

Stinchcombe, A. L., & Taylor, D. G. On democracy and school integration. In W. G. Stephan & J. R. Feagin (Eds.), *School desegregation: Past, present and future.* New York: Plenum Press, 1980.

Taylor, D. G., Sheatsley, P. B., & Greeley, A. M. Attitudes toward racial integration. *Scientific American*, 1978, *238*, *6*, 42–49.

Tetlock, P. E., & Levi, A. Attribution bias: On the inconclusiveness of the cognition–motivation debate. *Journal of Experimental Social Psychology*, 1982, *18*, 68–88.

Tyler, T. R., & Sears, D. O. Coming to like obnoxious people when we must live with them. *Journal of Personality and Social Psychology*, 1977, *35*, 200–211.

Vanneman, R. D., & Pettigrew, T. F. Race and relative deprivation in the urban United States. *Race*, 1972, *13*, 461–486.

Weatherford, M. S. *Popular participation and representation in the urban environment: The school desegregation issue in Los Angeles.* Paper presented at the annual meeting of the American Political Science Association, New York, 1978.

Weidman, J. C. Resistance of white adults to the busing of school children. *Journal of Research and Development in Education*, 1975, *9*, 123–129.

Part II

*Improving Outcomes of
Desegregation in Specific Settings*

8

Cooperative Interaction in Multiethnic Contexts*

Stuart W. Cook

Early studies of the *contact hypothesis* concerning ethnic relations in the United States employed survey methods. Using interviews and questionnaires these studies related respondents' associations with minority groups to their attitudes toward such groups. Other studies exploited natural experiments: as desegregation in recreation, housing, employment, and education began to occur, this presented the opportunity to compare persons who had had one type of interracial contact with those who had had another—or with those who had had none (e.g., Wilner, Walkley, & Cook, 1955). On the one hand this represented one of the major assets of research on the contact hypothesis. It meant, for example, that the effects of contact have been studied in a variety of contexts and this, in turn, has prevented premature generalization of findings without adequate qualification. On the other hand, the utilization of natural experiments brought with it a persistent interpretive problem. Almost all studies have been carried out in situations in which whites and blacks were already in contact at the time of the investigation. Consequently, when attitudinal differences have been found between groups of subjects who differed in the amount and nature of interracial contact, it has usually difficult to guarantee that these differences

*The research reviewed was supported by funds from the following sources: Research Scientist Award, N.I.M.H., MH 43358; Office of Education contract, OEC-4-7-051320-0273; N.I.M.H. grant, MH 17495; Army Research Institute grant, DAH 19-76-G-0010; Office of Naval Research grant, N00014-80-C-0044.

Permission has been granted by the *Journal of Research and Development in Education* to include excerpts from an article by the author in Volume 12, 1, 1978 of the Journal.

GROUPS IN CONTACT:
THE PSYCHOLOGY OF DESEGREGATION

did not result from selective entry of favorable subjects into the contact experience—or from withdrawal of unfavorable subjects.

Although investigators have often dealt with this problem of interpretation in a convincing manner, the uncertainties to which it has given rise might be reduced still further were the contact hypothesis is to be tested under conditions approximating those of laboratory control. The purpose of this chapter is to review a series of studies in which this was done. The first of these studies assessed the attitudinal effect of an intergroup contact experience that was characterized by all the conditions of contact believed to encourage favorable attitude change. The next two focused on cooperative interdependence, comparing equal-status intergroup contact with and without interracial cooperation. These were followed by a series of experiments on cooperating interracial groups in which variables thought to influence respect and liking among group members were studied. These variables were task success–failure, participation in group decision making, relative task competence of group members, helping a groupmate, and receiving help from a groupmate.

A Laboratory Test of the Overall Contact Hypothesis

The requirements of the initial study (Cook, 1969, 1971) called for creating under laboratory control the set of conditions postulated in the contact hypothesis to produce favorable attitude change. This was accomplished as follows:

1. Equality of status in the contact situation was achieved through the use of a group task and the assignment of white and black participants to task roles of equivalent responsibility.
2. Contact with stereotype-disconfirming blacks was insured through the experimenter's selection of black confederates of educational background equivalent to that of the research subjects.
3. A cooperative relationship was encouraged by choice of a task that required interdependence in its execution and provided a reward (financial bonus) for group success.
4. The contact situation was given a high acquaintance potential by arranging for lunch-break conversations during which the black confederates brought out individualizing information about themselves.
5. Social norms favoring equalitarian interracial relations and racial equality were introduced, in part by the use of racially integrated supervisory staff, in part by the actions of the work supervisor, and in part through the support of desegregation by a white confederate.

The task that involved the research participant in an interdependent relationship with two co-workers (experimental confederates) was a type of management game. The task was to operate an imaginary railroad system composed of 10 cities and 500 freight cars of six different types. Successful operation involved learning how to maintain an appropriate distribution of these cars so that they were available when shipping orders were placed with the railroad. When the team received requests to ship merchandise of specified types from one station to another, it made decisions regarding the route to follow and the types of cars to use.

The management task, as used, lasted for 40 periods or "work days." A period covered 20–30 minutes. Two such periods separated by a 30-minute break made up an experimental session. The break was explained to the subject as giving the supervisor time to prepare materials for the second period. At intervals of 3–4 calendar days, the team learned how its profits compared with those of an earlier team whom it had to surpass to earn a bonus. Although its fortunes varied from report to report, it was prearranged that the team finally won out and earned the hoped-for bonus money.

To summarize, the interdependence requirements and reward structure of the management task were such as to involve the subject in efforts to achieve a goal in common with the black participant. The task required collaborative efforts, and success and failure came to the management team as a whole. The confederates were trained to share responsibility for decisions with the subject. All this led to close interaction and mutual assistance, especially when the subject and the black confederate were paired in job assignments requiring collaboration. They discussed their procedures and decided together on changes that would be helpful. They shared reverses as well as successes day by day for 20 days. Rotation of team assignments put the subject in the position both of teaching and being taught by the black confederate.

Persons with strongly negative scores on self-report tests of racial attitude were exposed to this experimental environment, whereas others with equally negative scores were not. This made it possible to control for a number of nonexperimental influences on changes in attitude test scores. Among these were the effect of taking the attitude measures a second time, the effect of regression to the mean on second testing associated with extreme scores on first testing, contemporaneous life experiences during the period of several months between pretest and posttest, and so forth.

The research subjects were white female students from colleges in Nashville, Tennessee. During the 5 academic years required to collect data for the study and a subsequent replication of it, numerous pools of potential subjects were established. This was done by administering a 12-hour battery of ability, interest, personality, and attitude tests throughout which racial attitude measures were dispersed. The battery was administered at colleges whose students had no contact with the college at which the study was conducted. From these pools the most prejudiced pair of individuals who had not yet participated in the experiment were assigned to the experimental and control groups.

The subjects were hired for part-time work, discovering only after they began work that they were to have black co-workers. The experiment was conducted in this manner in order to preserve the natural character of the experience as it might be encountered on a job.

Included in the preexperimental test battery were items ascertaining the subject's positions on race relations policies. During the course of the experiment a white student co-worker (a confederate) made known her integrationist positions on these same policies. This was done in the course of a series of 10 seemingly natural, but actually preplanned, conversations in which mention by the black co-worker (also a confederate) of a personal experience with discrimination gave the white co-worker an opportunity to express disapproval of the discriminatory practice or policy. The positions taken by the subject in subsequent conversations with this white co-worker were recorded and compared with her initial test positions. Changes in the direction of the views presented by the confederate offer an opportunity to explore situational influences on attitude-related social behavior.

At the end of the final session, after saying goodbye to her co-workers, the subject rated each one on various aspects of competence, character, and personality. This provided an opportunity to examine the effect of the experimental experience on the development of liking and respect of white subjects for their black co-workers.

Several months later the subject was retested in a setting removed from that of the part-time job described above by a person unconnected with her job experience (a person representing a fictional Educational Testing Institute engaged in test development). Here in the company of other students, including the equally prejudiced control subjects, she again responded to the questions asked in the tests taken prior to her selection as a subject as well as to those asked in a number of new tests. Her opinions were compared with her preexperimental ones to determine whether changes had occurred.

Two studies utilizing this design were carried out. The initial study involved 23 subjects in the experimental condition, with an equal number of controls. Because each subject participated for approximately a month, it was possible to complete work with a maximum of nine subjects per academic year. Hence the study covered a total elapsed time of approximately 3 years. After another 3 years, a replication of the initial study was conducted. The replication involved 19 experimental subjects plus controls and lasted somewhat over 2 years.

Results

Although the design of the study focused upon a test of the hypothesis that prejudiced whites would change their racial attitudes as a result of cooperative interracial contact, it also provided an opportunity to observe the behavior of the subjects toward blacks they encountered in the contact situation. On the one hand, the subjects' negative racial attitudes should have predisposed them to be unfriendly and distant. On the other, the experimental contact experience was assembled of components thought to induce friendly and cooperative cross-racial behavior.

Actions toward Black Co-Workers

The research subjects displayed predominantly positive actions toward black co-workers.[1] Despite the strong overall tendency in this direction, it was somewhat less true of those who had said earlier in another setting that they would quit a job if given a black co-worker and somewhat more true of those who had said that, under these circumstances, they would either (1) continue working or (2) continue working and be friendly.

Positions Taken Publicly on Race-Related Matters

The subjects tended to remain silent in situations in which their negative views on race-related matters might be disapproved if expressed. When induced to take positions, they most often voiced the situationally approved view in contrast to the view they had earlier expressed privately. When the matter at issue involved a relatively extreme deviation from the subjects' positions, this acquiescence occurred less often. These findings, like those in the paragraph above, are consistent with the interpretation that the situational influences built into the experimental contact situation outweighed attitudinal influences in determining behavior toward persons from the disliked group. On the other hand, they also reveal some interplay between attitudinal and situational forces.

Postexperimental Evaluations of Black Co-Workers

The subjects with rare exceptions reported highly favorable evaluations of the individuals they had come to know from a racial group they disliked.

Attitude Change

Whether or not the experience of cooperative interracial contact had changed the racial attitudes of the prejudiced whites who participated in the research was examined by several methods. The first utilized difference scores between pre- and postexperimental administration of the same attitude scales. These were computed for each participant in both the experimental and control groups and

---

[1]Staff members recorded systematic observations of positive and negative actions. Positive actions were complimentary statements, friendly personal questions, joking, sharing food, taking initiative in work collaboration, physical contact, doing favors, and extending sympathy.

the averages were compared. This was done separately for each attitude measure—three in the initial experiment and two in the replication—and for composite scores derived from the total set of measures. The experimental group in the initial experiment changed significantly more in a favorable direction on one of the three individual measures ($p < .05$) and on the composite measure ($p < .05$). In the replication experiment significant differences in favor of the experimental group were obtained on one of the two individual attitude measures ($p < .05$) and on the composite measure ($p < .05$). Analysis of covariance confirmed these results for the replication experiment but not for the original study.[2]

A third method of analysis was suggested by the fact that the change in self-described attitudes tended to be large when it occurred. Expressing change in average standard score units of change over the three tests, there appeared in the initial experiment a natural break in the distribution of average standard scores at .82. Eight experimental subjects changed this much or more (six were above a change of one standard score), whereas the next highest subject changed an average of .55 standard score units. Interestingly, exactly the same values were found in the replication experiment, where nine experimental subjects changed an average of .82 standard score units or more, with the next highest subject again at .55 units. In both experiments other subjects clustered around zero change with one or two in each experiment showing substantial negative change. For the controls in the two experiments, a clear contrast with the above pattern emerged. In the first experiment, only two control subjects reached the .82 standard score change; three changed to this extent in the second study. Taking the two experiments together, 17 of 42 experimental subjects (40%) showed impressive change of potential practical significance, whereas 5 of 42 controls (12%) show change of similar magnitude. A comparison of these frequencies by the chi-square test showed the difference between experimental and control groups to be statistically significant ($p < .01$).

Cooperation in the Attainment of Personal Goals among Mothers in an Interracial Preschool

Although these initial studies of the overall contact hypothesis confirmed conclusions drawn from the surveys and natural experiments that had preceded it, they left unanswered the contribution of the cooperation component of the

[2]The second method of analyzing the data was by analysis of covariance with postexperimental scores as the dependent variable and preexperimental scores as the covariant. In the initial experiment (but not in the replication) assignment of participants to experimental and control groups had resulted in somewhat more prejudiced preexperimental scores for the former. Pre-

contact experience. As had been true in the field studies, the factor of cooperation in these studies was accompanied by other experiences (such as contact with stereotype-disconfirming individuals) that may have been responsible for the observed behavioral and attitudinal outcomes.

The next step was to examine the effect of cooperation when these other factors were held constant. This was done in the two field experiments described below.

The first study involved a comparison of two conditions of unintended equal-status interracial contact (Cook, Gray, & Vietze, 1973). One condition maximized the extent of collaborative activity in the attainment of shared goals, whereas the other minimized it (without minimizing interracial contact or introducing competition).

The research subjects were mothers from low-socioeconomic backgrounds whose children attended an interracial preschool in Nashville, Tennessee. None had previously experienced equal-status, interracial contact. All were required as a condition of their childrens' enrollment to participate in once-weekly, day-long, child-rearing training sessions throughout the course of a school year. Training was conducted in racially balanced groups of five or six members by co-trainers, one black and one white.

The following illustrates the differences between the two treatment conditions. Under the cooperative, high-interdependence condition the staff always discussed children with all mothers (10 black and 11 white) rather than only with the child's own mother. The staff encouraged mother-to-mother discussions and diagnoses of their childrens' difficulties. Training exercises (e.g., for giving children positive reinforcement for desired behavior) were conducted in mother pairs.

By contrast, when staff members implemented the low-interdependence condition they discussed a given child only with his or her own mother (10 black and 10 white). Staff conducted diagnoses of childrens' difficulties in staff-to-mother pairs. These pairs were also used for training exercises. Note however that all training of mothers in a given group occurred during the same period in the same room and that, during breaks from training, the mothers remained in this room. These arrangements facilitated cross-racial association without inducing interdependence.

Assignment of subjects to treatments was random with two constraints: (1) the groups were racially balanced, and (2) mothers who knew each other previously or who lived close enough together to make neighborhood encounters a possibility were not permitted in the same training group.

---

sumably due to this, the covariance analysis did not confirm the finding of a greater change in the experimental group. In the replication experiment, on the other hand, the greater change in the experimental group was confirmed.

Three types of measures were taken: (1) observations of the proportion of cross-racial to total mother-to-mother interactions within the training groups; (2) realistically confidential postexperimental intermember-attraction ratings and -partner choices; and (3) structured, preexperimental and postexperimental racial attitude interviews conducted in the participants' homes and carefully disassociated from the preschool experience.

Results

Given the almost totally segregated prior experience of the research subjects, the findings with respect to the proportion of cross-racial mother-to-mother interaction were surprising. In a group of three blacks and three whites there were six same-race pairs and nine cross-race pairs. Thus if interactions of pairs were unrelated to color, one would expect 60% to be cross-racial. Instead, beginning with the early gatherings of the training groups, cross-racial interactions approached 80%. Probably because of this high initial figure there was no change in proportion over time.

This pattern is reminiscent of the overwhelmingly positive character of the cross-racial interactions in the initial and replication studies described in the first part of the chapter. A possible explanation in both cases might be as follows: newcomers to a situation may interpret the people and arrangements they find there as reflecting strong social expectations for equalitarian race relations. If they do, they are likely to react in such a way as to overshoot a pattern of unbiased behavior.

The findings, with respect to intermember attraction are also clear: there was an extremely strong tendency for each experimental subject to rate highly and to choose preferentially other subjects who had been rated highly on the same characteristics (e.g., concern for others) by the joint assessment of three staff members (black trainer, white trainer, and black observer). Thus if these combined staff ratings are taken as accurate reflections of the mothers' characteristics, we may infer that attraction ratings of the subjects by one another were based upon personal attributes other than race.

Given that no differences were found between experimental treatments in relative attraction for own-race and other-race group members, it might still be the case that the absolute level of attraction ratings, regardless of color, was higher in the means-interdependent groups than in the means-independent groups. Examination of the average ratings of a mother by the members of her group suggests this was the case: 75% of the means-interdependent mothers received higher average ratings than the median average rating of the means-independent mothers.

Analysis of preexperimental and postexperimental attitude interviews of mothers in the cooperative groups as well as those in the control groups showed no evidence of attitude change in the mothers of either race.

From these results one is led to infer the following: (1) Persons holding negative attitudes to another racial group may be influenced by certain types of sustained interracial contact to develop liking and respect for members of that group. The degree of liking and respect developed will be minimally affected by race and maximally affected by the presence or absence of generally valued personal attributes. (2) This will happen when the contact situation is characterized by strong norms favoring equalitarian race relations and by equality in status for representatives of the two racial groups and when the contact is close enough and of long enough duration (in this case a school year) to develop intimate personal acquaintance. (3) In such a context, means-interdependence in the achievement of shared goals will have no additional measurable influence on relative attraction to own-race and other-race associates, although it may affect the absolute level of attraction to both.

One must infer in addition, however, that an experience that has the above effect is not sufficient under some circumstances to produce change in racial attitudes in general. A comparison with the conditions introduced into the studies of the overall contact hypothesis, reported above, may be instructive. Recall that despite the considerably shorter duration of contact in those studies—40 hours versus 36 days in the present study—substantial racial attitude change was found. This leads one to suspect that attitude change will result from cooperative interracial contact only when such contact is accompanied by a supplementary influence that promotes the process of generalization from favorable contact with individuals to positive attitudes toward the group from which the individual comes. The supplementary influence in the earlier research was one of relating explicit peer-group norms supporting equalitarian race relations to pleasant experiences with black individuals. This took the form of advocacy of desegregation and racial equality by an own-group peer immediately following accounts of discrimination suffered by a well-liked black coworker.

Cooperative Interdependence in Ethnically Heterogeneous Classroom Groups

The second of the two field experiments on cooperating interracial groups was carried out in a school setting. Its focus was upon the impact of cooperative learning experiences on cross-ethnic and interracial relations and attitudes in newly desegregated school classrooms (Weigel, Wiser, & Cook, 1975).[3] The objective was to induce cooperative interdependence in the classroom by means of a teaching method that emphasized the use of small interracial and cross-ethnic groups. The resulting social relations and attitudes were compared to similar behaviors and dispositions resulting from contact in classes taught by traditional lecture and whole-class discussion techniques.

The newly desegregated schools in which the study took place had segregated or predominantly segregated feeder schools. The students who participated in the research were 7th graders in a junior-high school or 10th graders in a senior-high school who had just moved into the desegregated setting. These grade levels were selected to minimize previous interracial and cross-ethnic contact. Most of the minority group students were bused to the schools.

Ten English teachers participated in the experiment. Each taught one of her class sections by the whole-class method, with students carrying out assignments individually, and one by the small-group method, with students working in multiethnic teams of four to six members, cooperating in assignments and projects. (One teacher taught two pairs of classes.) The two sections taught by a given teacher were closely comparable in racial mix; that is, 60% Anglo, 20% black, 20% Hispanic. Racial and ethnic balance across sections had been arranged by assignment of children to sections during the previous summer, and the class section in each pair to be taught by the small-group method was chosen by random assignment.

Dropouts of minority group students during the course of the year (from either the experimental or control section of a pair) reduced the number of pairs of classes that remained adequately matched from 11 to 6. Only these six were included in the analysis of results. Of these six, three pairs of classes were in the junior high school and three in the senior high school.

The group-method classes were so structured as to foster cooperative interracial and cross-ethnic activities. These activities involved working toward common goals and required mutual interdependence among group members. Although some material, such as films and recordings, was presented to the class as a whole, much gathering and interpreting of information was done by the interracial groups. Discussion of the material was carried out by the students in their small groups; afterward they made group reports to the rest of the class. Membership in groups remained constant throughout the study. The control classes involved a great deal of whole-class instruction with students gaining most of their information about the course content from lectures and individual reading. Discussions involved the entire class and were led by the teacher. Dialogue tended to be between teacher and student rather than between two or

[3]This study received the 1973 Gordon Allport Intergroup Relations Prize awarded by the Society for the Psychological Study of Social Issues.

more students. Projects and other assignments were usually carried out on an individual basis.

Two methods of monitoring the implementation of the contrasting teaching methods were used. The first involved systematic observation by research staff members. The second involved weekly interviews by research staff of participating teachers. Deviations from planned teaching procedures were remedied by periodic training sessions with the teachers.

Groups within a given group-taught class were put into competition with each other in order to induce motivation for mutual assistance among team members. Rewards were given to winning groups in order to maximize satisfaction in group success.

In interviews following the study, teachers were asked to recall their preexperimental expectations of outcomes in the pairs of classes they had taught. Nothing in the way of shared expectations emerged; no anticipation of outcomes with respect to race relations was reported.

Results

Seven of the 10 teachers characterized their group-taught classes as showing somewhat more, or much more, interracial and cross-ethnic interaction. Seven of the 10 reported group-taught classes as having a more supportive classroom atmosphere. Nine of the 10 recommended using the group method in newly desegregated schools.

Tabulation of reports from weekly interviews with teachers showed crossethnic conflict to be significantly less frequent ($p < .001$) and cross-ethnic helping to be significantly more frequent ($p < .001$) in group-taught classes.

The students rated their classmates on a number of desirable personal attributes. In order to minimize situational influences on response associated with the presence of the teacher and with close classroom contact with classmates, these ratings were obtained in an auditorium or library setting by persons not associated with the school. No school personnel were present. When ratings of own-ethnic-group classmates were compared with ratings of other-ethnicgroup classmates, the following results were obtained. Anglo students in the group-taught classes gave equally high ratings to their Hispanic and own-group (Anglo) classmates. In contrast, Anglo students in the traditional whole-class method rated their Anglo classmates higher than their Hispanic classmates. Difference scores reflecting a comparison of the ratings of own-ethnic group (Anglo) and other-ethnic-group (Hispanic) were computed for each of the Anglo students in each type of class. An analysis of variance (subjects-within classeswithin treatments) showed the difference scores for Anglo students in the grouptaught classes to be less (and thus less biased) than those in the traditional classes

($p < .001$). However, when the ratings by Anglos of their Anglo classmates and black classmates were compared the result was different. In this case the Anglo students in the two types of classes behave similarly; that is, in both types of classes Anglo students rate their Anglo classmates higher than their black classmates.

Similar comparisons across the two teaching methods were made for the classmate ratings made by black and by Hispanic students. Here no advantage was found for the experimental classrooms. The fact that even in the traditional classrooms the ratings of Anglo classmates by blacks and Hispanics were as favorable as their ratings of classmates from their own-ethnic groups indicates that "color-blind" rating behavior was either already present preexperimentally or was produced under the noncooperative contact experienced in the control classes.

On a second measure of interpersonal attraction, students chose 10 schoolmates from their entire grade (7th or 10th) with whom to share each of two activities, one task-oriented and one social in nature. Percentage of cross-ethnic choices made by Anglo students of Hispanic schoolmates was higher in the group-taught classes than in the classes taught by traditional methods ($p < .04$). Percentage of choices by Anglos of black schoolmates, by contrast, was equivalent in the two types of classes.

Data on racial attitudes of the research subjects were obtained from an interview administered to students in their homes. The interviews were in the form of public opinion polls and were not associated in any way with the school system. From these data scale scores were derived for the following attitudinal components: (1) integration–segregation policy, (2) gradualism in desegregation, (3) reactions to militant protest by minority groups, (4) acceptance of minority groups into close personal relationships, (5) derogatory beliefs about blacks, and (6) derogatory beliefs about Hispanics. A total attitude score was computed by combining derogatory beliefs items, social acceptance items, and social policy items (desegregation, gradualism and militance), with equal weight assigned to the three clusters. Mean scores on the subscales and the total scale did not differ between the Anglo students in the two types of classes. Examination of means makes it clear that this failure to find a difference was not due to ceiling effects. In most cases, the means approximated the mid-point of the scale score ranges.

Other Studies of Cooperating Groups in Multiethnic Schools

Within the decade, 1972–1982, classroom experiments similar to the one just described were published by a number of investigators. Several examples illustrate the procedural variations that developed and the results obtained.

A group at the Center for the Social Organization of Schools, Johns Hopkins University, conducted a study that shared the emphasis of the Weigel, Wiser, and Cook (1975) study on motivating classroom performance through team competition (DeVries, Edwards, & Slavin, 1978, Experiment 2). However, their study differed from the Weigel *et al.* (1975) study both in the nature of the cooperative learning activity and in the manner of choosing which teams in a classroom were to be rewarded.

The study involved four classes of seventh grade students; the subject matter was social studies and mathematics. One hundred twenty-eight students were allocated to these classes by stratified random assignment. Stratification was based on past achievement, race, and sex. Fifty-one percent of the students were black. Three of the four classes constituted the experimental group; each class was subdivided into teams made up of 4 or 5 students. Students in the fourth class served as a control group; they studied as individuals in a traditional classroom arrangement. A single mathematics teacher taught mathematics to the four classes; a single social studies teacher taught the classes in social studies. Both teachers were white.

The task for all students was the same, that is, to master informational and skill units in the subject matter area. Following the teacher's initial presentation of a curriculum unit, student teams in the three experimental classes began practice sessions in which they helped their teammates in various ways. Later in the week they engaged in a classroom tournament covering the material they had been studying. In the tournament, groups of three students, each comparable in achievement level, competed with one another to answer quiz questions that they drew from a question pool. Each of the three was representing his/her team against members of other teams. The one of the trio who answered the most questions correctly earned six points for his/her team. The second place student earned four points and the last place student, two points. Of note is the fact that this procedure provides low-achieving students as much opportunity to contribute to team scores as high-achieving students have. As time passes this equality of opportunity is updated by ''bumping'' the first place winner in a trio to the next highest tournament level and the last place loser to the next lowest level. Inventors of this procedure have labelled it Teams-Games-Tournaments (TGT) (DeVries, Slavin, Fennessey, Edwards, & Lombardo, 1980).

In two of the three experimental classes, team scores were calculated and leading teams were praised in a class newsletter. Also, for students in these groups, the team score became a component of their individual course grade. In the third experimental class the identification of team winners in a newsletter was omitted. Instead, each team received a newsletter describing only the performance of its own members and comparing this performance to earlier performance by these same individuals. For these students the course grade was determined entirely by individual performance.

The result was a three condition design: (1) cooperative group study plus team praise and publicity based on interteam competition, (2) cooperative group study with individual praise but no team reward, and (3) control, in which individuals studied alone and were praised as individuals. The ethnic proportions across conditions were equivalent, thus controlling for situational opportunities for cross-ethnic interaction.

The dependent variables were the number and the percentage of choices that were cross-race when participants listed best friends, friends outside school, friends in school, and classmates with whom they would like to work. Only posttest measures were obtained. On the percentage measures, students in both experimental treatments exceeded the control group significantly in percentage of cross-race "best friends" ($p < .05$), and marginally in percentage of cross-race friends outside school ($p < .10$) and in cross-race classmates "to work with" ($p < .10$). No difference was found for "friends in school." (On two measures, cross-race "best friends" and "classmates to work with", students in the second experimental condition, cooperative group study without team rewards, showed a higher percentage of cross-race choices than did those in the experimental condition with team rewards.)

Differences in number (rather than percentage) of cross-race friends named were also reported. However, this measure is subject to ambiguous interpretation. Number alone can increase in equal proportion for within-race and cross-race responses—and thus have no implications for reduction in cross-race bias. On the other hand, as the investigators argued, the increase in number of cross-race student friends represents a highly desirable outcome even if it is part of a general increase in students felt to be friends. With number as the criterion, the three TGT groups combined, that is, the two experimental treatments, exceeded the control group on cross-race choices for "best friends in school."

A second study (Slavin, 1979) paralleled the above study in its use of co-operative team learning and motivation based on team competition. The principal difference was that team rewards were based on points earned by team members on paper and pencil quizzes. The opportunity for lower-achieving students to contribute equally to higher-achieving ones, provided in the above study by the different levels of the classroom tournament, was ensured in this study by basing a student's team points on a comparison of his quiz score with that of other classmates at a similar level of past performance. This scoring procedure is called Student Teams-Achievement Divisions (Slavin, 1978).

The study involved students in 12 seventh- and eighth-grade English classes. The five volunteer teachers, one white male, two black females, two white females, taught either one experimental and one control section, or two of each. Intact classes were randomly assigned within teacher to experimental or control conditions. Experimental classes contained 226 students of whom approximately 40% were black and 60% white. Control classes contained 198 students; approximately 37% were black and 61% white (2% were oriental; their scores were not included in the analysis). Experimental classes ranged from 19% black to 70% black. Parallel percentages in the control classes were 17% to 60%.

For 10 weeks experimental students studied grammar, punctuation and English usage in interracial teams. Two quizzes were given per week. On each quiz team winners were determined and announced in newsletters distributed to the class as a whole. Students in control classes studied the same materials individually and took the same quizzes. Evaluations of their performance were directed to them as individuals.

The criterion measure was the number and race of classmates written down in response to a question about "your friends in this class." Nothing was said to the students about the race relations focus of the study.

Results indicated that the team learning classes showed a greater increase in the proportion of cross-ethnic friends than did control classes ($p < .001$). The same was true for number of cross-ethnic friends. Black students and white students showed an equivalent amount of increase.

Not all studies of cooperative contact in desegregated schools employ classroom competition between teams. A study by Johnson and Johnson (1981) provides an example. The experiment involved two classes of fourth grade children. One of the classes was divided into ethnically mixed four-person teams and instructed to complete an assignment sheet as a group. The teams studied social studies in this way for an hour per day for 16 instructional days. The second of the two classes studied the same material as individuals. The students in this class were instructed to work on their own.

In contrast to the three previous experiments described above, in which rewards were based on team competition, the teacher in the cooperative condition praised and rewarded all teams. In the individualistic condition the teacher praised and rewarded each student individually. Johnson and Johnson describe these procedures in their book, *Learning Together and Alone* (1975).

Fifty-one students in the study were randomly assigned to the two conditions, stratifying for ethnic membership, past general achievement, and sex. Eleven of the students were minority (9 black, 1 American Indian, 1 Hispanic). The ethnic membership of teams in the cooperative condition followed as closely as possible the ethnic proportions of the class.

Systematic time-sampled observations confirmed that the experimental and control classrooms differed in ways called for by the experimental manipulation: while the classes were in session there was more cross-ethnic verbal interaction in the cooperative classroom than in the individualistic one ($p < .05$) and students in the former also reported more cross-ethnic helping ($p < .01$). Additional confirmation of the experimental manipulation came from a post-experimental questionnaire in which students in the cooperative condition were found to perceive more cooperative behavior among their classmates than did their counterparts in the individualistic condition ($p < .01$).

In this study the dependent variable of relevance to ethnic relations was an observational measure of cross-ethnic interaction taken during 10 minutes of free time following the 45-minute study session. Such interaction was found to be more frequent in the cooperative condition ($p < .01$). The difficulty in interpreting this finding arises from the fact that the observations were made in the classrooms in the presence of the same teachers who had instructed the students to work together or alone. A free-time interaction measure taken away from such potential influences would have been more persuasive, but the finding is perhaps strengthened somewhat by the results of a postexperimental questionnaire. When asked to place stickers containing the names of classmates on a diagram of the probable free-time location of their classmates in the classroom, students in the cooperative condition placed more majority and minority students together ($p < .05$).

Yet another approach to the study of cooperative contact in multiethnic classrooms involves structuring classroom process in such a way that students in small groups must teach and learn from one another. In the seminal study of this approach the purpose was to assess its effect on liking for cooperating classmates, liking for school, and, more important, the self-esteem of minority students (Blaney, Stephan, Rosenfield, Aronson, & Sikes, 1977). The study explicitly avoided any use of rewards for group achievement (except in the form of teacher encouragement and approval for effectively carrying out the interdependent learning procedure.) Tested achievement was reported only to individuals and team scores were not calculated.

Interdependent learning was induced by dividing the material to be learned, for example, a biography, into as many parts as there were students in the learning teams. Each student learned one part of the total material and was, in turn, responsible for teaching that part to his or her groupmates. This arrangement assured that each member was dependent on every other group member to achieve mastery of all material. This feature of the procedure was highlighted by calling it the *Jigsaw method* (Aronson, 1978).

Two hundred forty-five students from 10 classes were taught social studies by this procedure. A control group of 59 students in 3 classes was taught the same material by traditional teacher-to-class and teacher-to-individual procedures.

The student participants were in the fifth grade and came from Anglo, black, and Hispanic ethnic groups. Most teams contained 5–6 individuals. Volunteer teachers were trained to carry out the experimental teaching. Equally competent teachers volunteered to teach the control classes. The experiment lasted six weeks, with classes meeting for 45 minutes per day, three days a week.

Data on liking for school and self-esteem were gathered by pre- and postexperimental questionnaires administered in the classrooms. Sociometric data on liking for groupmates and for other classmates were obtained with an instrument that allowed students to indicate the order in which they would take classmates on a fantasy boat trip.

Because there were no learning teams in the control condition, the variable, liking for groupmates in comparison to liking for other classmates, could only be analyzed in the classes in the experimental condition. A significant liking-by-trial interaction was obtained ($p < .05$): liking for groupmates was lower than liking for other classmates on the pretest but higher on the posttest.[4]

As may be seen from the description of the preceding classroom experiments, procedures employed to encourage cooperation and mutual assistance among team members differ both with respect to the nature of the task (task structure) and the distribution of rewards for performance (reward structure). Group tasks may be defined in such a way that team members have different subtasks, for example, each may prepare a section of a team report. In other cases the group character of the task is established by giving each team member sole access to an aspect of a total set of material on which each team member will eventually be individually tested and graded. In still other cases, each team member has the same task, for example, to learn to solve mathematics problems. Here, in order to make the team members interdependent, the teacher must adopt some method of aggregating the test scores of team members into a team score.

Rewards for team members may be based either upon their performance as individuals or upon their team's performance. In the case of rewards based on individual performance, the cooperative team activity has usually been induced by some such arrangement as making team members dependent on their team-mates for information they need to pass tests. When rewards are based on a team score, the team members' common fate tends to induce cooperation. Sometimes investigators have provided preexperimental training in how to work together.

The fact that student teams are characteristically heterogeneous in achievement poses a problem when team scores are computed by summing the scores of team members. The problem arises from the concern that the lower-achieving team members may contribute insignificantly to the team total. The danger is that repeated experience of this sort may further enhance the low self-concept to which earlier school failure has already contributed. To avoid this, the Johns Hopkins investigators, as illustrated in the DeVries *et al.* (1978) and Slavin

---

[4]As anticipated, the change in self-esteem from pretest to posttest favored the experimental condition ($p < .01$). (Experimental students increased while control subjects decreased.) Change in liking for school resulted in a three-factor interaction: (a) experimental Anglos increased in liking for school whereas control Anglos decreased; (b) experimental blacks showed little change whereas control blacks decreased markedly; (c) experimental Hispanics showed little change whereas control Hispanics increased markedly. The suspicion that the Hispanic result reflected a local reticence—in Austin, Texas—of students from this ethnic group to speak in class was supported in a later study of Hispanics in Southern California who had a history of longer residence in the United States (Gonzales, 1979). In that study Hispanic children in interdependent study groups increased in self-esteem by a signficantly greater amount that did other Hispanics in traditional classes.

(1979) studies, have used methods that made it possible for lower-achieving children to contribute as much as higher-achieving ones to their team scores. They have done this either by arranging for lower-achieving students from different teams to compete against each other or by scoring tests in such a way that team points were earned for improvement, that is, for exceeding a base line or expected score established on the basis of each student's own past achievement.

When investigators use team rewards they must decide what criterion of success is to be used. One alternative has been to put teams within a classroom into competition and reward the winners. Another has been to have the teacher set a criterion score in advance of a test; teams that achieve this score are rewarded. A third has been to reward (usually with teacher praise) any team that has made constructive effort. Team rewards, when used, have varied from teacher praise to consumable items such as candy and pencils. Included are privileges (e.g., first in line for lunch), school publicity (e.g., team name on a bulletin board; wearing winner buttons), and take-home winning team certificates. Although rare, grades may be assigned either totally or partially on the basis of team performance.

In newly desegregated schools white Anglo students in cooperating interracial and cross-ethnic learning groups, by comparison with those in equally heterogeneous traditional classrooms, show more respect and liking for non-Anglo classmates and more frequently choose friends from outside the Anglo group. They do not, however, change their attitudes toward the minority groups from which their classmates come—at least not in the course of the limited amount and duration of cooperation characterizing the school experiments described. Hence, although it is evident that participation in cooperating interracial and cross-ethnic groups may have favorable behavioral and attitudinal outcomes, it remains to be determined what conditions maximize such outcomes. This task stimulated the series of laboratory experiments to be described below.

Experiments on the Determinants of Respect and Liking in Cooperating Interracial Laboratory Groups

An analysis of the makeup and activities of cooperating interracial groups calls attention to two features that are difficult to control in natural settings in which cooperating groups might be activated. These are (1) group task outcome (success, failure, uncertainty) and (2) the relative adequacy of performance of group members from different ethnic groups (relatively less competent, of equal competence, and relatively more competent). Should it be learned, as one might anticipate, that group task failure or the presence in the group of an inadequately performing member from an ethnic minority inhibits the development of positive cross-ethnic relationships, this knowledge should stimulate a search for preventive and/or compensating arrangements and procedures.

An example of such a compensating arrangement is participation in significant aspects of the group's operating procedures, that is, participation that arouses a sense of contributing meaningfully to achieving the group's goals. Research on both task-oriented laboratory groups and industrial work groups has underscored the effect of significant participation on morale and intermember attraction.

A second example of a preventive or compensatory procedure is that of contributing to the achievement of group goals by helping a less competent group member with his or her part of the group task. The potential relevance of such helping derives from the fact that, in cooperating interracial groups formed in newly desegregated settings, members from disadvantaged minority groups may enter the situation with performance handicaps that retard the group's progress. Although no directly relevant research is available, a reasonable theoretical inference is that contributing to group progress by helping such a teammate would generate a sense of personal satisfaction that might increase liking for the helped individual. However, the converse is also possible, namely that helping might increase the perceived incompetence of the person helped and, consequently, lead to lesser attraction for him or her. Of course, personal satisfaction in helping a teammate and perceived incompetence of the teammate may be enhanced concurrently and, as a consequence, leave liking and respect for the teammate unchanged.

Finally, research on the recipient of help indicates that this side of the helping relationship in teams must also be examined. A potential problem is suggested by the fact that research on dyads has shown that the recipient of help sometimes likes the donor less than he or she would in the absence of such help.

The writer and his associates have conducted eight experiments on the effect on respect and liking for teammates of each of the five variables enumerated, that is, group success–failure, teammate incompetence–competence, amount of significant participation in the group's activity, the helping of an inadequately performing teammate, and the receipt of help from a more competent teammate. In addition, the effect of race of teammate on respect and liking for him or her has been examined. The results of these studies are described below.

Design and Methods of the Experiments

The cooperative setting employed was the railroad management task described above in reporting the initial experiments on the contact hypothesis. However, in these experiments the three-man management team conducted its business during a series of five contiguous 15-minute sessions called *workdays;* the total experimental period, including time for team training and practice, lasted approximately 2 hours. There were three positions in the railroad business; these were filled by the research subject, one white confederate, and one black confederate.

The primary dependent variable in all experiments was the degree of respect and liking developed by the white research subject for one of the two confederates, for example, the one in the role of performing less competently. Respect and liking for the second confederate was also measured and used in some analyses. The instrument used to measure respect and liking contained 20 items. Nine items were adjective ratings from the evaluative dimension of the semantic differential (e.g., "friendly–unfriendly," "valuable–worthless"). Five items requested ratings of respect and liking; for example, subjects were asked whether they would like to be friends with the stimulus person. The final six items specified real-life choices for the subjects; for example, subjects were asked whether they would like to work again with the stimulus person on a similar project. The scale based on all 20 items exhibited high reliability (Cronbach's alpha = .95).

After the group task had been completed, subjects were separated from the confederates and a postexperimental questionnaire containing the respect and liking items was administered. (Other components of the questionnaire are noted in discussing the results.) Before they responded to the questionnaire the subjects were told that they would not meet with their groupmates again. Administration of the questionnaire was prefaced with guarantees of confidentiality and anonymity. While providing his ratings for each of the two confederates, the subject believed that he was being rated in other rooms by them.

The research participants in seven of the eight experiments were young white males, typically just out of high school, who had recently finished 6 weeks of basic training in the Air Force and were stationed at the Lowry Air Force Base in Denver awaiting technical training. The participants in the eighth experiment were white female students at the University of Colorado. The latter were selected from the more prejudiced extreme of a pool of persons on whom racial attitude measures were available, although they were unaware of this basis of selection. In the Air Force setting, however, it proved impossible to administer attitude scales without running the risk of sensitizing the participants to the experimenter's interest in the race variable. Instead, geographical background was used as an indicator of antiblack attitudes. Since public opinion surveys have shown that such attitudes are most prevalent in the rural South (Brink & Harris, 1964; Greeley & Sheatsley, 1971; Maykovitch, 1975), white airmen from this region were selected from the large pool of airmen who volunteered to participate.

In all except one of the experiments with airmen as research participants, the confederates were dressed in Air Force uniforms and identified as airmen from different sections of the large air base (10,000 men). In the other experiment, the confederates were presented as employees of other nearby U.S. government installations.

Each of the experiments employed either a three-variable or four-variable factorial design. Since a given variable sometimes appears in more than one experiment it will be most efficient to describe the results for each variable across all the experiments in which it appears.

Results of Experiments on Subject Attributes

Two variables were attributes of teammates: ethnic membership and competence to perform a share of the team task well enough not to handicap the team's performance. The effect upon respect and liking for a teammate of competence in carrying out his assignment has been studied in three experiments (Blanchard, Weigel, & Cook, 1975; Cook & Pelfrey, 1978; Mumpower & Cook, 1978). The competence variable was manipulated through the behavior of the confederates. At prescribed points throughout the experiment the confederate in the less-competent role made serious and costly errors in the performance of his duties. The errors, which were obvious to the subject, resulted in fines against the group and in significant losses in profits. In all three experiments the level of competence of the black confederate significantly affected the subjects' liking and respect for him ($p < .007$ to $p < .001$). In two of the three experiments a parallel effect was also found for the white confederate ($p < .001$).

The race of the less competent groupmate was unrelated to respect and liking for him in three of the five experiments in which the effect of this variable was assessed (Blanchard & Cook, 1976; Blanchard, Weigel, & Cook, 1975; Cook & Pelfrey, 1980). In two experiments respect and liking for the less-competent white teammate was greater than that for the less-competent black teammate (Cook & Pelfrey, 1978; Mumpower & Cook, 1978). These differences, although statistically significant ($p < .05$), were small in magnitude by comparison with the main effect for competence itself. (The reader should remember that these are statements of *relative* liking and respect. Lower scores for black groupmates imply neither low interpersonal attraction nor lesser attraction than would be felt for blacks outside the cooperating groups context.)

The effect of race on respect–liking for the more competent groupmate was also assessed. In the five experiments in which this was included, no relationship was found in four (Blanchard, Adelman, & Cook, 1975; Cook & Pelfrey, 1978; Cook & Pelfrey, 1980; Weigel & Cook, 1975). In one of the experiments respect and liking for the white groupmate was greater than for the black groupmate, $p < .005$ (Mumpower & Cook, 1978). This deviant result occurred in the only experiment with airmen subjects in which a monetary reward was not provided for success. In this same experiment the investigators also failed to replicate the otherwise well-established effect of success in elevating respect and liking for groupmates of both races (see below for additional discussion of this experiment).

The development of equal attraction for groupmates from own- and from disliked-ethnic groups is consistent with the results of experiments reported in earlier sections of this chapter. In most of those studies, white Anglos in cooperating interracial or cross-ethnic groups increased their respect–liking for minority groupmates and/or classmates and, in some cases, showed attraction for minority group associates equivalent to that for associates from their own ethnic background.

Results of Experiments on Task Success–Failure

A third variable in the series of experiments was the outcome of the group's assigned task. In natural settings task-oriented groups may succeed in achieving their goals or they may fail to do so. The latter can happen because the task is difficult, their competitors do well, they function ineffectively as a group, and for other reasons. Those in positions of responsibility, such as teachers, are likely to take ameliorative or preventive measures only if they are aware of the possible consequences of team success and failure for relationships among team members.

The effect of group success versus failure on respect and liking for teammates was assessed in seven studies. In five of these the research participants were told in advance that each would receive a $5 reward if their team exceeded the performance of comparison groups (Blanchard, Adelman, & Cook, 1975; Blanchard & Cook, 1976; Blanchard, Weigel, & Cook, 1975; Cook & Pelfrey, 1978; Cook & Pelfrey, 1980). The comparison groups for the success condition were Air Force officers, whereas for the failure condition, they were Army draftees. Pilot work had shown that for airmen these groups were high and low status, respectively. At the end of each work day (15 minutes) the team was given a report of its earnings and told where it stood in relation to the comparison group's progress during an equivalent period. In these five experiments, research participants in successful groups were found to have markedly higher respect and liking for their less-competent groupmates than did those in unsuccessful groups ($p < .001$). In the two remaining experiments (Mumpower & Cook, 1978; Weigel & Cook, 1975) the monetary reward was omitted. This change had major consequences: subjects in successful and unsuccessful groups no longer differed in the respect and liking they reported for their teammates.

The task-outcome variable had little effect on respect–liking for competent teammates. The single experiment in which it was statistically significant differed from the five in which it was not, in the absence from the teams of a confederate in the less-competent role. A possible inference from this is that when the team has a less-competent member the satisfaction accompanying success attaches to the person to whom lack of success might otherwise be attributed, that is, the less competent teammate. However, in the absence of such a teammate, this sense of satisfaction raises the respect and liking for both the competent teammates.

A possible interpretation of the contrasting outcomes for respect–liking for less- competent teammates emerged from a comparison of data from two experiments in which the variable of task outcome was studied (Mumpower & Cook, 1978). In one of the experiments there was a financial incentive for team success. In the other there was only the satisfaction of excelling the comparison group of Air Force officers—or the disappointment of falling below the performance of Army draftees. (Identical experimental procedures were followed and research subjects were drawn from highly similar subject-pools.) The comparison revealed that the difference between subjects' liking for their less competent teammates occurred only in the success condition: that is, members of teams who succeeded and received a financial reward liked their groupmates significantly more than did members of teams who succeeded but did not receive a financial reward. By contrast, failing teams in the experiment in which failure led to loss of financial reward did not differ in liking for teammates from failing teams not penalized by financial loss.

These results are of considerable significance for the management of cooperating interracial groups. If it were thought that failure resulting in loss of a salient, meaningful reward (for example, a financial reward) led to lesser attraction than when there was no possibility of such a reward, then those responsible for managing integrated activities would be reluctant to establish strong incentives for group performance. When group success could not be ensured they might fear that failure would inhibit the development of cross-racial respect and liking. The data from this program of research suggest, however, that when a reward contingent on group performance is obtained, the development of attraction for group members (including those from other ethnic groups) is facilitated; failure to obtain such rewards, however, has no significant inhibiting effect on attraction—although it may lessen the degree of satisfaction felt in the group experience.

Results of Experiments on the Subject's Role in the Group

Several variables examined in this series of experiments concerned aspects of the individual's own role as a team member: the level of participation by the individual in the group's operational decisions, giving help to a teammate who was delaying the group's progress, and the experience of needing and receiving help. Level of participation was controlled by the behavior of the two trained confederates. Throughout the course of the task, major changes in the way the group operated its business were needed in order to increase the group's efficiency. In the low-participation condition, the insights underlying these changes were "discovered" in discussions between the two confederates and then implemented by the confederate who was the "executive" officer. The subject neither participated in the discussions leading to the discovery nor exercised any say in the decision to implement it. By contrast, in the high-participation condition, the confederates guided discussions in such a way that the subject contributed to the discovery of the principles of efficient operation. Furthermore, the executive officer urged the subject to propose changes that the team should make. The confederates' skill in guiding the discussions in the direction required by the two treatment conditions was developed through an intensive training program and practice sessions with pilot subjects.

In one experiment (Weigel & Cook, 1975) subjects experiencing a high level of participation showed significantly greater respect and liking for groupmates than did subjects with a low participation level ($p < .001$). In another (Blanchard, & Adelman, & Cook, 1975), no difference was obtained. A possible clue to the discrepancy lies in the fact that, in the first experiment, success was not accompanied by a substantial reward whereas in the second it was. If, as has been shown in several of the experiments in this series, success accompanied by a meaningful reward is strongly associated with degree of satisfaction with the group experience—and this, in turn, with extent of respect and liking for groupmates—it seems likely that in the second experiment the success–failure factor controlled the variation in liking for groupmates while in the first it did not. (Recall that in the first experiment the success incentive was weaker than in the second.) This made it possible in the first experiment to measure the effect of level of participation; in the second, presumably, the effect was masked by the large difference associated with success versus failure.

The second of the individual role variables, that of helping a teammate, derives its interest in part from the repeated observation that members of interdependent groups are very likely to help one another when this is needed to promote a group goal. Interest in helping behavior has been spurred also by the discovery that less-competent teammates are liked and respected less than competent ones. This arouses concern that the experience of helping teammates who have difficulty will further lessen attraction for them. Such concern has special significance in recently desegregated schools in which minority members of cooperating groups may be the least well-prepared academically. We should emphasize at this point, however, that we are asking the question about helping within the context of cooperative groups—a context that relates helping to group success and consequent self-interest rather than to sympathy for others. We already know from many studies, including the student-team learning studies reviewed in the previous section, that persons in cooperating multiethnic groups form more positive cross-ethnic relationships than do comparable persons working individually and competitively.

In the several experiments in which helping effects were examined, helping was sometimes provided by the research subject and sometimes by one of the teammate confederates. Voluntary helping by the subject was induced by (1) experimenter endorsement of teammate helping in general, introduced during the instructions for the task, (2) requests for help by the less-competent confederate, and (3) if needed, subtle suggestions by the second confederate that helping would be appropriate. Because the inadequate confederate always performed his duties less competently, committing numerous errors, working extremely slowly, and causing losses and fines against the group because of his performance, the need for and extent of help was constant across conditions, regardless of the source of help. Helping behaviors included checking and correcting the less competent confederate's arithmetic, solving problems related to the manner in which his duties should be performed, and taking over several of his duties. The performance of the less-competent confederate improved somewhat over the course of the activity; his response to help was appreciative and accepting. Detailed scripts specified not only how and when each error should be made, but also when and the manner in which helping was to be induced.

In one experiment, subjects' respect and liking for less-competent teammates who were not helped (because the experimenter gave instructions that this was not permitted) was compared with that for equally incompetent teammates who were helped. The help was given either (1) "voluntarily" by the subject, (2) by the subject because the experimenter directed him to, or (3) by the more-competent third teammate, also because directed by the experimenter (Cook & Pelfrey, 1980). Personal helping, either voluntary or directed, was found to be associated with lower respect and liking for the less-competent teammate than was the absence of helping (for voluntary helping, $p < .02$; for direct helping, $p < .04$), whereas help given by a third teammate produced an intermediate level of attraction for the helped team-member. An interpretation of this result was suggested by the discovery that personal helping also led to lowered perceptions of the helped teammate's task competence and general ability.

One experiment in this series found a borderline difference in respect–liking ($p < .07$) in favor of personal helping over helping by a third teammate (Blanchard & Cook, 1976). This difference was paralleled by a significant difference between helping and nonhelping subjects in their feelings of satisfaction with their group experience and was interpreted as following from these feelings. However, in three subsequent experiments neither of these findings was confirmed (Cook & Pelfrey, 1978; Cook & Pelfrey, 1980; Mumpower & Cook, 1978). Hence, the weight of the evidence indicates that the effect on a team member's attraction to a helped teammate will be neither enhanced nor diminished by the fact that he is the personal agent of help.

Given this equivalence of personal and observed helping, it could still be the case that the consequences of personal helping might depend on whether such helping was given voluntarily or directed by someone in authority. Theoretical grounds for apprehension about directed helping come from reactance theory, that is, resentment at the dimunition of personal autonomy (Brehm, 1966) or from either dissonance or self-perception theory, that is, lower liking for the helped teammate if there are external motives for helping than if help is given by choice (Bem, 1972; Brehm & Cohen, 1962). Comparisons of voluntary and directed helping by the subject were made in two experiments (Cook & Pelfrey, 1980; Mumpower & Cook, 1978). No differences in respect and liking for the helped teammate were found. Moreover in these comparisons there were no differences on subjective experience variables such as satisfaction with the group experience or perceived competence of the helped teammate.

A final experiment related to a team member's role in a cooperating interracial group focused on the experience of being the recipient of help rather than the helper. Previous research on the recipient of help in dyadic relationships (Gross, Wallston, & Piliavin, 1979) as well as at the level of international aid (Gergen, Ellsworth, Maslach, & Seipel, 1975) has called attention to the possibility that persons receiving help may show a decrement in liking for their helpers. One of the circumstances under which this is likely to occur is that in which the helped person is unable to reciprocate the assistance he has received. Such reciprocation is difficult to arrange when team members are unequal in abilities needed for the group task. When such differences exist most help will be given by more-accomplished teammates and received by less-accomplished ones. This is especially likely to happen in learning teams in which all team members must master the same skills.

In the experiment in which he was the recipient of help, the research subject was put in the position of needing help by assigning him an overload of duties. Being unfamiliar with the duties of his teammates, he was unaware that this had happened. Consequently, when he found himself delaying the team's progress he experienced considerable embarrassment and discomfort. In one experimental condition the subject received no help despite the fact that one teammate regularly finished his duties early and was available to help; in this condition team members had been instructed to do only their own work. In a second experimental condition the early-finishing teammate voluntarily helped the subject by doing part of his work. In a third condition the same teammate helped under instructions to do so by the experimenter.

The results indicated there was a significant relationship between the helping condition variable and respect–liking for the helper ($p < .03$). Respect–liking under the voluntary helping condition was high whereas that in the absence of helping was low ($p < .05$). (Attraction for the helper in the directed helping condition was intermediate). Perceptions of the helper's competence and ability again appeared to be the mediating variables, that is, the direction of the relationship between level of perceived competence and respect–liking exactly paralleled that for the relationship between the helping variable and respect–liking. Examination of these relationships within race of the helping teammate indicated that white and black helpers contributed equally to the experimental effects. There was no interaction between type of help and race of helper, and within-race means indicated that both whites and blacks contributed to the main effects. One implication of this, of course, is that within the context of an interdependent group a prejudiced white who has received help from a black teammate will have greater respect and liking for him than would be the case if he has not received the help. This is the opposite of what we might have predicted from the conclusion reached in a recent review of research on the recipient of aid (Fisher, Nadler, & Whitcher-Alagna, 1982) that threat to self-esteem is the most likely antecedent of negative affect toward the donor. From our results we may infer that, even when the donor is a peer from a low-status group, unreciprocated help may be received without loss of self-esteem if this happens in the context of a cooperating group with a common goal.

Implications of the Experiments

In concluding this section exploring determinants of respect and liking within cooperating interracial groups, several precautions should be noted with regard to generalization to parallel phenomena in natural settings. These precautions have special relevance to programs employing classroom learning teams in multiethnic schools.

The primary warning, of course, is against a literal generalization. As always, the conclusions of laboratory studies should be taken only as directing one's attention to potential influential features of natural settings. Before conclusions are reached about determinants of cross-ethnic relationships in such settings, confirmatory studies should be carried out under field conditions.

The second warning is against generalizing to cooperating groups that do not share key features of the laboratory teams. For example, the latter often employ the motivating incentive of team competition for success and rewards. Although this is characteristic of student learning teams in many classrooms, in others, team achievement is either rewarded with praise in all teams or in none. To take a second example, the laboratory studies assessed the effect of team member competence on respect and liking under the condition that the team members's inadequacy handicapped team performance. Hence, the finding that competence had a major impact may not be relevant for learning teams in which lesser-achieving team members aid their teams considerably by contributing points based on improvement over their past achievement levels.

Given that we keep such precautions in mind, it would appear that several aspects of multiethnic teams in natural settings warrant the attention of teachers and other supervisory personnel. One of these is the success of the team in its assigned task. Success and the satisfaction that accompanies it clearly enhance team members' regard for their less-competent teammates.

A second is the competence of groupmates to carry out their team tasks. Lesser competence produces markedly less respect and liking and this effect may be exaggerated either by giving or observing the giving of help to the teammate who needs it. Several ways of ameliorating the impact of lower competence have already been explored, although not evaluated, for example, scoring team members for improvement, rewarding teams for the quality of mutual help, and so forth. One of the clear-cut advantages of learning teams that are heterogeneous in past achievement is that of accelerating achievement gains in the historically lesser-achieving students (and doing this without handicapping the progress of higher-achieving students). Because this argues strongly for a mix of more- and less-competent students, it is imperative to continue the search for ways to ameliorate the negative effects of relative competence on social relationships.

A third matter deserving continued examination is the participation of students in determining the working procedure of learning teams. The laboratory research suggests that cooperating groups should be urged to share decision making regarding working procedures. It is not known to what extent this is encouraged by teachers at the present time.

Finally, both the laboratory research and the field research indicate that race and ethnic background do not introduce insurmountable barriers to the development of cross-ethnic respect and liking in cooperating groups. When such respect and liking develops, however, it often fails to generalize to intergroup attitudes. Full realization of the potential of cooperating interracial groups would include generalized attitude change toward members of minority groups not present in the contact setting. It has long been supposed that negative attitudes survive intergroup contact experiences because of the tendency to perceive liked individuals as exceptions to the ethnic group from which they come. This would imply the need to introduce some element into the cooperative experience to serve as a ''cognitive booster'' for generalization to ethnic attitudes. Among the studies reviewed in this chapter, such an element was present only in the initial experiments on the overall contact hypothesis. The element in question was a guided conversation between the prejudiced research subject and a peer group confederate. The starting point in these conversations was shared disapproval of discriminatory treatment of a minority individual who had become a friend in the course of the experiment. When the peer group confederate voiced opposition to policies that permitted the discriminatory treatment in question, the research subject could relate this to the experience of her new minority group friend. Once this had happened the subject often joined in condemning the discriminatory policy or practice. Although a direct application of this procedure to a public school setting is not possible, it should be feasible to develop an analogous approach. For example, at some point during the second half of the school year the positive cross-ethnic relationships within cooperating work groups might be utilized to add a dimension of affect to discussion of the effects of prejudice and discrimination. A staff member or teacher might begin a discussion with a learning team on the topic of a previously assigned story, newspaper article, or movie that illustrates the problem of discrimination or social rejection. This person would attempt, gradually, to relate the abstract principles evolved in such a discussion to the discriminatory experiences of individuals in the team itself.

Summary

Experiments on multiethnic groups show that task interdependence induces cooperative, friendly behavior and develops liking and respect for one's groupmates. For white Anglo subjects these outcomes are enhanced by task success, participation in group decisions, the task competence of groupmates, and the experience of receiving needed help with one's own performance. With rare exceptions these favorable outcomes apply equally strongly to other-ethnic and to own-ethnic groupmates.

Cooperating multiethnic groups may also have the potential for bringing about generalized intergroup attitude change. The research described in this chapter suggests one avenue by which this potential may be realized. This is to make explicit for persons who have formed cross-ethnic friendships the fact that adoption of equalitarian social policies would make it less likely that their new friends would experience prejudice and discrimination. Such assistance in recognizing the relationship between societal practices and the welfare of individuals may be viewed as promoting the generalization of positive affect felt for other-ethnic friends to race-relations policies that would benefit them.

References

Aronson, E. *The jigsaw classroom.* Beverly Hills, CA: Sage, 1978.

Bem, D. J. Self-perception theory. In L. Berkowitz (Ed.), *Advances in experimental social psychology* (Vol. 6) New York: Academic Press, 1972.

Blanchard, F. A., Adelman, L., & Cook, S. W. Effect of group success and failure upon interpersonal attraction in cooperating interracial groups. *Journal of Personality and Social Psychology,* 1975, *31,* 1020–1030.

Blanchard, F. A., & Cook, S. W. Effects of helping a less competent member of a cooperating interracial group on the development of interpersonal attraction. *Journal of Personality and Social Psychology,* 1976, *34,* 1245–1255.

Blanchard, F. A., Weigel, R. H., & Cook, S. W. The effect of relative competence of group members upon interpersonal attraction in cooperating interracial groups. *Journal of Personality and Social Psychology,* 1975, *32,* 519–530.

Blaney, N. T., Stephan, S., Rosenfield, D., Aronson, E., & Sikes, J. Interdependence in the classroom: A field study. *Journal of Educational Psychology,* 1977, *69,* 121–128.

Brehm, J. W. *A theory of psychological reactance.* New York: Academic Press, 1966.

Brehm, J. W., & Cohen, A. R. *Explorations in cognitive dissonance.* New York: Wiley, 1962.

Brink, W., & Harris, I. *The negro revolution in America.* New York: Simon and Schuster, 1964.

Cook, S. W. Motives in a conceptual analysis of attitude-related behavior. In W. J. Arnold & D. Levine (Eds.), *Nebraska symposium on motivation.* Lincoln, NE: University of Nebraska Press, 1969.

Cook. S. W. *The effect of unintended interracial contact upon racial interaction and attitude change.* (Final report, Project No. 5–1320). Washington, D.C.: U.S. Department of Health, Education and Welfare, Office of Education, 1971. (Mimeo).

Cook, S. W., Gray, S., & Vietze, P. *Cooperation in the attainment of personal goals among mothers in an interracial pre-school.* Institute of Behavioral Science, University of Colorado, 1973. (Mimeo).

Cook, S. W., & Pelfrey, M. C. *Determinants of respect and liking in cooperating interracial groups: The effects of group success, race of less competent groupmate, and helping behavior.* Institute of Behavioral Science, University of Colorado, 1978. (Mimeo).

Cook, S. W., & Pelfrey, M. C. *Effects of voluntary and directed helping upon interpersonal attraction in cooperating interracial groups.* Institute of Behavioral Science, University of Colorado, 1980. (Mimeo).

DeVries, D. L., Edwards, K. J., & Slavin, R. E. Biracial learning teams and race relations in the classroom: Four field experiments on Teams-Games-Tournament. *Journal of Educational Psychology,* 1978, *70,* 356–362.

DeVries, D. L., Slavin, R. E., Fennessey, G. M., Edwards, K. J., & Lombardo, M. M. *Teams-Games-Tournament: The team learning approach.* Englewood Cliffs, NJ: Educational Technology Publications, 1980.

Fisher, J. D., Nadler, A., & Whitcher-Alagna, S. Recipient reactions to aid. *Psychological Bulletin,* 1982, *91,* 27–54.

Gergen, K. J., Ellsworth, P., Maslach, C., & Seipel, M. Obligation, donor resources, and reactions to aid in three nations. *Journal of Personality and Social Psychology,* 1975, *3,* 390–400.

Gonzales, A. *Classroom cooperation and ethnic balance.* Paper presented at the Annual Convention of the American Psychological Association, New York, 1979. (Mimeo).

Greeley, A. M., & Sheatsley, P. B. Attitudes toward racial integration. *Scientific American,* 1971, *225*(6), 13–19.

Gross, A. E., Wallston, B. S., & Piliavin, I. Reactance, attribution, equity, and help recipient. *Journal of Applied Social Psychology,* 1979, *9,* 297–313.

Johnson, D. W., & Johnson, R. T. *Learning together and alone.* Englewood Cliffs, NJ: Prentice–Hall, 1975.

Johnson, D. W., & Johnson, R. T. Effects of cooperative and individualistic learning experiences on interethnic interaction. *Journal of Educational Psychology,* 1981, *73,* 444–449.

Maykovitch, M. K. Correlates of racial prejudice. *Journal of Personality and Social Psychology,* 1975, *32,* 1014–1020.

Mumpower, J. L., & Cook, S. W. The development of interpersonal attraction in cooperating interracial groups: The effects of success–failure, race and competence of groupmates, and helping a less competent groupmate. *International Journal of Group Tensions,* 1978, *8*(3,4), 18–50.

Slavin, R. E. Student teams and achievement divisions. *Journal of Research and Development in Education,* 1978, *12,* 39–49.

Slavin, R. E. Effects of biracial learning teams on cross-racial friendships. *Journal of Educational Psychology,* 1979, *71,* 381–387.

Weigel, R. H., & Cook, S. W. Participation in decision-making: A determinant of interpersonal attraction in cooperating interracial groups. *International Journal of Group Tensions,* 1975, *5,* 179–195.

Weigel, R. H., Wiser, P. I., & Cook, S. W. The impact of cooperative learning experiences on cross-ethnic relations and attitudes. *Journal of Social Issues,* 1975, *31,* 219–244.

Wilner, D. M., Walkley, R. P., & Cook, S. W. *Human relations in interracial housing.* Minneapolis, MN: University of Minnesota Press, 1955.

9

Goal Interdependence and Interpersonal Attraction in Heterogeneous Classrooms: A Metanalysis*

David W. Johnson
Roger Johnson
and Geoffrey Maruyama

Goal Interdependence

Proponents of school desegregation and mainstreaming often assume that placing heterogeneous students (in terms of ethnic membership and handicapping conditions) in the same school and classroom will facilitate positive relationships and attitudes among the students. A lack of theoretical models and apparently inconsistent research findings, however, may have left the impression that desegregation and mainstreaming do not have constructive effects on interpersonal relations. It is our conclusion that a key factor in determining whether desegregation and mainstreaming promote positive or negative relationships among heterogeneous students is the way in which classroom teachers structure goal interdependence among students as they work on academic assignments. By structuring positive, negative, or no goal interdependence among heterogeneous students during academic learning situations, teachers can influence the pattern of interaction among students and the interpersonal attraction that results (Deutsch, 1962; Johnson & Johnson, 1975, 1980).

Lewin's (1935) theory of motivation postulates that a state of tension within

*This research was supported in part by the United States Department of Education, National Institute of Education, Grant = NIE G–90–0192.

an individual motivates movement toward the accomplishment of desired goals and that it is a drive for goal accomplishment that motivates cooperative, competitive, and individualistic behavior. Deutsch (1949, 1962), in formalizing a theory of how the tension systems of different people may be interrelated, conceptualized three types of goal structures that organize interpersonal behavior—cooperative, competitive, and individualistic. In a *cooperative* goal structure the goals of the separate individuals are so linked together that there is a positive correlation among their goal attainments. Under purely cooperative conditions an individual can attain his or her goal if and only if the other participants can attain their goals. Thus a person seeks an outcome that is beneficial to all those with whom he or she is cooperative linked. In a *competitive* social situation the goals of the separate participants are so linked that there is a negative correlation among their goal attainments. An individual can attain his or her goal if and only if the other participants cannot attain their goals. Thus a person seeks an outcome that is personally beneficial but is detrimental to the others with whom he or she is competitively linked. Finally, in an *individualistic* situation there is no correlation among the goal attainments of the participants. Whether an individual accomplishes his or her goal has no influence on whether other individuals achieve their goals. Thus a person seeks an outcome that is personally beneficial, ignoring as irrelevant the efforts of goal achievement of other participants in the situation.

Much of the research conducted on intergroup relations between 1930 and 1970 indicated that cooperative interdependence was a key aspect in structuring interaction among heterogeneous individuals in a way that promoted positive relationships. However, very little theorizing about the processes through which cooperative experiences promoted interpersonal attraction accompanied this research. Consequently, the research on desegregation and mainstreaming has lacked an appropriate theoretical framework within which to organize the existing research and to direct future research.

In response to this need for a theoretical framework, Johnson and Johnson (1980) proposed a model that posits:

1. There are preinteraction negative attitudes existing between students from different ethnic groups and between handicapped and nonhandicapped students.
2. Physical proximity is a necessary but not sufficient condition for a reduction of this negativity.
3. Depending on whether instruction is organized cooperatively, competitively, or individualistically, attitudes become more positive or more negative. A cooperative, compared with a competitive or individualistic, context promotes greater interpersonal attraction among heterogeneous individuals.

4. Part of the relationship between cooperative experiences and interpersonal attraction may be explained by more constructive interaction patterns, greater feelings of support and acceptance, more accurate perspective-taking, more differentiated view of others, higher self-esteem, and greater success promoted by cooperation.

Preinteraction Attitudes

The first proposition states that students from different ethnic groups and students who are handicapped and nonhandicapped have negative attitudes toward each other even before they interact. There can be little doubt that in the United States there is considerable prejudice and mistrust between members of majority and minority groups (Scott, 1979). When schools are desegregated, therefore, both majority and minority students have initial prejudices and negative attitudes toward each other. Own ethnic-group sociometric choices, for example, are more common than other ethnic-group nominations in the 1930s (Criswell, 1939), the 1940s (Radke, Sutherland, & Rosenberg, 1950), consistently throughout the 1950s and 1960s (Springer, 1953; Morland, 1966), and in the 1970s (Gerard, Jackson, & Connolley, 1975). Even when students are asked to rate their associates as preferred playmates or work companions rather than as best friends, own ethnic-group choices dominate other ethnic-group choices (Singleton & Asher, 1979). Furthermore, as students get older, there is an increasing solidification of own ethnic-group choices over other ethnic-group choices (Jelinek & Brittan, 1975; Singleton & Asher, 1979). White students often have negative stereotypes of black students and vice versa (Bartel, Bartel, & Brill, 1973; Duncan, 1976; Patchen, Hofman, & Davison, 1976; Sagar & Schofield, 1980).

Handicapped students are viewed by the nonhandicapped peers, furthermore, in negative and prejudiced ways, whether or not the handicapped children and adolescents are in the same or separate classrooms (Johnson, Johnson, & Maruyama, 1983). Many teachers and nonhandicapped students have negative evaluations of handicapped students and low expectations for their performance (Combs & Harper, 1967; Guerin & Szatlocky, 1974; Jones, 1972; Kelley, 1973). This appears to be the case regardless of the amount of time spent in close physical proximity (Gottlieb, Semmel, & Veldman, 1978), despite the fact that the behavior of handicapped students has often been documented to be no different from the behavior of nonhandicapped students (Semmel, Gottlieb, & Robinson, 1979), and that the presence of students with a history of engaging in inappropriate behavior (i.e., emotionally disturbed) does not necessarily create a disrupting effect on the regular class (Saunders, 1971). Furthermore the stigmas attached to handicaps transfer across settings. Even when learning-disabled children attend new schools with new classmates they continue to be rejected (Bryan, 1974; Siperstein, Bopp, & Bak, 1978).

When initial contact is made among heterogeneous students, first impressions are formed on the basis of potent characteristics that overshadow much observed behavior. Such first impressions may become monopolistic (taking into account only a few characteristics), static (remaining unchanged from situation to situation), and stereotyped; or they may become differentiated (taking into account many different characteristics), dynamic (in a constant state of change), and realistic, depending on nature of the interaction that subsequently takes place among the heterogeneous students. For many majority students and teachers, the perception of a student as being a member of a minority or as being handicapped results in a monopolistic, static, and stereotyped impression that leads to a negative evaluation and low expectations for performance. Once labeled as being a minority or handicapped, the strong possibility exists that the student will be rejected by majority and nonhandicapped classmates. The same is true for majority and nonhandicapped students being labeled by minority and handicapped students.

Physical Proximity

Physical proximity among heterogeneous students (in terms of ethnic membership and handicapping conditions) is the beginning of an opportunity, but like all opportunities it carries a risk of making things worse as well as the possibility of making things better. Physical proximity does not mean that heterogeneous students will like and accept each other.

The ethnic desegregation that has occurred in the United States' schools has produced a mixture of positive, negative, and neutral results (Carithers, 1970; Cohen, 1975; St. John, 1975; Stephan, 1978). Some reviewers conclude that negative outcomes occur more frequently than positive ones (St. John, 1975; Stephan, 1978), whereas others find mixed results with no predominant effect (Carithers, 1970; Cohen, 1975; Schofield, 1978). Relatively few cross-ethnic friendships seem to emerge in desegregated classrooms. Studies of direct interaction between majority and ethnic minority students indicate that contact within the same ethnic group is more frequent than cross-ethnic interaction among children from preschool (McCandless & Hoyt, 1961) through early adolescence (Schofield & Sagar, 1977). Elementary children are significantly more likely to nominate as friends other children from their own ethnic group than from other groups (Criswell, 1939). Third grade students rated a majority of same ethnic group peers as best liked (Singleton, 1974). Ethnic membership is found to be a significant grouping criterion even though the students and their families have chosen to attend an integrated rather than a segregated school

(Schofield & Sagar, 1977). Rosenberg and Simmons (1971) report that as many as 92% of even third choices for friends by black students in a desegregated school are within their own ethnic group. Among fourth, fifth, and sixth grades in a recently desegregated school (in a study that lasted over a year), association with members of the other ethnic group led to less acceptance of members of that group (Shaw, 1973). Even after several years of voluntary desegregation, black, white, and Mexican-American students tended not to associate with each other and relatively few cross-ethnic friendships emerged (Gerard et al., 1975).

Consistent with the research on ethnic integration, several studies indicate that placing handicapped and nonhandicapped students in close physical proximity (e.g., the same classroom) may increase nonhandicapped students' prejudice toward and stereotyping and rejection of their handicapped peers (Goodman, Gottlieb, & Harrison, 1972; Gottlieb & Budoff, 1973; Gottlieb, Cohen, & Goldstein, 1974; Iano, Ayers, Heller, McGettigan, & Walker, 1974; Panda & Bartel, 1972; Porter, Ramsey, Trembly, Iaccobo, & Crawley, 1978). On the other hand, there is also evidence that placing handicapped and nonhandicapped students in the same classroom may result in more positive attitudes of nonhandicapped students toward their handicapped peers (Ballard, Corman, Gottlieb, & Kaufman, 1977; Higgs, 1975; Jaffe, 1966; Lapp, 1957; Sheare, 1975; Wechsler, Suarez, & McFadden, 1975).

During the initial interaction between handicapped and nonhandicapped classmates, the nonhandicapped students may feel discomfort and show *interaction strain*. Davis (1961), Jones, (1970), Siller and Chipman (1967), and Whiteman and Lukoff (1964) found that physically nonhandicapped persons reported discomfort and uncertainty in interaction with physically handicapped peers. Nonhandicapped individuals interacting with a physically handicapped (as opposed to physically nonhandicapped) person have been found to exhibit greater motoric inhibition (Kleck, 1968); greater physiological arousal (Kleck, 1966); less variability in their behavior, the quick termination of interaction, the expression of opinions not representative of their actual beliefs, fewer gestures, and more reported discomfort in the interaction (Kleck, Ono, & Hastorf, 1966); and in the case of a person said to have epilepsy, greater maintenance of physical distance (Kleck, Buck, Goller, London, Pfeiffer, & Vukcevic, 1968). Jones (1970), furthermore, found that nonhandicapped college students who performed a learning task in the presence of a blind confederate (as opposed to a sighted confederate) reported stronger beliefs that they would have performed better on the task if the blind person had not been present, even when the actual performance data indicated that the presence of a blind or sighted person had no significant effects of performance.

The nonhandicapped students may not be the only ones who experience interaction strain in the mainstreaming situation. Comer and Piliavin (1972) found that handicapped students feel tension and discomfort when interacting with nonhandicapped peers. Farina and associates (1971) found that when mental patients believed that another person knew of their psychiatric history (as opposed to believing that another person did not know) they felt less appreciated, found the task more difficult, and performed at a lower level. Moreover, objective observers perceived them to be more tense, anxious, and poorly adjusted than the patients who believed that their partners did not know their psychiatric status. In a previous study, Farina, Allen, and Saul (1969) demonstrated that merely believing that another person views one in a stigmatized way creates expectations of being viewed negatively and rejected by others.

Another aspect of interaction between nonhandicapped and handicapped students is that the norm to be kind to the handicapped may result in overfriendliness by nonhandicapped students in initial encounters, which usually decreases with further interaction (Kleck, 1968). Handicapped students tend not to receive accurate feedback concerning the appropriateness of their own behavior and tend not to experience the normal interaction behavior of nonhandicapped peers (Hastorf, Wildfogel, & Cassman, 1979). They may as a result become socially handicapped and believe that the other people like them less the more they get to know them.

Both the research on cross-ethnic and cross-handicap interaction are consistent. Promoting constructive interaction and relationships requires something more than simple proximity. Placing heterogeneous students in the same classroom may be a necessary condition for promoting positive relationships, but it does not seem to be a sufficient condition.

Goal Interdependence and Interpersonal Attraction

The third proposition is that the type of goal interdependence used to structure classroom learning determines whether the attitudes of heterogeneous students toward each other become more negative or more positive. In order to determine the validity of this proposition a metanalysis was undertaken of all research known to the authors comparing the relative impact of cooperative, competitive, and individualistic situations on interpersonal attraction between individuals from different ethnic groups and between handicapped and nonhandicapped individuals in school settings. Given the disagreement among social scientists as to whether desegregation and mainstreaming can produce constructive relationships among heterogeneous students, and the limitations of the summary–impression methodology used in previous reviews, there is a need for a comprehensive review of the existing research that examines the magnitude of any differences between goal structures as well as the probability of finding such differences.

Metanalysis

Traditionally, research reviews in psychology and education have focused on the summary impressions gleaned by the reviewer from a reading of related studies. Metanalysis provides a quantitative alternative to this approach. Glass (1976) defines *metanalysis* as the combining of the results of independent experiments for the purpose of integrating the findings. A metanalysis is conducted on a group of studies that are related through sharing a common conceptual hypothesis or operational definitions of independent or dependent variables. A metanalysis usually (1) results in a significance level that gives the probability that a set of studies exhibiting the obtained results could have been generated if no actual relation existed, or (2) describes the degree of overlap between experimental groups. Thus, when used to examine a complete survey of studies from a specific research area, metanalysis procedures allow both a characterization of the tendencies of the research as well as information about the magnitude of any differences among conditions.

Metanalysis Procedures

Three methods of metanalysis were used: the voting method, the effect-size method, and the z-score method. For the *voting method,* each study was read carefully and all findings considered by the original author(s) to be significantly positive, significantly negative, or nonsignificant were counted. If a plurality of findings fall into one of these three categories, the modal category is declared the winner and assumed to give the best estimate of the direction of the true relation between the independent and dependent variables. Although this is a common method of reviewing literature, the practice of declaring the modal category ignores sample size. Large samples produce more statistically significant findings than do small samples. The voting method also disregards information about the strength and importance of relations among variables.

For the *effect-size method* the difference between the means of pairs of treatment conditions is divided by the within-group standard deviation of the treatment conditions, yielding a standardized mean difference (Glass, 1976). In this review, the estimate of the within-group total standard deviation is the sample size average of standard deviations for all groups weighted by condition. The effect size for each finding of a study is treated as an observation and examined statistically in relation to characteristics of the study. The effect size allows for the examination of the strengths of the relations between the independent and dependent variables.

The *z-score method* was originally developed by Strouffer (1949) and comprises the following steps: (1) compute the exact p value of the test statistic used by the author(s) of each study, obtaining a one-tailed p by dividing exact p value by two if a two-tailed test was reported; (2) compute the exact z-score of each p value; (3) sum these z scores, and divide this sum by the square root of the number of findings involved; and (4) refer this z-score back to the table and record the appropriate probability level. This probability describes the likelihood that the results of all studies are generated by chance. The z-score results are understated, as many studies did not include the specific t, F, or chi-square scores; therefore, nominal rather than exact p values have to be used. A failsafe n was also calculated; this procedure determined how many additional studies with summed z-scores totaling zero are needed to raise the overall probability level of a significant Stouffer score to nonsignificance.

Selection of Studies

Over a period of 3 years we engaged in several searches of the literature to obtain all relevant studies. Our metanalysis include every study that (1) was available to us, (2) contained interpersonal attraction data, and (3) compared two or more of the three goal structures. A few additional studies, in which we judged the independent variables to be cooperative, competitive, or individualistic, were included even though the conditions were not so labeled by the authors. Although the majority of the studies were field studies conducted in schools, any relevant laboratory study and field studies conducted in other settings (such as housing projects and work settings) were also included. No study was excluded on the basis of poor methodology or quality.

Conditions

Four conditions were compared. The first is *intragroup cooperation without intergroup competition* in which participants are structured to cooperate with each other through positive goal interdependence, resource interdependence, or reward interdependence. The second condition was *intragroup cooperation with intergroup competition* in which participants were not only structured to cooperate with other members of their group but also to compete with other groups to determine which group was best. *Interpersonal competition* was the third condition; this condition was structured so that all subjects were supposed to attempt to outperform the other subjects to see who was best. The fourth condition was *individual effort* in which subjects performed individually to reach a preset criteria for excellence.

Rater Reliability

Two judges independently read all of the articles and made the 20 ratings needed for each study. To compute interrater reliability 10 articles were randomly selected and the 200 ratings were compared. The interrater agreement was 95%.

Dependent Measures

Within the studies reviewed a variety of measures of interpersonal attraction were used. Both nomination and roster-rating sociometric measures appeared in the studies, as well as Likert-type items indicating liking, multiitem attitude scales indicating liking, attitude scales indicating perceptions of being liked or accepted by peers, and direct observation of positive interaction during instruction and free-time. These measures were basically for interpersonal attraction for any other subject in the condition.

Cross-Ethnic Relationships

Thirty-one studies were found and reviewed comparing the relative effects of two or more goal structures on interpersonal attraction between majority and minority students. These studies yielded 107 findings. The results are summarized in Table 9.1 and indicate:

1. There are not enough studies that have compared intragroup cooperation without intergroup competition and intragroup cooperation with inter-

TABLE 9.1

Metanalyses of Cross-Ethnic Findings[a]

	Voting			Effect size			z score		
	N	ND	P	M	SD	n	z	n	Fail-safe (n)
Cooperative vs. intergroup competitive	0	1	0	—	—	—	—	—	—
Cooperative vs. intragroup competitive	1	24	29	0.54	0.50	42	10.33	42	1617
Intergroup competitive vs. intragroup competitive	0	11	18	0.40	0.13	7	9.15	17	509
Cooperative vs. individualistic	0	5	22	0.68	0.41	17	10.08	19	695
Intergroup competitive vs. individualistic	0	1	3	0.60	0.18	2	5.36	3	29
Intragroup competitive vs. individualistic	1	2	4	0.21	0.71	7	3.05	7	17

[a]A positive finding favors the first goal structure of each pair; a negative finding favors the second goal structure of each pair.
N = negative, ND = no difference, P = positive.

group competition to draw any reliable conclusions as to their relative effects on cross-ethnic interpersonal attraction.

2. Intragroup cooperation without intergroup competition tends to promote more positive attitudes and relationships between majority and minority students than either interpersonal competition or individualistic efforts.

3. Intragroup cooperation with intergroup competition promotes more positive attitudes and relationships between majority and minority students than does either interpersonal competition or individualistic efforts.

4. Interpersonal competition tends to promote more positive attitudes and relationships between majority and minority students than do individualistic efforts.

Mainstreaming

Twenty-six studies comparing the relative effects of two or more goal structures on interpersonal attraction between handicapped and nonhandicapped students were found and reviewed. These studies yielded 105 findings. There were seven studies that contained data concerning both cross-ethnic and cross-handicap interpersonal attraction or cross-handicap and homogeneous interpersonal attraction. These studies are included in both analyses. There is, therefore, some overlap between the cross-ethnic and the mainstreaming findings. From Table 9.2 it may be seen that:

TABLE 9.2

Metanalyses of Mainstreaming Findings[a]

	Voting			Effect size			z score		
	N	ND	P	M	SD	n	z	n	Fail-safe (n)
Cooperative vs. intergroup competitive	0	0	0	—	—	—	—	—	—
Cooperative vs. intragroup competitive	0	9	14	0.86	0.54	16	7.88	17	373
Intergroup competitive vs. intragroup competitive	0	5	3	0.41	0.55	2	1.97	2	1
Cooperative vs. individualistic	0	6	48	0.96	0.55	30	15.39	33	2856
Intergroup competitive vs. individualistic	0	1	3	0.82	0.15	3	5.87	4	47
Intragroup competitive vs. individualistic	0	5	1	0.27	0.63	5	2.41	5	6

[a]N = negative, ND = no difference, P = positive.

1. There were no findings comparing intragroup cooperation without intergroup competition with intragroup cooperation with intergroup competition.
2. Intragroup cooperation without intergroup competition tends to promote more positive attitudes and relationships between handicapped and non-handicapped students than do either interpersonal competition or individualistic attitudes.
3. Intragroup cooperation with intergroup competition tends to promote more positive attitudes and relationships between handicapped and non-handicapped students than do either interpersonal competition or individualistic efforts.
4. Interpersonal competition tends to promote more positive attitudes and relationships between handicapped and nonhandicapped students than do individualistic efforts.

Findings from Other Studies[1]

In addition to studies involving desegregation and mainstreaming, we reviewed 48 studies comparing the relation of two or more goal structures on interpersonal attraction among homogeneous subject populations (in terms of ethnic membership and handicap status). These studies yielded 66 findings. No significant differences were found between the homogeneous and the heterogeneous results (Johnson, Johnson, & Maruyama, 1983). The results from all the studies, therefore, were combined to present an overall picture of the relative impact of the goal structures on interpersonal attraction and to permit further analyses. Because 7 of the studies reviewed had either both cross-ethnic and mainstreaming data of mainstreaming and homogeneous data, they were counted only once in the summary of the total findings. Overall, there were 98 studies yielding 251 findings, which are summarized in Table 9.3.

1. When cooperation with and without intergroup competition are compared, the results favor cooperation without intergroup competition.
2. When cooperation without intergroup competition is compared with in-

[1]When the number of findings are analyzed, studies that have numerous findings end up having more weight than do studies with only one measure of interpersonal attraction. In order to control for a possible bias resulting from studies with multiple measures of interpersonal attraction, the effect-size and z-score findings were reanalyzed so that each finding was weighted inversely proportionally to the number of findings from that study. This resulted in each study being given the same overall weight in the analysis. There are generally no significant differences between the unweighted and the weighted results and, therefore, the weighted results are not presented in this chapter (Johnson, Johnson, & Maruyama, 1983).

TABLE 9.3

Metanalyses of Total Findings[a]

	Voting			Effect size			z score		
	N	ND	P	M	SD	n	z	n	Fail-safe (n)
Cooperative vs. intergroup competitive	3	3	14	1.10	1.98	12	8.06	16	419
Cooperative vs. intragroup competitive	1	29	72	0.77	0.66	71	20.09	77	11,408
Intergroup competitive vs. intragroup competitive	0	19	23	0.57	0.62	14	12.17	30	1,611
Cooperative vs. individualistic	2	12	82	0.97	0.87	6	20.94	62	10,028
Intergroup competitive vs. individualistic	3	10	13	0.72	1.75	11	9.93	15	531
Intragroup competitive vs. individualistic	1	15	4	0.14	0.52	5	2.56	14	20

[a]Several studies contained both either cross-ethnic data and mainstreaming data or mainstreaming and homogeneous data. When conducting the metanalyses for the total findings, they were included only once and, therefore, there are nonsumming n's in this table. N = negative, ND = no difference, P = positive.

terpersonal competition and individualistic efforts, the results strongly favor cooperation without intergroup competition.

3. When cooperation with intergroup competition is compared with interpersonal competition and individualistic efforts, the results favor cooperation.

4. When interpersonal competition is compared with individualistic efforts the results somewhat favor interpersonal competition.

Relationship between Cooperation and Interpersonal Attraction

The fourth proposition of the Johnson, Johnson, and Maruyama model (1983) is that some of the relationship between cooperation and interpersonal attraction may be explained at least in part by (1) more constructive interaction patterns, (2) greater feelings of support and acceptance, (3) more accurate perspective-taking, (4) more differentiated view of others, (5) higher self-esteem, and (6) greater success promoted by cooperation. Since metanalysis results were not sufficient to address each of these propositions, relevant literature was examined for evidence in support of those mediating variables.

Promotive versus Oppositional or No Interaction

One reason why cooperative experiences may promote more interpersonal attraction among heterogeneous individuals than do competitive or individualistic experiences is that within cooperative situations participants benefit from encouraging others to achieve whereas in competitive situations participants benefit from obstructing others' efforts to achieve, and in individualistic situations the success of others is irrelevant. Hence, promotive interaction tends to be greater within cooperative situations than in competitive and individualistic ones (Johnson, Johnson, & Maruyama, 1983; Johnson & Johnson, 1983). There is, for example, more cross-ethnic and cross-handicap helping in cooperative than in competitive situations. Stuart Cook reviews many studies relevant to this proposition in Chapter 8, this volume.

One of the problems with the research on desegregation and mainstreaming is that there is very little evidence concerning the actual interaction taking place among heterogeneous students during instruction. Johnson & Johnson (1981a, 1982a), found that considerably more cross-ethnic interaction occurred within cooperative than in competitive or individualistic instruction situations, and this interaction was aimed at supporting and regulating students' efforts to learn and at ensuring that everyone was actively involved in the group's work (Johnson, Johnson, Tiffany, & Zaidman, 1983). Similarly, in a related series of studies on mainstreaming, cooperative learning experiences promoted more cross-handicapped helping than did competitive learning experiences, as well as the perception that the class was more cohesive (Johnson & Johnson, 1982b). More positive and less negative interaction with handicapped children occurred during instruction in cooperative than in competitive and individualistic conditions (Johnson & Johnson, 1982a; Johnson, Rynders, Johnson, Schmidt, & Haider, 1979; R. Johnson & Johnson, 1981; Nevin, Johnson, & Johnson, 1982; and Rynders, Johnson, Johnson, & Schmidt, 1980).

Even though heterogeneous students interact more frequently and in more positive ways with cooperative than in competitive and individualistic situations, that does not mean that the relationships formed within instructional experiences will generalize to postinstructional, free-time situations. A number of recent studies have demonstrated that when students are placed in postinstructional, free-choice situations there is more cross-ethnic interaction (Johnson & Johnson, 1981a, 1982a; Johnson, Johnson, Tiffany, & Zaidman, 1983) and more cross-handicap interaction (Johnson & Johnson, 1981a, 1981b, 1982a, 1982b, in press-a; Martino & Johnson, 1979) when students are in a cooperative rather than a competitive or individualistic situation. These findings are qualified by the fact that the teacher is always present, the free-time takes place in the same classroom the study is conducted in, and the situation does not involve new peers in new settings.

Perceived Peer Support and Acceptance

Cooperative learning experiences, compared with competitive and individu-alistic ones, have been found to result in stronger beliefs that one is personally liked, supported, and accepted by other students, that other students care about how much one learns, and that other students want to help one learn (Cooper, Johnson, Johnson, & Wilderson, 1980; Gunderson & Johnson, 1980; Johnson & Johnson, 1981a, 1981b, 1982b, in press-b; Johnson, Johnson, DeWeerdt, Lyons, & Zaidman, 1983; Johnson, Johnson, Johnson, & Anderson, 1976; Johnson, Johnson, Roy, & Zaidman, 1983; Johnson, Johnson, Tiffany, & Zaidman, 1983; Johnson, Skon, & Johnson, 1980; Skon, Johnson, & Johnson, 1981; Smith, Johnson, & Johnson, 1981; Tjosvold, Marino, & Johnson, 1977). Attitudes toward cooperation, furthermore, are significantly related to believing that one is liked by other students and to wanting to listen to, help, and do schoolwork with other students (Johnson & Ahlgren, 1976; Johnson, Johnson, & Anderson, 1978). Many of these same studies found evidence that students within cooperative learning situations or with cooperative attitudes perceive teachers as being more supportive and accepting, both academically and personally, than do students in competitive or individualistic learning situations. Finally, there is some evidence that cooperation promotes a lower fear of failure and higher feelings of safety than do the other two goal structures (Johnson & Johnson, 1975).

Accuracy of Perspective-Taking

A potentially important influence on the building of constructive relation-ships among heterogeneous students is their ability to take each other's per-spectives. *Social perspective-taking* is the ability to understand how a situation appears to another person and how that person is reacting cognitively and emo-tionally to it. The opposite of perspective-taking is *egocentrism*, the embed-dedness in one's own viewpoint to the extent that one is unaware of other points of view and of the limitations of one's perspective. A number of studies have found that cooperativeness is positively related to the ability to take the emotional perspective of others (Johnson, 1975a; 1975b; Murphy, 1937), al-though Levine and Hoffman (1975) found no relationship. Competitiveness, on the other hand, has been found to be related to egocentrism (Barnett, Mat-thews, & Howard, 1979). Cooperative learning experiences, furthermore, have been found to promote greater cognitive and emotional perspective-taking abil-ities than either competitive or individualistic learning experiences (Bridgeman, 1977; Johnson & Johnson, in press-b; Johnson, Johnson, Johnson, & Anderson, 1976; R. Johnson & Johnson, 1981; Lowry & Johnson, 1981; Smith, Johnson,

& Johnson, 1981; Tjosvold & Johnson, 1978; Tjosvold, Johnson, & Johnson, in press).

Differentiation of View of Others

Stephan and Rosenfield (1980) contend that varied experiences with different members of other ethnic groups should increase the complexity of one's perceptions of the ethnic group and undermine any belief that most members of the ethnic group fit one stereotype. Armstrong, Johnson, & Balow (1981) found a more differentiated view of handicapped peers resulting from a cooperative, compared with an individualistic, learning experience. Ames (1981) found that within a cooperative situation participants seemed to have a differentiated view of collaborators and tended to minimize perceived differences in ability and view all collaborators as being equally worthwhile, regardless of their performance level or ability. Johnson, Johnson, and Scott (1978) found that when given a choice of future collaborators, low achievers were picked by classmates just as frequently as high achievers.

Self-Esteem

There is evidence that self-esteem and prejudice are negatively related (Stephan & Rosenfield, 1978b, 1979; Trent, 1957) and increases in self-esteem are associated with decreases in prejudice (Stephan & Rosenfield, 1978a). It may be, therefore, that self-esteem explains some of the relationship between cooperation and interpersonal attraction among heterogeneous individuals. There is evidence that cooperative learning situations, compared with competitive and individualistic ones, promote higher levels of self-esteem and healthier processes for deriving conclusions about one's self-worth (Johnson, Johnson, & Maruyama, 1983). The impact of positive peer evaluations (frequently found in cooperative situations) may be especially powerful for individuals who have a history of failure (Turnure & Zigler, 1958).

Academic Success

There is considerable evidence that cooperative, compared with competitive and individualistic learning situations promotes higher achievement (Johnson, Maruyama, Johnson, Nelson, & Skon, 1981). A number of these studies, furthermore, find more on-task behavior and higher perceptions of personal success as a student in cooperative than in competitive or individualistic learning situations. Such achievement success has been found to foster the development of cross-ethnic liking (Blanchard & Cook, 1976; Blanchard, Adleman, & Cook,

1975; Blanchard, Weigel, & Cook, 1975; Cook & Pelfrey, 1981; Mumpower & Cook, 1978). In studies on homogeneous populations, liking for collaborators has been found to become progressively more favorable as the groups' success increases (Kahn & Ryen, 1972; Worchel, Andreoli, & Folger, 1977; Worchel & Norvell, 1980).

Summary and Conclusions

There seems to be considerable evidence that negative attitudes exist among heterogeneous (in terms of ethnic membership and handicapping conditions) students prior to their interacting with one another. When students from different groups are placed in the same classroom and school, these negative attitudes may become more extreme, or they may be modified into liking and respect for one another. One of the factors determining whether negative attitudes become more extreme or become positive depends on how instruction is organized. A cooperative, compared with a competitive or an individualistic, learning situation promotes greater cross-ethnic and cross-handicap interpersonal attraction. Part of the relationship between cooperative experiences and interpersonal attraction may be explained by the more constructive interaction patterns, the greater feelings of support and acceptance, the more accurate perspective-taking, the more differentiated views of others, the higher self-esteem, and the greater academic success promoted by cooperation (in comparison to competitive and individualistic learning situations).

Practical Implications

Social psychology has often been criticized for generating extensive but trivial knowledge. It has been noted that although social psychological theorizing and research has generated much information, they have not provided the concise answers required to solve even the simplest social problems. As can be seen from this chapter, one of the areas of inquiry within social psychology least deserving of such criticism is the study of cooperative, competitive, and individualistic situations. For not only have theory development, the validation of theory, and the summarization of existing knowledge been addressed, but the specific bridges to practice have also been built. The practical procedures for implementing cooperative learning procedures in the classroom and school have been specified and considerable training of teachers has taken place (Chasnoff, 1979; Johnson & Johnson, 1975: Lyons, 1980; Roy, 1982). The productivity of this area is largely due to the interaction between theory, research, and application.

Both desegregation and mainstreaming are required by law and are being implemented through North America. In many classrooms, however, desegregation and mainstreaming are being conducted in a highly individualistic way. Students work on their own, on individualized materials, and with a minimum of interaction with their classmates. The contents of this chapter provide some basis for recommending that cooperative learning procedures should be utilized in desegregated and mainstreamed classrooms if the goal of improved intergroup acceptance is to be achieved.

Acknowledgments

The authors thank Susan Green for her help and assistance in compiling these data. An earlier draft of this chapter was awarded the Gordon Allport Award for 1981 by the Society for the Psychological Study of Social Issues.

References

Ames, C. Effects of group reward structures on children's attributions and affect. *American Educational Research Journal*, 1981, *18*, 273–288.

Armstrong, B., Johnson, D. W., & Balow, B. Effects of cooperative versus individualistic learning experiences on interpersonal attraction between learning-disabled and normal-progress elementary school students. *Contemporary Educational Psychology*, 1981, *6*, 102–109.

Ballard, M., Corman, L., Gottlieb, J., & Kaufman, M. Improving the social status of mainstreamed retarded children. *Journal of Educational Psychology*, 1977, *69*, 605–611.

Barnett, M., Matthews, K., & Howard, J. Relationship between competitiveness and empathy in 6- and 7-year-olds. *Developmental Psychology*, 1979, *15*, 221–222.

Bartel, H., Bartel, N., & Brill, J. A sociometric view of some integrated open classrooms. *Journal of Social Issues*, 1973, *29*, 143–157.

Blanchard, F. A., Adelman, L., & Cook, S. W. The effect of group success and failure upon interpersonal attraction in cooperating interracial groups. *Journal of Personality and Social Psychology*, 1975, *31*, 1020–1030.

Blanchard, F. A., & Cook, S. W. Effects of helping a less competent member of a cooperating interracial group on the development of interpersonal attraction. *Journal of Personality and Social Psychology*, 1976, *34*, 1211–1218.

Blanchard, F. W., Weigel, R. H., & Cook, S. W. The effect of relative competence of group members upon interpersonal attraction in cooperating interracial groups. *Journal of Personality and Social Psychology*, 1975, *32*, 519–530.

Bridgeman, D. *The influence of cooperative, interdependent learning on role taking and moral reasoning: A theoretical and empirical field study with fifth grade students.* Unpublished doctoral dissertation, University of California, Santa Cruz, 1977.

Bryan, T. Peer popularity of learning disabled students. *Journal of Learning Disabilities*, 1974, *9*, 307–311.

Carithers, M. School desegregation and racial cleavage, 1954–1970: A review of the literature. *Journal of Social Issues*, 1970, *26*, 25–47.

Chasnoff, R. (Ed.). *Structuring cooperative learning in the classroom: The 1979 handbook.* Minneapolis, MN: Cooperative Network, 1979.

Cohen, E. The effects of desegregation on race relations. *Law and Contemporary Problems,* 1975, *39,* 271–299.

Combs, R., & Harper, J. Effects of labels on attitudes of educators toward handicapped children. *Exceptional Children,* 1967, *34,* 399–406.

Comer, R., & Piliavin, J. The effects of deviance upon face-to-face interaction: The other side. *Journal of Personality and Social Psychology,* 1972, *55,* 33–39.

Cook, S., & Pelfrey, M. *Determinants of respect and liking in cooperative interracial groups.* Paper presented at the American Psychological Association, Los Angeles, August 1981.

Cooper, L., Johnson, D. W., Johnson, R., & Wilderson, F. Effects of cooperative, competitive, and individualistic experiences on interpersonal attraction among heterogeneous peers. *Journal of Social Psychology,* 1980, *111,* 243–252.

Criswell, J. Social structure revealed in a sociometric test. *Sociometry,* 1939, *2,* 69–75.

Davis, F. Deviance disavowal: The management of strained interaction by the visibly handicapped. *Social Problems,* 1961, *9,* 120–132.

Deutsch, M. An experimental study of the effects of cooperation and competition upon group process. *Human Relations,* 1949, *2,* 199–232.

Deutsch, M. Cooperation and trust: Some theoretical notes. In M. R. Jones (Ed.), *Nebraska symposium on motivation,* Lincoln, NE: University of Nebraska Press, 1962, Pp. 275–319.

Duncan, G. Differential social perceptions and attribution of intergroup violence: Testing the lower limits of stereotyping of blacks. *Journal of Personality and Social Psychology,* 1976, *34,* 590–598.

Farina, A., Allen, J., & Saul, B. The role of the stigmatized in affecting social relationships. *Journal of Personality,* 1968, *36,* 196–182.

Farina, A., Gliha, D., Boudreau, L., Allen, J., & Sherman, M. Mental illness and the impact of believing others know about it. *Journal of Abnormal Psychology,* 1971, *77,* 1–5.

Gerard, H., Jackson, T., & Connolley, E. Social contact in the desegregated classroom. In H. Gerard & N. Miller (Eds.), *School desegregation.* New York: Plenum, 1975, 211–242.

Glass, G. Primary, secondary, and meta-analysis of research. *Educational Researcher,* 1976, *5,* 3–8.

Goodman, H., Gottlieb, J., & Harrison, R. Social acceptance of EMR's integrated into a nongraded elementary school. *American Journal of Mental Deficiency,* 1972, *76,* 412–417.

Gottlieb, J., & Budoff, A. Social acceptability of retarded children in nongraded schools differing in architecture. *American Journal of Mental Deficiency,* 1973, *78,* 15–19.

Gottlieb, J., Cohen, L., & Goldstein, L. Social contact and personal adjustment as variables relating to attitudes toward educable mentally retarded children. *Training School Bulletin,* 1974, *71,* 9–16.

Gottlieb, J., Semmel, M., & Veldman, A. Correlates of social status among mainstreamed mentally retarded children. *Journal of Educational Psychology,* 1978, *70,* 396–405.

Guerin, G., & Szatlocky, K. Integration programs for the mildly retarded. *Exceptional Children,* 1974, *41,* 173–179.

Gunderson, G., & Johnson, D. W. Building positive attitudes by using cooperative learning groups. *Foreign Language Annals,* 1980, *13,* 39–46.

Hastorf, Wildfogel, J., & Cassman, T. Acknowledgement of handicap as a tactic in social interaction. *Journal of Personality and Social Psychology,* 1979, 37, 1790–1797.

Higgs, R. Attitude formation—contact or information? *Exceptional Children,* 1975, *41,* 496–497.

Iano, R., Ayers, D., Heller, H., McGettigan, J., & Walker, V. Sociometric status of retarded children in an integrated program. *Exceptional Children*, 1974, *40*, 267–271.

Jaffe, J. Attitudes of adolescents toward the mentally retarded. *American Journal of Mental Deficiency*, 1966, *70*, 907–912.

Jelinek, M., & Brittan, E. Multiracial education I: Inter-ethnic friendship patterns. *Educational Research*, 1975, *18*, 44–53.

Johnson, D. W. Affective perspective-taking and cooperative predisposition. *Developmental Psychology*, 1975, *11*, 869–870. (a)

Johnson, D. W. Cooperativeness and social perspective taking. *Journal of Personality and Social Psychology*, 1975, *31*, 241–244. (b)

Johnson, D. W., & Ahlgren, A. Relationship between students' attitudes about cooperation and competition and attitudes toward schooling. *Journal of Educational Psychology*, 1976, *68*, 92–102.

Johnson, D. W., & Johnson, R. *Learning together and alone: Cooperation, competition, and individualization.* Englewood Cliffs, NJ: Prentice-Hall, 1975.

Johnson, D. W., & Johnson, R. Integrating handicapped students into the mainstream. *Exceptional Children*, 1980, *46*, 89–98.

Johnson, D. W., & Johnson, R. Effects of cooperative and individualistic learning experiences on interethnic interactions. *Journal of Educational Psychology.* 1981, *73*, 454–459. (a)

Johnson, D. W., & Johnson, R. The integration of the handicapped into the regular classroom: Effects of cooperative and individualistic instruction. *Contemporary Educational Psychology*, 1981, *6*, 344–353, (b)

Johnson, D. W., & Johnson, R. Effects of cooperative, competitive, and individualistic learning experiences on cross-ethnic interaction and friendships. *Journal of Social Psychology*, 1982, *118*, 47–58. (a)

Johnson, D. W., & Johnson, R. Effects of cooperative and individualistic instruction on handicapped and nonhandicapped students. *Journal of Social Psychology*, 1982, *118*, 257–268. (b)

Johnson, D. W., & Johnson, R. Mainstreaming hearing-impaired students: The effect of effort in communicating on cooperation. *Journal of Speech and Hearing Disorders*, in press. (a)

Johnson, D. W., & Johnson, R. Building acceptance of differences between handicapped and nonhandicapped students: The effects of cooperative and individualistic problems. *The Journal of Social Psychology*, in press. (b)

Johnson, D. W., & Johnson, R. The socialization and achievement crises: Are cooperative learning experiences the solution? In L. Bickman (Ed.), *Applied social psychology annual 4.* Beverly Hills, CA: Sage Publications, 1983.

Johnson, D. W., Johnson, R., & Anderson, D. Relationships between student cooperative, competitive, and individualistic attitudes and attitudes toward schooling. *Journal of Psychology*, 1978, *100*, 183–199.

Johnson, D. W., Johnson, R., & Johnson, J., & Anderson, D. The effects of cooperative vs. individualized instruction on student prosocial behavior, attitudes toward learning and achievement. *Journal of Educational Psychology*, 1976, *68*, 446–452.

Johnson, D. W., Johnson, R., & Maruyama, G. Interdependence and interpersonal attraction among heterogeneous and homogeneous individuals: A theoretical formulation and a meta-analysis of the research. *Review of Educational Research*, 1983, *52*, 5–54.

Johnson, D. W., Johnson, R., Roy, P., & Zaidman, B. Analysis of verbal interaction in cooperative and individualistic learning situations. Manuscript submitted for publication, University of Minnesota, 1983.

Johnson, D. W., Johnson, R., & Scott, L. The effects of cooperative and individualized instruction on student attitudes and achievement. *Journal of Social Psychology,* 1978, *104,* 207–216.

Johnson, D. W., Johnson, R., Tiffany, M., & Zaidman, B. Are low achievers disliked in a cooperative situation? A test of rival theories in a mixed ethnic situation. *Contemporary Educational Psychology,* 1983, *8,* 189–200.

Johnson, D. W., Maruyama, G., Johnson, R., Nelson, D., & Skon, L. The effects of cooperative, competitive, and individualistic goal structures on achievement: A meta-analysis. *Psychological Bulletin,* 1981, *89,* 47–62.

Johnson, D. W., Skon, L., & Johnson, R. Effects of cooperative, competitive, and individualistic conditions on children's problem-solving performance. *American Educational Research Journal,* 1980, *17,* 83–94.

Johnson, R., & Johnson, D. W. Building friendships between handicapped and nonhandicapped students: Effects of cooperative and individualistic instruction. *American Educational Research Journal,* 1981, *18,* 415–424.

Johnson, R., Johnson, D. W., DeWeerdt, N., Lyons, V., & Zaidman, B. Integrating severely adaptively handicapped seventh-grade students into constructive relationships with nonhandicapped peers in science class. *American Journal of Mental Deficiency,* 1983, *87,* 611–618.

Johnson, R., Rynders, R., Johnson, D. W., Schmidt, B., & Haider, S. Producing positive interaction between handicapped and nonhandicapped teenagers through cooperative goal structuring: Implications for mainstreaming. *American Educational Research Journal,* 1979, *16,* 161–168.

Jones, R. Learning and association in the presence of the blind. *The New Outlook,* December 1970, Pp. 317–329.

Jones, R. Labels and stigma in special education. *Exceptional Children,* 1972, *38,* 553–564.

Kahn, A., & Ryen, A. Factors influencing the bias towards one's own group. *International Journal of Group Tensions,* 1972, *2,* 33–50.

Kelley, H. The processes of causal attribution. *American Psychologist,* 1973, *28,* 107–128.

Kleck, R. Emotional arousal in interaction with stigmatized persons. *Psychological Reports,* 1966, *19,* 1226.

Kleck, R. Physical stigma and nonverbal cues emitted in face-to-face interaction. *Human Relations,* 1968, *21,* 19–28.

Kleck, R., Buck, P., Goller, W., London, R., Pfeiffer, J., & Vukcevic, D. Effect of stigmatizing conditions on the use of personal space. *Psychological Reports,* 1968, *23,* 111–118.

Kleck, R., Ono, H., & Hastorf, A. The effects of physical deviance upon face-to-face interaction. *Human Relations,* 1966, *19,* 425–436.

Lapp, E. A study of the social adjustment of slow learning children who were assigned parttime to regular classes. *American Journal of Mental Deficiency,* 1957, *62,* 254–262.

Levine, L., & Hoffman, M. Empathy and cooperation in four year olds. *Developmental Psychology,* 1975, *11,* 533–534.

Lewin, K. *A dynamic theory of personality.* New York: McGraw-Hill, 1935.

Lowry, N., & Johnson, D. W. The effects of controversy on students' motivation and learning. *Journal of Social Psychology,* 1981, *115,* 31–43.

Lyons, V. (Ed.). *Structuring cooperative learning in the classroom: The 1980 handbook.* Minneapolis, MN: Cooperative Network, 1980.

Martino, L., & Johnson, D. W. Cooperative and individualistic experiences among disabled and normal children. *The Journal of Social Psychology,* 1979, *107,* 177–183.

McCandless, B., & Hoyt, J. Sex, ethnicity and play preferences of preschool children. *Journal of Abnormal and Social Psychology,* 1961, *62,* 683–685.

Morland, J. A comparison of race awareness in northern and southern children. *American Journal of Orthopsychiatry,* 1966, *36,* 22–31.

Mumpower, J., & Cook, S. The development of interpersonal attraction in cooperating interracial groups: The effects of success–failure, race, and competence of groupmates. *International Journal of Group Tension*, 1978, *38*, 18–50.

Murphy, L. *Social behavior and child personality*. New York: Columbia University Press, 1937.

Nevin, A., Johnson, D. W., & Johnson, R. Effects of group and individual contingencies on academic performance and social relations of special needs students. *Journal of Social Psychology*, 1982, *116*, 41–59.

Panda, K., & Bartel, N. Teacher perception of exceptional children. *Journal of Special Education*, 1972, *6*, 261–266.

Patchen, M., Hofman, G., & Davison, J. Interracial perceptions among high school students. *Sociometry*, 1976, *39*, 341–354.

Porter, R., Ramsey, B., Trembly, A., Iaccobo, M., & Crawley, S. Social interactions in heterogeneous groups of retarded and normally developing children: An observational study. In B. Sackett (Ed.), *Observing behavior: Theory and applications in mental retardation*. Baltimore, MD: University Park Press, 1978, 311–328.

Radke, M., Sutherland, J., & Rosenberg, P. Racial attitudes of children. *Sociometry*, 1950, *13*, 154–171.

Rosenberg, M., & Simmons, R. *Black and white self-esteem: The urban school child*. Washington, D.C.: American Sociological Association, 1971.

Roy, P. (Ed.). *Structuring cooperative learning in the classroom: The 1982 handbook*. Minneapolis, MN: Interaction Books, 1982.

Rynders, J., Johnson, R., Johnson, D. W., & Schmidt, B. Effects of cooperative goal structuring in producing positive interaction between Down's Syndrome and nonhandicapped teenagers: Implications for mainstreaming. *American Journal of Mental Deficiency*, 1980, *85*, 268–273.

Sagar, H., & Schofield, J. Racial and behavioral cues in black and white children's perceptions of ambiguously aggressive acts. *Journal of Personality and Social Psychology*, 1980, *39*, 590–598.

St. John, N. *School desegregation*. New York: John Wiley, 1975.

Saunders, B. The effect of the emotionally disturbed child in the public school classroom. *Psychology in the Schools*, 1971, *8*, 23–26.

Schofield, J. School desegregation and intergroup relations. In D. Bar-Tal, & L. Saxe (Eds.), *The social psychology of education*. Washington, D. C.: Hemisphere, 1978, Pp. 329–363.

Schofield, J., & Sagar, H. Peer interaction patterns in an integrated middle school. *Sociometry*, 1977, *40*, 130–138.

Scott, R. *National comparisons of racial attitudes of segregated and desegregated students*. (Report 279). Baltimore, NY: Johns Hopkins University, Center for Social Organization of Schools, July 1979.

Semmel, M., Gottlieb, J., & Robinson, N. Mainstreaming: Perspectives on educating handicapped children in the public school. In D. Berliner (Ed.), *Review of research in education*, (Vol. 7) Washington, D.C.: American Educational Research Association, 1979.

Shaw, M. Changes in sociometric choices following forced integration of an elementary school. *Journal of Social Issues*, 1973, *29*, 143–159.

Sheare, J. *The relationship between peer acceptance and self-concept of children in grades 3 through 6*. Doctoral dissertation, Penn State University, 1975. (University Microfilms, N. 76-10, 783).

Siller, J., & Chipman, A. *Attitudes of the nondisabled toward the physically disabled*. New York: New York University, 1967.

Singleton, L. *The effects of sex and race in children's sociometric choices for play and work*.

Urbana, IL: University of Illinois, 1974 (ERIC Document Reproduction Service No. ED 100 520).

Singleton, L., & Asher, S. Racial integration and children's peer preferences: An investigation of developmental and cohort differences. *Child Development*, 1979, *50*, 939–941.

Siperstein, F., Bopp, M., & Bak, J. Social status of learning disabled students. *Journal of Learning Disabilities*, 1978, *11*, 49–53.

Skon, L., Johnson, D. W., & Johnson, R. Cooperative peer interaction versus individual competition and individualistic efforts: Effects on the acquisition of cognitive reasoning strategies. *Journal of Educational Psychology*, 1981, *73*, 83–92.

Smith, K., Johnson, D. W., & Johnson, R. Can conflict be constructive? Controversy versus concurrence seeking in learning groups. *Journal of Educational Psychology*, 1981, *73*, 651–663.

Springer, D. National-racial preferences of fifth-grade children in Hawaii. *Journal of Genetic Psychology*, 1953, *83*, 121–136.

Stephan, W. School desegregation: An evaluation of predictions made in Brown vs. Board of Education. *Psychological Bulletin*, 1978, *85*, 217–238.

Stephan, W., & Rosenfield, D. Effects of desegregation on racial attitudes. *Journal of Personality and Social Psychology*, 1978, *36*, 795–804. (a)

Stephan, W., & Rosenfield, D. The effects of desegregation on racial relations and self-esteem. *Journal of Educational Psychology*, 1978, *70*, 670–679. (b)

Stephan, W., & Rosenfield, D. Black self-rejection: Another look. *Journal of Educational Psychology*, 1979, *71*, 706–716.

Stephan, W., & Rosenfield, D. Racial and ethnic stereotypes. In A. Miller (Ed.), *In the eye of the beholder: Contemporary issues in stereotyping.* New York: Holt, Rinehart & Winston, 1980.

Stouffer, S. *The American soldier: Vol. I: Adjustment during army life.* Princeton, NJ: Princeton University Press, 1949.

Tjosvold, D., & Johnson, D. W. Controversy within a cooperative or competitive context and cognitive perspective-taking. *Contemporary Educational Psychology*, 1978, *3*, 376–386.

Tjosvold, D., Johnson, D. W., & Johnson, R. Influence strategy, perspective-taking, and relationships between high and low power individuals in cooperative and competitive contexts. *The Journal of Psychology*, in press.

Tjosvold, D., Marino, P., & Johnson, S. The effects of cooperation and competition on student reactions to inquiry and didactic learning. *Journal of Research in Science Teaching*, 1977, *14*, 281–288.

Trent, R. The relation between expressed self acceptance and expressed attitudes towards Negros and whites among Negro children. *Journal of Genetic Psychology*, 1957, *91*, 25–31.

Turnure, J., & Zigler, E. Outer-directedness in the problem-solving of normal and retarded students. *Journal of Abnormal and Social Psychology*, 1958, *57*, 379–388.

Wechsler, H., Suarez, A., & McFadden, M. Teachers' attitudes toward the education of physically handicapped children: Implications for implementation of Massachusetts Chapter 766. *Journal of Education*, 1975, *157*, 17–24.

Whiteman, M., & Lukoff, I. A factorial study of sighted people's attitudes toward blindness. *Journal of Social Psychology*, 1964, *64*, 339–353.

Worchel, W., Andreolli, V., & Folger, R. Intergroup cooperation and intergroup attraction: The effects of previous interaction and outcome of combined effort. *Journal of Experimental Social Psychology*, 1977, *13*, 131–140.

Worchel, S., & Norvell, N. Effect of perceived environmental conditions during cooperation on intergroup attraction. *Journal of Personality and Social Psychology*, 1980, *5*, 764–772.

Appendix A:
Studies Included in Metanalysis:
Cross-Ethnic

Ballard, M., Cornam, L., Gottlieb, J., & Kaufman, M. Improving the social status of mainstreamed retarded children. *Journal of Educational Psychology*, 1977, *69*(5), 605–611.

Blaney, N., Stephan, C., Rosenfield, D., Aronson, E., & Sikes, J. Interdependence in the classroom. *Journal of Educational Psychology*, 1977, *69*(2), 121–128.

Chalip, P., & Chalip, L. Interaction between cooperative and individual learning. *New Zealand Journal of Educational Studies*, 1978, *13*(2), 174–184.

Cook, S. The effect of unintended interracial contact upon racial interaction and attitude change. (Final Report 5-1320) Washington, D.C.: U.S. Department of Health, Education and Welfare, Office of Education, August, 1971.

Cook, S., Gray, S., & Vietze, R. *Cooperation in the attainment of personal goals among mothers in an interracial preschool.* Unpublished report, University of Colorado, 1973.

Cooper, L., Johnson, D. W., Johnson, R., & Wilderson, R. The effects of cooperative, competitive and individualistic experiences on interpersonal attraction among heterogeneous peers. *The Journal of Social Psychology*, 1980, *111*, 243–253.

DeVries, D., & Edwards, K. Learning games and student teams: Their effects on classroom process. *American Journal of Educational Research*, 1973(Fall), *10*(4), 307–318.

DeVries, D., & Edwards, K. Student teams and learning games: Their effects on cross-race and cross-sex interaction. *Journal of Educational Psychology*, 1974, *66*(5), 741–749.

Devries, D., Edwards, K., & Slavin, R. Biracial learning teams and race relations in the classroom: Four field experiments on teams-games-tournament. *Journal of Educational Psychology*, 1978, *70*, 356–362.

DeVries, D., Edwards, K., & Wells, E. *Team competition effects on classroom group process.* (Report 174). Baltimore, MD: John Hopkins University, Center for Social Organization of Schools, April, 1974.

Edinger, J., Bailey, K., & Lira, F. Effects of team play on racial prejudice. *Psychological Reports*, 1977, *40*, 887–898.

Edwards, K., & DeVries, D. *The effects of teams-games-tournament and two instructional variations on classroom process, students' attitudes, and student achievement.* (Report 172). Baltimore, MD: John Hopkins University, Center for Social Organization of Schools, 1974.

Fulcher, D., & Perry, D. Cooperation and competition in inter-ethnic evaluation in preschool children. *Psychological Reports*, 1973, *33*, 795–800.

Hansell, S., & Slavin, R. *Cooperative learning and interracial friendships* (Report 285). Baltimore, MD: Center for Social Organization of Schools, John Hopkins University, September 1979.

Hansell, S., Tackaberry, S., & Slavin, R. *Cooperation, competition and the structure of student cliques* (Report 309). Baltimore, MD: Center for Social Organization of Schools, Johns Hopkins University, April 1981.

Johnson, S., & Johnson, D. W. The effect of other's actions, attitude similarity, and race on attraction towards others. *Human Relations*, 1972, *25*, 121–130.

Johnson, D. W., & Johnson, R. Effects of cooperative and individualistic learning experiences on interethnic interaction. *Journal of Educational Psychology*, 1981, *73*, 454–459. (a)

Johnson, D. W., & Johnson, R. Effects of cooperative, competitive, and individualistic learning experiences on cross-ethnic interaction and friendships. *Journal of Social Psychology*, 1982, *118*, 47–58.

Johnson, D. W., Johnson, R., Tiffany, M., & Zaidman, B. Are low achievers disliked in a cooperative situation? A test of rival theories in a mixed ethnic situation. *Contemporary Educational Psychology*, 1983, *8*, 189–200.

Katz, I., Goldston, J., & Benjamin, L. Behavior and productivity in biracial work groups. *Human Relations*, 1958, *11*, 123–141.

Rogers, M., Miller, N., & Hennigan, K. Cooperative games as an intervention to promote cross-racial acceptance. *American Educational Research Journal*, 1981, *18*, 513–516.

Schofield, J. The impact of positively structured contact on intergroup behavior: Does it last under adverse conditions? *Social Psychological Quarterly*, 1979, *42*(3), 280–284.

Schofield, J., & Sagar, H. Peer interaction patterns in an integrated middle school. *Sociometry*, 1977, *40*(2), 130–138.

Silverthorne, C., Chelune, G., & Imada, A. The effects of competition and cooperation on level of prejudice. *Journal of Social Psychology*, 1974, *92*, 293–301.

Slavin, R. How student learning teams can integrate the desegregated classroom. *Integrated Education*, 1977, *15*, 56–58. (a)

Slavin, R. *Using student learning teams to desegregate the classroom* (Report *321*) Baltimore, MD: Center for Social Organization of Schools, Johns Hopkins University, 1977. (b)

Slavin, R. Effects of biracial learning teams on cross-racial friendships. *Journal of Educational Psychology*, 1979, *71*, 381–387.

Slavin, R., & Oickle, E. Effects of cooperative learning teams on student achievement and race relations: Treatment by race interactions. *Sociology of Education*, 1981, *54*, 174–180.

Weigel, R., Wiser, P., & Cook, S. The impact of cooperative learning experiences on cross-ethnic relations and attitudes. *Journal of Social Issues*, 1975, *31*, 219–243.

Wilner, D., Walkey, R., & Cook, S. Residential proximity intergroup relations in public housing project. *Journal of Social Issues*, 1952, *8*, 45–69.

Witte, P. *The effects of group reward structure on interracial acceptance, peer tutoring, and academic performance.* Unpublished dissertation, Washington University, St. Louis, Missouri: 1972.

Appendix B:
Studies Included in Metanalysis:
Mainstreaming

Alden, S., Pettigrew, L., & Skiba, E. The effect of individual-contingent group reinforcement on popularity. *Child Development*, 1970, *41*, 1191–1196.

Armstrong, B., Balow, B., & Johnson, D. Cooperative goal structures as a means of integrating learning disabled with normal progress elementary school pupils. *Contemporary Educational Psychology*, 1981, *6*, 102–109.

Ballard, M., Corman, L., Gottlieb, J., & Kaufman, M. Improving the social status of mainstreamed retarded children. *Journal of Educational Psychology*, 1977, *69*, 605–611.

Chennault, M. Improving the social acceptance of unpopular educable mentally retarded students in special classes. *American Journal of Mental Deficiency*, 1967, *72*, 455–458.

Colby, M. The early development of social attitudes toward exceptional children. *Journal of Genetic Psychology*, 1944, *64*, 105–110.

Cooper, L., Johnson, D. W., Johnson, R., & Wilderson, R. The effects of cooperative, competitive, and individualistic experiences on interpersonal attraction among heterogeneous peers. *The Journal of Social Psychology*, 1980, *111*, 243–253.

Drabman, R., Spitalnik, R., & Spitalnik, K. Sociometric and disruptive behavior as a function of four types of token reinforcement programs. *Journal of Applied Behavior Analysis*, 1974, *7*, 93–101.

Fahl, M. Emotionally disturbed children: Effects of cooperative and competitive activity on peer interaction. *American Journal of Occupational Therapy*, 1970, *24*, 31–33.

Johnson, D. W., & Johnson, R. The integration of the handicapped into the regular classroom: Effects of cooperative and individualistic instruction. *Contemporary Educational Psychology*, 1981, *6*, 344–353.

Johnson, D. W., & Johnson, R. Effects of cooperative and individualistic instruction on handicapped and nonhandicapped students. *Journal of Social Psychology*, 1982, *118*, 257–268.

Johnson, D. W., & Johnson, R. Mainstreaming hearing-impaired students: The effect of effort in communicating on cooperation. *Journal of Speech and Hearing Disorders*, in press. (a)

Johnson, D. W., & Johnson, R. Building acceptance of differences between handicapped and nonhandicapped students: The effects of cooperative and individualistic problems. *The Journal of Social Psychology*, in press. (b)

Johnson, R., & Johnson, D. W. Building friendships between handicapped and nonhandicapped students: Effects of cooperative and individualistic instruction. *American Educational Research Journal*, 1981, *18*, 415–424. (a)

Johnson, R., & Johnson, D. W. Effects of cooperative and competitive learning experiences on interpersonal attraction between handicapped and nonhandicapped students. *Journal of Social Psychology*, 1981, *116*, 211–219. (b)

Johnson, R., & Johnson, D. W. Effects of cooperative, competitive, and individualistic learning experiences on cross-handicap relations in social development. *Exceptional Children*, 1983, *49*, 323–331.

Johnson, R., Johnson, D. W., DeWeerdt, N., Lyons, V., & Zaidman, B. Integrating educable mentally retarded seventh-grade students into constructive relationships with nonhandicapped peers in science class. *American Journal of Mental Deficiency*, 1983, *87*, 611–618.

Johnson, R., Rynders, J. R., Johnson, D. W., Schmidt, B., & Haider, S. Interaction between handicapped and nonhandicapped teenagers as a function of situational goal structuring: Implications for mainstreaming. *American Educational Research Journal*, 1979, *16*, 161–167.

Madden, N., & Slavin, R. Effects of cooperative learning on the social acceptance of mainstreamed academically handicapped students. *Journal of Special Education*, in press.

Martino, L., & Johnson, D. W. Cooperative and individualistic experiences among disabled and normal children. *The Journal of Social Psychology*, 1979, *107*, 177–183.

Nevin, A., Johnson, D. W., & Johnson, R. Effects of group and individual contingencies on academic performance and social relations of special needs students. *Journal of Social Psychology*, 1982, *116*, 41–59.

Rucker, C., & Vincenzo, R. Maintaining social acceptance gains made by mentally retarded children. *Exceptional Children*, 1970, *36*(9), 679–680.

Rynders, J., Johnson, R., Johnson, D. W., & Schmidt, B. Effects of cooperative goal structuring in producing positive interactions between Down's Syndrome and nonhandicapped teenagers: Implications for mainstreaming. *American Journal of Mental Deficiency*, 1980, *85*, 268–273.

Slavin, R. A student team approach to teaching adolescents with special emotional and behavioral needs. *Psychology in the Schools*, 1977, *14*, 76–84.

Slavin, R., & Madden, N., & Leavy, M. Effects of cooperative learning and individualistic instruction on the social acceptance, achievement, and behavior of mainstreamed academically handicapped students. *Exceptional Children*, in press.

Smith, K., Johnson, D. W., & Johnson, R. Effects of cooperative and individualistic instruction on the achievement of handicapped, regular and gifted students. *Journal of Social Psychology*, 1982, *116*, 277–283.

Worchel, S., Andreoli, V., & Folger, R. Intergroup cooperation and intergroup attraction: The effect of previous interaction and outcome of combined effort. *Journal of Experimental Social Psychology*, 1977, *13*, 131–140.

10

Intergroup Acceptance in Classroom and Playground Settings*

Marian Rogers
Karen Hennigan
Craig Bowman
and Norman Miller

As others have noted (Pettigrew, Useem, Normand, & Smith, 1973), school desegregation typically occurs in an environmental context that fails to meet the criteria that Allport (1954) delineated as necessary for producing intergroup social acceptance. The original *contact hypothesis* proposed that within the contact situation ingroup and outgroup members must share equal status, cooperative interdependence, intimate as opposed to superficial contact, and receive social approval from authority figures for their intergroup contact. The academic and social class disparities that typically exist between majority and minority students, however, often preclude equal status contact. Additionally the academic environment provided by most public school systems fosters competitive or individualistic interactions, not cooperative relations. Moreover overt hostility toward racial–ethnic minority groups by authority figures (including parents) often accompanies nonvoluntary desegregation.

In light of these circumstances it is not surprising that many studies show that school desegregation frequently exerts a minimal, if not negative, influence on intergroup relations. These pessimistic findings stem from studies spanning both space and time and using a variety of methodological techniques. Gerard and Miller's (1975) longitudinal study, for example, reveals that school deseg-

*A grant in Aid from the Society for the Psychological Study of Social Issues helped support the research reported in this chapter.

213

regation in Riverside, California promoted ethnic encapsulation in sociometric choice over time and Rist's (1978) ethnographic study shows that whites exhibited pronounced interracial hostility towards black children. Studies using quantitative observational procedures report similar findings (e.g., Schofield & Sagar, 1977).

Preliminary Field Studies

We recently conducted a pair of observational studies in two desegregated classrooms that came close to meeting at least two of the conditions specified by Allport's contact theory (1954). First, within the limitations set by our present day social environment, the children shared equal status. Most of the children had similarly high academic abilities; indeed, most of them had I.Q. levels exceeding 132. Many of them also shared an upper-middle class background. Admittedly, in comparison to upper-middle class white children, upper-middle class black children typically are still relatively disadvantaged. In this case, however, both groups held a similar economic position within their respective racial–ethnic group, and by virtue of this equivalence it seems reasonable to assume that they probably shared many similar attitudes and behaviors.

Second, the significant authority figures in the situation were unusually supportive of desegregation. During the course of litigation that eventually produced a court-ordered busing plan, the parents of children from two predominantly white suburban schools initiated contact with parents of children attending a predominantly black school located over 20 miles away and together representatives from the three schools drew up a voluntary integration plan that received district approval. The plan was formulated by cooperative interactions between the parents and the school administrators. The resistance and hostile rhetoric that often accompanies court initiated desegregation was essentially absent. The plan specified that each of the upper-level classrooms in the three schools combine to form two integrated classrooms. Each integrated classroom spent one half of each school year in a black receiving school and the other half at a white receiving school.

Even under these conditions, we found that children resegregated themselves by racial group during their classroom and recess activities. In comparison to girls, however, boys exhibited less ingroup preference, and their prosocial cross-racial behavior was more strongly affected by the setting (classroom versus playground). Among white males in particular the percentage of their positive interactions that was cross-racial was substantially greater on the playground (approximately 50%) than in the classroom (approximately 30%). Among black girls hostility was suppressed in the classroom but was dramatically higher in the play yard. White girls exhibited virtually no cross-racial interaction in either setting. Many other studies also reveal that boys typically display greater outgroup acceptance in desegregated settings than do girls (e.g., Jansen & Gallagher, 1966; Singleton & Asher, 1977; Schofield & Sagar, 1977). These findings intrigued us because we believed that if we could understand the factors that contributed to the interracial behavior of males we could potentially reduce the greater ethnocentrism displayed by females.

Researchers have offered at least two related hypotheses to explain the difference in male and female cross-racial interactions. Hallinan (1980) suggests that characteristics associated with the social network of female relationships impede intergroup contact. This perspective receives support from data showing that, in contrast to girls, boys interact in larger social units and display a stronger propensity to accept newcomers (Lever, 1974).

A second explanation suggests that the importance that boys place on physical competition and prowess leads to intergroup contact whereas girls' interest in their beauty and attractiveness to the opposite sex detracts from it (Schofield and Sagar, 1977). This viewpoint argues that for males to achieve physical superiority they must prove their dominance over both ingroup and outgroup members. In contrast females need only attract boys to attain status and thus they can shun female outgroup members.

Based on our own formal and informal observations, we hypothesized that the observed sex difference in intergroup acceptance is due largely to the nature of the physical games boys learn to play. The structure of males' organized activities at recess generally requires more participants than the usual number of available ingroup members. Thus simply because black and white boys need each other to form complete sports teams, they are more likely than girls to interact across racial barriers at recess. More important however is the fact that the goal structure of males' sport activities fosters further contact between team members representing different racial groups. Team sports have a mixed reward structure in that both competition and cooperation are elicited. In a game of basketball or softball each team member is expected to contribute his best effort to achieve a goal that all team members share in common. Interteam bickering or other acts of hostility will only result in defeat for all team members. Thus in accord with Sherif's (1961) analysis, teammates should show enhanced attraction towards one another across time.

The positive goal-interdependence invoked by team sports corresponds structurally to cooperative learning procedures such as Teams-Games-Tournaments (TGT) (DeVries & Edwards, 1976) and Student Teams and Academic Divisions (STAD) (Slavin, 1977), which require within group cooperation and between group competition. Experimental tests of the effectiveness of both STAD and TGT show that, in comparison to children in control classes, (who presumably engage in primarily individualistic or competitive tasks), students participating in cooperative learning teams exhibit wider friendship circles and greater mutual concern for each other (DeVries & Edwards 1974), stronger group cohesiveness (DeVries & Slavin, 1976), and increased interracial contact (Slavin, 1977).

Thus we believed that the goal structure of the sports males play at recess contributes to the greater prosocial interracial contact they display relative to females. To begin to test this hypothesis, we conducted an exploratory study that examined the influence of cooperative games on girls' cross-racial interaction (Rogers, Miller & Hennigan, 1981). Under the direction of an interracial team of activity directors, sixth-grade girls from a desegregated classroom were actively encouraged to participate in specially designed cooperative games at recess for a 2-week period. As Table 10.1 indicates, observations collected prior to the intervention during recess showed that only 13% of the social interactions of black girls, and 2% of those of white girls were with members of a racial outgroup. In contrast, observations gathered during the intervention period, (on days when the games were not in progress) revealed that 74% of the social interactions of black girls and 65% of those of white girls crossed racial boundaries. Analysis of the difference between these two periods suggests that the games had a strong, immediate, and positive effect on intergroup interaction.

During the two weeks following the games, the girls continued to make cross-racial choices in their peer interaction. At recess, 66% of the interactions of black girls and 43% of those of white girls were cross-racial. Thus it appeared that 2 weeks after the intervention, cooperative games continued to have an impact on interracial contact, especially for white girls. Four weeks after the intervention, however, the interracial behavior of black females had substantially declined. Although 16% of their interaction choices involved outgroup members, this level did not differ from their pretreatment rate. In contrast, white females did show marginal evidence of an increase from their pretreatment rates; 25% of their recess interactions continued to be directed towards black children.

TABLE 10.1

Mean Proportion of Cross-Racial Interactions[a]

Race	Time period			
	2 Weeks before	Concurrent	2 Weeks after	4 Weeks after
White	.02 (.008)	.65 (.20)*	.43 (.098)*	.25 (.08)*
Black	.12 (.03)	.75 (.06)*	.63 (.10)*	.14 (.05)
Total	.09 (.06)	.71 (.13)*	.56 (.14)*	.17 (.022)*

[a] Standard deviations are in parentheses.
*Significantly different from baseline rate at $p < .01$

The results of our pilot effort indicate that cooperatively oriented games are potentially effective for increasing intergroup contact among young girls. The duration of the effect, however, is relatively short-lived and the absence of a control group made our findings somewhat equivocal. Thus we decided to undertake an extended field experiment to test the hypothesis further and to gain some understanding of the processes that underlie the relationship between cooperative interaction and intergroup acceptance.

A Field Experiment

Influenced by the increasing amount of research showing that social categorization processes affect intergroup attitudes and behaviors, we hypothesized that the cognitive processes associated with categorization mediate the relationship between cooperation and ingroup bias. In particular, researchers have identified two concomitants of social categorization that may promote ingroup bias: (1) perceptions of outgroup homogeneity, and (2) perceptions of similarity to ingroup members and dissimilarity to outgroup members.

A series of studies by Park and Rothbart (1982) indicates that outgroup members are perceived as possessing stereotypic traits more consistently than are members of one's own group. Perceptions of outgroup homogeneity may be one basis for the negative evaluations and lack of social acceptance of outgroup members. Recent research by Linville (Linville & Jones, 1980; Linville, 1982) demonstrates that we tend (1) to view outgroup members in a more cognitively simplistic fashion than ingroup members; and (2) to be more extreme in our evaluations of them. In explaining these findings, Linville suggests that positive or negative information about a person has a greater impact on judgments when applied to a member of a group with whom one has little, as opposed to extensive contact. Thus equally positive information about ingroup and outgroup members results in outgroup favoritism whereas equally negative information produces ingroup favoritism. Alternatively, Wilder and Allen (1978) suggest that perceiving outgroup members as a homogeneous unit serves to deindividuate them. This in turn allows them to become easy targets for hostility.

Turning to the second categorization process, a number of studies show that perceiving one's self as similar to ingroup members and dissimilar to outgroup members promotes ingroup favoritism. In the absence of specific information, individuals tend to assume that members of outgroups are dissimilar to themselves and to seek out information that confirms ingroup similarity and intergroup dissimilarity (Wilder and Allen, 1978). Based on extensive evidence that people feel more attracted to similar than dissimilar others (e.g., Byrne, 1969), perceived similarity with ingroup members should lead to preferences for interactions with them in preference to members of outgroups.

Cooperative interaction may reduce ingroup bias by affecting both of these social categorization processes. Extended contact under conditions of interdependence should provide opportunities for acquiring information about outgroup members that counteracts both biases. Because the interaction takes place around common interests, similarities between the self and outgroup teammates should be evident. In addition, the necessity to attend and respond to outgroup members should reveal individual differences among them that reduce stereotypic homogenization.

Given this background of theory and research we began fieldwork in two desegregated schools, expecting to find the following characteristics in intergroup relations between black and white children:

1. Ingroup members favor themselves over outgroup members in their evaluative ratings and social interactions.
2. Outgroup members are perceived more homogeneously than are ingroup members.
3. Perceptions of outgroup homogeneity are positively associated with social rejection of outgroup members.
4. Outgroup members are perceived as less similar to self than ingroup members.
5. Perceptions of similarity of self to ingroup members and dissimilarity to outgroup members are positively associated with social rejection of outgroup members.

In comparison to these initial conditions, we expected that cooperative games, as opposed to individualistic games, would (1) reduce perceptions of outgroup homogeneity, dissimilarity of self with outgroup members, and similarity of self with ingroup members, and (2) promote intergroup acceptance.

Our research design included eight classes of fifth and sixth grade children at two schools in the urban Los Angeles area. One school was in its third year of desegregation. We gathered data during the second semester of the school's participation in a mandatory desegregation plan that entailed busing upper-middle class white children to a predominately lower-middle class black school. During the previous 2 years, the school had participated in a voluntary desegregation effort that involved students from the same schools engaged in the mandatory plan. The second school was also part of the mandatory desegregation plan, but in this case lower-middle class black and Hispanic students were bused to a predominantly middle class white and Asian school. Thus the two schools differed dramatically on a number of dimensions of desegregation, a condition we hoped would contribute to the external validity of any effects obtained from our experimental intervention.

Description of Intervention

The pretest–posttest design contains two treatment conditions: cooperative and individualistic games that were initiated and supervised by an activity director 3 days per week during recess. The individualistically oriented games were used rather than a no-treatment control group in order to control for Hawthorne-like effects. Within each school, the girls in each of two classes were randomly assigned to one of the two treatment conditions. In one school, one and a half weeks of observations preceded 2 weeks of intervention, followed by 10 weeks of postintervention observation. In the second, 4 weeks of preintervention observation preceded 5 weeks of intervention, followed again by 2 weeks of postintervention observation. The asymmetry in the lengths of treatments and observations reflects our attempt to "save" the experiment after learning that in response to a higher-court overruling, the school board planned to terminate the court-ordered desegregation plan.

Dependent Measures

Both before and after introduction of the experimental games, we used a number of measures to evaluate intergroup social acceptance and categorization processes. To assess social acceptance, we gathered observational data of actual social interaction as well as paper and pencil measures of liking. Categorization processes were examined with paper and pencil measures of perceived similarity. Although the cooperative games were designed to facilitate intergroup acceptance among girls specifically, we were also interested in examining the relationship between categorization processes and intergroup acceptance among both male and female students. Thus all paper and pencil measures were administered to students of both sexes. Due to staff limitations, however, observational measures were collected only for the female students. Also, because there were only small numbers of Asian and Hispanic students in our sample, we excluded their responses from the analyses.

Observations

Trained observers watched and systematically recorded a sample of the voluntary and spontaneous social interactions of the girls from participating classrooms during morning recess twice a week for 10 weeks. Using a variation of the observational technique developed in previous work (Rogers, Miller, & Hennigan, 1981), observers coded interactions into two major qualitative categories—prosocial and antagonistic. An additional category contained ambiguous behaviors. Less than 5% of all interactions were coded as ambiguous or antagonistic. Due to the potential problems with sampling unreliability generated by the low occurrence of such interactions, we decided to analyze only the prosocial interactions.

From this large body of observational data, we computed two indices of cross-racial social interaction. One assessed the proportion of all social interactions that were prosocial. The second only included individual (i.e., one-to-one) prosocial interactions. We chose to single out individual level interactions because such one on one cross-racial contact may reflect true social acceptance more accurately than group interaction.

Paper and Pencil Measures

During the ninth week of observations, a researcher from our group, who was unknown to the children, visited each classroom. The researcher stated that she was gathering information for a research project being conducted by some professors at the University of Southern California. She explained that the information was confidential and thus neither the teacher nor the student's fellow classmates would see it.

Each child was provided with a list of all their same sex classmates and asked to indicate how much he or she liked or disliked each on a 5-point scale. The use of the scale was explained and demonstrated with examples. Next, each child was given a prepared booklet which asked how similar all possible pairs of three randomly chosen black female, white female, black male, and white male classmates were to each other and to the child herself or himself. Again a 5-point scale was used, which was explained and demonstrated with examples.

Results and Discussion

Analyses of both the observational and paper and pencil measures suggested that the games produced little or no effect on the girls' intergroup acceptance. The mean proportions of cross-racial prosocial interactions during preintervention, intervention, and postintervention periods were .54, .53, and .44 for black and white girls in the cooperative treatment; for those who received the individualistic treatments the respective proportions were .33, .40, and .49. These means weight the black and white samples equally but are weighted by sample size within class and school. They mask very substantial between-school and between-class variability, some of which is undoubtedly due to the very small sample sizes within these subcategories. Additionally they mask strong racial-ethnic differences within the individualistic treatment.

A number of factors associated with the implementation of the experimental procedures and with historical events occurring during the course of the experiment contribute to the failure of the intervention. As indicated above, one critical factor was that a higher court reversed the lower-court's desegregation order, thereby permitting the school board to authorize children to withdraw from ongoing desegregation programs if they chose to do so after the Easter recess. Although only a few children accepted this option we suspect that it had several adverse effects upon the experimental component of our study. First, the threat that the desegregation program would terminate altogether forced us to shorten our baseline premeasures as well as the length of our interventions in order to be sure that some postintervention observations could be obtained. Other problems arose in conjunction with our implementation of the interventions. Many of our undergraduate activity directors lacked sufficient experience and skill in dealing with the children. Our use of novel equipment attracted on-lookers, which probably acted to maintain existing norms of separation among the racial–ethnic groups; and the fact that the equipment was removed the 3 days of the week that the activity director was not there meant that on those days the major cue or vehicle for cross-racial interaction was not present for those in the cooperative treatment condition. These and other implementation problems are discussed more fully by Miller, Rogers, and Hennigan (1983); taken together, they suggest inadequate control and implementation of the treatments.

Despite the failure to replicate previous findings with respect to effects of the cooperative games, our data collection did provide a rich body of information about natural variations in intergroup acceptance within very different school settings. We therefore analyzed the interrelationships among our various measures of intergroup attitudes and perceptions both within and between schools.

Ingroup Favoritism

To examine ingroup favoritism in the desegregated schools, we generated separate ingroup and outgroup liking scores from the children's responses to the paper and pencil measure of liking, and then subtracted the outgroup scores from the ingroup scores. These difference scores were then entered into a 2 (race of rater) × 2 (sex of rater) × 2 (black majority school versus white plurality school) mixed-design analysis of variance. As shown by the means presented in Table 10.2, and as confirmed in the analysis of variance outcomes, the different groups of children exhibited interesting variation in the extent of their ingroup favoritism.

An interaction between school and race, $F(1,111) = 16.86$, $p < .001$, qualified a main effect for race, $F(1,111) = 3.96$, $p < .049$. This higher-order effect is due to the fact that children who belonged to the racial group that was in the numerical minority in their school setting exhibited more ingroup bias than did those who belonged to the racial majority group. To gain a better

TABLE 10.2

Mean Ingroup Bias as a Function of School, Race, and Sex of the Ruler[a]

	Female		Male	
	$\overline{X}$	(N)	$\overline{X}$	(N)
White plurality school				
White	−.01	(19)	−.12	(17)
Black	.39	(13)	.18	(17)
Black majority school				
Black	−.24	(21)	−.26	(23)
White	.92	(9)	1.23	(7)

[a] Higher numbers reflect greater ingroup bias and negative numbers reflect favoritism toward out group members.

understanding of the nature of this effect, we performed separate analyses of responses to the measures concerned with ingroup and outgroup liking. The means associated with these responses appear in Table 10.3.

In the analysis of ingroup liking, two out of three main effects reached significance. The main effect for race of the rater, $F(1,112) = 12.34$, $p < .001$, indicated that blacks overall $(\overline{X} = 3.50)$ favored their ingroup less than did

TABLE 10.3

Mean Liking for Racial Ingroup and Outgroup as a Function of School, Race, and Sex of the Rater[a]

	Female		Male	
	$\overline{X}$	(N)	$\overline{X}$	(N)
Ingroup liking				
White plurality school				
White	3.71	(19)	3.59	(18)
Black	3.86	(13)	3.15	(10)
Black majority school				
Black	3.61	(21)	3.37	(23)
White	4.34	(9)	4.36	(7)
Outgroup liking				
White plurality school				
White	3.80	(19)	3.60	(18)
Black	3.42	(13)	3.01	(10)
Black majority school				
Black	3.85	(21)	3.63	(23)
White	3.43	(9)	3.12	(7)

[a] Liking is measured on a 1–5 scale with higher numbers indicating greater liking.

whites ($\overline{X}$ = 4.0). The main effect for school, $F(1,112)$ = 5.71, p < .02, revealed that students at the white plurality school expressed less liking for their racial ingroup than did those at the black majority school ($\overline{X}$ = 3.58; $\overline{X}$ = 3.92, respectively). These outcomes were qualified by an interaction between race and school, $F(1,112)$ = 6.30, p < .02, that indicated that white children expressed greater ingroup liking when they were numerically in a minority position as opposed to a plurality position, whereas black children's liking for ingroup members did not vary as a function of their numerical position.

The analysis of outgroup liking did not reveal any significant main effects, but the interaction between race and school, $F(1,111)$ = 8.11, p < .006. It showed that the racial group occupying a numerical minority position in their school setting liked the outgroup less than did those in the majority or plurality position.

To summarize, the analyses of responses to the measure of liking revealed that children in a numerical minority expressed greater ingroup bias than did those in a majority or plurality position and that differences in both ingroup and outgroup liking contributed to this effect. These results are consistent with findings showing that minority group status escalates the tendency to favor ingroup members over outgroup members (Branthwaite and Jones, 1975; Gerard and Hoyt, 1974). As Brewer (1979) suggests, in comparison to majority group status, being in a minority position may increase the salience of intergroup distinctions and thereby make it easier for minorities to categorize others along dimensions associated with group membership. The mechanism by which this particular categorization process promotes ingroup bias is explained by Turner's (1975) social comparison theory of ingroup bias. He postulates that the presence of a salient basis for distinguishing between ingroup and outgroup members generates social competition that in turn leads to a search for differences between the ingroup and the outgroup along dimensions that favor the ingroup. This search is motivated by the need to maintain the positive self-esteem that results from a favorable social identity. This interpretation therefore suggests that, relative to majority-group status, minority-group status elicits greater insecurity about the favorability of one's social group, and consequentially, produces a stronger need to differentiate between ingroup and outgroup members in favor of the ingroup.

Similarity of Ingroup and Outgroup to Self

To test the prediction that the children would perceive themselves as more similar to ingroup members than to outgroup members, we entered indexes of similarity of these targets to self into a 2 (race of rater) × 2 (sex of rater) × 2 (black majority school versus white plurality school) mixed-design analysis of variance. As implied by inspection of the means in Table 10.4, the main effect

TABLE 10.4

Mean Perceived Similarity of Self to Ingroup and Outgroup Members
as a Function of School, Race, and Sex of the Rater[a]

	Female		Male	
	$\overline{X}$	(N)	$\overline{X}$	(N)
Ingroup members				
White plurality				
White	2.41	(19)	2.47	(19)
Black	2.50	(12)	2.58	(10)
Black majority				
Black	2.47	(21)	3.99	(19)
White	4.35	(9)	3.28	(7)
Outgroup members				
White plurality				
White	2.56	(19)	2.28	(19)
Black	2.40	(12)	2.40	(10)
Black majority				
Black	2.35	(21)	3.50	(19)
White	2.59	(9)	3.04	(7)

[a] Higher scores indicate greater preceived similarity.

for the ingroup and outgroup responses, $F(1,108) = 5.77$, $p < .042$, shows that, as expected, both black and white children perceived themselves as more similar to ingroup members than to outgroup members. Additionally, the main effect for school, $F(1,108) = 11.18$, $p < .001$, reflects the fact that children at the white plurality school tend to perceive less similarity between themselves and both ingroup and outgroup members than do those at the black majority school.

Thus, of the two research sites, students attending the more heterogeneously composed school show a weaker tendency to perceptually align themselves with either ingroup or outgroup members. Perhaps a diversified student body impedes the formation of perceptually well-defined social groups and thus allows the self to remain differentiated from others. Alternatively, other characteristics associated with the more diversified of the two schools may have contributed to this effect. The fact that it is a middle-class receiving school suggests that its teachers may have been less willing to tolerate the formation of strong social boundaries among the student body than may have their counterparts in the lower-middle class receiving school (Brookover, Beady, Flood, Schweitzer, & Wisenbaker, 1979). To the extent that these teachers serve as role models, their relatively nonprejudicial behavior may have inhibited the formation of strong ingroup identification among pupils (Fraser, 1981). The fact that a similar main effect for school did not emerge from the analysis of the ingroup bias scores, however, partially contradicts this interpretation.

Perceptions of Ingroup and Outgroup Homogeneity

To examine whether the children perceived stronger homogeneity among outgroup members than among ingroup members, indexes of intragroup similarity were entered into a 2 (race of rater) × 2 (sex of rater) × 2 (school) mixed-design analysis of variance. As the means displayed in Table 10.5 suggest, the resulting main effect for ingroup and outgroup responses, $F(1,157) = 13.36$, $p < .001$, show that, as expected, the children perceived greater similarity among outgroup members than among ingroup members. No other effects reached significance.

Association between Liking and Categorization Variables

To examine the relationship between responses to the measure of liking and responses to the categorization measures, we inspected the Pearson product moment correlations between the two sets of responses. An inspection of them indicates that, as expected, perceiving oneself as similar to either ingroup or outgroup members is positively associated with liking for these targets. How-

TABLE 10.5

Mean Perceptions of Ingroup and Outgroup Homogeneity
as a Function of School, Race, and Sex of the Rater[a]

	Female		Male	
	$\overline{X}$	(N)	$\overline{X}$	(N)
Ingroup homogeneity				
White plurality school				
White	2.50	(16)	1.95	(13)
Black	2.67	(11)	3.04	(9)
Black majority school				
Black	2.70	(22)	3.71	(21)
White	3.67	(8)	3.10	(5)
Outgroup homogeneity				
White plurality school				
White	3.29	(16)	4.33	(15)
Black	2.97	(11)	2.44	(9)
Black majority school				
Black	3.83	(22)	4.54	(21)
White	3.77	(18)	4.01	(13)

[a] Higher numbers indicate stronger perceptions of homogeneity.

ever disconfirming our expectations, perceived similarity of self with ingroup members generally is not associated with decreased attraction towards outgroup members. Additionally only one out of the four corresponding correlations show that perceptions of outgroup homogeneity are related to decreased liking for outgroup members. These findings suggest that interventions that help to decrease the social distance between self and outgroup members may be the most effective technique for improving intergroup relations among desegregated school children.

In general, the results suggest that desegregation involving schools in which one social group strongly outnumbers another can produce deleterious effects on intergroup relations. Caution must be exercised in accepting this conclusion, however, because in the present study the majority versus plurality variable is confounded with whether the children attended a white and Asian middle-class receiving school or a black lower-middle class receiving school. Evidence suggesting that teachers and administrators in lower-class black schools behave in more prejudicial ways than do those in middle-class schools implies that these school differences may contribute substantially to the impact of desegregation on intergroup relations.

References

Allport, G. W. *The Nature of Prejudice*, Cambridge, MA: Addison-Wesley, 1954.

Branthwaite, A. & Jones, J. E. Fairness and discrimination: English versus Welsh. *European Journal of Social Psychology*, 1975, *5*, 323–338.

Brewer, M. In-group bias in the minimal intergroup situation. A cognitive-motivational analysis, *Psychological Bulletin*, 1979, *86*, 307–324.

Brookover, W., Beady, C., Flood, P., Schweitzer, J., & Wisenbaker, J. *School Social Systems and Student Achievement: Schools can make a difference*. New York: Praeger, 1979.

Bryne, D. *The attraction paradigm*. New York: Academic Press, 1969.

DeVries, D. L., & Edwards, K. J. Learning games and student teams: Their effects on classroom process. *American Educational Research Journal*, 1973, *10*, 307–318.

DeVries, D. L., & Edwards, K. *Student teams and learning games: Their effects on cross-race and cross-sex interaction*. Journal of Educational Psychology, 1974, *66*(5), 741–749.

DeVries, D. L., & Slavin, R. E. *Teams-Games-Tournament: A final report on the research* (Report = 217) Baltimore, MD: The Johns Hopkins University, Center for Social Organization of schools, August 1976.

Entwisle, D. R., and Hayduk, L. *Early Schooling: Cognitive and Affective Outcomes*. Baltimore, MD: Johns Hopkins University Press, 1982.

Fraser, R. W. *Behavioral and attitudinal differences between teachers in desegregated classrooms*. Unpublished Doctoral dissertation, University of Southern California, 1981.

Gerard, H. B. & Hoyt, M. F. Distinctiveness of social categorization and attitude toward ingroup members. *Journal of Personality and Social Psychology*, 1974, *29*, 836–842.

Gerard, H. & Miller, N. *School Desegregation*. New York: Plenum Press, 1975.

Hallinan, M. Patterns of cliquing among youth. In H. C. Foot, A. J. Chapman, & J. R. Smith (Eds.), *Friendship and Social Relations in Children*. New York: Wiley, 1980.

Jansen, V. G., & Gallagher, J. J. The social choices of students in racially integrated classes for the culturally disadvantaged talented. *Exceptional Children*, 1966, *33*, 222–226.

Lever, J. *Games children play: Sex differences and the development of role skills.* Unpublished doctoral dissertation, Yale University, 1974.

Linville, P. The complexity-extremity effect and age based stereotyping. *Journal of Personality and Social Psychology, 42*, 1982, 193–211.

Linville, P., & Jones, E. E., Polarized appraisals of outgroup members. *Journal of Personality and Social Psychology*, 1980, *38*, 689–703.

Miller, N., Rogers, M., & Hennigan, K., Cooperative games as an intervention to promote interracial contact. In L. Bickman (Ed.), *Annual Review of Applied Social Psychology*, 1983, *3.*

Park, B. & Rothbart, M., Perception of outgroup homogeneity and levels of social categorization: Memory for the subordinate attributes of in-group and out group members. *Journal of Personality and Social Psychology*, 1982, *42*, 1051–1068.

Pettigrew, T. F., Useem, E. L., Normand, C., and Smith, M., Busing: A review of "the evidence", *Public Interest*, 1973, *30*, 88–118.

Rist, R. The Invisible Children: School Integration in American Society. Cambridge, MA: Harvard University Press, 1978.

Rogers, M., Miller, N., & Hennigan, K., Cooperative games as an intervention to promote cross-racial acceptance. *American Educational Research Journal*, 1981, *18*(4), 513–516.

Schofield, J. & Sagar, H. Peer interaction patterns in an integrated middle school, *Sociometry*, 1977, *40*, 130–138.

Sherif, M. A preliminary experimental study of intergroup relation. In J. H. Rohen & M. Sherif (Eds.), *Social Psychology at the Crossroads*. New York: Harper, 1961.

Singleton, L. C. & Asher, S. R. Peer preferences and social interaction among third grade children in an integrated school district. *Journal of Education Psychology*, 1977, *69*, 330–336.

Slavin, R. E. How student learning teams can integrate the desegregated classroom. *Integrated Education*, 1977, *15*, 56–58.

Turner, J. C. Social comparison and social identity: Some prospects for intergroup behavior. *European Journal of Social Psychology*, 1975, *5*, 5–34.

Wilder, D. A., and Allen V. L. Group membership and preference for information about others. *Personality and Social Psychology Bulletin*, 1978, *4*, 106–110.

11

The Role of Ignorance in Intergroup Relations*

Walter G. Stephan
and
Cookie White Stephan

> *See that man over there?*
> *Yes.*
> *Well, I hate him.*
> *But you don't know him.*
> *That's why I hate him.*
> *(Allport, 1954, p. 253)*

This chapter is dedicated to the resurrection of one of the oldest hypotheses in intergroup relations. The hypothesis is simply this: ignorance causes prejudice. We will not adopt the position that it is the only cause or even the most important cause of prejudice, but we do regard it as one of the easiest causes to undermine in school settings. For this reason we believe that this neglected idea deserves reconsideration. In this chapter we review research that can be used to assess this hypothesis. Then we discuss and test a causal model that specifies the pivotal role of ignorance as a cause of prejudice.

Ignorance and Prejudice: Early Work

In his classic study, *An American Dilemma*, Myrdal (1944) makes the point clearly: "The race prejudice of the typical Northerner . . . is based mainly on

*The research reported in this chapter was supported by grants from the College of Arts and Sciences at New Mexico State University and by the Society for the Psychological Study of Social Issues.

229

ignorance, both simple and opportune, and is much less bound up with fundamental conceptions of society and self. . . . The Southerner's prejudice toward whites is based partly on ignorance, but it is much more a matter of fear and hatred of the oppressor'' (pp. 1142–1143). Similarly, in discussing the most prevalent assumptions underlying intergroup relations programs, Williams (1947) wrote: ''Insofar as it is assumed that presentation of facts will reduce intergroup prejudice, a further premise is necessary: That prejudice is unrealistic, a function of ignorance or of 'distorted stereotypes' '' (p. 13).

Four early studies of ignorance of ethnic outgroups and prejudice provide some support for the idea that these two concepts are related. The first study found that factual knowledge of black history and demography was highly correlated with positive attitudes toward blacks in a large sample of college students ($r = .64$) (Reckless & Bringen, 1933). The second study found correlations of .18 and .25 between factual knowledge of blacks and positive attitudes toward blacks in two samples of college students (Bolton, 1935). One of these groups subsequently received a course covering black history. After this course knowledge and attitudes were uncorrelated ($r = .02$). The meaning of this lack of relationship is unclear because it may have been the result of differential changes in knowledge or attitudes or other factors, such as differential responsiveness to demand characteristics or social desirability. In the third study a measure of evaluations of blacks and attitudes toward social norms concerning blacks showed moderate ($r = .35$) to low ($r = .12$) correlations with factual knowledge about blacks in two separate samples of college students (Murphy & Likert, 1938). In a fourth study, knowledge of the demography and social life of Japanese-Americans was moderately correlated ($r = .31$) with a measure of attitudes toward them in a large sample consisting mostly of college students (Nettler, 1946).

Effects of Programs Designed to Reduce Intergroup Ignorance

In further support of the hypothesis that ignorance causes prejudice, we review interventions designed to attack intergroup ignorance. Direct attacks on intergroup ignorance have been a topic of research for half a century. Two direct approaches have been extensively studied—propaganda and the provision of educational materials, either through interethnic curricula in school settings or in cross-cultural programs.

Propaganda

Studies of propaganda typically involve examining the effects of movies, oral presentations, written materials, and television programs. Williams (1947) reviewed the early studies of propaganda designed to reduce prejudice. Seven of the nine studies he reviewed found positive effects. He concluded that in the short run most types of propaganda do reduce prejudice. Williams offered eight conclusions based on his review: auditory stimuli are more effective than visual stimuli; speakers are more effective than printed material; emotional appeals are less effective than rational appeals when the audience is well-educated or holds views opposing those of the speaker; oral propaganda is more effective in small than in large groups; propaganda is more effective when the speaker is prestigious; using several communication channels is better than using only one; pictures and cartoons are effective in communicating simple ideas; and each successive presentation in a series has less effect (Williams, 1977).

More recent empirical research on propaganda designed to change racial attitudes has added little to these conclusions. Several additional studies suggested that movies on intergroup relations issues reduce prejudice (Goldberg, 1956; Kraus, 1960; Rosen, 1948), but others have found no effects (Cooper & Dinerman, 1951; Rath & Trager, 1948). A study employing high school students as subjects found that a film treating prejudice as a communicable disease was successful in reducing prejudice by itself and when accompanied by a group discussion (Mitnick & McGinnies, 1958). The film-plus-discussion-group condition was somewhat more effective than the film-only condition. In another study, reading the Kerner report on civil disorders led to more positive attitudes toward school desegregation and residential integration (Davis & Fine, 1975). A study of the effects of sermons on racial hatred and injustice found no changes in prejudice among the Catholic parishioners who heard the sermons (Crawford, 1974). Studies of the television series "Holocaust" revealed mixed effects on attitudes (Ahren & Melchers, 1979; American Jewish Committee, 1979; Brunkhorst & Lissman, 1979; Ernst, 1979; Hormuth & Stephan, 1981). Likewise, the effects of the Archie Bunker series on intergroup attitudes are mixed (Brigham, 1977; Brigham & Giesbrecht, 1976; Vidmar & Rokeach, 1974).

The problem with propaganda is that people who do not wish to be influenced by it will avoid it, and, if they are exposed to it, will distort it (Berelson & Steiner, 1964). Cooper and Jahoda (1947) trace this problem to ethnocentrism:

> Consider the fact that most people agree with the ideas of their own group; they are conditioned by the people with whom they live and, in turn, they choose to be with people whose attitudes are compatible with their own. Adopting a conflicting attitude would create antagonisms in inter-personal relationships . . . . Even considering an opposing point of view may create great discomforts. (p. 24)

The changes in attitudes brought about by brief exposure to propaganda are likely to be equally brief, if such changes occur at all. Many studies finding positive effects may merely demonstrate social desirability effects. Thus, while the evidence concerning propaganda is consistent with the hypothesis that reducing ignorance reduces prejudice, the magnitude of the effects is probably not large. The potential seems great—educating the public about the nature of American racial, ethnic, and religious groups—but the reality is likely to be that the enlightened lead the enlightened. Nonetheless we would argue that the mass media have an obligation to contribute to the creation of an egalitarian pluralistic society and not to reinforce ignorance, fear, and bigotry.

Educational Materials: Interethnic Curricula Stressing Group Similarities

We have found 39 studies that have examined the effects of interethnic curricula on prejudice.[1] Most of these programs focus on the history of different groups in our society, especially blacks, and highlight the achievements of members of minority groups.

While the majority (24) of these 39 studies found that educational materials can reduce prejudice, a number of studies (14) found that such programs had no effects on prejudice and one found an increase in prejudice. The authors of this last study (Schon, et al., 1980) argue that their results are due to the increasing honesty of the students' responses to their anonymous racial attitude measures, an argument made plausible by progressive changes in responses to a social desirability scale.

One study of 51 high schools found that the use of multiethnic curricula was not associated with racial attitudes for whites or blacks (Slavin & Madden, 1979). Reports of classroom discussions of racial issues were related to lower levels of prejudice for whites but not for blacks. In addition, working together in biracial work teams was associated with positive racial attitudes in both groups.

Those programs that employed the most extensive multiethnic courses were most successful (Leslie et al., 1972; Litcher & Johnson, 1969; Singh & Yancy, 1974; Yawkey & Blackwell, 1974). Such courses employed multiethnic readers supplemented by discussions, speakers, films, and field trips. Generally, longer courses of about 3 months, 1 hour per day (Campbell et al., 1980; Lee, 1978; Robertson, 1979) were more successful than shorter ones. Age does not appear to be a significant factor in the success of the programs. Educational programs have failed with very young students (Best et al., 1975) and older students (Greenberg et al., 1957), but they have also succeeded with both young children (Yawkey, 1973) and older students (Glass & Trent, 1982). The more actively

[1]Best, Smith, Graves & Williams, 1975; Campbell, Hoggens & Murphy, 1980; Glass & Trent, 1982; Greenberg, Pierson & Sherman, 1957; Jackson, 1944; Katz & Zalk, 1978; Lee, 1978; Leslie, Leslie & Penfield, 1972; Litcher & Johnson, 1969; Litcher, Johnson & Ryan, 1973; Robertson, 1979; Schon, Hopkins & Vojir, 1980; Singh & Yancy, 1974; Slavin & Madden, 1979; Smith, 1943; Vassiliou, Triandis & Oncken, 1968, cited in Brislin & Pedersen, 1976; Yawkey, 1973; Yawkey & Blackwell, 1974; see also a multistudy book edited by Cook, 1970, and a multistudy review by Williams, 1947.

the students were involved in the multiethnic education programs, the more positive the results. The success of studies employing role-playing techniques and discussions of students' values and behavior supports this conclusion (Carlson, 1956; Culbertson, 1957; DeKock, 1969; Rokeach, 1971).

Our evaluation of these studies must be accompanied by a few cautionary notes. Some of these studies have severe methodological flaws. For example, some studies did not employ adequate control groups. Few studies included follow-up data that would permit an assessment of the duration of the effects. Nearly all of these studies employed white subjects only. Further, most studies showing favorable changes may be interpreted in terms of social desirability effects. Finally, studies finding no differences are not as likely to be published as studies showing positive effects as a result of a program.

These methodological shortcomings make a more detailed analysis of these studies impractical. It might be useful to apply the techniques of meta-analysis to this literature (Glass, 1976) to examine in greater detail the correlates of successful attempts to change attitudes. However, it is impossible to determine effect sizes in many of these studies and the lack of adequate control groups renders suspect many of the effect sizes that can be determined.

Educational Materials: Cross-Cultural Programs Stressing Group Differences

Other researchers have created programs stressing group differences. This emphasis contrasts with that of multiethnic curricula programs in which there has been a tendency to deny that group differences exist. The principal reason for this denial appears to be the problems associated with presenting differences in a nonevaluative way. The sometimes acrimonious debate over racial differences in intelligence, self esteem, and locus of control suggests that the presentation of any group difference runs the risk of being interpreted as an indication that one group is inferior to another (Adam, 1978).

Researchers in this tradition note that it is not the similarities between groups that create conflict. Misperceived and real dissimilarities create conflict and prejudice. Even if misperceptions are eliminated, cultural differences may remain. Because these researchers believe that there are real differences between groups, they feel that programs should explain and legitimize these differences rather than ignore them.

The vast majority of such programs are used in cross-cultural situations. When faced with the real differences that exist between cultures, cross-cultural researchers have provided participants in training programs with information on cultural differences. In addition, however, participants are typically provided with information on similarities among cultures and among peoples of these cultures.

In addition to their emphasis on group differences, cross-cultural training programs typically differ from multiethnic curriculum programs in the type of information they provide. Triandis' (1975) term for the type of information provided by cross-cultural training programs is *subjective culture*. By this he means the often unrecognized, implicit value premises, roles, norms, and attitudes of a given group. Triandis attempts to present this type of information in his own training programs. Other programs provide information on other cultural differences, such as differences in nonverbal behavior patterns. An underlying assumption common to these techniques is that members of one group must understand the cultural system of the other group before they can understand individual members of this group. We will review work using Triandis' technique, the Cultural Assimilator, and then review studies dealing with other cross-cultural training programs designed to reduce ignorance.

The principal goal of Cultural Assimilator training is to create parallel attribution patterns between cultural groups (Triandis, 1976). Thus, after training, ingroup members should make the same attributions to explain the behavior of outgroup members as does the outgroup and vice versa. In order to achieve this goal, members of one group read a self-paced assimilator, consisting of 75–100 incidents in which members of the two groups often make different attributions for behavior due to differences between the groups in values, roles, and norms. For each incident the readers are asked to choose among a set of attributions for the behavior of members of the other group until they have selected the same attribution selected by members of the other cultural group. The readers' correct choices are followed by explanations regarding elements of the subjective culture of the other group that make the selected attribution correct.

Assimilators have been developed to teach Americans about foreign cultures, including Saudi Arabia, Thailand, Honduras, and Greece (Chemers, Lekhyananda, Fiedler & Stolurow, 1966; Foa, Mitchell, Santhai, Wichiarajote, & Wichiarajote, 1967; Mitchell, Gagerman & Schwartz, 1967; O'Brien, Fiedler & Hewlett, 1970). Assimilators have also been designed for multicultural domestic use. Several studies have examined the effectiveness of assimilators in teaching whites about blacks. Assimilators designed to teach whites about blacks do lead to increasingly isomorphic attributions, suggesting that whites learn to view these incidents in the same way as do blacks (Landis, Day, McGrew, Thomas & Miller, 1976; Weldon, Carlston, Rissman, Slobodin & Triandis, 1975). In the Weldon et al. (1975) study, white subjects who had received 6 to 8 hours of training with an assimilator about blacks stereotyped blacks less than untrained subjects. In conflict situations the trained subjects also perceived the attitudes of blacks and whites to be more positive than the untrained subjects. A measure of racial attitudes yielded no differences. Another study of a shorter assimilator training program found that trained whites enjoyed working with a black confederate more than did untrained whites (Randolph, Landis & Tzeng, 1977). No effects were found for measures of racial attitudes. Thus these studies suggest that Cultural Assimilator training may reduce stereotyping and anxiety about interacting with outgroup members. However neither study found changes in prejudice.

A variety of other cross-cultural training programs have been developed over the last 25 years (see Brislin & Pedersen, 1976, for a review). We review only those that deal specifically with overcoming intercultural ignorance. Among these, we focus only on those that have attempted some type of evaluation of the program's effectiveness. Using these criteria, the number of studies to be considered is unfortunately rather small. Still more unfortunate is the fact that many of these studies are available only as technical reports, although they have been summarized in a number of sources (e.g., Brislin & Pedersen, 1976). Much of this research has been conducted in military settings.

Researchers working for the Army have developed a program, the *alien presence program,* to train troops for overseas assignment. The goals of the program are similar to the goals of many cross-cultural training programs. The goals are to develop habits of dealing with each host national on an individual rather than a stereotyped level, to prepare trainees to withstand culture shock, and to give specific information about host-national attitudes and customs (Brislin & Pedersen, 1976). During the alien presence program, junior officers and enlisted men receive 16 hours of briefings in specific ways in which U.S. culture and those of other countries differ. This cognitive information may be supplemented by contact with material aspects of the foreign culture and by contact with the foreign people. In a set of three studies of troops going to Korea, trained troops had more favorable attitudes toward host nationals than untrained troops. Further, Korean soldiers reported better relations with Americans who had received more training in the alien presence program than with Americans who had received less of this training (Spector, 1969; Spector, Parris, Humphrey, Aronson & Williams, 1969, cited in Brislin & Pedersen, 1976).

A second Army program, the *contrast American program,* presents participants with a member of another culture whose values contrast with those of the average American. The goal is to enable the participants to learn about their own cultural values and the ways these values affect their attitudes and behavior toward people who differ from them. The results of one study indicated that Westinghouse executives were better able to predict the behavior of contrast Americans after several days of reading about them and role-playing interactions involving them than they were initially (Stewart, Danielman & Foster, 1969, cited in Brislin & Pedersen, 1976).

The Air Force has also developed a technique that focuses on self-awareness

(Eachus, 1966, cited in Brislin & Pedersen, 1976). In this technique individuals read about and then role-play cross-cultural encounters. Next they review and discuss the videotape of their verbal and nonverbal behaviors, and finally they role-play the situation again. Compared to subjects who only read materials about the other culture, role-playing subjects subsequently performed better at the verbal and nonverbal behaviors demanded by the encounter. The results again suggest that active participation in learning information about other groups is more effective than passively acquiring information.

A technique developed by the Navy employs a three-day seminar that uses a variety of approaches, including contrast American role-playing, teaching of values and behavior of the foreign culture, a field trip, and explanations of cultural relativity and culture shock. One group of trained participants reported enjoying their tours in Japan more than an untrained control group (Gudykunst, Hammer & Wiseman, 1977).

A final study involved training Englishmen in the nonverbal behavior of Arabs (Collett, 1971). In this study it was found that Arabs preferred the trained subjects to subjects who had only read about Arab culture. Katz (1978) has developed a program that incorporates many of the features of the cross-cultural programs outlined above. This 5-stage program is designed to expose and then reduce racism among whites. In the initial stages participants are confronted with the discrepancies between the myth and reality of American racial ideology. Films and tapes of Third World peoples are presented along with structured group exercises. In the intermediate stages participants process their reactions to this information. In one study (Katz & Ivey, 1977) participants kept a journal and read assigned readings in the interim between 2 weekend workshops. In the latter stages participants explore white ethnocentrism and the ways this ethnocentrism has influenced both American society and their own perspectives. Participants also discuss strategies that can be adopted to change individual and institutional racism. Finally, additional readings are given to the participants.

An evaluation of the workshop showed that it increased the participants' awareness of racism as a white problem and led to more positive attitudes toward blacks. The authors also report qualitative evidence indicating that the workshop continued to have an impact on the participants one year later. Other programs similar to this one have been developed but, to our knowledge, their effectiveness has not been empirically tested (Baptiste & Baptiste, 1979; Fromkin & Sherwood, 1976; Gabelko & Michealis, 1981).

The cross-cultural programs have a number of similarities. All involve relatively brief interventions, varying from 1 or 2 to 15 or 20 hours. Their goal is to create greater empathy for members of the outgroup. All attempt to overcome ethnocentrism and ignorance by providing information designed to create a greater understanding of cultural differences.

The programs also differ on several dimensions. Some provide specific suggestions as to how participants should change their behavior and interpretations of the behavior of members of another culture, whereas other programs provide the participants with considerable latitude to draw their own inferences. Several of the techniques explicitly emphasize insight into the culture of the ingroup; others emphasize the culture of the outgroup. A few programs provide general information about ways in which most outgroups differ from the ingroup, whereas others provide information about a specific outgroup.

Most of these programs are attended prior to the participants' entry into a foreign culture, but some have been applied in multiethnic domestic settings. The success of Cultural Assimilators in domestic use with black and white work relations suggests that they are applicable to other multiethnic domestic settings, such as desegregated schools. It seems likely that these techniques would be most effective in intergroup relations programs involving relatively unassimilated groups because the intergroup differences are greater between such groups and the dominant group. Overall, these comprehensive programs focusing on group differences show positive effects on intergroup relations.

Reexamination of Ignorance as a Cause of Prejudice

If we take seriously the proposition that ignorance causes prejudice, the question becomes one of understanding the types of information that will reduce prejudice and the process by which such prejudice reduction works. We will examine each of these issues in turn.

Ignorance and Prejudice: Types of Information

The most fundamental issue with respect to the types of information and experiences that reduce prejudice is the degree to which intergroup relations programs should focus on group similarities or differences. The idea that intergroup relations programs should stress similarities between groups is consistent with admonishments such as those offered by Williams (1947): "The likelihood of conflict is reduced by education and propaganda emphases upon characteristics and values common to various groups rather than upon group differences" (p. 64) and Allport (1954): "Is it well, for example, for children to discuss the "Negro problem" as such, or is it better for them to approach it through more incidental methods? . . . . Why sharpen in the child a sense of conflict? Far better for him to learn the similarities among human groups" (p. 452). Stressing group similarities seems reasonable given the general agreement among blacks and whites in basic values, at least when social class differences are controlled (Rokeach, 1973; Triandis, 1972). Also emphasizing similarities capitalizes on the tendency for perceived similarity to create liking for similar others (Byrne, 1961).

In contrast, our review of cross-cultural studies suggests that knowledge and understanding of differences as well as similarities among groups is important in reducing prejudice. It is obvious that the effect of presenting group differences is determined by the manner in which these differences are presented. One could present information regarding outgroups in such a way that the outgroup culture appeared flawed or pathological. To promote intergroup understanding, knowledge regarding group differences must be presented in a way that shows respect for the customs, traditions, and culture of all groups. Further, presentation of differences alone is not sufficient to reduce prejudice. Individuals need training to appreciate and accept such differences. At this point, information regarding group similarities becomes important. Differing customs, traditions, and culture should be presented as ways of meeting basic human goals and needs that are similar among all groups. Actual similarities among the groups should be noted and attempts should be made to eliminate myths about differences that do not exist.

Ignorance and Prejudice: Mediators

In this section we examine three variables that we believe mediate the relationship between ignorance and prejudice. They are *anxiety, assumed dissimilarity,* and *stereotyping.*

Anxiety

Ignorance of outgroups promotes prejudice because people tend to fear and reject what they do not understand. Ignorance of outgroups creates anxiety about how members of outgroups will behave and how ingroup members should behave toward them. Lack of knowledge of outgroup norms, values, and attitudes, and in some cases, language and nonverbal behaviors, can create a relatively high level of frustration when interacting with outgroup members. Given the availability of the outgroup as a suitable target for hostility and the lack of sanctions against expressing it, the hostility may be turned toward its source. As Park (1950) describes it:

> On the whole, we may define the situation in which races meet, as one of vague apprehension. The first effect is to provoke a state of tension . . . . It is in such situations, I suspect, that those antipathies arise which seem to constitute the most irrational . . . elements in racial prejudice. The sense of insecurity which the presence

of the stranger implies, when not dispelled by more intimate acquaintance, crystallizes into [a negative] attitude. (p. 238)

GSR (galvanic skin response) recordings and self-reports have both shown that anxiety is created by interaction with outgroup members (Heiss & Nash, 1967; Hendricks & Bootzin, 1976; Porier & Lott, 1967; Rankin & Campbell, 1955; Vidulich & Krevanick, 1966). Anxiety based on interaction with outgroup members is regarded as the basis of *culture shock*, a reaction of strong rejection to foreign cultures (Brislin & Pedersen, 1976). According to Oberg (1960), culture shock is caused by the anxiety that results from losing one's cues to social interaction. This idea seems applicable to group relations within a culture. The degree of anxiety engendered by interacting with outgroup members is likely to be a function of the perceived differences between the groups in values, norms, attitudes, and in verbal and nonverbal behaviors. A hostile or rejecting attitude from the outgroup would also contribute to ingroup anxiety and consequent rejection of the outgroup (Rosenfield, Sheehan, Marcus & Stephan, 1981).

Whereas a number of the cross-cultural training programs have been designed to reduce intercultural interaction anxiety, only a few have measured anxiety levels. In the study by Randolph, et al. (1977), Cultural Assimilator training initially raised the anxiety of white subjects about interactions with blacks. However, 1 week later these anxiety levels were significantly lower than the baseline rates. The authors' interpretation of these results is that the training sensitized the subjects to differences between blacks and whites and this made interacting with blacks seem more problematical to trained than to untrained whites. These initial fears then dissipated as the white subjects began to consolidate their newly acquired knowledge of blacks.

One investigator has attempted to reduce anxiety as a means of reducing prejudice and improving intergroup relations. Sappington (1976) used systematic desensitization to reduce the anxiety of prejudiced whites about interacting with blacks. The students individually developed hierarchies of increasingly threatening racial situations and then visualized these situations while listening to tapes of relaxation instructions. After five sessions the subjects in this experimental condition had decreased in prejudice, whereas subjects in an untreated control condition had not.

Several other studies have used classical conditioning procedures in an attempt to alter the negative affect associated with outgroups. In a study by Parish and Fleetwood (1975), exposing white students to pairings of the color black with positive adjectives resulted in unbiased attributions of positive qualities to blacks and whites, but only when the procedure was used repeatedly (eight sessions). Less extensive classical conditioning failed to produce any changes (Collins, 1972; Parish, 1972). One study found that pairing the word ''Negro'' with positive adjectives led to more negative evaluations of Negroes (Sappington, 1976). The college students in this study were selected because they were high in prejudice and may have reacted negatively to the conditioning procedure, which they were informed was an attempt to change their attitudes. In a study using instrumental verbal conditioning, Primac (1980) found that the frequency of positive adjectives in response to pictures of blacks increased. However, when the conditioning ceased, the subjects returned to baseline levels. Taken together, these studies of the relationship between anxiety and prejudice suggest that, as intergroup anxiety is reduced, prejudice is likely to be decreased.

Assumed Dissimilarity

The effect of ignorance on prejudice can also be explained in terms of the assumption made by ingroup members that outgroups differ from the ingroup. This assumed dissimilarity stems from the basic categorization processes of assimilation and contrast, the tendencies to see groups as more homogeneous than they actually are and to see greater differences between them than actually exist (Doise, Deschamps & Meyer, 1978; Tajfel, Sheikh & Gardner, 1964; for a review, see Stephan in press).

Several studies illustrate these processes. Byrne and Wong (1962) showed that highly prejudiced whites assume greater attitudinal dissimilarity between themselves and a black stranger than between themselves and a white stranger (Dienstbier, 1972). Wilder and Allen (1978) found that students who were randomly assigned to one of two groups predicted that the beliefs of members of their own group would be more similar to theirs than would be the beliefs of members of the other group. Thus, this study indicates that categorization alone leads to assumed dissimilarity.

Other studies indicate that biased encoding and retrieval of information about outgroups also contributes to the perception that outgroup members differ from ingroup members. For instance, Wilder and Allen (1978) found that people who were given an opportunity to review information about arbitrarily created ingroups and outgroups chose to see information indicating that ingroup members were similar to them and that outgroup members were dissimilar to them. Another study found that people were better able to recall information indicating that ingroup members were similar and outgroup members were dissimilar than information indicating ingroup dissimilarity and outgroup similarity (Wilder, 1982).

The assumption that outgroups differ from ingroups leads to the formation of prejudice in at least three ways. First, as trait-by-trait comparisons are made between the ingroup and the outgroup, there tends to be a selective focus on comparisons that favor the ingroup. Traits on which the ingroup and outgroup do not differ or those on which the outgroup is perceived to excel tend not to become part of the outgroup stereotype (Brewer, 1979a). This leads to a selective focus on negative intergroup differences and thus promotes prejudice. In addition, an extensive literature indicates that categorization leads to evaluative and behavioral discrimination in favor of the ingroup (Billig, 1976; Brewer, 1979b; Doise, 1978; Tajfel, 1978; Turner, 1978). These effects have been found for arbitrarily created laboratory groups. They indicate that, in the absence of any information about outgroups, prejudice and discrimination will occur. Finally, as is amply illustrated in the work of Byrne (1961) and others (Hensley & Duval, 1976; Rokeach, 1960), dissimilarity leads to disliking.

Studies of the belief versus racial similarity issue provide indirect evidence that similarity information reduces prejudice. There are dozens of studies on this issue and the results are complex. The majority of these studies find that belief similarity is more important than racial similarity as a determinant of liking (Dienstbier, 1972; Wrightsman, 1977). However, as the interaction context becomes more intimate, the importance of racial similarity increases.

A corollary of the perception that outgroups have dissimilar beliefs is the belief that outgroups are homogeneous with respect to values, attitudes, and traits (Hensley & Duval, 1976; Tajfel et al., 1964; Wilder, 1978). Attempts to inform the ingroup of the complexity of the outgroup may have the effect of reducing prejudice toward the outgroup by reducing the degree of perceived dissimilarity between groups. In a direct test of this hypothesis (Katz, 1973), prejudiced black and white children were assigned to one of three conditions: learning to associate names with the faces of children from the other race, making perceptual judgments of same or different to pairs of faces of children from the other race, or simply observing the faces of children from the other race. Subjects in the first two conditions decreased in prejudice as a result of the treatment, but subjects in the third condition did not. The implications of this study for intergroup relations programs are that such programs should not only present similarities and differences, but they should also help the students to perceive the outgroup as internally differentiated on values, attitudes, and traits.

Stereotyping

A third reason that ignorance causes prejudice is that the information void created by ignorance of outgroups is often filled with trait information supplied by stereotypes. Stereotypes are simplifications of social reality. The overgeneralized traits that comprise stereotypes are most easily maintained in the absence of information that might reveal the internal diversity of outgroups and their similarities to the ingroup.

Stereotypes lead to prejudice because they tend not to be neutral dispassionate analyses of outgroup traits. Lippman (1922), in introducing the concept of stereotyping, mentions this aspect of stereotypes.

> A pattern of stereotypes is not neutral. It is not merely a way of substituting order for the great blooming, buzzing confusion of reality. It is not merely a short cut. It is all these things and something more. It is the guarantee of our self respect; it is the projection upon the world of our own position and our own rights. The stereotypes are, therefore, highly charged with the feelings that are attached to them. (pp. 95–96)

Stereotypes tend to reflect ethnocentric biases (Campbell, 1967). As a result, they are typically composed of more negative than positive traits.

There are several reasons why stereotypes are important in the production of prejudice and discrimination. First, they lead people to treat others as members of groups rather than as individuals. Second, stereotypes establish expectancies that lead to biased processes of attention, encoding, and retrieval of information about others. Stereotype-generated expectancies lead to a search for expectancy confirming evidence, selective encoding of confirming evidence, and recall of more confirming than nonconfirming evidence, including supplying evidence that was not actually observed (see Stephan, in press, and Stephan & Rosenfield, 1982, for reviews). Third, expectancies set in motion self-fulfilling prophecies that influence the treatment of outgroup members by ingroup members. The result is that outgroup members often respond in ways that confirm the expectancy. The outgroup behaviors that are thus induced may convince outgroup members that the outgroup possesses the stereotypic traits attributed to them (see Stephan, in press, for a review). Finally, it appears that stereotypes bias the explanations that ingroup members use to explain outgroup behavior (Campbell, 1967; Pettigrew, 1979).

The idea that stereotypes and prejudice are related is supported by several laboratory studies suggesting that stereotyped expectancies can be offset with specific information about members of stereotyped groups. These studies have been based on the "base rate fallacy" (Kahneman & Tversky, 1973), the fact that people often ignore information about the base rate of a phenomenon in a given population when presented with information about an individual member of the population (Nisbett & Borgida, 1975). A study by Fiske (1982) found that when individual members of stereotyped groups (e.g., ROTC cadets) acted in stereotype-inconsistent ways (e.g., cooking, arranging flowers), they were evaluated more favorably than when they engaged in evaluatively neutral but stereotype-consistent ways (e.g., dating, playing football). Another study found that stereotype-inconsistent information about one group member changed the perception of traits possessed by the group (Hamill, Wilson, & Nisbett, 1980). In this study, information about a single prison guard who was characterized as humane led subjects to regard prison guards as more humane, even though this guard was presented as atypical of prison guards. The results of this study are particularly interesting because they suggest that knowledge about individual outgroup members may reduce negative stereotyping of the group as well as modifying attitudes toward individual group members.

Ignorance and Contact

If ignorance causes prejudice, then we must be concerned with the causes of ignorance. We will focus primarily on one cause of ignorance, lack of contact with outgroup members.

We have previously argued that anticipated contact with outgroups can lead to anxiety and frustration. We now argue that, under the proper conditions, contact with outgroups can have the opposite effect: contact that reduces ignorance will reduce prejudice.

Contact has been studied intensively in school desegregation settings and in other settings as well. The studies of school desegregation settings have had mixed results. A small number of studies has found predominantly positive effects, a greater number has found predominantly negative effects, and most have found mixed or no effects (Stephan, 1978). However, studies that have examined levels of contact among groups in desegregated schools typically reveal an association between lack of contact and prejudice (Campbell, 1956; Smith, Griffith, Griffith, & Steger, 1980; Stephan & Rosenfield, 1978a, 1979; Webster, 1961). Contact in other situations, including contact at summer camps, in the military, the workplace, and in housing, has generally led to positive effects.

Factors related to the situation and characteristics of the participants are important in determining the outcome of contact (Allport, 1954; Amir, 1969, 1976; Ashmore, 1970; Cook, 1970; Pettigrew, 1969, 1973, 1975; Rose, 1981; Williams, 1947, 1977). Where contact has failed, typically the setting is competitive, there is institutional opposition to the contact, and the statuses and competencies among groups are unequal; where contact has succeeded, typically the setting is cooperative, there is institutional support for the contact, and statuses and competencies among groups are equal. Thus, where the characteristics of the situation and the participants produce contact that allows members of each group to become better acquainted, prejudice is reduced. The evidence from these studies, then, suggests that contact has an indirect effect on prejudice by reducing ignorance of the outgroup.

In addition, contact may have a direct effect on prejudice. For instance, the mere exposure effect suggests that simple exposure to outgroups will lead to more favorable attitudes toward them (Zajonc, 1968). In two studies whites exposed to blacks' faces evaluated blacks more favorably as exposure increased

(Cantor, 1972; Perlman & Oskamp, 1971). However, this effect occurred only when blacks were presented in a positive context.

Causal Model of Ignorance and Prejudice

The foregoing arguments can be viewed as a causal model. In this model (see Figure 11.1), lack of contact has a direct effect on prejudice as well as an indirect effect acting through ignorance of outgroups. Ignorance of outgroups causes people to feel anxiety and frustration in the presence of outgroup members. Ignorance also leads to the assumption that outgroups are dissimilar to the ingroup and it leads to negative stereotyping. Thus ignorance has indirect effects on prejudice acting through the direct effects of anxiety and frustration, negative stereotyping, and assumed dissimilarity on prejudice.

This highly simplified model ignores causes of prejudice that are not influenced by ignorance and excludes other factors that influence stereotyping and lack of contact. It also presents the causal influence of the factors as being unidirectional, an assumption that is unwarranted in some cases, particularly the relationships between contact and ignorance and between stereotyping and prejudice. Nonetheless, the model does represent our basic arguments concerning the role that reducing ignorance can play in decreasing prejudice.

An Empirical Study of the Model

Our model suggests that lack of contact with outgroups is a primary cause of ignorance of the outgroup and that ignorance is a determinant of prejudice, mediated in the full model by anxiety, assumed dissimilarity, and stereotyping. As an initial exploratory test of these assumptions, we examined the proposed causal links with a path analysis representing a reduced version of the model. Contact and amount of knowledge about another group were hypothesized to have direct effects on prejudice. Contact was also hypothesized to have an in-

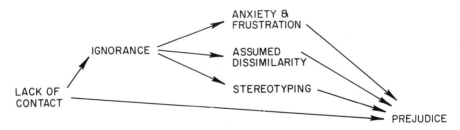

Figure 11.1. Causal model of the role of ignorance as a cause of prejudice.

direct effect on prejudice acting through amount of knowledge. In addition, we included two determinants of contact and prejudice that are not in our general model, parental attitudes toward the outgroup and peer group attitudes toward the outgroup. An extensive literature suggests that parental and peer group attitudes are related to both contact and prejudice (Epstein & Komorita, 1966a, 1966b; Mosher & Scodel, 1960; Patchen, Davidson, Hofman & Brown, 1977; Stephan & Rosenfield, 1978a). Friends' attitudes and parents' attitudes were hypothesized to have direct effects on prejudice and indirect effects acting through contact. The path model we tested is presented in Figure 11.2.

The subjects for our study consisted of 107 Anglo and 132 Chicano students enrolled in ninth-grade classes in two junior-high schools in Las Cruces, New Mexico.[2] The students completed questionnaires during their social studies classes. The measure of prejudice consisted of eight bipolar trait items. The students were asked to indicate the degree to which most Chicano (Anglo) students could be characterized by the bipolar traits (e.g., mean-kind).[3]

The measure of knowledge of the other group was derived from a Cultural Assimilator designed to teach Anglo students about Chicano culture. Cultural Assimilators present incidents involving members of another cultural group that are likely to be misunderstood by members of the reader's cultural group due to cultural differences. The reader is asked to choose an explanation for the behavior of the outgroup member from several possibilities. From the perspective of the other cultural group one of the attributions is correct and three are incorrect. Although Cultural Assimilators are typically used as an intervention technique to reduce ignorance of the outgroup, Cultural Assimilators can also be used as a tool to measure knowledge of another group.

Ten items were selected from our Anglo-Chicano assimilator, each of which

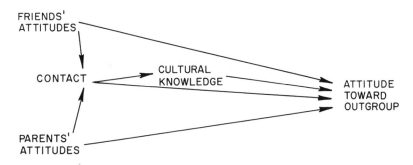

Figure 11.2. Path model of causes of prejudice.

[2]Ethnicity was determined by asking the students to provide information on the ethnic background of their parents. Only students who said that both parents were Anglo or Chicano were included in the analyses.

[3]The other seven dimensions used were: easy to get along with, loud, helpful, learn quickly, like you, honest, and hard working.

had previously been shown to differentiate between junior-high-school Anglos and Chicanos in this population. The situations included school and extracurricular situations. The themes for the 10 items were: respect for women, the authority of the father, open expressions of emotion, closeness of the family, modesty, speaking Spanish in class, sex roles, home responsibilities, cooperativeness, and dependence on others. For example, the item concerning the authority of the father in Chicano families read:

> David asked Francisco if he wanted to go to the college baseball game on Saturday. Francisco really wanted to go so he asked his father. His father said no. Francisco told David that he couldn't go.
>
> WHY DIDN'T FRANCISCO ARGUE WITH HIS FATHER?

The response options for this question are:

> A. Because Francisco didn't get along with his father.
> B. Because he thought his father would punish him if he did.
> C. Because a son shouldn't question his father's decision.
> D. Because he changed his mind about going to the ballgame.

From the Chicano perspective, the correct answer to this item is C.[4] The Anglo students' scores for knowledge of Chicano culture were calculated by determining the frequency with which they gave the answer that Chicanos typically viewed as correct. This measure of knowledge of another group differs considerably from those employed in earlier studies. Whereas the measure in other studies typically relies on factual demographic information, our measure relies more heavily on knowledge of the roles, norms, and values of the other group.

Contact with the other group was measured with 12 items. Ten of the items concerned informal positive contact (e.g., called and talked to on the telephone) and two concerned informal negative contact (e.g., having arguments with

---

[4]The answer provided by the cultural assimilator is: You have selected option C. which says: "Francisco didn't argue with his father because a son shouldn't question his father's decision."

Good choice. Children in Chicano families are usually taught to obey their parents and not to question them even if they think their parents are wrong. Young children are punished if they argue with their parents so they learn not to do this. Chicano parents more frequently punish their children when the children do something they shouldn't do than Anglo parents do. For this reason, the children learn to believe that their parents are usually right. Anglo parents are usually not as strict with their children and they tend to discuss their decisions more often with their children. In the story Francisco didn't question his father because he had learned not to.

If a Chicano friend of yours says he can't do something because his parents won't let him, you probably shouldn't press him. If you do it will only make things more difficult for him.

TABLE 11.1

Intergroup Attitudes and Contact

	Attitudes toward		Contact with	
Ethnic group	Anglos	Chicanos	Anglos	Chicanos
Anglo	19.33	14.04	14.19	8.90
Chicano	17.44	19.53	8.14	14.84

outgroup members).[5] The perceived attitudes of parents and peers toward outgroup members were measured with two items each.[6]

As can be seen in Table 11.1, both the Anglos and the Chicanos had more positive attitudes toward the ingroup than toward the outgroup $F(1,235) = 79.02$, $p < .001$. Also, each group had more positive informal contact with ingroup than with outgroup members $F(1,240) = 206.32$, $p < .001$. Thus, both groups were ethnocentric in attitudes and behavior, suggesting that there is a need for intergroup relations training for these students.

We conducted the path analysis using data from the Anglo students. The correlations among the variables in the path analysis are presented in Table 11.2. The significant paths from the analysis are presented in Figure 11.3. The results of the path analysis support the model reasonably well. The model accounted for 30% of the variance in Anglos' attitudes toward Chicanos. Perhaps the

TABLE 11.2

Correlation Matrix for the Path Analysis

	1	2	3	4	5
1. Friends' attitudes	—	—	—	—	—
2. Parents' attitudes	.51*	—	—	—	—
3. Contact with Chicanos	.55**	.36**	—	—	—
4. Knowledge of Chicano culture	.12	.11	.19*	—	—
5. Attitudes toward Chicanos	.40**	.36**	.43**	.32**	—

*p .05
**p .01

[5]The positive contact items were: talked to on the telephone, been to a Chicano's (Anglo's) house to visit, confided in Chicanos (Anglos), gone someplace with Chicanos (Anglos), invited Chicanos (Anglos) to your house, played on the same team together, sat next to in the cafeteria, worked on a project with, helped on a school assignment, and lent them something. The two negative contact items were: had arguments or fights with Chicanos (Anglos) and been called names by Chicanos (Anglos).

[6]The two items were: How do your parents (friends) think you should behave toward Chicanos? and How do your parents (friends) seem to feel about Chicanos?

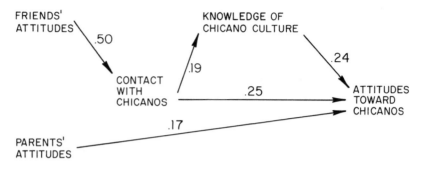

Figure 11.3. Path model for Anglo students.

most important link in the path model is the hypothesized relationship between knowledge of another group and attitudes toward that group. This path was significant, indicating that the more the Anglos knew about Chicano culture, the more favorable were their attitudes toward Chicanos.[7] Consistent with most earlier studies, contact was significantly related to prejudice.[8] Contact with Chicanos was also related to knowledge of Chicano culture.[9] This latter finding supports the hypothesis suggesting that positive informal contact can provide opportunities to learn about the subjective culture of an ethnic outgroup.

Although parents' attitudes were not significantly related to contact, they were significantly related to prejudice, replicating previous studies. Friends' attitudes were significantly related to contact but fell just short of significance for prejudice. These results suggest that contact with outgroup members may be determined to a greater extent by peers than by parents. This may reflect the fact that peers were present to approve or disapprove of most of the contact situations that comprised this contact index, so it was the peer's perceived attitudes that were related to contact as measured here.

The results of the path analysis are consistent with the basic assumptions in our general model. Whereas strong causal statements are unwarranted at this time, these confirmatory results suggest the value of further research exploring the links between contact, knowledge, and prejudice.

[7]This finding was replicated in a second study in which the subjects were 101 Anglo college students. In this study the correlation between knowledge of Chicano culture and an item measuring attitudes toward Chicanos was .27 ($p < .01$).

[8]Stephan and Rosenfield (1978b) present cross-leg correlational evidence that contact is a more powerful determinant of prejudice than the reverse in desegregated schools.

[9]In the second study of Anglo college students it was also found that contact with Chicano culture, as measured by percentage of friends who are Chicano, was correlated with knowledge of Chicano culture ($r = .28$, $p < .01$).

Conclusion

In this chapter we have presented a causal model that specifies the pivotal role of ignorance as a cause of prejudice. We reviewed the early literature relevant to that hypothesis and the literature concerning the effects of interventions designed to overcome intergroup ignorance. These studies show that simple intergroup contact, such as the contact that typically occurs in desegregated schools, is not likely to improve intergroup relations. However, specially designed educational programs designed to reduce ignorance of the outgroup do appear to improve intergroup relations.

The optimal educational program to attack intergroup ignorance should present both group similarities and differences. Such a program should explain real differences in the subjective culture of the differing groups, such as differences in values, norms, roles, attitudes, language, and nonverbal behavior. The differences should be presented in a nonevaluative manner. Further, attempts should be made to eliminate myths about differences that do not exist. An attempt should also be made to present the diversity within the outgroup. In addition, actual similarities between the groups should be noted and the similarities in goals and needs among all humans should be highlighted. The optimal program would employ multiple materials and media, such as books, films, slides, lectures, and field trips, and would include participative techniques such as role playing. It should be a rather extensive program.

We proposed three processes by which ignorance causes prejudice. We suggested that ignorance causes prejudice because ignorance creates anxiety about outgroups, because outgroups are presumed to be dissimilar from the ingroup, and because the information void regarding outgroups is filled with negative stereotypes.

Our causal model of the relationship between ignorance and prejudice suggests that lack of contact has a direct effect on prejudice and an indirect effect acting through ignorance. Ignorance leads to anxiety, assumed dissimilarity, and stereotyping all of which have a direct effect on prejudice. We tested a reduced version of this model and found support for the hypothesized links between contact and ignorance, contact and prejudice, and ignorance and prejudice. These confirmatory results suggest the value of further research exploring the links between contact, knowledge, and prejudice.

Acknowledgments

The authors thank Deanna Nielson, Lynette Menefee, Deborah Orozco, Maria Telles-McGeagh, Debbie Valverde, Wayne Whitmore, Deb Zigler and the principals, teachers, and students of Alameda and Court Junior High for their assistance.

References

Adam, B. D. Interiorization and "self-esteem." *Social Psychology*, 1978, *1*, 47–53.

Ahren, Y., & Melchers, C. B. Die entdeckung der leiche im eigenen keller. *Tribune*, 1979, *72*, 46–62.

Allport, G. W. *The nature of prejudice.* Cambridge, MA: Addison-Wesley, 1954.

American Jewish Committee. *Americans confront the holocaust.* New York: American Jewish Committee, Institute of Human Relations, 1979.

Amir, Y. Contact hypothesis in ethnic relations. *Psychological Bulletin* 1969, *71*, 319–342.

Amir, Y. The role of intergroup contact in changes of prejudice and ethnic relations. In P. A. Katz (Ed.), *Towards the elimination of racism.* New York: Pergamon Press, 1976.

Ashmore, R. D. In B. E. Collins (Ed.), *Social psychology.* MA: Addison-Wesley, 1970.

Baptiste, H. P., Jr., & Baptiste, M. L. *Developing the multicultural process in classroom instruction.* Washington, D.C.: University Press, 1979.

Berelson, B., & Steiner, G. A. *Human behavior, an intentory of scientific findings.* New York: Harcourt, Brace and World, 1964.

Best, D. L., Smith, S. C., Graves, D. J., & Williams, J. E. The modification of racial bias in preschool children. *Journal of Experimental Child Psychology*, 1975, *20*, 193–205.

Billig, M. *Social psychology and intergroup relations.* London: Academic Press, 1976.

Bolton, E. B. Effects of knowledge upon attitudes towards the Negro. *Journal of Social Psychology*, 1935, *6*, 68–90.

Brewer, M. B. The role of ethnocentrism in intergroup conflict. In W. Austin and S. Worchel (Eds.), *The Social Psychology of Intergroup Conflict.* Monterey, CA: Brooks/Cole, 1979. (a)

Brewer, M. B. In-group bias in the minimal intergroup situation: A cognitive-motivational analysis. *Psychological Bulletin*, 1979, *86*, 307–324. (b)

Brigham, J. C. Verbal aggression and ethnic humor: What is their effect? In J. C. Brigham & L. S. Wrightsman (Eds.), *Contemporary issues in social psychology* (3rd edition). Monterey, CA: Brooks/Cole, 1977.

Brigham, J. C., & Giesbrecht, L. W. "All in the family": Racial attitudes. *Journal of Communication*, 1976, *26*,(4) 69–74.

Brislin, R. W., & Pedersen, P. *Cross-cultural orientation programs.* New York: Gardner Press, 1976.

Brunkhorst, H., & Lissmann, H. J. Ich finde es falsch, dass man saggt: "Die amerikaner haben auch bomben geworfen" . . . *Paed. Extr*, 1979, *4*, 58–61.

Bryne, D. Interpersonal attraction and attitude similarity. *Journal of Abnormal and Social Psychology*, 1961, *62*, 713–715.

Byrne, D., & Wong, T. J. Racial prejudice, interpersonal attraction, and assumed dissimilarity of attitudes. *Journal of Abnormal and Social Psychology*, 1962, *65*, 246–253.

Campbell, E. Q. *The attitude effects of educational desegregation in a Southern community.* Unpublished doctoral dissertation, Vanderbilt University, Tennessee, 1956.

Campbell, D. T. Stereotypes and the perception of group differences. *American Psychologist*, 1967, *22*, 812–829.

Campbell, R. L., Hoggens, R., & Murphy, D. *The effect of information about famous Black scientists on the closed-mindedness of preservice teachers.* Paper presented at the annual meeting of the National Association for Research in Science Teaching, Boston, April 1980.

Cantor, G. Z. Effects of familiarization on children's ratings of pictures of whites and blacks. *Child Development*, 1972, *43*, 1219–1229.

Carlson, E. R. Attitude change through modification of attitude structure. *Journal of Abnormal Social Psychology*, 1956, *52*, 256–261.

Chemers, M. M., Lekhyananha, D., Fiedler, F. E., & Stolurow, L. M. Some effects of cultural training on leadership in heterocultural task groups. *International Journal of Psychology*, 1966, *1*, 301–314.

Collins, J. L. *The effect of differential frequency of color adjective pairings on the subsequent retaining of color meaning and racial attitude in preschool children.* Unpublished M.A. thesis. East Tennessee State University, 1972.

Collett, P. Training Englishmen in the non-verbal behavior of Arabs. *International Journal of Psychology*, 1971, *6*, 209–215.

Cook. S. W. Motives in a conceptual analysis of attitude-related behavior. In W. J. Arnold & D. Levine (Eds.), *Nebraska Symposium on Motivation* (Vol. 18). Lincoln, NE: University of Nebraska Press, 1970.

Cooper, E., & Dinerman, H. Analysis of the film, "Don't be a Sucker": A study in communication. *Public Opinion Quarterly*, 1951, *15*, 243–264.

Cooper, E., & Jahoda, M. The evasion of propaganda: How prejudiced people respond to anti-prejudice propaganda. *Journal of Psychology*, 1947, *23*, 15–25.

Crawford, T. J. Sermons on racial tolerance and the parish neighborhod context. *Journal of Applied Social Psychology*, 1974, *4*, 1–23.

Culbertson, F. M. Modification of an emotionally held attitude through role playing. *Journal of Abnormal and Social Psychology*, 1957, *54*, 230–233.

Davis, E. E., & Fine, M. The effects of the findings of the U.S. National Advisory Commission on Civil Disorders: An experimental study of attitude change. *Human Relations*, 1975, *28*, 209–227.

DeKock, D. Simulations and change in racial attitudes. *Social Education*, 1969, 181–183.

Dienstbier, R. A. A modified belief theory of prejudice emphasizing the mutual causality of racial prejudice and anticipated belief differences. *Psychological Review*, 1972, *79*, 146–160.

Doise, W. *Groups and individuals: Explanations in social psychology.* Cambridge, MA: Cambridge University Press, 1978.

Doise, W., Deschamps, J. C., & Meyer, G. The accentuation of intracategory similarities. In H. Tajfel (Ed.), *Differentiation between social groups*. New York: Academic Press, 1978.

Eachus, H. *Comparison of various approaches to training for culture contact.* Wright-Patterson Air Force Base. OH Air Force Systems Command, March 1966.

Epstein, R., & Kormorita, S. S. Childhood prejudice as a function of parental ethnocentrism, punitiveness, and outgroup characteristics. *Journal of Personality and Social Psychology*, 1966, *3*, 259–264. (a)

Epstein, R., & Komorita, S. S. Prejudice among Negro children as related to parental ethnocentrism and punitiveness. *Journal of Personality and Social Psychology*, 1966, 643–647.

Ernst, T. "Holocaust" und politische bildung. *Media Perspektiven*, 1979, *4*, 230.

Fiske, S. T. Schema triggered affect: Applications to social perception. In M. S. Clark and S. T. Fiske (Eds.), *Affect and cognition: The 17th annual Carnegie Symposium on Cognition*. Hillsdale, NJ: Erlbaum, 1982.

Foa, U. G., Mitchell, T. R., Santhai, S., Wichiarajote, N., & Wichiarajote, W. *Thai culture assimilator.* Urbana, IL: Group Effectiveness Research Laboratory, University of Illinois, 1967.

Fromkin, H. L., & Sherwood, J. J. *Intergroup and minority relations: An experimental handbook.* La Jolla, CA: University Associates, Inc., 1976.

Gabelko, N. H., & Michaelis, J. U. *Reducing adolescent prejudice.* New York: Teacher's College Press, 1981.

Glass, G. V. Primary, secondary, and meta analysis of research. *Educational Researcher*, 1976, *5*, 3–8.

Glass, J. C., & Trent, C. Changing student's attitudes toward older persons. In J. Keating (Ed.), *Annual editions: Social psychology 82/83*. Guilford, CN: Dushkin, 1982.

Goldberg, A. L. The effects of two types of sound motion pictures on the attitudes of adults toward minorities. *Journal of Educational Sociology*, 1956, *29*, 386–391.

Greenberg, H., Pierson, J., & Sherman, S. The effects of single-session education techniques on prejudice attitudes. *Journal of Educational Sociology*, 1957, *31*. 82–86.

Gudykunst, W. B., Hammer, M. R., & Wiseman, R. L. An analysis of an integrated approach to cross-cultural training. *International Journal of Intercultural Relations*, 1977, *1*, 99–110.

Hamill, R., Wilson, T. D., & Nisbett, R. E. Insensitivity to sample bias: Generalizing from atypical cases. *Journal of Personality and Social Psychology*, 1980, *39*, 578–589.

Heiss, J., & Nash, D. The stranger in laboratory culture revisited. *Human Organization*, 1967, *26*, 47–51.

Hendricks, M., & Bootzin, R. Race and sex as stimuli for negative affect and physical avoidance. *Journal of Social Psychology*, 1976, *98*, 111–120.

Hensley, V., & Duval, S. Some perceptual determinants of perceived similarity, liking, and correctness. *Journal of Personality and Social Psychology*, 1976, *34*, 159–168.

Hormuth, S. E., & Stephan, W. G. Effects of viewing "Holocaust" on Germans and Americans: A just-world analysis. *Journal of Applied Social Psychology*. 1981, *11*, 240–251.

Jackson, E. P. Effects of reading upon attitudes toward the negro race. *The Library Quarterly*, 1944, *14*, 47–54.

Kahneman, D., & Tversky, A. On the psychology of prediction. *Psychological Review*, 1973, *80*, 237–251.

Katz, J. H. *White awareness*. Norman, OK: University of Oklahoma Press, 1978.

Katz, J. H., & Ivey, A. White awareness: the frontier of racism awareness training. *Personnel and Guidance Journal*, 1977, *55*, 485–489.

Katz, P. A. Stimulus predifferentiation and modification of children's racial attitudes. *Child Development*, 1973, *44*, 232–237.

Katz, P. A., & Zalk, S. R. Modification of children's racial attitudes. *Developmental Psychology*, 1978, *14*, 447–461.

Kraus, S. Modifying prejudice: Attitude change as a function of the race of the communicator. *AV Communication Review*, 1960, *10*, 14–22.

Landis, D., Day, H. R., McGrew, P. L., Thomas, J. A., & Miller, A. B. Can a Black "culture assimilator" increase racial understanding? *Journal of Social Issues*, 1976, *32*, 169–183.

Lee, M. K. Attitudinal changes in a cultural heritage course about Black Americans. National Institute of Education, Washington, D.C., 1980 (*Eric Document Reproduction Service*, 195 622, 1978).

Leslie, L. L., Leslie, J. W., & Penfield, D. A. The effects of a student centered special curriculum upon the racial attitudes of sixth graders. *Journal of Experimental Education*, 1972, *41*, 63–67.

Lippman, W. *Public Opinion*. New York: Harcourt Brace, 1922.

Litcher, J. H., & Johnson, D. W. Changes in attitudes toward Negroes or White elementary school students after use of multiethnic readers. *Journal of Educational Psychology*, 1969, *60*, 148–152.

Litcher, J. H., Johnson, D. W., & Ryan, F. L. Use of pictures of multiethnic interaction to change attitudes of white elementary school students toward blacks. *Psychological Reports*, 1973, *33*, 376–372.

Mitchell, T. R., Gagerman, J., & Schwartz, S. *Greek cultural assimilator*, Urbana, IL: Group Effectiveness Research Laboratory, University of Illinois, 1967.

Mitnick, L. L., & McGinnies, E. Influencing ethnocentrism in small discussion groups through a film communication. *Journal of Abnormal and Social Psychology*, 1958, *56*, 82–90.

Mosher, D., & Scodel, A. Relationships between ethnocentrism in children and the ethnocentrism and authoritarian rearing practices of their mothers. *Child Development*, 1960, *31*, 369–376.

Murphy, G., & Likert, R. *Public opinion and the individual*. New York: Russell & Russell, 1938.

Myrdal, G. *An American dilemma*. New York: Harper & Row, 1944.

Nettler, G. The relationship between attitude and information concerning the Japanese in America. *American Sociological Review*, 1946, *11*, 177–191.

Nisbett, R. E., & Borgida, E. Attribution and the psychology of prediction. *Journal of Personality and Social Psychology*, 1975, *32*, 932–943.

Oberg, K. Cultural shock: Adjustment to new cultural environments. *Practical Anthropology*, 1960, *7*, 177–182.

O'Brien, G. E., Fiedler, F. E., & Hewlett, T. The effects of programmed training upon the performance of volunteer medical teams in Central America. Seattle, WA: Organizational Research, University of Washington, 1970.

Parish, T. S. *Changing anti-Negro attitudes in Caucasian children through mediated stimulus generalization*. Unpublished doctoral dissertation, University of Illinois, 1972.

Parish, T. S. & Fleetwood, R. S. Amount of conditioning and subsequent change in racial attitudes of children. *Perceptual and Motor Skills*, 1975, *40*, 79–86.

Patchen, M., Davidson, J. D., Hofmann, G., & Brown, W. R. Determinants of student interracial behavior and opinion change. *Sociology of Education*, 1977, *50*, 55–75.

Perlman, D., & Oskamp, S. The effects of picture content and exposure frequency on evaluations of Negroes and Whites. *Journal of Experimental Social Psychology*, 1971, *7*, 503–514.

Pettigrew, T. F. Racially separate or together? *Journal of Experimental Social Issues*, 1969, *25*, 43–69.

Pettigrew, T. F. Busing: A review of the evidence. *Public Interest*, 1973, *30*, 88–118.

Pettigrew, T. F. Preface. In T. F. Pettigrew (Ed.), *Racial discrimination in the United States*. New York: Harper & Row, 1975.

Pettigrew, T. F. The ultimate attribution error: Extending Allport's cognitive analysis of prejudice. *Personality and Social Psychology Bulletin*, 1979, *5*, 461–476.

Porier, G. W., & Lott, A. J. Galvanic skin responses and prejudice. *Journal of Personality and Social Psychology*, 1967, *5*, 253–259.

Primac, D. W. Reducing racial prejudice by verbal operant conditioning. *Psychological Reports*, 1980, *46*, 655–669.

Randolph, G., Landis, D., & Tzeng, O. C. S. The effects of time and practice upon culture assimilator training. *International Journal of Intercultural Relations*, 1977, *1*, 105–119.

Rankin, R. E., & Campbell, D. T. Galvanic skin response to Negro and White experimenters. *Journal of Abnormal and Social Psychology*, 1955, *51*, 30–33.

Rath, L. E., & Trager, F. N. Public opinion and crossfire. *Journal of Educational Sociology*, 1948, *21*, 345–349.

Reckless, W. G., & Bringen, H. L. Racial attitudes and information about the Negro. *Journal of Negro Education*, 1933, *2*, 128–138.

Robertson, I. H. *An investigation of the effects of reading literature on the racial attitudes of elementary school children*. Unpublished M.A. Ed. thesis, University of Illinois at Urbana-Champaign, 1979.

Rokeach, M. *The open and closed mind*. New York: Basic Books, 1960.

Rokeach, M. Long range experimental modification of values, attitudes and behavior. *American Psychologist*, 1971, *26*, 453–459.

Rokeach, M. *The nature of human values*. New York: Free Press, 1973.

Rose, T. L. Cognitive and dyadic processes in intergroup contact. In D. Hamilton (Ed.), *Cognitive processes in stereotyping and intergroup behavior*. Hillsdale, NJ: Erlbaum, 1981.

Rosen, I. C. The effect of the motion picture "Gentleman's Agreement" on attitudes toward Jews. *Journal of Psychology*, 1948, *26*, 525–536.

Rosenfield, D., Sheehan, D. S., Marcus, M. M., & Stephan, W. G. Classroom structure and prejudice in desegregated schools. *Journal of Educational Psychology*, 1981, *73*, 17–26.

Sappington, A. A. Effects of desensitization of prejudiced whites to blacks upon subjects' stereotypes of blacks. *Perceptual and Motor Skills*, 1976, *43*, 938.

Schon, I., Hopkins, K. D., & Vojir, C. *The effects of special curricular study of Mexican culture on Anglo and Mexican-American students' perceptions of Mexican-Americans.* Paper presented to the American Educational Research Association, Boston, April 1980.

Singh, J. M., & Yancy, A. V. Racial attitudes in white first grade children. *Journal of Educational Research*, 1974, *67*, 370–372.

Slavin, R. E., & Madden, N. A. School practices that improve race relations. *American Educational Research Journal*, 1979, *16*, 169–180.

Smith, F. T. An experiment in modifying attitudes toward the Negro. *Teachers College Contributions to Education*, 1943, *887*.

Smith, R. J., Griffith, J. E., Griffith, H. K., & Steger, M. J. When is a stereotype a stereotype? *Psychological Reports*, 1980, *46*, 643–651.

Spector, R. *Troop-community training.* NATO Conference on Special Training for Multilateral Forces, Brussels, July 1969.

Spector, P. Parris, T., Humphrey, R., Aronson, J., & Williams, C. *Troop-community relations research in Korea* (Technical Report). Washington, D.C., American Institutes for Research, April 1969.

Stephan, W. G. School desegregation: An evaluation of predictions made in Brown vs. the Board of Education. *Psychological Bulletin*, 1978, *85*, 217–238.

Stephan, W. G. Intergroup relations. In G. Lindzey & E. Aronson (Eds.), *The handbook of social psychology* (3rd edition). Reading, MA: Addison-Wesley, in press.

Stephan, W. G., & Rosenfield, D. Effects of desegregation on race relations and self-esteem. *Journal of Educational Psychology*, 1978, *70*, 670–679. (a)

Stephan, W. G., & Rosenfield, D. Effects of desegregation on racial attitudes. *Journal of Personality and Social Psychology*, 1978, *36*, 795–804. (b)

Stephan, W. G., & Rosenfield, D. Black self-rejection: Another look. *Journal of Educational Psychology*, 1979, *71*, 708–716.

Stephan, W. G., & Rosenfield, D. Racial and ethnic stereotypes. In A. G. Miller (Ed.), *In the eye of the beholder: Contemporary issues in stereotyping.* New York: Praeger, 1982.

Stewart, E., Danielman, J., & Foster, R. *Simulating intercultural communication through role playing* (HumRRO Technical Report 69-7) Alexandria, VA: Human Resources Research Organization, May 1969.

Tajfel, H. La categorisation sociale. Cited in H. Tajfel, *Differentiation between social groups.* London: Academic Press, 1978.

Tajfel, H., Skeikh, A. A., & Gardner, R. C. Content of stereotypes and the inference of similarity between members of stereotyped groups. *Acta Psychologica*, 1964, *22*, 191–201.

Triandis, H. C. Interpersonal attitudes and behavior in race relations. In P. Watson (Ed.), *Psychology and race.* London: Penguin, 1972. Pp. 242–256.

Triandis, H. C. Culture training, cognitive complexity, and interpersonal attitudes. In R. Brislin, S. Bochner & W. Lonner (Eds.), *Cross-cultural perspectives on learning.* Beverly Hills, CA: Sage and Wiley/Halstead, 1975. Pp. 39–77.

Triandis, H. C. *Variations in Black and White perceptions of the social environment.* Urbana, IL: University of Illinois Press, 1976.

Turner, J. C. Social categorization and social discrimination in the minimal group paradigm. In H. Tajfel, *Differentiation between social groups.* New York: Academic Press, 1978.

Vassiliou V., Triandis, H., & Oncken, G. *Intercultural attitudes after reading ethnographic essay: An exploratory study* Technical Report, 68 (68–13). University of Illinois, Group Effectiveness Research Laboratory, 1968.

Vidmar, N., & Rokeach, M. "Archie Bunker's bigotry: A study in selective perception and exposure." *Journal of Communication,* 1974, *24,* 36–47.

Vidulich, R. N., & Krevanick, F. W. Racial attitudes and emotional response to visual representation of the Negro. *Journal of Social Psychology,* 1966, *68,* 82–93.

Webster, S. W. The influence of interracial contact on social acceptance in a newly integrated school. *Journal of Educational Psychology,* 1961, *52,* 292–296.

Weldon, D. E., Carlston, A., Rissman, A. K., Slobodin, L., Triandis, H. C. A laboratory test of effects of culture assimilator training. *Journal of Personality and Social Psychology,* 1975, *32,* 300–310.

Wilder, D. A. Perceiving persons as a group: Categorization and intergroup relations. In D. Hamilton (Ed.), *Cognitive processes in stereotyping and intergroup behavior,* Hillsdale, NJ: Erlbaum Associates, 1982.

Wilder, D. A., & Allen, V. L. Group membership and preference for information about others. *Personality and Social Psychology Bulletin,* 1978, *4,* 106–110.

Williams, R. M., Jr. *The reduction of intergroup tensions: A survey of research on problems of ethnic, racial, and religious group relations* (Bulletin 57), New York: Social Science Research Council, 1947.

Williams, R. M., Jr. *Mutual accommodation: Ethnic conflict and cooperation.* Minneapolis, MN: University of Minnesota Press, 1977.

Wrightsman, L. S. *Social Psychology* (2nd ed). CA: Brooks/Cole, 1977.

Yawkey, T. D. Attitudes toward Black Americans held by rural and urban white early childhood subjects based upon multi-ethnic social studies materials. *Journal of Negro Education,* 1973, *42,* 164–169.

Yawkey, T. D., & Blackwell, J. Attitudes of four-year old urban black children toward themselves and whites based upon multi-ethnic social materials and experiences. *Journal of Educational Research,* 1974, *67,* 373–377.

Zajonc, R. B. Attitudinal effects of mere exposure. *Journal of Personality and Social Psychology Monograph Supplement,* 1968, *9,* (2: Part 2), 2–27.

12

Training for Desegregation in the Military*

Dan Landis
Richard O. Hope
and
Harry R. Day

This chapter has three aims: First, a theory of interethnic behavior is presented and related to the military situation. In keeping with the focus of this book, the theory is appropriately psychologically and behaviorally based. Second, we describe the history and current status of race relations and equal opportunity training programs in the U.S. military. We also take a look at the evaluations that have been performed on these programs and attempt to relate those findings to the theory developed here. We say attempt because the evaluations rarely, if ever, have a clearly defined and articulated theoretical base. Finally, we make some recommendations for the future conduct of training for desegregation in the military. It is not our purpose to review completely the many and varied attempts by the military to make desegregation a practical reality. That has been done elsewhere (Day, 1983; Hope, 1979). Rather, our focus is on the presentation of a model of interethnic behavior that could be used to guide desegregation training efforts in the military and other similar situations.

*Preparation of this chapter was facilitated by Contract N0014–83–K–0021 from the Office of Naval Research to the first author. The opinions here are those of the authors and do not necessarily represent those of the Department of the Navy, the Department of Defense, the United States Government, or its agencies. The writing of the chapter was also facilitated by the first author's tenure as Fellow at the Culture Learning Institute, East–West Center, Honolulu, Hawaii, during 1983.

A Model of Interethnic Behavior

It seems quite clear from the various reports reviewed both here and elsewhere that the race-relations programs in the military have suffered from a lack of consistent theoretical guidance. Thus there have been, in reality, a number of programs, the total only limited by the unique character of each base and commander. Not only has the behavior that is desired been unclear but so also is any conceptualization of the links between the desired behavior and possible program modules. We demonstrated the importance of looking at these links in a recent study (Hulgus and Landis, 1979) in which counterbalancing the order of two common types of cross-cultural training produced quite different results.

If we take the luxury of standing back from the organizational constraints (Dinges & Maynard, 1983; Mumford, 1983), we can sketch the outlines of a model of interethnic behavior. For a variety of reasons (e.g., our own disciplinary backgrounds) the focus of the model is individualistic. That is, we are concerned with defining interethnic competent behaviors (Dinges, 1983) at the level of an individual's actions. To be sure, there will be organizational impacts and restrictions on this behavior. We include where ever possible such variables in our model.

The model presented below also draws some of its inspiration from the discussion and research on the contact hypothesis (Allport, 1954; Amir, 1969, 1976). That is, it is taken as axiomatic that the aim of interethnic training is to produce interpersonal contact situations that are positive and lead to further interactions of the same type. However as Amir (1976) has pointed out, not all contact situations produce positive results and the findings particularly in the military have been mixed (Amir, Bizman, & Rivner, 1973; MacKenzie, 1948). Further, contact does not occur as a full-blown act without history and preparation. That is, a rich and complex set of cognitions and behaviors precede any contact situation and act to set up expectancies and behaviors on the part of the actor as well as the others in the situation. The contact hypothesis provides a critical but not very complete backdrop to understanding the integration situation. For without a clear idea of the cognitive history of the person, we cannot predict how he or she will categorize the behavior of the other and thus how those actions will reinforce the actor. We are left simply with the fact of contact, good or bad. We feel that we must go beyond the surface and somewhat naive analyses and attempt to see the integration situation from the point of view of the actor. The model in this section is put forward in that spirit.

It is our basic thesis that desegregation becomes a reality when people feel, as well as become, interethnically competent. That competence comes about when appropriate behaviors are elicited and reinforced. This rather facile statement begs the real issues, of course: how are the ''appropriate behaviors'' elicited and, once emitted, how is the reinforcement provided and by whom? To provide a beginning for an answer, we use a model of intercultural behavior[1] recently proposed by Brislin, Landis and Brandt (1983). This model is schematically shown in Figure 12.1.

As the criterion behavior, Brislin *et al.* propose that actions should be defined in terms of their impact on others. These authors see "intercultural behavior as action that produces a significant change in the judgments of the actor's social or skill competence by people from *another* cultural background" (p. 3; emphasis in the original). Thus as the actors, cultures, and settings change, the desired behavior may and should change. Further, the definition leaves open the possibility that the behavior may be judged positively, negatively, or neutrally from time to time. We would argue, however, that the relevant set of interethnic behaviors are those that result in a positive change in minority perceptions of whites' social or skill competence. For as that subset of positive behaviors is emitted, it is likely to be reinforced by minorities and become part of the actor's preferred repetoire. Now, how does this desired set come about?

The model proposed by Brislin *et al.* (1983) suggests a number of factors needed to elicit the desired set of behaviors. Some of the antecedent variables are conceptually and temporally close to the desired action and some are quite distant. All, however, are hypothesized to contribute to the nature of the in-

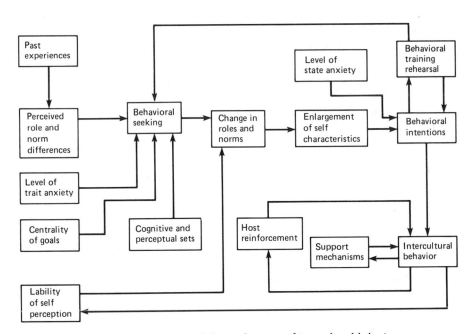

Figure 12.1. Cognitive behavioral picture of intercultural behavior.

[1]We use the words *intercultural* and *interethnic* interchangeably.

tercultural act. As we discuss each variable in the model, we shall relate it to the military setting—as we understand that setting.

The person entering the integrated situation is not, in most cases, without intercultural experiences. He or she comes complete with a packet of experiences, beliefs, and expectations about people of all other racial groups. These originate deep in the past as well as just yesterday. The most salient variables are:

1. The *affect* that is associated with the sum total of past interactions with members of the other group. These experiences may be real or imagined. So a person who comes from an urban area in which he or she had negative experiences with members of a minority group would have one set of experiences; similarly a person whose experiences were positive would have another view.

2. The past experiences lead to certain expectations of *differences* in role and norm behaviors. The contrast here is between the actor and the perceived other (Jones & Nisbett, 1972; Ross, 1977). If the difference is perceived to be great, there may be little attempt to interact so that relevant behavior rarely, if ever, occurs. For example, a soldier who sees blacks as being very different, wanting different things from the military, and sharing few values might avoid interaction whenever possible. When avoiding is not possible, the interaction would be kept on a task basis with little cognitive or affective evaluation of the experiences.

On the other hand, when no differences are perceived, parodoxically the same result might be obtained. That is, a belief of sameness might lead to a loss of any motivation to associate except as necessary and accidental during the normal work day. The often used statement in the Army "there is no black or white, only (Army) green" is, perhaps, an expression of this idea.

The preceding observations suggest something like the Yerkes-Dodson curve. There is some optimum perceived difference that is a motivation for a person to engage in behavior directed at changing the other's perception.

3. Intercultural behavior is arousing. This statement finds some theoretical support in the speculations of George Kelly (1955; Diamond, 1982). Kelly's suggestion was that if personal constructs are in danger of being changed due to external experience, anxiety is the affective state that results. Later we discuss the directional properties of this state. However, here we note that there are individual differences in the normal level of arousal, in particular, *anxiety*. If a person is chronically highly anxious, his or her willingness to engage in intercultural behavior may well be compromised. This *trait* anxiety (Spielberger, 1966) probably functions in a more linear fashion than anxiety associated with a particular event. So, we might predict that the level of anxiety is inversely related to willingness to enter intercultural settings. For examples, all things being equal, if a white soldier is invited for a drink by two other persons, one

white and one black, and he has a choice of going with one or the other, level of state anxiety will affect the choice.

4. Intercultural behavior is only one category of activities that may engage a person's attention at any given time. Each such set of activities is viewed by the person as more or less important to achieve more or less critical goals. To the extent that the behaviors are perceived as related to central goals, the person will be more likely to engage in such behaviors. The major effect of the various military directives regarding interethnic relations has probably been to increase the centrality (i.e., perceived relationship to promotion) of positive intercultural behaviors. We would suspect that the perceived centrality of goals is quite similar and related to the perceived consequences of behavior that Triandis (1976) has included in his model.

All of the above distal variables are alike in one important respect. Each has some impact on the individual's inclination to seek new social situation, which Brislin et al. (1983) call behavioral seeking. We believe that this tendency is critical and central to an understanding and maintenance of intercultural behavior.

Behavioral seeking involves the deliberate placing of oneself in situations for which the interpersonal action cues are ambiguous, at best. Because these are situations that are likely to be anxiety arousing, there are good reasons for them to be avoided. Yet, without this volitional behavior, the individual may never have the opportunity to try out new responses and have them potentially reinforced. In the military setting, we would note that behavior seeking is taking place when individuals begin to interact with others on matters not strictly related to the mission at hand. Those activities may be social or work focused but extended in time, involving new behaviors that are not required and occur in place of previous learned activities. Our caveat that the critical new behaviors are those that are not focused solely on work has support in the many studies that have found little or no reduction in prejudice when contact is restricted to occupational interaction (Minard, 1952).

Behavioral seeking is affected by another set of individual traits. These have to do with the way in which the person constructs social reality. In particular, we would point to the tendency to use wide or narrow categories to deal with people, things, and situations. Detweiler (1980) has presented some evidence that wide categorizers (a trait that seems quite similar to cognitive complexity [Mayo & Crockett, 1964]) are able to function more effectively in an intercultural situation. On the other hand, Kealey and Ruben (1982) have been unable to find such a relationship when dealing with people being sent overseas to provide technical assistance. Indeed, the latter authors find just the opposite relationship from that reported by Detweiler (1980). Perhaps, the cognitive–perceptual set (Gardner, Holzman, Klein, Linton, & Spence, 1959) is moderated by the situation (Detweiler, Brislin, & McCormack, 1983) to a greater extent than previously suspected. It thus seems reasonable to suggest that these "sets" are related to the tendency to overstereotype and, we would suspect, maintain the belief in the face of overwhelming evidence.

Behavioral seeking, by virtue of generating new experiences, leads to changes in expected roles and normative behaviors. By this we mean that new conceptions of the "oughts" and "shoulds" of behavior become consolidated, or even take the place of old ideas about what are proper intercultural behaviors. Critical to the occurrence of these new beliefs is the flexibility of the person's conception of him- or herself. If there are rigid boundaries to the behaviors that he or she considers proper for the self, then the new experiences may be reinterpreted in a limited fashion. The results of behavioral seeking (e.g., social interaction with black soldiers) can often be misinterpreted when the minority individuals express a tolerance for behavior that seems unacceptable. The willingness to accept traits in others—to take the viewpoint of others—is what we mean by the term *lability* of self-perception.

Under favorable circumstances, not only is there a change in perceived role and norm difference but also the individual's self-conception shifts. This shift is toward the inclusion of others' characteristics in the person's own view of him- or herself in such a way that the person can visualize engaging in behaviors and being judged as a member of another cultural group. Most importantly, he or she can take the view of others and judge it in the same terms that others would. This move away from egocentrism is a critical element in the development of desegregation supportive behaviors.

Despite important changes in the world view of the person, appropriate intercultural behaviors may still not occur; and not occurring, their failure to be reinforced will lead to fewer and fewer such behaviors in the future. We hypothesize that an important precursor to the intention to engage in intercultural acts (which the studies and conceptualizations of Fishbein and Triandis [1976] have shown to be highly related to behavior) is the engaging in *behavioral training rehearsal*. We have captured the description of this variable from the early learning literature. Cognitive rehearsal of lists is shown to be effective in their later recall. Related here is Piaget's Law of Relative Centrations in which the interaction of sensory mechanisms and stimuli are shown to underlie illusions. Landis and Harrison (1967) show that similar effects occur through use of fantasy. Planning potential intercultural behaviors in an imaginary situation may not only produce more stable behaviors but allow a relative emphasis on certain aspects. So a soldier may think about how he will give an order to a black man, or how he will respond to being insulted, or any one of a myriad of possible and imagined situations. In any case, for each, he can rehearse actions and contemplate possible reactions and rewards.

Once the desired behavior has occurred, its future course depends almost entirely on the reactions from the "others" and the surrounding social network. If the other reacts negatively—as Japanese often do for someone imperfectly speaking their language (Ramsey & Birk, 1983)—then the future responses may be considerably muted. Similarly, if the social system (e.g., the "chain of command") is not supportive, then also the responses will degrade (Brislin, 1981; Fontaine, 1982). Over the past decade, the military has been attempting to provide appropriate support mechanisms for the kind of desegregative behaviors that are desired.

It is safe to say that the U.S. military, despite room for improvement, represents the most desegregated sector of American society. This has not always been true. For example, Abraham Lincoln accepted black soldiers only when casualty rates became so high it was politically inexpedient not to use them (Forner, 1974). Black Buffalo Soldiers were set against another minority, the Native Americans. In both world wars, although extensively represented among American soldiers, all-black units were commanded by white officers and were rarely relied upon for important duty.

The modern period of race relations in the military began clearly with President Truman's Executive Order 9981 on July 26, 1948. This order, which took undoubtedly a great deal of political courage, made it the policy of the government that integration and equal opportunity were to be the norm rather than the exception in the armed forces. One of the factors contributing to this decision was able performance of black soldiers in the European and Pacific campaigns; this performance was documented by the now-classic Stouffer Report (Stouffer, Lumsdaine, Lumsdaine, Williams, Smith, Janis, Star & Cottrell, 1949) and the later Gillian Committee Report (Quarles, 1961). Unlike the aftermath of previous wars in which outstanding black performance had been denigrated upon cessation of hostilities, these reports must have contributed to a new perception (Hope, 1979). In any case, Mr. Truman must have been convinced that no degradation of military efficiency would result from racial integration of the armed forces.

The army's response to Truman's order was the adoption of a policy statement issued in January, 1950. Coincident with this policy statement, and probably due to the training demands of the Korean "police action," the commander of Fort Ord, California, began integrating training companies (Hope, 1979). Other similar actions were taken and desegregation, at least at the lower ranks, became the norm rather than the exception. However desegregation at this level did not lead to similar action at other levels. During the 1950s, blacks, although found in all units, remained concentrated in the lower enlisted ranks and in certain military occupational specialities (e.g., food service). The army's lead in desegregation was followed by similar, though often not as effective, actions by the other services.

The black–white tensions during the 1960s were reflected in the military as one might expect. The growing awareness of the facts of disadvantagement among blacks in the military led to an assertion of demands for equal treatment as well as a rise of racial sensitivity, white anxiety, and open hostility. The increased tension and continually escalating hostilities throughout the 1960s, exacerbated by the disproportionate numbers of blacks among the lower enlisted ranks, a dearth of black officers[2], and the high casuality rates for blacks in the Vietnam war culminated in open conflicts within the military that were often described as "race riots." These conflicts were experienced by all branches of the service. However those occurring in the army (e.g., in Germany) and in the navy (e.g., the U.S.S. *Kittyhawk*) received the greatest attention (Hope, 1979; Day, 1983).

This situation led to a series of investigations and appointment of task forces in an attempt to resolve the problems. For example, an investigating team was sent to Europe by President Nixon and found a high level of frustration and anger among black troops. The team concluded that the problem lay in the perceived failure of the military leadership to exercise adequate authority and responsibility in monitoring the equal opportunity aspects of military regulations. At about the same time, an Interservice Task Force on Education (created by the Secretary of Defense), was assigned responsibility for developing an effective race relations education program that would be applicable to all the services. The Task Force called for: (1) creation of a mandatory program in race relations education for all military personnel, (2) establishment of a Defense Race Relations Institute, and (3) formation of an interservice race relations board.

All these recommendations were officially implemented by Department of Defense (DoD) Directive 1322.11 issued in June, 1971. The program that resulted included a formal DoD support structure, key components of which were the Defense Race Relations Institute (DRRI) and the Race Relations Board. In addition, local units were required to provide race relations training (instructors coming from the Defense Race Relations Institute) to all troops under their control.

The existence of racial discrimination in the military can be attributed to the fact that individuals who enter the military service bring with them the prejudices and stereotypes acquired prior to enlistment. Further, the military services, like other types of institutions in American society tend to reinforce discriminatory attitudes and behaviors by not recognizing the possibility of an institutional racist aspect to many policies and practices. Hence despite equal opportunity directives throughout the 1950s and 1960s, the United States mil-

---

[2]The black officers in the Army held steady at a little over 3%, the highest of all branches, whereas the percentage of blacks in both the enlisted military population and American society was at least four times as large.

itary services simply reflected discrimination found in the society as a whole. When the racial situation became serious enough to threaten the survival and efficiency of the military, the institution reacted with an ambitious and comprehensive program. (For a more detailed history of race relations in the U.S. military, the reader is referred to Day, 1983, and Hope, 1979).

Even though military organizations are highly authoritarian and hierarchical social structures, the statements of policies and directives by no means assure automatic implementation and achievement of goals. In reality, military personnel have considerable latitude for noncompliant and self-directed behavior. This latitude, although present at all times, is even more obvious during peace time. On the other hand, most other American institutions are hardly governed by laissez faire rules allowing full and unrestrained individual freedom and autonomy. Thus, while the military has some unique organizational aspects, these, we believe, tend to be more matters of degree than quantitative differences. On this basis it seems reasonable to look at the military's experience with race relations and desegregation for lessons to be applied in other sections of our society.

The Response to the Problem: Inception of the Program at the Defense Department[3]

One cannot understand the current program of race relations and its effects without understanding the organization that was created to develop that program. Further, since the implementors of the race-relations program were all trained, initially at least, by the DRRI, much of what has happened subsequently to both the trainees and the trainers can be better understood by looking at that institution. For that reason, we shall rather carefully describe the training institute and its history within the military establishment.

The mandate of the DRRI[4] upon its creation, was to develop and implement a program of classes in race relations. These classes were to be designed to prevent "racial unrest, tension or conflict" from impairing "combat readiness and efficiency." The following specific tasks were identified, although the emphasis has always been on the first of these responsibilities: (1) educate and train instructors in race relations, (2) develop doctrine and curricula, (3) evaluate

---

[3]The authors are indebted to the recent and extensive report of Adelman and her colleagues (Adelman & Larkin, 1980; Adelman, Jarkin, Carleton, & Olmpia, 1980) on EO as practiced in DoD.
[4]This institute is now known (since 1978) as the Defense Equal Opportunity Management Institute (EOMI), reflective of a new stage in the military training program (i.e., a shift toward a management-oriented approach).

program effectiveness, and (4) develop and disseminate guidelines and materials to be used throughout the military services.

While there is some question about the achievement of the last two goals, there is no question that an educational program was developed and implemented. The instructional program to be given to individuals who were to become race-relations trainers at bases of the U.S. Army, Navy, and Air Force was described as follows:

> The program of instruction consists of 75 hours of instruction in the history and contributions of major minority groups, 42 hours of instruction in the psychological, social, and cultural factors directly related to the dynamics of race-relations, 40 hours of community interaction activities, four hours for guest speakers, 70 hours devoted to practicum in group leadership dynamics and reentry into their military units, and an added four hours for orientation, critique, and graduation. A total of 235 hours over a six week period. (Commander's Notebook, 1971)

In 1974 the training was expanded to two phases. Phase I emphasizes the use of small-group discussion or seminar methods as a means of exposing students to the differing racial and ethnic life styles and cultures. The objective is to open channels of communication among individuals, identify potential intergroup problems, and provide an arena in which constructive recommendations can be made to appropriate local commanders. Phase II is the more service-specific portion of training. Instruction is carried out by personnel assigned by the individual services. The instruction in Phase II provides training in educational techniques and other service-unique areas of instruction. Students receive information on small group leadership, specific service policies and procedures, and special preparation required for carrying out the unique race-relations and equal-opportunity programs of the individual service.

The Phase I program lasts between 5 and 7 weeks with instruction in minority studies and behavioral science and basically includes the original 6-week instructional material. The Phase II portion varies in length in accordance with service requirements. Currently the total training program, including Phase II, does not exceed 16 weeks.

In 1982, DoD and the military services were implementing comprehensive Equal Opportunity and Human Relations programs with varying degrees of intensity. The chain of command within each service has the primary responsibility to promote and support the equal opportunity program. As one component of the program, current and potential commanders, commanding officers, and other senior commissioned and noncommissioned personnel are to be provided education and training specifically related to their equal opportunity responsibilities. This education is to be included as part of the curricula of various institutions within the military system (e.g., the Command and General Staff School at Ft. Leavenworth, Kansas).

All the military services currently seem intent on phasing out their race relations training as an approach to desegregation and turning toward a management approach to equal opportunity. Whether the new directions taken by the military prove to be efficacious and sufficient remains to be seen. The next section of this chapter examines the evidence of program effectiveness during the first decade.

Military Race Relations Training Evaluated

In evaluating the success of the military establishment's attempts at integration, we find ourselves hampered by a clear lack of specific behavioral goals. The program was instituted without much thought being given to evaluation, either at the base or DRRI/Defense Equal Opportunity Institute (EOMI) level. Indeed, as Hope (1979) notes, DRRI was specifically prohibited from assessing training effectiveness once the students had left the training site. So many of the evaluative reports were based on goals which were retrospectively formulated and imperfectly measured. For the most part, the evaluations focus on attitudinal and self-report measures, with occasional forays into archival (e.g., incident report) data. At the same time, there appears to be a dearth of model formulation that would tie the various dimensions together in meaningful fashion. This lack will remain, we fear, the major obstacle to determining the worth of the military's integration efforts.

The model that we presented earlier suggests the importance of societal norms in the development and maintenance of interethnic behaviors. The presence of social support groups at both the peer and superordinate levels seem to be quite important, if not critical. It is not surprising, therefore, that a good deal of the military evaluation effort has been devoted to an examination of commander support.

Command Support and the Impact of the Race Relations/Equal Opportunity Programs

As the Race Relations/Equal Opportunity (RR/EO) programs are reviewed and evaluated over the last 11 years, it becomes clear that the commander's support is critical to the success of these programs. Because the importance of administrative support is a factor well recognized in social action programs (Allport, 1954; Brislin, 1981; Fontaine, 1982), we included it as a critical aspect of the model presented earlier. Within the military most of our information is focused on the role of the commander. However, the behavior of peers and, in particular, members of the minority groups is critical to the maintenance of behaviors that lead to good race relations. So, the comments that follow in this section are, of necessity, quite limited.

During the period when race relations seminars were the primary focus, attendance, involvement, and ultimately improved understanding between minority and majority, black and white, male and female was directly influenced by the degree of participation of commanders at all levels of administration (Day, 1983; Hope 1979). The vital importance of the commander in the effectiveness of the RR/EO program was emphasized in an analysis of the army unit race relations training program in 1976 (Hiett and Nordlie, 1978). Perceptions of DRRI/EOMI graduates in the study further reinforced the critical role of command. The amount of command support most strongly distinguished higher and lower quality RE/EO programs, and it also correlated strongly with the overall job satisfaction of the graduate (Hope, 1979).

Awareness of the important role of the commander in this process of improving intergroup behavior has lead to the services shifting emphasis on the role of the professional RR/EO person. The role has become more of a consultant to the commander and less involved in direct instruction with service personnel. Whereas some DRRI/EOMI graduates still serve in the instructor role, this is not their exclusive role, and time spent in other roles, especially the equal opportunity staff role, often takes precedence.

In recognition of the changed role of the RR/EO person, the instructional program at the Equal Opportunity Management Institute appears to be gradually shifting to reflect the current situation. The focus on the chain of command presupposes an awareness on the part of the commander. Thus the final question of evaluation must rest with the commander and his or her knowledge and appreciation of the requirements of a military free of discrimination. Most commanders are not sent to DRRI/EOMI today. It is assumed that what awareness there is comes primarily from the traditional military schools that have added courses on the Affirmative Action/Equal Opportunity Program of the services. Preliminary indications are that the more voluntary instructional programs of these schools are limited in the detail and scope necessary for a fully informed commander.

Quality of the Trainer's Training

The seeing of oneself as a person who is interethnically competent and who, therefore, has the skills for positive interactions appears in several parts of the model presented earlier. For example, we would expect that as one feels more competent, the boundaries of the self-image expand and include other points of view. We might also expect that competence and behavioral seeking and rehearsal are intimately related, even prior to actual interethnic behavior. Although these relationships seem reasonable, the emphasis on one set of evaluations on the perceptions by DRRI graduates of their training is not based on such a theoretical statement. Rather, the interest is in providing a mechanism of feedback to the instructional and evaluation staff of DRRI (as well, perhaps, to serve as an early warning system on the attitudes of field commanders toward this new and largely untried function).

Perceptions of the nature of the Defense Race Relations Institute/Equal Opportunity Management Institute training held by students, faculty, graduates, and service personnel are quite clear and consistent. Based on agreement-type items, Phase I training is dramatically endorsed as highly satisfactory training experience, with between 85 and 90% of all graduates claiming satisfaction with the training. (Hope, 1979, p. 65). It is seen by most students of the Institute as an important life experience leading to changes in racial and sex-role awareness and profound changes in feelings about one's self.

Criticisms of Phase I training are fairly consistent throughout the 11 years of evaluations. Graduates emphasize the need for more nonblack minority group content and practical, job-relevant, skills training. More continuous contact after graduation is desired in order to remain current in the field, including new educational literature and periodic refresher courses. In response to these evaluations, training staff have repeatedly requested data from the field describing the specific job requirements and the effectiveness with which the graduates perform their jobs. Unfortunately, the assessment of these graduates was always considered the prerogative of the services and not DRRI/EOMI. Consequently, measurements of performance in the field are difficult if not impossible to obtain. Without such measurements, it is impossible to relate program components to personnel statistics.

Phase II training has been in even greater flux than Phase I. Graduate assessments of Phase II training, although generally positive, have been mixed and are indicative of the confusion associated with these changes. One study conducted in 1977 noted:

> Since Phase II training emphasizes skills development, it is particularly vulnerable to criticism about the lack of instructor job experiences. The large variation in training RR/EO job experience and intellectual aptitude has resulted in some difficulties for Phase II in developing an optimal training program for all trainees. Separate training models based on rank have not been sensitive to the more important dimensions of trainee experience and aptitude. Also the Phase I—Phase II integration of the overall DRRI training experience has not been entirely successful in taking advantage of the changes in awareness and self, associated with Phase I. (Fiman, 1978, p. 84).

In evaluating the impact of the DRRI/EOMI program, the gap between mission or objectives and application looms large. The basic mission of the training programs changed very little since the inception of DRRI but the uses of its graduates changed drastically between 1971 and the present. The mission of

DRRI/EOMI is established by the Department of Defense but the role of the graduates is defined by each branch of the services in accordance with their own requirements.

This gap between mission and application often results in DRRI/EOMI graduates being assigned to jobs and activities for which they are untrained. For example, the original Army Race Relations and Equal Opportunities Training Program (RAP #1) was a mandatory 18-hour course taught by DRRI graduates. The primary responsibility for graduates at that time was as race-relations instructors. DRRI training was geared toward developing "instructors in race relations," as required by the mission statement.

By early 1974 the program was changed by revised Army regulation to create RAP #2 which placed the primary responsibility for conducting training in the chain of command and required seminars to be conducted with platoon-sized units. This regulation effectively took the DRRI/EOMI graduate out of the training business. Most of the RAP #2 became discussions led by a commander or his designee who rarely was DRRI/EOMI trained. Indeed, an evaluation conducted by Hiett and Nordlie (1978) found that race relations training conducted by the commander rather than DRRI-trained instructors had limited impact. Many commanders, not being trained as race-relations instructors, were often not appreciative of the possible benefits of an effective race-relations instructional program, and, as a consequence, treated this program requirement as just another bureaucratic requirement on top of an already overburdened set of role expectations.

Other regulations continued to make these graduates advisors to the chain of command. These new rules increasingly defined DRRI/EOMI graduates as administrators and managers and not instructors. During all of these changes in the role of these graduates, the basic mission of training instructors in race relations was not changed to comply with new regulations. As Hope (1979) demonstrated, this conflict has produced occupational stress and burnout in DRRI/EOMI graduates. Because individuals under such stress are likely to be less effective in what they perceive their mission to be, the impact on the program is most likely negative.

On the other side of this issue, the services rarely made decisions to change the role of the DRRI/EOMI graduate on the grounds of improving the effective utilization of this resource. Rather, these decisions were made primarily to protect the management decision making within the chain of command. It was felt that the proliferation of these graduates throughout the services was undermining the authority of the unit commander. (Hiett & Nordlie, 1978). In the early days of DRRI this was accurate to some extent. Given the lack of precedent for this type of job in the military, independent actions were taken by the trained graduates without consulting the commander. After 1974 this behavior did not persist because of the addition of Phase II, which was designed to concentrate on service-specific requirements. Presumably, as the unit commanders began to take over responsibility for training, independent action by DRRI graduates was not reinforced.

Field Evaluations

Few field evaluations were conducted to determine the impact of the intergroup relations training program on the average soldier. Part of this was due to the inability of the DRRI staff to follow-up on their graduates, and part was due to the difficulty of the research problem. However, one such study, representing the only replication investigation, sought to analyze attitudes of army personnel in 1972 as compared to 1974 (Brown, Nordlie, & Thomas, 1977). This study concluded that "sharp and pervasive differences" still existed 2 years later in 1974 between blacks and whites; however most of the changes in the difference were in the direction of a reduction of prejudice. Blacks continued to see a great deal of racial discrimination (as measured by forced-choice attitude-type items) but whites saw little or no evidence of discrimination against blacks. Blacks did see the state of race relations more favorably in 1974 than the 2 previous years. The training programs had shown little impact on the perceived importance of accepting race relations and equal opportunity as part of leadership responsibility. Lower-ranking enlisted personnel did not see officers and noncommissioned officers using this definition of leadership in annual evaluations even though this was a policy requirement.

Although we discussed the findings on command support earlier, the Brown, Nordlie and Thomas (1977) study also had some things to say on this issue. They noted that the chain of command was pushing the program as indicated by a significant increase in the knowledge of the program by the enlisted respondents.

> Large numbers of both blacks and whites continue to report that they have personally benefitted from the Army's race relations training program. At the same time, however, there is still an absence of any widespread feelings that race relations training and education programs will achieve the objective set for them." (Brown, Nordlie and Thomas, 1977, p. V)

The second major field evaluation (Hiett & Nordlie, 1978), looked at the Army Unit Race Relations Training Program. This was an attempt to put the training and leadership back in the hands of the unit commander, and remove it from the primary responsibility of the DRRI/EOMI graduate.

The evaluation of Hiett and Nordlie (1978) of this unit training program was not favorable. The Army had reported in 1976 that less than half of all companies in the United States were conducting monthly unit race relations seminars that were required by policy. They went on to say:

The quality of training is low and its relationship to RR/EO (race relations/equal opportunity) often minimal. There is much evidence that the unit training program is largely a "paper program" and for most company commanders its priority is extremely low. It seldom reaches personnel above the rank of E5: those persons who (by virtue of their role in the organization) have the most power to effect change, if change is needed, are least likely to participate in the seminars. The sensitive nature of the subject matter coupled with the specialized background knowledge required make it nearly impossible for untrained chain-of-command personnel to conduct effective RR/EO seminars. (Hiett and Nordlie, 1978, p. 4)

This 1976 data-gathering also found the racial climate to be steadily declining from its high in 1972. Hiett and Nordlie noted that despite the low frequency of overt violence, perceptions of race-related tension persists and may be increasing.

Whereas field evaluations based on clear linkages between training components and the attitudes and behaviors of personnel are not available, there is some data on the change in perceptions over the time period (1972–1980) in question. During this period, Nordlie and his colleagues performed a number of surveys designed to probe the perceptions of race relations in various Army commands. Data were gathered in 1972, 1974, 1976 (Continental United States—CONUS—only), Korea in 1976, U.S. Army in Europe (USAREUR) in 1976, and a sample of Army Leaders in 1977. Because there were a number of items common to all of these surveys, it is possible to track at least two dimensions over time and location (Day, 1983).

Table 12.1 (taken from Day, 1983) presents data on the perceptions of the status of race relations and the perceptions of trends in the same variable. It should be noted that the time period covered represents the most active period in the army's program. The general impression from the data in Table 12.1 is that the positivity of whites' perceptions about race relations reached a peak around 1976 and has declined somewhat since then. The perceptions of blacks followed a similar trend. Another impression is the apparently unrealistic perception by army leaders in 1977 who see the situation as much better than do the mass of personnel. It should be noted that the downturn appears at about the same time as the shift from a race relations focus to a management concern was taking place, although the causal connection between these events is difficult to document.

Similar data appear in evaluations of the other services. We concentrate here on the Army for two reasons: (1) the Army has had the most active research and evaluation program, perhaps due to the obvious fact that it is the largest of the services and, (2) the documentation of the evaluation efforts within the Army are easily available to the scholarly community. Furthermore the racial distribution in the Army represents a closer approximation than the other services to that in the general population.

A fair assessment of the evaluations carried out on the various services' equal

TABLE 12.1

Differences in Static and Dynamic Perceptions of Race Relations in the Army

	Total 1972	Army[a] 1974	CONUS[b] 1976	Korea[c] 1976	USAREUR[d] 1976	USAREUR: junior enlisted	1977[e] Leaders
		Perceptions of army race relations across time and location					
White responses							
Good	20	23	23	16	21	15	45
Fair	55	55	49	45	55	52	50
Poor	25	22	28	39	24	33	5
Black responses							
Good	10	20	24	15	16	18	33
Fair	50	52	45	43	46	51	55
Poor	39	27	31	42	38	33	12
		Perceptions of trends in race relations across time and location					
White responses							
Getting better	39	41	30	28	34	20	44
No change	36	41	56	43	50	62	51
Getting worse	24	18	14	29	16	18	5
Black responses							
Getting better	42	48	39	35	39	35	54
No change	39	39	49	42	47	52	40
Getting worse	18	11	12	23	14	13	6

[a]From Brown, Nordlie, and Thomas, 1977.
[b]From Hiett and Nordlie, 1978
[c]From Edmonds and Nordlie, 1977
[d]From Gilbert and Nordlie, 1978
[e]From Brown, Edmonds, White, Sevilla, and Nordlie, 1979

opportunity/race-relations programs would find a focus on attitudinal measures divorced from a clear theoretical conception or model. Self-report measures loom large with little serious attempt at multitrait and multimode measurement. Further, there is often a failure to relate the effects of training (obtained through attitudinal and self-report) to the putative objectives of the training. Thus it is difficult, if not impossible, to form any reasonable judgment of the effectiveness of the vast and complicated structure that the military has developed to deal with the goal of integration. What does seem clear, however, is that as the race-relations training programs (at least in the U.S. Army) were turned over to the generally untrained unit leadership, the racial climate deteriorated. Our earlier model would suggest that what happened was a decrease in the black and white enlisted personnel's perception of the interethnic competence of the commanders. Thus we could note that as professional intergroup training increased between the late 1960s and early 1970s, racial harmony, as measured by attitudinal as well as archival measures, improved. However, as this training was put in the hands of less well-trained unit leaders, the level of intergroup competence decreased along with the interracial climate.

Gross Measures of DoD-Wide Impact

One can, of course, evaluate the gross effect of the total Department of Defense program by examining minority representation figures. These figures, available in Nordlie (1973) and Adelman, Larkin, Carleton, & Olmpia (1980), make a comparison between 1972 and 1979 possible. Such data suggest that each service increased its representation of minorities at all levels over that period with the greatest change being at the enlisted ranks. The Army apparently was the most successful in attracting and retaining minority personnel. For example, in 1972, 17.5% of Army enlisted personnel were black; in 1979 this figure had increased to 32%. Comparable figures for the Navy were 7.2 and 11%. Summaries of these figures are given by Day (1983).

These figures should not be overinterpreted. Just as Amir (1976) has suggested that not all contact situations produce reductions in prejudice, so a rise in minority representation may not indicate success of the desegregation program. Indeed, the suggestion made earlier, that racial climate, at least in the Army units, seems to be deteriorating over the same time period would suggest that not enough attention has been paid to the conditions of interethnic interaction. Because we have no information on actual interethnic behavior, it is difficult to predict the joint effect of increase in minority representation and decrease in racial climate under present training models.

Theory as a Guide to Training Design in the Military Program

The qualitative data clearly show that the military's program, although ambitious, was often of the "shotgun" variety. There is often a distressing emphasis on structure to the detriment of clearly defined objectives and training modules tied to these goals. Quite different and perhaps conflictual programs are mixed with little thought or attention to their interactions or even how to evaluate their effects. Further, there has, as far as we can tell, been little cross-fertilization from the field of cross-cultural training (Landis & Brislin, 1983; Weeks, Pederson & Brislin, 1979). To be sure, the Army Research Institute did sponsor a number of projects in which some new approaches were developed (e.g., Landis, Day, McGrew, Miller, & Thomas, 1976; Landis, Tzeng, &

Thomas, 1981) and subjected to field evaluation. These efforts involve a use of the Culture Assimilator approach derived from the work by Triandis (1976) and focus on producing an increase in behavioral rehearsals of intercultural behaviors. These studies would bear a closer look because they represent, to our knowledge, the only attempt in the decade and a half of serious military desegregation programs to develop a training program based on a reasonable theoretical formulation. However, these efforts do not seem to have become institutionalized and do not play a significant part in the military program at this time. Thus they are somewhat beyond the scope of this chapter. (Good summaries are available in Albert, 1983.)

Recommendations

The above observations lead us to make a number of recommendations:

1. We suggest that the military critically evaluate its programs in terms of developing and stating just what behaviors are desired.
2. Once a clear conception of desired behavior is made, then consider what are the potent precursors of those behaviors. Some models like the one presented in the first section of this chapter might be useful.
3. Develop exemplary programs around the desired behaviors and their precursors and allow those programs to operate a reasonable length of time.
4. Evaluate the program using the model. To be sure, other measurements can and should be taken, but the conceptual model should be the critical underpinning for the evaluative strategy.
5. Recognize that the similarities in military service are greater than the differences, at least at the desegregation level. The interservice rivalries that have surfaced from time to time have given a patina of difference, based on uniform color, which hides the true state of affairs. So, unified policies and training, using common models and techniques, will show a greater commitment to desegregation than the present fractionated approach.
6. It is imperative that more attention be given to increasing the fit between the training models and the requirements in the field for the Equal Opportunity Management Institute graduate.
7. The development of a professional and well-trained cadre cannot be overestimated. Having people who are committed to the goal of integration will help as both role and training models to the large mass of military personnel. Whereas this may mean returning to the professional race-relations training school concept, the military should recognize that any objective levied on the commander that does not directly relate to his or her combat mission will not enjoy a high priority. To believe otherwise

flies in the face of not only the psychological facts but also the evaluations that have been performed.

References

Adelman, J. & Larkin, T. F. *Functional assessment of military equal opportunity staffs: policy and personnel analysis.* Volume II of a Final Report to the Deputy Assistant Secretary of Defense (Equal Opportunity), Logical Technical Services Corporation, Vienna, VA, 1980.

Adelman, J., Larkin, T. F., Carleton, D., & Olmpia, P. *Functional assessment of military equal opportunity staffs: field research and job analysis.* Volume I of Final Report to the Deputy Assistant Secretary of Defense (Equal Opportunity), Logical Technical Services Corporation, Vienna, VA, 1980.

Albert, R. D. The intercultural sensitizer or culture assimilator: cognitive approach to training. In D. Landis and R. W. Brislin (Eds.), *Handbook of intercultural training Vol. II: Issues in training methodology.* Elmsford, NY: Pergamon Press, 1983.

Allport, G. W. *The nature of prejudice.* Reading, MA: Addison-Wesley, 1954.

Amir, Y. Contact hypothesis in ethnic relations. *Psychological bulletin.,* 1969, *71,* 319–342.

Amir, Y. The role of intergroup contact in change of prejudice and ethnic relations. In P. A. Katz (Ed.), *Towards the elimination of racism.* New York: Pergamon Press, 1976.

Amir, Y., Bizman, A., & Rivner, M. Effects of interethnic contact on friendship choices in the military. *Journal of Cross-cultural Psychology,* 1973, *4,* 361–373.

Brislin, R. W. *Cross-cultural encounters.* New York: Pergamon Press, 1981.

Brislin, R. W., Landis, D., & Brandt, M. E. Conceptualizations of intercultural behavior and training. In D. Landis and R. W. Brislin (Eds.), *Handbook of Intercultural Training. Vol. I: Issues in theory and design.* Elmsford, NY: Pregamon Press, 1983. Pp. 1–35.

Brown, D. K., Edmonds, W. S., White, S. J., Sevilla, E. R., Jr., & Nordlie, P. G. *A second study of race relations/equal opportunity training in USAREUR.* McLean, VA: HSR, January, 1979.

Brown, D. K., Nordlie, P. G., & Thomas, J. A. *Changes in black and white perceptions of the Army's race relations/equal opportunity program—1972–74* (ARI Technical Report TR 77–83). Alexandria, VA: U.S. Army Research Institute for the Behavioral and Social Sciences, 1977.

Day, H. R. Race relations training in the U.S. Military. In D. Landis & R. W. Brislin (Eds.), *Handbook of Intercultural Training. Vol II: Issues in training methodology.* Elsmford, NY: Pergamon Press, 1983.

Defense Race Relations Institute (DRRI). *Commander's notebook.* Melbourne, FL: Patrick Air Force Base, 1971.

Department of Defense. *Directive 1322.11. Subject: Education and training in Human/Race Relations for military personnel,* 1971. (Revised [September 12, 1978]).

Detweiler, R. Intercultural intervention and the categorization process: A conceptual analysis and behavioral outcome. *International Journal of Intercultural Relations,* 1980, *4,* 277–295.

Detweiler, R., Brislin, R. W., & McCormack, W. Situational analysis. In D. Landis & R. W. Brislin (Eds.), *Handbook of intercultural training. Vol. II: Issues in training methodology.* Elmsford, NY: Pergamon Press, 1983.

Diamond, C. T. P. Understanding others: Kellyian theory, methodology and application. *International Journal of Intercultural Relations,* 1982, *6,* 395–419.

Dinges, N. Intercultural competence. In D. Landis and R. W. Brislin (Eds.), *Handbook of intercultural training. Vol I: Issues in theory and design.* Elmsford, NY: Pergamon Press, 1983.

Dinges, N. & Maynard, W. Intercultural aspects or organizational effectiveness. In D. Landis & R. W. Brislin (Eds.), *Handbook of intercultural training. Vol II: Issues in training methodology.* Elmsford, NY: Pergamon Press, 1983.

Edmonds, W. S. & Nordlie, P. G. *Analysis of race relations/equal opportunity training in Korea.* McLean, VA: HSR, 1977.

Fiman, B. G. *An analysis of the training of Army personnel at the Defense Race Relations Institute.* Army Research Institute Technical Report TR78–B14. Alexandria, VA: U.S. Army Institute for the Behavioral and Social Sciences, 1978.

Forner, J. D. *Blacks and the military in American history.* New York: Praeger, 1974.

Fontaine, G. *Social support system in intercultural experiences.* Unpublished manuscript, Honolulu: University of Hawaii, 1982.

Gardner, R. W., Holzman, P. S., Klein, G. S., Linton, H. & Spence, D. P. Cognitive control: A study of individual consistencies in cognitive behavior. *Psychological Issues,* 1959, *1*(4).

Gilbert, M. A. & Nordlie, P. G. *An analysis of race relations/equal opportunity training in USAREUR* (ARI Technical Report TR 78–810). Alexandria, VA: U.S. Army Research Institute for the Behavioral and Social Sciences, 1978.

Hiett, R. L. & Nordlie, P. G. *An analysis of the unit race relations training program in the U.S. Army* (ARI Technical Report TR78–99). Alexandria, Va: U.S. Army Research Institute for the Behavioral and Social Sciences, 1978.

Hope, R. O. *Racial strife in the U.S. Military.* New York: Praeger, 1979.

Hulgas, J. & Landis, D. *The interaction of two types of acculturative training.* Indianapolis, IN: Center for Applied Research and Evaluation, 1979.

Jones, E. E. & Nisbett, R. E. The actor and the observer: divergent perceptions of the causes of behavior. In E. E. Jones, D. E. Kanouse, H. H. Kelley, R. E. Nisbett, S. Valins, and B. Weiner (Eds.), *Attribution: Perceiving the causes of behavior.* Morristown, NJ: General Learning Corporation, 1972.

Kealey, D. & Ruben, B. Cross-cultural personnel selection criteria, issues and methods. In D. Landis and R. W. Brislin (Eds.), *Handbook of intercultural training. Vol. I: Issues in Theory and Design.* Elmsford, NY: Pergamon Press, 1982.

Kelly, G. A. *The psychology of personal constructs.* New York: Norton, 1955.

Landis, D. & Brislin, R. W. (Eds.), *Handbook of intercultural training.* Elmsford, NY: Pergamon Press, 1983 (3 Vols).

Landis, D., Day, H. R., McGrew, P. L., Miller, A. B. & Thomas, J. A. Can a black culture assimilator increase racial understanding? *Journal of Social Issues,* 1976, *32,* 169–183.

Landis, D. & Harrison, S. Effect of amount of scanning from memory on phenomenal size of objects. *Psychological Record,* 1967, *17,* 77–80.

Landis, D., Tzeng, D. C. S. & Thomas, J. A. *Some effects of acculturative training: A field evaluation.* Paper presented at the Third Annual Intercultural Training Conference. Bradford, England, 1981.

MacKenzie, B. K. The importance of contact in determining attitudes towards Negroes. *Journal of Abnormal and Social Psychology.,* 1948, *43,* 417–441.

Mayo C. W. & Crockett, W. H. Cognitive complexity and primary-recency effects in impression formation. *Journal of Abnormal and Social Psychology,* 1964, *68,* 335–338.

Minard, R. D. Race relationships in the Pocahontas coal field. *Journal of Social Issues,* 1952, *8,* 29–44.

Mumford, S. Intercultural training from the program manager's perspective In D. Landis & R. W. Brislin (Eds.), *Handbook of intercultural training. Vol II: Issues in training methodology.* Elmsford, NY: Pergamon Press, 1983.

Nordlie, P. G. Black and white perceptions of the Army's Equal Opportunity and Treatment programs. TR HSR-RR-73/6-Sd. McLean, VA: Human Services Research, 1973.

Osgood, C. E. *Method and theory in experimental psychology.* New York: Oxford University Press, 1953.

Piaget, J. *Les mécanismes perceptifs.* Paris: Presses Universitaires France, 1961.

Quaries, B. *The Negro in the American revolution.* Chapel Hill, NC: University of North Carolina Press, 1961.

Ramsey, S. & Birk, J. Preparation of North Americans for interaction with Japanese: considerations of language and communication style. In D. Landis & R. W. Brislin (Eds.), *Handbook of intercultural training. Vol. III: Area studies in intercultural training.* Elmsford, NY: Pergamon Press, 1983.

Ross, I. The intuitive psychologist and his shortcomings: Distortion in the attribution process. in L. Berkowitz (Ed.), *Advances in experimental social psychology* (Vol. 10). New York: Academic Press, 1977.

Spielberger, C. (Ed.) *Anxiety and behavior.* New York: Academic Press, 1966.

Stouffer, S. A., Lumsdaine, A. A., Lumsdaine, M. H., Williams, R. M., Jr., *The American soldier* (2 Vols.) Princeton, NJ: Princeton University Press, 1949.

Triandis, H. C. *Interpersonal behavior.* Monterey, CA: Brooks/Cole, 1976.

Weeks, W. H., Pedersen, P. B. & Brislin, R. W. (Eds.). *A manual of structured experiences for cross-cultural learning.* Washington, D.C.: Society for Intercultural Education, Training and Research, 1979.

Part III

Conclusion

13

Beyond the Contact Hypothesis: Theoretical Perspectives on Desegregation

Marilynn B. Brewer
and
Norman Miller

In order to provide a conceptual framework for integrating the contributions of the present volume, we first review the premises of "social identity theory" as elaborated by Henri Tajfel and his colleagues (Tajfel, 1978a; Tajfel & Turner, 1979), add some conceptual distinctions of our own, and then reexamine the original "contact hypothesis" and its derivatives in light of these theoretical contributions. Finally, we shall suggest a program of research for analyzing the processes underlying the effects of contact on intergroup acceptance.

Social Identity Theory

Social identity theory represents the convergence of two independent traditions in the study of intergroup attitudes and behavior—social categorization, as represented in the work by Doise (1978), Doise and Sinclair (1973), Tajfel (1969), and Wilder (1978), and social comparison, as exemplified by Pettigrew (1967), Vanneman and Pettigrew (1972), and Lemaine (1974). The theory holds that an individual's personal identity is highly differentiated and based in part on membership in significant social categories, along with the value and emotional significance attached to that membership. When a particular social category distinction is highly relevant or salient in a given situation, the individual will respond with respect to that aspect of his or her social identity, acting

GROUPS IN CONTACT:
THE PSYCHOLOGY OF DESEGREGATION

towards others in terms of their corresponding group membership rather than their personal identity.

A primary consequence of such categorical responding is the depersonalization of members of the outgroup categories. Social behavior in such situations is characterized by a tendency to treat individual members of the outgroup as undifferentiated items in a unified social category, independent of individual differences that may exist within groups and independent also of any personal relationships that may exist between members of the two groups in other situations (Tajfel, 1978b). More importantly, in these settings the processes of social comparison operate to maintain and enhance the group distinctiveness. Categorical responding, accompanied by a need for *positive self-identity* (Turner, 1975), causes group members to differentiate members of their own group (ingroup) from those of the outgroup along dimensions that allow comparisons favorable to the ingroup. Thus the need for social identity creates a kind of social competition in which individuals are motivated to define the situation—and the characteristics of other participants—in terms that are associated with positive ingroup status and to avoid comparisons on characteristics that are unfavorable or irrelevant to ingroup identity. This in turn promotes intergroup differentiation as members of each group strive to establish various forms of positively valued group distinctiveness. This competitive process not only creates a depersonalized view of outgroup members but also leads to relatively homogenous, undifferentiated perceptions of one another on the part of ingroup members (Brown & Turner, 1981, p. 39). Other data suggest, however, that perception's of one's ingroup do not become as undifferentiated as do perceptions of the outgroup (Park & Rothbart, 1982).

It is important to note that social identity theory incorporates both perceptual and motivational components. The perception of group differences alone is not sufficient to account for pervasive biases in ingroup–outgroup evaluations. Motivational factors associated with the drive for social comparison and positive self-identity must be invoked in order to explain the selective nature of intergroup comparisons and the prevalence of ingroup favoritism (Brewer, 1979). Thus based on the assumption that the positive value attached to category membership is derived through comparison with other relevant groups, the notion of social comparison serves as the critical link between social categorization and social identity.

Social identity theory also provides an interface between psychological and societal explanations for prejudice and discrimination. Institutional arrangements and group norms are translated at the individual level into aspects of social identity. According to Tajfel (1978b), the basic conditions for extreme forms of category-based social identity lie in the existence of various forms of intergroup conflict at the societal level and in the belief that relevant social boundaries between categories are ''sharply drawn and immutable''(p. 51). The concept of social identity represents the social psychological processes that intervene between objective conditions of the structure of intergroup relations and the construction of widely held beliefs about ingroups and outgroups.

Because it deals with the reciprocal relationship between structural features of the social environment and perceptions and motivations at the individual level, social identity theory provides a useful integrative framework for the study of intergroup contact and its effects. Considerable elaboration of the basic theory is required, however, to make it an adequate basis for understanding the processes and outcomes characteristic of desegregation situations. Most conspicuous is the need for further explication of the determinants of social-category salience and the conditions that trigger categorical responding in some social exchanges but not others. Large complex societies are characterized by multiple cross-cutting systems of social categorization, and individuals have corresponding multiple social identities, any one of which may be activated in a given social situation. Of interest to us is what factors make particular social categories more salient than others across a wide range of social occasions and settings.

Determinants of Category-Based Interaction

Categories are more likely to be generally salient if they are characterized by what Brewer and Campbell (1976) call *convergent boundaries,* in which group identities based on many different distinctions—for example, religious, economic, political—all coincide. When social category membership is so multiply determined, the probability is high that at least one cue to category identity will be relevant in almost any social situation. To some extent, the coincidence of category boundaries may arise from natural covariation among various dimensions of social differentiation. Language differences, for instance, create barriers to social exchange that may lead to concommitant differences in life style, education, and related social distinctions. Distinctive physical features may be easily linked to cultural differences, so that one automatically cues the other. Convergent categories may also be imposed by artificial constraints within a social system. Constraints on geographical or economic mobility, for instance, may lead to ethnic specialization of occupational roles and a correspondence between social categorization based on ethnic origin and those based on socioeconomic indicators (Levine & Campbell, 1972, Chapter 10).

Convergent category boundaries may also be situation-specific. Schwarzwald and Amir (Chapter 4 in this volume), for instance, describe the situation in Israeli religious schools as one in which cultural distinctions between children from Western and Middle Eastern backgrounds are compounded in that setting by distinctions in economic advantage, residential neighborhood, and religious identity. Similarly, in the United States, when school desegregation is achieved by busing, distinctions based on preexisting ethnic and racial identity become correlated with other situationally specific differences, such as distance and mode of transportation to school, which contribute to category salience and significance.

Even social categories based on single, arbitary distinctions can coalesce into salient social-identities if members of different categories are subjected to differential treatment by outside agents. Results of laboratory studies (Rabbie & Horwitz, 1969) indicate that, although mere assignment of individuals to different group labels is not sufficient to create ingroup–outgroup distinctions, differential treatment of groups by the experimenter does produce disjunction in perceptions of own-versus other-group members. Experiments with the "minimal intergroup situation" (Brewer, 1979; Tajfel, 1970) attest to the powerful impact that perception by external authorities can have on the formation of subjective group-identity on the part of those who are lumped together as a category. This effect can lead to a type of self-fulfilling prophesy. The perception that an aggregate of individuals constitutes a social category leads to common treatment of members of that category. This in turn produces a correlation between similarity (on some arbitrary dimension) and "common fate" that enhances group identification (Campbell, 1958). This process highlights the important role that political factors and social policies that officially recognize certain group distinction can play in determining the salience of category membership for situations in which those policies are relevant (Sears & Allen, Chapter 7 in this volume).

Tajfel (1978b) gives particular emphasis to the structure of intergroup relations at the societal level as a critical determinant of category salience. Of most relevance is the presence of intense conflict of interest between groups (as in the relation between rival football teams) or the existence of a fairly rigid system of social stratification within the society that is paralleled by established differences in the status accorded to the social categories. According to Tajfel, the available modes of achievement of positively valued social distinctiveness are deeply affected by the perceived status relationships between the groups involved. For those who belong to categories with superior status, the importance of category distinctions to positive identity will depend on the security of the established status-differential. When high status is secure, category identity will not be salient in most social situations, but if status differentials are perceived to be insecure or threatened, the need to preserve category distinctiveness may be high and category identity commensurately salient. For the member of inferior-status groups, category salience will depend on the extent to which category membership creates barriers to individual achievement of positive social identity. If status mobility is possible on an individual level, members of low-status groups will tend to minimize category identity and avoid category-based social behavior. But if category membership is perceived as unchangeable and a deterrent to status mobility, high category salience may be functional to group-based efforts to achieve a change in the basis of evaluation that determines relative status. Elizabeth Cohen's chapter in this volume highlights the effects of preexisting status differentials on intergroup behavior and suggests conditions under which low-status groups may successfully achieve changes in status evaluation within the contact situation.

Group structure within a specific setting is also an important factor in category salience, particularly the relative proportion of members of different social categories represented in the group composition. In general, in fairly large social groupings, a relatively equal representation of two social categories will make category distinctions less salient, whereas the presence of a clear minority will enhance category salience. Findings from Hamilton, Carpenter, and Bishop's research on neighborhood desegregation (see Chapter 6 in this volume) illustrate the so-called solo effect, that is, the salience of category identity of a single member of a distinctive social group in an otherwise homogeneous social environment. Results of the research by Rogers, Hennigan, Bowman, and Miller (Chapter 10 in this volume) in desegregated school settings also demonstrate the effect of minority status on awareness of ingroup–outgroup distinctions.

The effects of minority–majority representation tend to interact with differences in group status to determine the extent to which category differentiation is important or salient to members of the respective groups. Majority groups with insecure or negative self-image and minority groups with positive self-image have been found to display the greatest degree of discrimination against outgroups, whereas majority groups with secure positive self-image and minority groups with negative self-image show relatively little discrimination (Moscovici & Paicheler, 1978).

Effects of category size and group composition are more complex in situations in which more than two distinguishable social categories are represented. Based on perceptual factors alone, we hypothesize that the salience of particular category distinctions will vary as a function of the ratio of category size to total group size. If a fairly large group is divided into several categories of relatively equal size, those categories will provide a useful way of "chunking" the social environment and category differentiation will be highly salient (each category is treated, in effect, as a distinctive minority). When several different social categories are equally represented in a much smaller total group, however, category salience should be low. When the representation of any one social category is small relative to other categories in the setting, differentiation of that category may be highly salient whereas distinctions among the other categories present are less salient.

In addition to structural features of the environment, certain characteristics of individuals may affect the salience of particular category identities across a wide range of social occasions. Wagner and Schönbach (See Chapter 3), for instance, discuss how low self-esteem on the part of individuals can enhance the importance of group identification as a means of achieving positive social identity. The greater the importance of a particular category identity to an individual's sense of self-worth, the more likely that individual is to respond in terms of that category in a variety of social situations. A general need for self-differentiation or personal identity (Snyder & Fromkin, 1980) may also influence awareness of particular category membership. In a given situation, individuals may be most inclined to define themselves in terms of that category identity that makes them most distinctive in that setting (McGuire & Padawer-Singer, 1976). If an individual's sex, ethnicity, or physical features are actuarily distinctive in a given social environment, this aspect of the self will be particularly salient and most likely to be mentioned in spontaneous self-descriptions (McGuire, McGuire, Child, & Fujioka, 1978).

As documented in the contributions to Part I of this volume, the conditions that characterize desegregation in a wide variety of settings have a number of features that predict a high likelihood of category-based social interaction. First of all, the groups involved are usually social categories that are differentiated by convergent boundaries, including distinctions in cultural, economic, linguistic, and physical features. In addition, these objective group differences tend to be confounded with status level within a larger social system, often under conditions in which the existing status structure is under threat, that increases the salience of group distinctiveness and promotes intergroup social comparison on the part of members of both the high- and low-status categories. Moreover, desegregation frequently occurs within a context of explicit political policies that affect groups differentially and bring individuals into the situation as representatives of their respective social categories. Finally, the immediate social structure tends to be one of disproportional (majority–minority) representation of the different groups that makes category identity perceptually salient as well as emotionally significant.

The Process of Decategorization

The importance of specifying the conditions and consequences of category salience in intergroup contact situations lies in its potential for clarifying processes whereby category-based social interactions may be replaced by social relations that are more interpersonally oriented and more consistent with the goals of desegregation. Of course such reduction of category differentiation may not be an appropriate goal in all social situations. The success of social movements and many other forms of collective problem-solving rest on a capacity for group identity to override, at least temporarily, individual self-interest. In situations in which group outcomes are highly interdependent, however, an emphasis on intergroup distinctions introduces dysfunctional social competition and out-group rejection that interferes with collective action and interpersonal acceptance. Under such circumstances it is our assumption that the intended goal of desegregation is not simply to redistribute members of different social categories but to promote intergroup acceptance and to reduce the role that category membership plays in creating barriers to individual social mobility and to the development of positive interpersonal relationships.

We have already indicated that the major symptoms or consequents of category-based social interaction are deindividuation and depersonalization of out-group-category members. Hence the reduction of categorical responding should be associated with social interactions based on increased differentiation and personalization. These two processes can be distinguished conceptually and do not necessarily co-occur. *Differentiation* refers to the distinctiveness of individual category members within that category; it is the perception of intracategory differences, but does not necessarily imply the elimination of category boundaries that differentiate ingroup from outgroup. *Personalization,* on the other hand, involves responding to other individuals in terms of their relationship to the self, which necessarily involves making direct self–other interpersonal comparisons that cross category boundaries.

Differentiation occurs when one learns information that is unique to individual outgroup members, allowing one to draw distinctions among them and organize them into smaller subgroups. Such differentiation, however, does not necessarily eliminate the tendency to view the subgroups as components of the larger social category. Thus one may differentiate old people into subtypes such as "elderly statesmen," "grandmothers," "senior citizens" (Brewer, Dull & Lui, 1981), or into even finer subcategories that reflect individual uniqueness. Nonetheless, one might continue to respond to elderly individuals as members of the larger umbrella category. In other instances one may acquire information that leads one to dissociate an individual from the category, as in the case in which one learns that a person who lives in a Jewish neighborhood and looks Jewish is in fact not a Jew. Depending on the information received, such persons may be assigned to another, more appropriate category, or simply left uncategorized. (The new information may even suggest that the person properly belongs in the ingroup.) Such differentiation may lead one to respond differently to the reclassified individual, but one's response to the original category remains unchanged.

Differentiation may occur without personalization. One may acquire information that differentiates outgroup members under circumstances that entail no involvement of the self. For instance, one may learn to discriminate accurately among different presidents of the United States but still relate to them all only as occupants of a specialized role. Interaction that is highly task oriented may encourage differentiation among category members in terms of their task contribution, but such differentiation may have no personal implications. As Deutsch (1982) has observed, "in task-oriented relations people are oriented to each other as *complexes of performance*—that is, in terms of what each *does*; in a social–emotional relationship people are oriented to each other as *complexes of qualities*—that is, in terms of what each *is*" (p. 32).

We consider differentiation a necessary but not sufficient condition for personalization. In our view the elimination of categorized responding in an intergroup social situation requires both elements. Differentiated and personalized interactions are necessary before intergroup contact can lead to intergroup acceptance and reduction of social competition.

Figure 13.1 provides a pictorial representation of three alternative models of the intergroup contact situation. In the figure, distances between the self (represented by the small dark circle) and others represent perceptual distinctiveness and affective distance; the size and connectedness of the boundary surrounding the different groupings represent degree of category-based responding.

In the first model (Figure 13.1A) pure *category-based* contact, a given ingroup member responds to outgroup members as interchangeable representatives of an undifferentiated category. Thus, in the diagram outgroup members are located closely adjacent to each other within a tightly bounded space, suggesting little room for noncategorical responding. Note also that in this model ingroup members tend also to be seen as relatively homogeneous, although not as much as outgroup members. Thus the self is not well-differentiated from other ingroup members.

In the second model (Figure 13.1B), *differentiation*, the outgroup members have greater spatial separation (as do ingroup members), indicating perceptual distinctiveness. Further, the self is represented as more distinct from other ingroup members than is the case in category-based contact. The enlarged and disconnected boundaries around each group reflect the differentiation of each group into subgroups (or individuals) that are associated to varying degrees with the larger category but the distinctiveness of the two categories remains clear.

In the third model (Figure 13.1C), *personalization*, the conditions of interaction in the contact situation encourage participants to attend to information that replaces category identity as the most useful basis for classifying each other. In other words, the contact experience reduces information processing and interaction decisions that are category-based and promotes attention to personalized information about others that is self-relevant and not correlated with category membership. We assume that such contact experiences are more likely to generalize to new situations because extended and frequent utilization of alternative informational features in interactions undermines the availability and usefulness of category identity as a basis for future interactions with the same

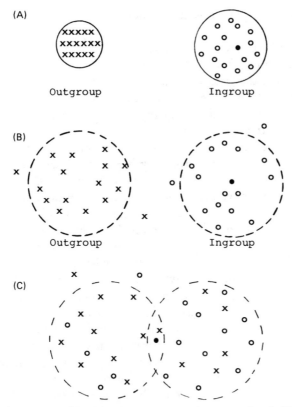

Figure 13.1. Alternative models of intergroup contact: (A) category-based, (B) differentiated, (C) personalized.

or different individuals. Thus permanent changes occur in both the cognitive and motivational aspects of social interaction with outgroup members.

It is of interest at this point to compare the concepts of category-based and personalized social interaction with the alternative models of intergroup relations discussed by John Berry (Chapter 2 in this volume). Obviously, segregation and separatism imply category-based social relations in which decisions to avoid or reject social contact are determined by category membership alone. It is important to note, however, that personalization does not necessarily imply adoption of the deculturation or assimilationist models of intergroup relations nor does it necessitate that real differences or perceived distinctions between groups be eliminated. Category identity may remain a feature of individuals that enters into—but does not solely determine—the formation of impressions, interpersonal evaluations, and interaction decisions. In our view, then, personalization is compatible with—indeed, probably essential to—the integration model of intergroup relations as described by Berry.

Reduction of Category-Based Interaction

Having specified the essential features of personalized social situations, we turn to a consideration of what conditions will promote such forms of social interaction. In general, the factors that promote personalization may be seen as the obverse of those that enhance the salience and relevance of category boundaries in particular settings. Social-identity theorists have emphasized the presence of multiple cross-cutting category distinctions as an important factor in reducing ingroup biases (Deschamps & Doise, 1978), and anthropologists have identified the existence of cross-cutting group loyalties as a critical factor in social integration (Levine & Campbell, 1972, Chapter 4; Murphy, 1957). When category boundaries are not convergent, competing bases for ingroup–outgroup categorization reduce the importance of any one category identity and force the perceiver to classify other individuals on multiple dimensions at the same time.

Cross-cutting categorization may be encouraged by enhancing the relevance in the immediate social setting of multiple existing uncorrelated systems of categorization, or by creating new social categories that are deliberately constructed to cross cut existing category memberships. The danger with these approaches is that a basis for category-based perceptions and interaction remains intact. Even if multiple categorizations are available, one category distinction may become dominant and form the primary basis for social identity in that setting. In situations involving large social groups, individuals may differentiate themselves into subcategories, based on shared cross-category identities (e.g., all Polish barbers), that then become the basis of intergroup distinctions and social competition. Only situations of extended interactions that force continual realignments of individuals based on different category identities at different times can reduce such category-based responding.

Another approach is for authorities in the contact situation to treat each individual differentially on the basis of multidimensional characteristics. Policies can be designed to reduce as much as possible the experience of common fate among members of a social category. Attempts to compose groups of equally large numbers of members of the relevant social categories should also be effective. Probably the single most critical aspect of the contact situation with respect to social identity is the reduction of status differentials correlated with category membership. Cohen (1982) has reviewed the bases for interventions designed to equalize or offset category-based status difference in desegregated classrooms.

In general we hypothesize that the effects of categorization on social interaction will be reduced most successfully (1) when the nature of the interaction in the contact situation promotes an interpersonal orientation rather than a task orientation to fellow participants, and (2) when the basis for assignment of roles, status, social functions, and subgroup composition in the situation is perceived to be category-independent rather than category-related. These two hypotheses subsume a large number of specific structural and psychological features of the contact situation that have been proposed as important determinants of intergroup acceptance.

The Contact Hypothesis Reconsidered

The elaborated version of the *contact hypothesis* (Cook, 1978) specifies a number of contingencies on the general hypothesis that association between members of different social groups will lead to an increase in liking and respect for outgroup members. These contingencies involve various characteristics of the contact situation that presumably affect the nature and quality of interpersonal interaction, including (1) equal status within the situation, (2) opportunities to disconfirm prevailing stereotypes about outgroup characteristics, (3) mutual interdependence such as cooperation in achievement of joint goals, (4) promotion of intimate interpersonal associations, and (5) presence of egalitarian social norms.

For the most part, this list was generated intuitively rather than derived from formal theory. Our analysis leads to a more theory-based approach to these same conditional specifications. We will consider each factor in turn, evaluating how our elaborated version of social identity theory may help to explain and qualify its expected effects on intergroup acceptance.

Equal Status

For a number of reasons, equal status between members of different social groups at the structural level may not correspond to equal status at the psychological level. Cohen's work (Chapter 5 in this volume), as well as that by Rogers *et al.* (Chapter 10), demonstrates the extent to which preexisting status differentials between groups tend to carry over into new situations, making equal-status interaction difficult or impossible. On the one hand, elimination of status differences within the contact setting may make category disctinctions less salient. However, systematic attempts to reduce or reverse existing status differences may threaten members of the initially high-status group, leading to active resistance and attempts to reestablish ingroup distinctiveness and positive status differentials. In a laboratory study of status-differential effects, Norvell and Worchel (1981) found that subjects uniformly thought that giving one group a status advantage within the experimental session was unfair, although it did lead to increased intergroup acceptance if it was perceived as compensating for past inequity. Unfortunately, the researchers' analytic procedures did not separate responses from the initially high- versus low-status groups so it is not possible to determine whether the increase in outgroup attraction occurred for both ingroups or only among members of the lower-status group.

According to social-identity theory, overcoming prior status differentials would require introducing into the contact situation alternative sources of status or positive social identity that cross-cut (rather than correspond to) category membership. Simply eliminating status differentials within the setting runs the risk of arousing social competition aimed at reestablishing preexisting status differences, especially on the part of the initially high status group. True equal-status interaction under these conditions is more likely to be a consequence of intergroup acceptance than its cause.

Disconfirmed Stereotypes

Maximizing the opportunity to learn stereotype-inconsistent information about outgroup members is closely related to the differentiation component of the decategorization process. It is not necessarily true, however, that successful differentiation among outgroup members is sufficient to produce personalization. That may depend on the amount and distribution of disconfirming information that the perceiver is exposed to, but also seems to depend heavily on motivational factors.

Recent research on the cognitive mechanisms underlying the formation and maintenance of intergroup stereotypes (Hamilton, 1979, 1981) suggests that a number of encoding and memory biases operate to make existing stereotypic beliefs difficult to disconfirm. Information about an individual that is irrelevant to existing stereotypes may fail to be noticed or represented in memory (Brewer, Dull, & Lui, 1981). Information that is highly inconsistent with stereotypic expectations is more likely to be salient and well remembered but not necessarily lead to changes in the group stereotype. Instead, the inconsistent individual may be subcategorized as a special case or a subtype within the social category (Lui & Brewer, 1983; Weber & Crocker, 1983) without any overall effect on categorization. Reduction of stereotyped expectations requires frequent exposure to multiple types of disconfirming information that is dispersed across a large number of outgroup members (Weber & Crocker, 1983). In our terms, such information reduces the usefulness of category identification as a basis for classifying individuals. As the category becomes more and more finely differentiated, the boundaries between categories become less salient, which increases the probability of more personalized interpersonal evaluations. For this to occur, the contact situation must include a diverse representation of outgroup-category members. Additionally, however, the conditions of interaction must encourage attending to individual differences on a number of dimensions. As has been suggested previously, highly task-focused interactions do not ordinarily lead to such attention.

Cooperative Interdependence

The effect of cooperative interaction on both interpersonal and intergroup acceptance has been widely researched in laboratory and field settings (see Chapters 8 and 9 in this volume). In considering the effects of cooperation on intergroup acceptance, it is important to distinguish between cooperation as a goal structure (i.e., that rewards in the situation are delivered to the group as whole rather than individualistically or competitively) and cooperation as a condition of interaction (i.e., interdependent or joint effort). A review of the experimental research indicates that the introduction of a cooperative intergroup reward-structure alone is not sufficient to eliminate ingroup bias or intergroup social competition (Brewer, 1979). Cooperative task interaction, on the other hand, has been found to reduce hostility between members of the cooperating social categories (Sherif, Harvey, White, Hood, & Sherif, 1961; Worchel, Andreoli, & Folger, 1977) and to increase intergroup friendships (Sherif et al., 1961; also see Chapter 9 in this volume) in comparison to competitive intergroup conditions. The effectiveness of cooperation as an intervention strategy in desegregation settings, however, is limited by a number of factors associated with task structure and outcomes. For one thing, the ameliorative effects of intergroup cooperation appear to hold up only under conditions of task success, whereas cooperative failure can actually decrease intergroup attraction (Worchel et al., 1977; Worchel & Norvell, 1980). Further, there is some evidence that when cooperative teams engage in competitive interaction with other teams the positive effects of intrateam cooperation on interpersonal acceptance of outgroup members may be reduced (Johnson, Johnson, & Maruyama, 1983; Sharan, 1980).

Even when positive intergroup acceptance is achieved in cooperative situations, there is little evidence that these effects generalize to other settings or to members of the outgroup category other than those involved in the cooperative venture (see Cook, Chapter 8 in this volume). Like equal status, cooperative goals provide an opportunity for reducing the salience of category membership as a relevant or important aspect of individual identity but whether it does so will depend on the task structure and the nature of the interaction it promotes among team members. Interteam competition, for instance, may have the effect of enhancing task focus and thus lead team members to ignore personalizing information because of its irrelevance to task objectives. As a consequence, such cooperation provides less opportunity to acquire information about fellow team-members that would counteract category identity. Actual or anticipated failure may have similar attentional consequences, along with arousing needs for reestablishing positive personal identity through intergroup comparisons.

The basis for assignment to team membership and to roles within teams may also be a significant factor in the effectiveness of cooperative interaction. Systematic and conscious efforts on the part of authorities to represent specific social categories in team composition may enhance rather than reduce the salience of category membership within the cooperative setting. Under such conditions, intrateam social competition may undermine effective cooperation or inhibit interpersonal interactions not directly associated with task performance. Thus, by itself, imposition of a superordinate goal structure may not be sufficient to eliminate the negative effects of category differentiation, although it does provide more opportunity for positive intergroup experiences than other forms of interdependence. To know when joint goals will lead to intergroup acceptance, we need to learn more about the processes that mediate the effects of reward structure on interpersonal attraction.

Intimacy

One effect that cooperative task-structure may have is to increase what Cook (1978) calls the "acquaintance potential" in the contact situation, that is, the promotion of interactions that reveal enough detail about members of the outgroup to encourage seeing them as individuals rather than as stereotyped group members. In our terms, this effect will depend on whether the focus of the interaction in the contact setting is primarily task oriented or interpersonally oriented.

In a task-oriented environment, the primary standard for evaluating fellow participants will be task requirements and contribution to task performance. This tends to narrow the range of information that is attended to and reduce perception of individual differences, thus limiting the opportunity to learn anything about group members other than their salient category identity. In addition, attraction toward other group members is likely to be heavily influenced by task success or failure.[1] In more socially oriented environments, on the other hand, evaluations of others will be made primarily with reference to the self. This orientation is associated with more complex information processing (Rogers, 1981; Rogers, Kuiper, & Kirker, 1977) with attraction determined by perceived similarities to the self at the individual rather than group level. Structural features of the contact situation that might promote such an interpersonal orientation include extension across time and contexts, informality, open communication, and the absence of a single group goal or formal group structure.

---

[1]In making this distinction between task orientation and interpersonal focus, we do not mean to ignore the fact that tasks can vary in the extent to which they naturally elicit attention to interpersonal characteristics. An additive, optimizing task, as compared to a nonadditive, maximizing task (Steiner, 1972), will be more likely to focus attention on individual characteristics and promote interpersonal responding. Indeed, attending to personal attributes of fellow group members can be made part of task requirements (Rogers, 1982).

Egalitarian Norms

Apart from structural features of the environment, the shared values that participants bring to or acquire in the contact situation will be of critical importance. When norms favoring intergroup equality and expression of individuality are salient, adherence to such values provides an alternate source of positive self-identity that may replace social category identity. Such values may be brought to the situation by participants who come together for that purpose, as in voluntary desegregation efforts. More often, however, participation in the contact situation is not motivated by egalitarian values and such values have to be superimposed on other goals and purposes in that setting. Stuart Cook's research (Chapter 8 in this volume) stresses the role of explicitly expressed egalitarian norms in determining the effect of contact on intergroup acceptance and its generalization to new settings.

Additional Factors

In its expanded version the contact hypothesis focuses on features of the contact situation itself, particularly those structural features that can be potentially manipulated or controlled. Somewhat ignored are those antecedent conditions, such as the history and intensity of intergroup conflict, ethnocentric value systems, and the personal characteristics and prior experience of the participants in the contact situation that might be expected to influence readiness for intergroup contact. A number of chapters in this volume have given attention to such antecedent factors, particularly those involving individual characteristics and prior experience. From our theoretical perspective, the most important personal factors will be those that determine the individuals' openness to information about other persons and the ability to integrate that information. The research reported by Berry (Chapter 2) and by Wagner and Schönbach (Chapter 3) both implicate cognitive complexity as a moderator variable in intergroup acceptance and adaptation to cultural contact. More specifically, Stephan and Stephan (Chapter 11) and Landis, Hope, and Day (Chapter 12) stress knowledge and acceptance of intergroup differences and feelings of competence in intergroup interactions as prior conditions to interpersonal acceptance. Research on human learning and reasoning points to the importance of "advance organizers" (Mayer, 1979) in the individual's ability to master complex new information. Information about outgroup members is likely to be rejected or assimilated to preexisting negative stereotypes unless alternative knowledge structures are available to process and organize the information effectively. Previous experience with and knowledge about outgroups probably acts to augment cognitive complexity and to provide such alternative structures.

Alternative Process Models

Our theoretical analysis thus far has stressed the interrelationships among perceptual–cognitive variables on the one hand and interactive behavior on the other. A more precise model would specify the causal relationships between these two types of variables and the predicted sequencing of changes in them over time. Three alternative basic models are available, each of which has been applied to the desegregation situation. The first model views structural factors in the contact setting as causally prior to changes in intergroup acceptance as a single underlying conceptual variable with perceptual, attitudinal, and behavioral components. This model is depicted in Figure 13.2A, using cooperative interdependence as an illustrative contact variable. The other two models view behavioral changes as causally mediating perceptual and attitudinal changes or vice versa. These alternatives are depicted in Figures 13.2B and 13.2C.

The second model, based on cognitive dissonance and self-perception theories, sees changes in attitudinal, perceptual, and cognitive variables as emerging from the behavioral changes in patterns of interaction induced by the contact situation. In this model personalization of the interaction is the end product of changes in affective variables arising from the need to justify or explain changes in intergroup behavior. The opposite causal sequence is represented in the third model, in which change in social categorization is viewed as prior to changes in affect that then lead to interpersonal social-interactions. In this model, participants must first abandon social-category identity as a primary basis for organizing information, replacing it with more individuated and personalized information processing before other changes in intergroup acceptance will emerge.

The three models depicted in Figure 13.2 are extreme in their incorporation of unidirectional causal assumptions. No doubt, complex, reciprocal causal relationships would better represent the processes actually underlying changes in intergroup relations. Whether one emphasizes the organizing and directing function of social behavior or social categorization as predominant, however, should influence which structural features of the desegregation environment are to be emphasized in the design of intervention strategies and how one would evaluate the effectiveness of those interventions. An emphasis on social categorization effects (Figure 13.2C, Model 3), for instance, would lead to programmatic interventions that alter the perceptual salience of group differences, with particular attention to the composition of groups and the salience of individual differences. An emphasis on Model 2 (Figure 13.2B), on the other hand, would lead to a focus on environmental conditions that elicit and reward prosocial behaviors between members of different groups. Unfortunately, field studies of intergroup contact rarely allow for the kind of process analysis that would permit teasing out the relative strengths of alternative causal-sequences

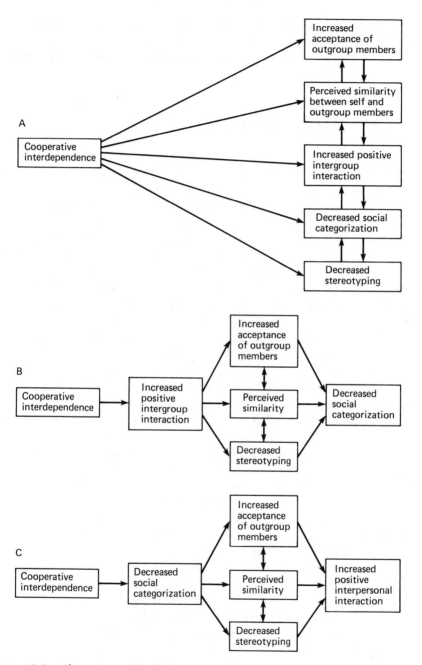

Figure 13.2. Alternative models of the process of intergroup contact effects: (A) Model 1, (B) Model 2, (C) Model 3.

that underlie different intervention approaches. Understanding the mediating processes involved requires a return to experimental research methodologies in which alternative process theories can be tested in simpler, controlled settings.

A Program of Laboratory Research

The social-category identities represented in most real-world desegregation settings involve category memberships vested with cultural, political, and affective significance. A decade of research with the minimal intergroup situation in laboratory settings, however, demonstrates that ingroup–outgroup categorization and subsequent social competition can be engaged, at least temporarily, by even the most trivial category differentiations (Brewer, 1979; Turner, 1978). Such situation-specific social categories may not have the full emotional significance of membership in natural categories such as gender or ethnic identity, but they do seem to replicate the perceptual and motivational properties of social identity over the short term. Taking advantage of this fact permits us to reproduce the essential features of the desegregation situation—members of two separate social categories, previously isolated from each other, coming together on some common ground—in a laboratory analogue.

The research paradigm we have been working with involves a three-phase experimental session. In the initial phase, groups of six to eight same-sex participants are arbitrarily divided into two separate groups with distinctive labels and names. Members of each of the groups are given identifying signs (in distinct colors) to wear, thereby assuring that a visible cue to category identity is available throughout the session. The two groups are then separated to work independently on a group problem-solving task. At the end of this phase, each group is asked to evaluate their own problem solution and then to give and receive evaluations from the other group. The objective of this phase of the experiment is to provide an opportunity for members of each category to establish a sense of ingroup identification and concomitant perception of the members of the other category as an outgroup.

In the second phase of the study, the two groups are reassembled and divided into two new teams (maintaining initial category membership identification) for further cooperative problem-solving efforts. The assignment to teams at this point is prearranged to represent members from the two initial categories on both teams in accord with experimental design. The conditions under which the second phase teams are constituted and the task instructions that they are given at this stage can be systematically varied to test our general hypotheses about effectiveness of contact experiences in reducing category-based responding. In particular, we are interested in experimental manipulations designed to affect the task versus interpersonal orientation of participants and the bases for category-dependent versus independent classifications of fellow team members.

The problem-solving task assigned to teams in the second phase is designed to permit both individual input and group decision making. The task consists of a first stage in which team members work individually to develop contributions for use in the group solution, a second stage in which the individual contributions are compared and discussed, and a third stage in which the group members arrive at a consensus on a single solution derived from the individual contributions. Thus the task induces cooperative interdependence under conditions in which there is ample opportunity for assessment of performance and personal characteristics of fellow team members.

In the final phase of the experiment, the effects of the cooperative team-experience on perceptions and evaluations of the original ingroup and outgroup category members are assessed. This phase is also divided into three subparts. First, participants are asked to make a series of ratings of the ingroup and outgroup members of their own team and its problem solution. These include measures of evaluative traits, perceived interpersonal similarity among team members, satisfaction with team performance, reward allocation to team members, and memory for individual contributions. Following that, each team is provided with information about the individual and group solutions to the problem-solving task generated by the other team in the session, and subjects then are asked to make evaluation, similarity, and reward–allocation judgments of the ingroup and outgroup members of that team.

A final set of measures provides an assessment of the generalization of attitudes toward ingroup and outgroup members acquired during the contact experience. Participants are given an opportunity to view a prepared videotape of a four-person team from another experimental session working on the final discussion phase of the cooperative problem-solving task. Persons shown on the videotape are clearly identified as to original category membership. After viewing the tape, participants are asked to make evaluation, similarity, reward allocation, and sociometric ratings of the video team members to determine the extent of continuing ingroup–outgroup (category-based) bias that remains toward strangers with whom the participants have not had contact.

Initial research utilizing this experimental paradigm (Rogers, 1982) indicates that it has many of the properties our theoretical analysis regards as essential to assessment of intergroup contact effects. Participants become involved in the group situation, attach significance to category membership, and respond differentially to ingroup and outgroup members. Although no laboratory analogue can be expected to map the full complexity of real-world desegregation situations, such a research paradigm can provide a relatively low-cost vehicle for testing the effects of context on intergroup contact and the potential effectiveness of various intervention strategies before attempting their implementation on a large scale. It is our hope that the conjunction of field and laboratory research within a common theoretical framework in the arena of intergroup relations will provide an effective model for social psychological research on all social issues.

References

Brewer, M. B. Ingroup bias in the minimal intergroup situation: A cognitive-motivational analysis. *Psychological Bulletin*, 1979, *86*, 307–324.

Brewer, M. B., & Campbell, D. T. *Ethnocentrism and intergroup attitudes: East African evidence*. New York: Halsted Press (Sage Publications), 1976.

Brewer, M. B., Dull, V., & Lui, L. Perceptions of the elderly: Stereotypes as prototypes. *Journal of Personality and Social Psychology*, 1981, *41*, 656–670.

Brown, R. J., & Turner, J. C. Interpersonal and intergroup behavior. In J. Turner & H. Giles (Eds.), *Intergroup behavior*. Chicago, IL: University of Chicago Press, 1981.

Campbell, D. T. Common fate, similarity, and other indices of the status of aggregates of persons as social entities. *Behavioral Science*, 1958, *3*, 14–25.

Cohen, E. G. Expectation states and interracial interaction in school settings. *Annual Review of Sociology*, 1982, *8*, 209–235.

Cook, S. W. Interpersonal and attitudinal outcomes in cooperating interracial groups. *Journal of Research and Development in Education*, 1978, *12*, 97–113.

Deschamps, J. C., & Doise, W. Crossed category memberships in intergroup relations. In H. Tajfel (Ed.), *Differentiation between social groups*. London: Academic Press, 1978, Pp. 141–158.

Deutsch, M. Interdependence and psychological orientation. In V. Derlaga & J. Grzelak (Eds.), *Cooperation and helping behavior*. New York: Academic Press, 1982, pp. 15–42.

Doise, W. *Groups and individuals: Explanations in social psychology*. Cambridge, MA: Cambridge University Press, 1978.

Doise, W., & Sinclair, A. The categorization process in intergroup relations. *European Journal of Social Psychology*, 1973, *3*, 145–157.

Hamilton, D. L. A cognitive-attributional analysis of stereotyping. In L. Berkowitz (Ed.), *Advances in experimental social psychology. Vol. 12*. New York: Academic Press, 1979. Pp. 53–84.

Hamilton, D. L. (Ed.) *Cognitive processes in stereotyping and intergroup behavior*. Hillsdale, NJ: Lawrence Erlbaum, 1981.

Johnson, D. W., Johnson, R., & Maruyama, G. Interdependence and interpersonal attraction among heterogeneous and homogeneous individuals: A theoretical formulation and meta-analysis of the research. *Review of Educational Research*, 1983, *52*.

Lemaine, G. Social differentiation and social originality. *European Journal of Social Psychology*, 1974, *4*, 17–52.

LeVine, R. A., & Campbell, D. T. *Ethnocentrism: Theories of conflict, ethnic attitudes and group behavior*. New York: Wiley, 1972.

Lui, L. & Brewer, M. B. Recognition accuracy as evidence of category consistency effects in person memory. *Social Cognition*, 1983, *2*, 89–107.

Mayer, R. E. Can advance organizers influence meaningful learning? *Review of Educational Research*, 1979, *49*, 371–383.

McGuire, W. J., McGuire, C. V., Child, P., & Fujioka, T. Salience of ethnicity in the spontaneous self-concept as a function of one's ethnic distinctiveness in the social environment. *Journal of Personality and Social Psychology*, 1978, *36*, 511–520.

McGuire, W. J., & Padawer-Singer, A. Trait salience in the spontaneous self-concept. *Journal of Personality and Social Psychology,* 1976, *33,* 743–754.

Moscovici, S., & Paicheler, G. Social comparison and social recognition: Two complementary processes of identification. In H. Tajfel (Ed.), *Differentiation between social groups.* London: Academic Press, 1978. Pp. 251–266.

Murphy, R. F. Intergroup hostility and social cohesion. *American Anthropologist,* 1957, *59,* 1018–1035.

Norvell, N., & Worchel, S. A reexamination of the relation between equal status contact and intergroup attraction. *Journal of Personality and Social Psychology,* 1981, *41,* 902–908.

Park, B., & Rothbart, M. Perception of out-group homogeneity and levels of social categorization: Memory for the subordinate attributes of in-group and out-group members. *Journal of Personality and Social Psychology,* 1982, *42,* 1051–1068.

Pettigrew, T. F. Social evaluation theory: Convergences and applications. In D. Levine (Ed.), *Nebraska symposium on motivation: 1967.* Lincoln, NE: University of Nebraska Press, 1967, Pp. 241–311.

Rabbie, J. M., & Horwitz, M. The arousal of ingroup-outgroup bias by a chance win or loss. *Journal of Personality and Social Psychology,* 1969, *13,* 269–277.

Rogers, M. *The effect of interteam reward structure on intragroup and intergroup perceptions and evaluative attitudes.* Unpublished dissertation, University of Southern California, December 1982.

Rogers, T. B. A model of the self as an aspect of the human information processing system. In N. Cantor & J. Kihlstrom (Eds.), *Personality, cognition, and social interaction.* Hillsdale, NJ: Lawrence Erlbaum, 1981. Pp. 193–214.

Rogers, T. B., Kuiper, N. A., & Kirker, W. S. Self-reference and the encoding of personal information. *Journal of Personality and Social Psychology,* 1977, *35,* 677–688.

Sharan, S. Cooperative learning in small groups: Recent methods and effects on achievement, attitudes and ethnic relations. *Review of Educational Research,* 1980, *50,* 241–271.

Sherif, M., Harvey, O. J., White, B. J., Hood, W. R., & Sherif, C. W. *Intergroup conflict and cooperation: The Robber's Cave experiment.* Norman, OK: University of Oklahoma Press, 1961.

Snyder, C. R., & Fromkin, H. L. *Uniqueness: The pursuit of human difference.* New York: Plenum Press, 1980.

Steiner, I. D. *Group processes and productivity.* New York: Academic Press, 1972.

Tajfel, H. Cognitive aspects of prejudice. *Journal of Social Issues,* 1969, *25* (4), pp. 79–97.

Tajfel, H. Experiments in intergroup discrimination. *Scientific American,* 1970, *223* (2), 96–102.

Tajfel, H. (Ed.) *Differentiation between social groups: Studies in the social psychology of intergroup relations.* London: Academic Press, 1978. (a)

Tajfel, H. Social categorization, social identity and social comparson. In H. Tajfel (Ed.), *Differentiation between social groups.* London: Academic Press, 1978. Pp. 61–76. (b)

Tajfel, H., & Turner, J. C. An integrative theory of intergroup conflict. In W. Austin & S. Worchel (Eds.), *The social psychology of intergroup relations.* Monterey, CA: Brooks/ Cole, 1979. Pp. 33–47.

Turner, J. C. Social comparison and social identity: Some prospects for intergroup behaviour. *European Journal of Social Psychology,* 1975, *5,* 5–34.

Turner, J. C. Social categorization and social discrimination in the minimal group paradigm. In H. Tajfel (Ed.), *Differentiation between social groups.* London: Academic Press, 1978. Pp. 101–140.

Vanneman, R. D., & Pettigrew, T. F. Race and relative deprivation in the urban United States. *Race,* 1972, *13,* 461–486.

Weber, R. & Crocker, J. Cognitive process in the revision of stereotypic beliefs. *Journal of Personality and Social Psychology,* 1983, *45,* 961–977.

Wilder, D. A. Reduction of intergroup discrimination through individuation of the out-group. *Journal of Personality and Social Psychology*, 1978, *36*, 1361–1374.

Worchel, S., Andreoli, V., & Folger, R. Intergroup cooperation and intergroup attraction: The effect of previous interaction and outcome of combined efforts. *Journal of Experimental Social Psychology*, 1977, *13*, 131–140.

Worchel, S., & Norvell, N. Effect of perceived environmental conditions during cooperation on intergroup attraction. *Journal of Personality and Social Psychology*, 1980, *38*, 764–772.

Author Index

Numbers in italics show the page on which the complete reference is cited.

Subject Index